Peter Liddle

MEN OF GALLIPOLI

The Dardanelles and Gallipoli Experience
August 1914 to January 1916

Allen Lane

Contents

6   Contents

List of Plates

List of Maps

Acknowledgements

For several years now British Gallipoli veterans have been providing me with the research material for this book and their faith and encouragement have been complemented by the help of French, Australian and New Zealand veterans. The Gallipoli Association in Britain and associations of Gallipoli veterans in their home countries have been of tremendous assistance in co-ordinating this work. Throughout Britain and France and in widely separated areas of Australia and New Zealand I have been honoured by warmly welcoming hospitality in the homes of men who served in the campaign. The affection and respect which grew from our co-operation convince me that these men would not wish me to take in hand the invidious task of selecting and naming those whose help was of outstanding benefit to the research; I am indebted to every one. I should also like to acknowledge here the generosity of a Western Front man, one from Salonika and a conscientious objector, which materially assisted me towards the completion of this work.

The second area of major assistance has been that of the Sunderland Polytechnic, where the Rector Dr M. Hutton, my late Head of Department Mr H. W. L. Miller and the Sabbatical Leave Committee have provided me with every encouragement and facility. This institutional and personal backing has been invaluable. The great privilege of a sabbatical year and of financial assistance gave me the magnificent opportunity to carry out research in Australia and New Zealand, the fruits of which are, I believe, clearly reflected in the text and illustrative material. The Priestman Trust in Sunderland also kindly assisted me in my travel commitments.

The British Academy provided me with the funds to work in Turkey itself and here the Turkish Veterans' Association was an appreciated source of aid and advice. Most of my contacts there were established through the help of Major-General H. G. Aran of Ankara, the President of this Union, and General J. F. Inal of Istanbul. Further guidance and assistance in interpretation were kindly provided by Bayan Nedime Inan, the protocol officer of the Istanbul branch of the Union.

In four study visits to France, the warmth of the hospitality at every place I visited, from Soissons to Albertville, Neuilly to Marseilles, will remain an abiding memory. The trust of the Guédet-Guépratte family in giving me full access to Admiral Guépratte's papers was a wonderful example of the sort of help that I received. I would also like to acknowledge the assistance of Mme Ruth Dubreuil in contacting French veterans through national and local newspapers. Further help in this work came from M. Tranie, Secretary of the Association of Veterans who fought in Gallipoli and Serbia. I also had valuable assistance with interpretation during tape-recording from M. Gilormini, himself a veteran, and M. Alain Ginet of the University of Grenoble. M. Ernest Roux, President of the Paris Region of French Gallipoli veterans, and Cdt Raymond Weil, the Vice-President, bestowed honour upon my research in France by inviting me to re-charge the Eternal Flame at the Arc de Triomphe at the annual commemorative ceremony on 25 April 1974.

In Australia I received generous and well-organized help from Lieut-Colonel G. Shaw and the West Australian Gallipoli Legion of Anzacs, C. A. Sharman, Nell and Sid Carr and Mr Scott in Tasmania, Howard Vinning of the Returned Services League H.Q. in Canberra, and Reg Nixon and Clyde Smythe in New South Wales.

In New Zealand, the outstanding debt in my research for veterans is owed to Colonel W. Murphy, whose wonderful efficiency was behind the intensive work carried out there. In Northland Mr Ken Stevens and Captain Harris, in Wellington Mr and Mrs Brosnahan and Mr Johnston, the President of the Returned Services Association, in Blenheim Mr O. L. Watson, in Christchurch Captain and Mrs Arthur Marris, and in Dunedin Mr Taverndale all willingly assisted research begun in Auckland under the care of Colonel Murphy and D. E. Stacey, President of the New Zealand Gallipoli Association. Everywhere I had cause to be grateful to the Gallipoli Association and the Returned Services Association.

At the Public Record Office, the battalion war diaries were essential sources of reference and at the Imperial War Museum the Drewry and Berridge letters gave outstandingly graphic accounts of particular events in the campaign. The Hamilton papers at King's College Library, London, gave much useful background material for my central theme. At the Château de Vincennes the riches of the French Military Archives were outstanding. Similarly rich, especially in personal experience material, were the Mitchell Library in Sydney and the Alexander Turnbull Library in Wellington. In the nine libraries or archives which I visited in Australasia I was received with a uniform courtesy and helpfulness for which I thank sincerely the librarians and staff concerned. I feel that I must mention that the State Assistant Librarian in South Australia,

Mr R. C. Sharman, who also helped me in my search for Gallipoli veterans, gave me the sort of support that deserves to make this library in Adelaide a model for those who cherish the goal of co-operation rather than imperialism in archival preservation.

In concluding my acknowledgements for the research stage of the work I should like to mention four former students of mine whose commitment to Gallipoli was reflected in the depth and breadth of their own research and the very pleasing dissertations that they produced: Mrs Margery Lindley, who also helped me in finding Australian and New Zealand contacts, Margaret Lightfoot, Gordon A. Jones and Michael Shafto.

At the Polytechnic my warmly respected History Division colleagues and indeed the staff of the Education Department have shown tolerance and understanding as so much of my time became concentrated on Gallipoli. Clerical staff, technical staff and former students have assisted at every stage of the work with typing, the xeroxing of documents, copying of photos and of maps. The typing from my dreadful script has been done by Mrs Sandra Proctor, with Mrs Mary Milburn, assisted by my brother, completing the final draft.

The guidance of my publishers has always been shrewd and expressed felicitously. In this respect I would like to thank David Duguid, Eleo Gordon and indeed everyone who has played a part in the publication.

In all these aspects I have been fortunate but in the two areas that I have left to the last I have particular reason to express my gratitude. The Dean of the Faculty of Arts, University of Newcastle, Mrs Joan Taylor, who has shown great interest in the development of my work, has given ready advice on the structure of my writing and close textual criticism which I trust has disciplined me and ensured the avoidance of much which would otherwise have been clumsy or lacked clarity.

Finally, I sincerely appreciate the loyal support of my family. They have accepted considerable periods of physical separation and a degree of mental or emotional separation as the pressure of the work has increased, but from the beginning they have been closely associated with the task. As veterans have stayed in our home or we have visited them, an enriching bond of friendship has grown to link my wife Sheila, Steven, Alison and myself with men from all walks of life who shared a common experience in 1915. It is my hope that the book recaptures something of the essence of this experience, as it is dedicated in affectionate respect to so many men who have become 'family friends'.

Sunderland Polytechnic 1976   Peter H. Liddle

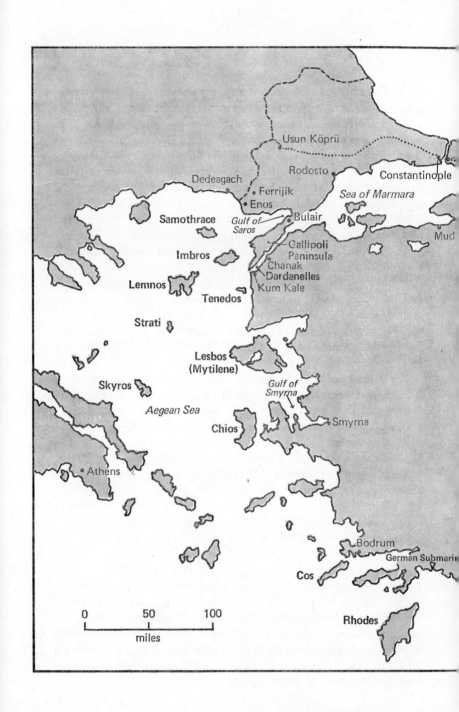

Usun Köprü

Rodosto

Constantinople

Dedeagach

Ferrijik

Enos

Sea of Marmara

Samothrace

Gulf of Saros

Bulair

Mud

Imbros

Gallipoli
Peninsula

Chanak

Dardanelles

Kum Kale

Lemnos

Tenedos

Strati

Lesbos
(Mytilene)

Skyros

*Gulf of
Smyrna*

Aegean Sea

Smyrna

Chios

Athens

Bodrum

German Submari

Cos

Rhodes

0   50   100

miles

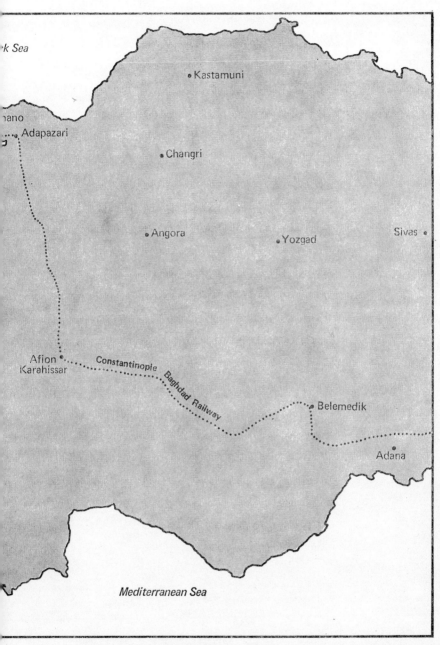

Map 1: Turkey and the Aegean

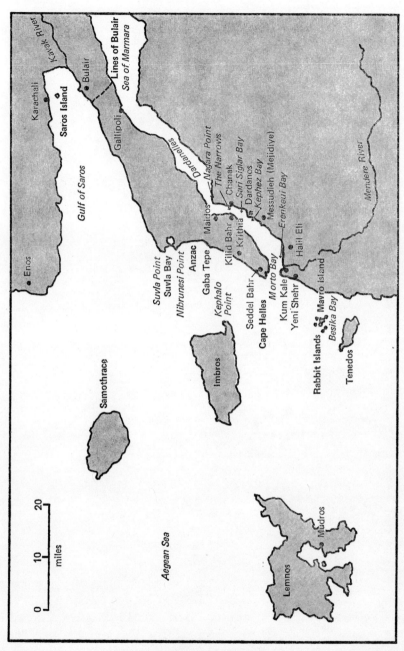

Map 2: Gallipoli and the Dardanelles

Introduction

This book has grown out of a long-held commitment to the Gallipoli campaign and to the men who served on the Peninsula or in the surrounding waters. Since 1967, I have been endeavouring to track down these men in the United Kingdom, in France, Australia, New Zealand, Eire and Newfoundland, and in Turkey, Germany and Austria. The research took me to France four times, to Australasia and to Turkey itself. A complete list of the 650 or so veterans with whom I made contact and who provided original diaries, letters and photographs, as well as recollections of service in 1915, appears at the end of the book. My work from the first had the dual purpose of building up an archive for posterity and of using the materials made available, in a book which would faithfully portray the personal experiences of the young officers, soldiers and sailors serving in and around the Peninsula.

In addition to the men with whom I was in touch I consulted many original personal and official documents in archives in Britain, France and Australasia. Further background information was contained in the official histories, biographies, monographs, unit histories, journal articles and published personal-experience accounts listed here in the bibliography.

The research itself was an exciting, enriching experience and I have, for example, satisfying memories of confirming the authenticity of a Marseilles citizen's dramatic story of escape from the sinking French battleship *Bouvet*, by finding evidence in a dusty file in the French Naval Archives in Paris. On a Tasmanian farmstead, in an elegant Parisian flat, in a South Shields council house and even on an empty Pacific beach in New Zealand, conversation with men who were at Helles, Anzac or Suvla in 1915 has, I feel, brought me close to this experience.

Of course, there are academic problems in using recollections. But when all account has been taken of the fallibility of memory with age, and physical or mental infirmity, there is still a conviction held by many veterans that the stark newness and intensity of their experience in 1915 left an ineffaceable impression on them. I believe this was because they were sufficiently young to be excited by the drama in which each was playing his small part and sufficiently mature to be aware of its significance.

My questions were restricted to what they themselves remembered having done, seen or experienced. The information given was checked against all other related reliable sources. From a really comprehensive collection of recorded testimony, the process of selection for inclusion in the text was rigorous. Similarly critical assessment was given to all the original personal documentation.

The careful examination I made of the Peninsula and of Kum Kale in 1972 helped enormously in placing this material into a physical geographical setting. Despite afforestation at Anzac and farming at Helles, it was easy to be carried back in eye and mind to 1915. A map shows Achi Baba's height to be insignificant, yet its shouldered bulk dominates the view from the cliffs above any of the Helles landing beaches. The contorted Anzac landscape reveals a forbidding stark face from the sea off Ari Burnu. The Suvla bowl or amphitheatre seen from either the Salt Lake or from the heights of Chunuk Bair takes on a new and unforgettable aspect from which any account of the events of August 1915 derives added significance. To see the still exposed Nek or the slightly raised shingle bank below Seddel Bahr castle and then, in the heat of the summer, the dried Salt Lake and the tinder-like scrub under a burning sun helps to dissolve the years which have passed since the soldier diarist made his record of the historic event in which he was engaged.

With regard to photographic illustration, I have tried to select examples which closely complement the text rather than show 'Gallipoli' in more general terms. Most of them are from private sources and are being published for the first time. I felt that the inclusion of certain 'fuzzy' ones is justified by their documentation of a certain aspect of personal experience seldom exemplified in this manner.

So much for the sources from which this book has been developed. What about its *raison d'être*? It may well be maintained that a British soldier almost invariably performed with characteristic stoicism under whatever difficulties and on whichever front he served. Can it be claimed that Gallipoli provided a sufficiently distinctive experience to justify a detailed concentration on personal experience of service there? I believe there is solid evidence to substantiate such a claim.

Gallipoli was the only major 'alternative' campaign which held the possibility of a quick dramatic victory. In those who took part there was an anticipation of great events. The sheer might of the naval commitment which the soldiers first glimpsed as they entered Mudros harbour was an inspiring sight engendering a consciousness of involvement in the challenge of a major enterprise. For most men it was to be their first experience under fire, precipitating a maturity which would leave its mark. Following the drama of the landings there were to be heroically fruitless assaults on entrenched positions in the tradition being established on the Western Front, but there were also distinctive operations, such as the night march and advance up the unreconnoitred Anzac gullies in August, or the aggressive mining activities so unlike the slow gestation of similar activity in France. There does not, for example, seem to be any parallel to the sheer concentrated ferocity of the hand bombing at Quinn's or Courtney's Post in May or of the prolonged fighting from entrenched positions where at some points only a sand-bagged barricade separated the opposing troops. Such conditions led to the construction and regular use of catapults, trench periscopes and rifles sighted by periscopes and operated by string. For an August attack at Anzac troops even dug assault tunnels to reduce further the narrow but fearsome no-man's land over which they were to charge. There was individual enterprise like that of John Simpson Kirkpatrick with his donkey for transporting men unable to walk to the dressing station, or that of the silent forays by Gurkhas to secure grim evidence of the sudden death of a Turkish sniper.

It is scarcely surprising that the geographical conditions which so dominated the campaign, strategically and tactically, should also affect living conditions. With Achi Baba, Sari Bair and the encircling hills at Suvla standing as a constant challenge, at once depressingly unreachable and demonstrably near, the allied soldiers were confined to very small beach-heads. Not even the Mesopotamian seasonal river flooding or the Bulgarian barrier of the Grand Couronné so circumscribed freedom of allied movement. The allied sectors on the Peninsula were all open to shell-fire. The land held by the British and French at Helles was, at its widest point, little more than two miles wide, and the distance from the front line to Cape Tekke Tepe was just over three miles. At Anzac the crescent-shaped wedge was still more restricted, particularly from the front line to the rear. At Suvla, sufficient of the plain was won to secure a greater degree of space, but concealment of men, material and tactical movement was even less possible, as the tiny hillocks were too low to hide any movement from Chunuk Bair observation. Within these three confined areas, attack and defence had to be planned and carried out, supplies accumulated and distributed, communications maintained, troop movements made, bomb factories and schools run, and field dressing and casualty clearing stations as well as field hospitals set up. Even a primitive aerodrome at Helles had to be constructed. A narrow-gauge railway, water-purifying plants, bakeries, cookhouses and plans for a funicular railway at Anzac are further evidence of an altogether remarkable situation.

For men on the Peninsula, mail was irregular, parcel contents were spoiled, and despite sea-bathing no one could keep clean. There was no proper leave, there were no real base areas. Shell-ruined Armentières in France or even Summerhill camp in Salonika held possibilities utterly beyond the reach of the Peninsula or the islands of Imbros or Lemnos, and a monastic seclusion from women was the lot of all who set foot on the Peninsula. There is significance in the late-August entry of a published Western Front diary. 'Whenever I get depressed . . . I keep repeating to myself, "Thank God I didn't go to the Dardanelles".'[1]

Permanently living in dugouts or trenches was something to which one simply had to become accustomed, but the summer heat and the impossibility of burying the dead who fell in no-man's land produced a plague of flies gorged from their feeding grounds of corpses, open latrines, mugs of tea and runny jam and bread. The resultant dysentery or enteric fever was a curse comparable to that of malaria in Salonika and un-paralleled in scale by disease on any other front except East Africa. Certainly on no front did such suffering occur as a result of suddenly severe weather conditions as at Suvla and Anzac in the November storm. In addition to all this, it was Gallipoli on 25 April and to some extent in August which shared with Mesopotamia the melancholy distinction of best illustrating the woefully ill-prepared wartime medical arrangements to deal with wounded. There was small compensation for these miseries in the unusual degree of informality in Peninsula service life. Away from the front line there was freedom to bathe, to scrounge, to visit friends in other units. Individual or collective cooking enterprise waged war against the deficiency of army rations and the near impossibility of cooking for and effectively supplying large units.

Viewed from a wider perspective than that of personal experience, the Dardanelles/Gallipoli campaign was of lasting significance. A combined operation involving a British and a French squadron and including the most powerful modern battleship afloat carried out seven separate land-ings with five divisions of troops from Britain, France, Africa, India and Australasia. The scale of such an operation was unmatched in the Great War and 25 April was a day of epic drama fit to rank with any day in the history of twentieth-century British warfare.

One of the most fascinating aspects of the campaign is the richly varied ethnic background of the troops involved. There were English, Scots,

[1] G. H. Greenwell, *An Infant in Arms*, Penguin Press, 1972, p. 46.

Welsh, Irish, Australians, New Zealanders including Maoris, New-foundlanders, Gurkhas, Sikhs, Palestinians, French, men of the varied races of the French Foreign Legion, Algerians, Moroccans and Senegalese. Their different languages and cultures, their prejudices and their ideals, their varied military training and experience, had to be fused to serve a common military purpose. For Australians and New Zealanders above all, Gallipoli earned a singular distinction; and 25 April, the day when Australian and New Zealand troops first saw action as separately identified units, despatched by the instruction of their own Governments, has been chosen as the day on which these two nations commemorate the service and sacrifice of their armed forces in two world wars.[2] Dr Gammage, in *The Broken Years*, writes: 'Anzac provided a glorious focus for specifically nationalist sentiment; it was a peculiarly Australian achievement which until then had been lacking and in the eyes of contemporaries it made Australia a nation at last with international recognition, national heroes, a national day and a worthy tradition. It established an ethos which seemed to express the best of both nation and Empire, and this inevitably reduced the imperial attachment of Australians.'[3] For Australia and New Zealand it is undeniable that their emergent nationhood had been forged in the crucible of Gallipoli.

In writing this book I have tried to emphasize the individual more than his unit and more than his country, while paying due concern to these factors when they seemed significant. I have endeavoured to let those who participated in the campaign speak for themselves. This concentration has meant that the political and military background is given only in outline. For readers who require this background in further detail there are the official British and Australian histories. Considering the difficulty of writing a detailed, interesting, critically objective official account, C. E. W. Bean's two-volume Australian *Official History* is an outstanding achievement and I recommend it highly. The books by John North, Alan Moorehead and R. R. James will interest and satisfy most readers, despite James's recurrent criticisms of Moorehead's work. For my book I drew much valuable information from the so-called *Mitchell Report*. This was a Government 'Confidential Book' published in 1919, the result of

[2] Technically, Australians in New Guinea and the New Zealanders in Samoa could claim to have been on active service before the Expeditionary Forces left Australasia, and the Nelson Company of the New Zealand Canterbury Battalion was in action on the Suez Canal in February.

[3] p. 277.

meticulous research by a specially appointed committee inquiring in great technical detail into every aspect of the naval, military and R.N.A.S. conduct of the campaign.

The whole question of political and military responsibility is dealt with in some detail in appendices to this book, but a very interesting top-level original commentary on the leadership and the development of the naval and military enterprise is provided by *The Keyes Papers*. This is a Navy Records Society publication of Keyes's correspondence with his wife and with naval contacts in London in 1914–18. Though I found that it increased my esteem neither of Keyes's judgement nor of his personal qualities, it is a fascinating record.

From Keyes it is appropriate to move to the distinguished American naval scholar, A. J. Marder's most recent book, *From the Dardanelles to Oran*, which persuasively argues that 'the stakes and the not impossible odds' justified the pursuit of a resumption of the naval assault in April. This is a stimulating and thought-provoking book even for those who do not incline towards the American's verdict.

The political background is well treated in S. Roskill's *Hankey: Man of Secrets*, and all the good general histories of the war provide an analysis of the Westerner/Easterner controversy. Volume III of Martin Gilbert's monumental biography of Churchill is an indispensable source, and George Cassar has written a valuable book on the less well-known French involvement (*The French and the Dardanelles*).

Many participants at all levels of experience have published memoirs of their service in 1915. The most recent example is Captain Bush, who has incorporated his naval memoirs into a history of the campaign. My preference is for two much older books, both by army chaplains. Creighton's *With the 29th Division in Gallipoli* and Foster's *At Antwerp and the Dardanelles* still read very well, and of course Ernest Raymond's *Tell England* is a deserved classic in which the author, himself a Gallipoli army chaplain, captures in the form of a novel the atmosphere of fresh enthusiasm and innocence true to the period.

No matter how thorough is the study undertaken by the researcher or general reader, he may still reach no final conclusion on the contentious issues of the campaign. His reading will, however, almost certainly have exposed the inadequacy of the verdict that the concept was within easy reach of fulfilment, but was brought to ruin entirely by disastrous naval and military leadership. I believe such a verdict to be a debasement of the real Gallipoli currency, the service of those who were there, who did their best in appalling circumstances and did it in a way which made history.

1.   Preliminaries

The Dardanelles is the narrow stretch of water which links the Sea of Marmara to the Aegean, separating the continents of Europe and Asia. This waterway, which provides the vital Mediterranean outlet for the Black Sea via the Bosphorus, has Turkish territory on both shores. The tongue of land which forms the northern shore is the Gallipoli Peninsula, named after the village of Gallipoli (Gelibolu) on its southern shore.

At the outbreak of the First World War on 4 August 1914 the area immediately became involved in the action owing to the presence in the Mediterranean of the German battle cruiser *Goeben* and the light cruiser *Breslau*, which escaped from the British and French Mediterranean squadrons, slipped through the Dardanelles and arrived off Constantinople on 9 August.

Chief Petty Officer Cave, serving in H.M.S. *Dublin*, the cruiser which, though far outmatched, had come nearest to forcing the *Goeben* to action in the chase for the Dardanelles, writes of the disappointment aboard the *Dublin* at that time. He had been range-taker on the upper navigating bridge, where he worked and slept during the search.

'Our gun crews were itching to justify our winning the Mediterranean Fleet Battle Practice Cup just prior to the outbreak of the war. The order of "All guns with lyddite – load" was greeted with cheers from all hands. Within I suppose ten seconds the breach workers had removed the fuse caps and "guns ready" was reported from all our 8- and 6-inch guns. Next came the torpedo orders "Flood out bar". Both port and starboard 21-inch torpedo tubes, previously loaded, were ready to fire. It was very early in the morning and I could only get approximate ranges in that light. Strangely *Goeben* and *Breslau* hadn't put out smoke screens and we could only presume they hadn't seen us. When we were within 6,000 yards and were positioning for torpedo attack, the two destroyers *Beagle* and *Bulldog* were ordered into position as at a boat race by Captain Kelly shouting through a megaphone from the starboard boat-deck "Back *Bulldog*", "Up *Beagle*". Then we were spotted and the German ships sheered off to port exposing only an end on view. As they could now turn if they so wished and have us at their mercy all we could do was to turn away and present our stern view to them. When we heard the order

"Cooks of messes to the galley for cocoa" we knew that we had failed in our chance secretly to approach and damage or sink *Goeben*. The guns remained loaded but not all the company showed frustration in cursing, some were actually in tears.'[1]

Stopping colliers from entering the Straits to coal the *Goeben* and the *Breslau*, range-keeping exercises and practice firings were to be poor compensation, though Cave asserts that the *Dublin* had drawn fire from the Peninsula even before the end of August. When preparing for 'hands to bathe', the ship had been shelled and thus could lay claim to being the war's first British target for Turkish shells.[2]

The story of the escape of the *Goeben* is told in a book by Redmond McLaughlin,[3] in which the author makes good use of Admiral Souchon's memoirs concerning the herculean efforts to coal the ship at Messina, when music in the form of martial airs, extra rations, stirring speeches, etc., had been used to increase the work rate. The exhaustion and danger from scalding to the overworked stokers are also mentioned in the book, which uses the evidence of a crew member's published memoirs to show that four stokers were killed during their labours in the chase.[4] Hans von Mohl, a gunnery officer in the *Breslau*, recalled the state of tension on the ship, exemplified by his reply on being asked what their destination was – 'Heaven or Hell!'

During this period numerous pertinent and impertinent articles appeared in *The Tenedos Times*, the monthly journal of the Mediterranean Destroyer Flotilla. An advertisement read, 'What offers? Two cross-bred Racers, *Goeben* and *Breslau*, both by Germany out of Kiel. Have been regularly hunted this season. Owing to the War, owner unable to use same. Apply B. F. Turk Esq., "The Dumping Ground", Chanak.' Then with apologies to Lewis Carroll there appeared a parody which included these verses:

The *Goeben* and the *Breslau*
    In the Sea of Marmara lay.
They wept like anything to see
    Those silent watchers grey.

---

[1] Diaries, letters, memoirs, etc whose provenance is not given in the footnotes to the text are in Peter Liddle's private collection (P.L.). A complete list of the contents of this collection is on pp. 291–307.

[2] The second of *Dublin*'s four funnels was hit in this action.

[3] *The Escape of the Goeben.*

[4] ibid., p. 72.

'We're sold to Turkey now,' they cried.
  'Why won't they go away?'

'If Turkey keeps the Straits shut up
  To ships for half a year
Do you suppose,' the *Breslau* said,
  'Those ships outside would clear?'
'I doubt it,' said the *Goeben*,
  'They'd still be there, I fear.'[5]

A signal from the Admiralty on 21 September to Vice-Admiral Carden, commander of the British Eastern Mediterranean Naval Squadron, affirmed that his 'sole duty is to sink *Goeben* and *Breslau*, no matter what flag they fly, if they come out of the Dardanelles',[6] but he was unable to put the order into effect. Government and Admiralty indicated their awareness of the approaching certainty of Turkey joining the Central Powers with a message to Carden on the 26th: 'You are authorized to attack any Turkish ships of war emerging from the Dardanelles',[7] and on the following day war was declared between Turkey and the Triple Entente of Britain, France and Russia, thus putting Egypt and the vital Suez Canal in real danger.

On 2 November a wireless message from the Admiralty informed Carden that 'without risking the ships, demonstration is to be made by bombardment on the earliest suitable day by your armoured ships against the forts at the entrance of the Dardanelles at a range of 14,000 to 12,000 yards. Ships should keep under way, approaching as soon after daylight as possible, retirement should be made before fire from the forts becomes effective.'[8] On the same day Carden prepared his orders, and they included the provision that ships were not to fire more than eight rounds per turret unless otherwise ordered by signal that rapid fire was necessary to keep the ships undamaged.

Petty Officer Cave has described his experience in a bombardment led by the flagship *Indefatigable* and the *Indomitable*, together with the French ships led by Admiral Guépratte's flagship *Suffren*. 'It seemed to me to be a deliberate bombardment of practically every building in sight [the

---

[5] *The Tenedos Times* original issues (P.L.) and published version, p. 63.
[6] Naval Official Papers, Admiralty to Vice-Admiral Carden (P.L.; classified in P.R.O. under ADM 137, vol. 881).
[7] ibid.
[8] Official Papers, Mediterranean Squadron (P.L.; classified at P.R.O. under ADM 137, vol. 881).

Seddel Bahr area of Cape Helles], care being taken not to hit the minaret. This would be because of its use for range-finding and also perhaps because of a wish not to offend religious sensibilities. The main target was certainly the fort, which we made a mess of, culminating in a huge explosion. There had been sporadic return fire from several positions but we certainly weren't hit and it was all a most one-sided affair.' (In April 1919 the Dardanelles Committee of investigators interviewed the Turkish officer in command of the defences of the Dardanelles in 1914, Djevad Pasha. He confirmed that the attack had 'caused more damage than any succeeding attack including that of 18 March',[9] and he accepted that the *Suffren*'s shelling of the Kum Kale battery had caused hits on the gun emplacements, though no casualties were caused.)

This bombardment was not followed up, and so the period of frustrating inaction was prolonged. The entrance to the Dardanelles was patrolled, as was the Gulf of Smyrna, and the French squadron was reinforced by the old battleships *Gaulois*, *Charlemagne*, *St Louis* and *Bouvet*. British destroyers attacked and drove back two Turkish gunboats and two torpedo boats on 5 November but otherwise it was the same interminable wait for the *Goeben* and the *Breslau* or for new Admiralty orders.

Surviving French officers from the *Gaulois* have accepted that the lack of any relations between the British and French crews increased the tendency of the young French officers to blame the British in general and the Admiralty in particular for the inaction. These sentiments were aggravated by technical disagreements over gunnery, in which the French preferred the effectiveness of salvoes to the more deliberate and economical British fire of turret by turret. The British method allowed for observation and correction. Unlike the French and British soldiers who were to serve on the Peninsula, the sailors had little opportunity for fraternization, but some necessary exchange did take place and it is pleasant to read of the enjoyable service of English signal officers and ratings in their letters of appreciation to Admiral Guépratte. In an undated letter from Mess 26 of the British flagship H.M.S. *Indefatigable* Signaller Madden wrote, 'Please excuse the liberty I am taking in writing to you but as you told us we would be always your friends perhaps you will not mind. When we left *Suffren* I was too moved and touched to say much and so I write now and express my gratitude for all the kindness of the Admiral, officers and men bestowed on me while serving aboard your flagship. Never as long as I live will I forget it. My wish is that you will get the opportunity

[9]   *Mitchell Report*, p. 25.

to distinguish yourself and so be able to rise to one of the highest in the French Navy.'[10]

An English officer, H. D. Farquharson, who served aboard the French cruiser *Jaureguiberry* in April 1915, wrote the first half of his letter in French and then continued, 'I can express myself better in English so I will tell you that I feel deeply indebted to you not only for your extreme kindness you showed to me and to my countrymen but for having given me the chance in assisting at a great event in history.' Farquharson concluded: 'Hoping we shall soon meet in Constantinople and that I may have the chance of entertaining you in London.'[11]

There is no doubt that this consciousness of participating in great events and the consequent sense of exhilaration were shared by many of the Army officers and men at the 25 April landings, and indeed there is abundant evidence that the Kitchener volunteers when they left England for the August Suvla landing were imbued with the same spirit.

In December and January two undersea exploits were successively to lift and then lower morale in the allied squadron, which was now officially under the command of Admiral Carden. The sinking by the British submarine *B 11* of the Turkish battleship *Messudieh* and the subsequent loss of the French submarine *Saphir* were the two events responsible for this fluctuating morale.

The submarine service was still in its infancy and the problems of mines, nets and currents facing the 143-foot-long *B 11*, built in 1906 with a complement of twelve or thirteen,[12] were serious. There was danger from petrol leaks and exhaust leak of carbon monoxide from the engine, which could cause, quite suddenly, the complete collapse of the crew members. The batteries had to be recharged on the surface, and submerged speed was not much more than $6\frac{1}{2}$ knots. There was no escape from the submarine except by surfacing and getting out through the conning-tower, and all these factors combined to make the task of using effectively one of her four precious torpedoes a difficult one. Nevertheless the competitive eagerness of officers and crew at this early date, and later in the wonderful exploits of Nasmith and Boyle, is both documented and remembered.

In 1972 Commander Holbrook gave a vivid account of the *B 11*'s successful mission, the substance of which is fully confirmed in the

---

[10] Guépratte Papers (P.L.).

[11] ibid.

[12] Commander Holbrook told me that he had a crew of twelve, which included an extra coxswain as the hydroplanes were too stiff to be manned by one man.

official naval history and in W. G. Carr's book *By Guess and by God*.[13]
With recently renewed batteries, *B 11* was sent up the Straits on 13
December. 'As a fisherman I knew that despite the strength of the current
in midstream if I crept in close to the [north] shore there would be slack
water. We dived to 60 feet at the Narrows, waited a while and then moved
up and through. I came up to periscope depth and saw on the starboard
quarter a large old Turkish battleship. We went down again but the tide
got us and swept us into Sari Siglar Bay and now the ship [*Messudieh*]
was on our port bow. I altered course and it needed full speed to combat
the current and get into position for a shot. I fired one torpedo and then
had to reduce speed because the lights were getting low and obviously
our batteries were failing. We then found ourselves aground stern first
and I could see the ship down by the stern and smoke from the shore
suggesting that fire was being directed at us. By using full revs. we got off
but I couldn't see the way out of the bay. I looked for the farthest bit of
land through the periscope but the coxswain said the spirit compass lenses
had packed up and all he could see was black spots. I told him to follow
them and at full [submerged] speed in twenty minutes a sea horizon
appeared on our port hand. We made for it and were more or less swept
out of the Straits having dived of course through the Narrows. We had
been under water for over nine hours. What a wonderful crew – each a
first class man – but we had been very very lucky.'

B 11 had successfully navigated and negotiated about forty-five miles
within the Straits on the entire trip, and avoided five lines of mines, nets
and Turkish patrolling torpedo boats, to say nothing of the shore batteries
which sighted her as she ran aground in Sari Siglar Bay. This in itself
was a major achievement, which the sinking of the *Messudieh* crowned.[14]
Lieutenant Holbrook was awarded the V.C. and all his crew were
decorated. Admiral Guépratte informed Vice-Admiral Carden that he
had recommended that Holbrook should become a Member of the Order
of the Legion of Honour, and in his appreciation of this distinction the
submarine commander wrote to the French Admiral, 'it is impossible for
me to tell you how much I appreciate receiving such a letter, especially
from the Admiral of our most noble allies. It is most gracious of you to
have written to the Commander in Chief about me and should the
Government of the French Republic confer upon me that high distinction,

---

[13] *Official History: Naval Operations*, vol. 2, pp. 72–3; *By Guess and by God*, pp. 19–20.
[14] Nearly all the crew were saved, because she sank in shallow water. Holes were cut in
the keel from which the trapped men escaped. Ten officers and twenty-seven men
had been killed.

the Legion of Honour, I shall be one of the proudest officers in His
Majesty's Navy. I am afraid the small service I have done is not worthy
of such high distinction.'[15]

Sadly, *B 11*'s success was balanced by the tragedy of the French
submarine *Saphir*. The *Saphir* ran aground in the Straits, near Chanak
and was lost on 15 January. English sources indicate that she was lost
owing to the failure to combat the bewildering change of water density
as the fresh waters of the Marmara meet the salt water at the Mediterranean end of the Straits. Paul Chack and Jean-Jacques Antier[16] give a
far fuller explanation. At first the *Saphir* had sprung a small leak and,
with the level of water rising, the pumps worked to keep the accumulation
of water to manageable proportions. In the middle of a minefield the
cables of the mines scraped the hull, then two mines bumped against the
thin sheet of the submarine without exploding. An hour later the same
noises were heard, and the Commander of the *Saphir* (Lieutenant Henri
Fournier) brought his submarine to periscope depth. His compass lenses
were obscured but he could see he was in the middle of a minefield. He
redescended and steering by auxiliary compass found himself aground on
a beach at an angle of 35°, with his hydroplanes on the beach in full view
of the enemy. The submarine began to slide down till it was at an angle
of 50°, the accumulators spilled their acid and the boat was filled with
noxious fumes. In this situation it settled on the bottom in sixty metres
of water. The leakage of water had become a cascade under a pressure
which threatened to split the hull. Emptying the ballast tanks failed to
raise the boat. Water was now entering from many leaks. All efforts to
move the *Saphir* failed, but then the bows rose and, totally out of control
and balance, broke the surface off Chanak. Two Turkish batteries started
firing. One of *Saphir*'s electric engines was still capable of work and
Fournier refilled the ballast tanks and went down to sixteen metres, but
could not keep on an even keel. The crew destroyed the secret code books
and slowly the *Saphir* resurfaced. Standing on the bridge while under
fire, Fournier directed his submarine into midstream to sink her in deep
water. As he was moving into midstream he attempted to fire torpedoes
at two gunboats firing on him but the boat's position in the water prevented this. With flag flying and the crew swimming to shore Fournier
remained standing under a hail of fire as the *Saphir*, with her ballast tanks
opened, sank beneath him. One of the sailors stayed till the end to help
him as Fournier couldn't swim, but it was cold and the man was obviously

[15] Guépratte Papers (P.L.).
[16] *Histoire maritime de la Première Guerre Mondiale*, vol. 2, p. 250.

exhausted. Fournier himself let go of his helper and drowned. Thirteen
of the crew of twenty-seven were saved. The differing fortunes of the
B 11 and the *Saphir* show the perils and strain which the crews of these
submarines suffered without the improved equipment of more modern
boats.

The loss of the *Saphir*[17] cast a particular shadow of concern which is
indicated by the earliest official intimation that something was wrong.
In a signal made at 11.9 a.m. on 16 January 1915 the destroyer *Blenheim*
reported to Vice-Admiral Carden, '*Saphir* has not been seen since 5.30
a.m. 15 January when she was seen to trim and dive near "Z" [a patrol
position]. I am searching Rabbit Island and coast of Imbros Island but I
consider she has gone up Dardanelles although she was informed not to
go without orders.'[18] On the same day Carden wrote to Guépratte, 'I am
sending you copy of a signal just received from *Blenheim* about *Saphir*. I
hope she is all right . . . I do not propose to make any signal as yet to the
Comm.-in-Chief but please do not let that affect your action if you wish
to do so.'[19] Within two days further information became available and
there is clearly no recrimination as Carden writes to Guépratte on the
18th, 'I am very unhappy about *your gallant Saphir*, it was most courage-
ous and dashing. I trust they are all saved,' and on 1 February, 'She had
done splendidly you see, having ascended so far.' However, before Carden
went with the *Indefatigable* to Malta for the ship's refit in temporarily
handing over command of the Eastern Mediterranean Squadron to
Guépratte, one of the requests he made in writing was that 'the submarines have orders that they are not to enter the Dardanelles without
permission from Captain Coode'.[20]

[17] The *Saphir* was in fact refloated by the Turks and seen in Constantinople by French
Army P.O.W.s, according to Maître Gondard, taken prisoner at Kum Kale, 26 April
1915.
[18] Eastern Mediterranean Naval Squadron Papers (P.L.; classified at P.R.O. under
ADM 137, vol. 382).
[19] Guépratte Papers (P.L.).
[20] Eastern Mediterranean Naval Squadron Papers (P.L.; classified at P.R.O. under
ADM 137, vol. 382). Captain Coode was in command of the British destroyers
maintaining a watch over the Dardanelles.

2. The February Bombardments

Meanwhile, on 25 November at a meeting of the War Council, Winston Churchill, the First Lord of the Admiralty, raised the question of safeguarding Egypt by striking at Turkey through the Dardanelles.[1] Though no decision was reached at this meeting, Churchill's thoughts received significant support in a memorandum of the secretary to the War Council, Lieut-Colonel Hankey. The naval historian Roskill[2] considers this Boxing Day memorandum the real inception of the Gallipoli campaign because in it Hankey argued for a blow at Germany's ally, Turkey: 'There ought to be no insuperable obstacle to the occupation of Constantinople, the Dardanelles and Bosphorus.'[3]

Whether Churchill and Hankey would have had sufficient support for their plan to be put into effect at that stage is by no means sure. For such a venture Hankey had laid down certain necessary conditions, such as the co-operation of Greece, Bulgaria and Russia, together with the involvement of three British army corps. But the question is hypothetical, because on 2 January 1915 a Russian appeal for action which would divert the Turks from concentrating on their offensive against the Russians in the Caucasus was made by Grand Duke Nicholas.

By letter to Churchill, Lord Kitchener, the Secretary of State for War, accepted that 'the only place that a demonstration might have some effect in stopping reinforcements going east would be the Dardanelles'.[4] The First Sea Lord, Fisher, who had previously favoured a North Sea landing in Germany, now saw an attack on the Dardanelles as an element in a new design for a major diplomatic, naval and military offensive on Turkey, but it was Churchill who provided the essential 'evidence' to support his own view. Churchill sent carefully worded telegrams to Admiral Carden raising the question of the feasibility of forcing the Dardanelles and leaving Carden with little option but to admit that the Dardanelles 'might be forced by extended operations with large numbers of ships'. Acquainted

---

[1] P.R.O. Cab. 22/1 3623.
[2] S. Roskill, *Hankey: Man of Secrets*, p. 149.
[3] P.R.O. W.O. 159 1/1 xi 3173.
[4] Letters, Kitchener to Churchill, 2 January 1915, quoted in W. S. Churchill, *World Crisis*, Mentor Edition, vol. 1, p. 362.

with Carden's reply, the War Council of 8 January resolved that an attempt should be made 'to bombard and take the Gallipoli Peninsula with Constantinople as its objective'.[5]

Apart from the immediate pressure of a Russian request for assistance, the case for an attempt on the Dardanelles was that the successful passage of the British Navy through the Straits into the Marmara and the navigation of these waters to Constantinople would stimulate the latent revolutionary atmosphere within the capital and lead to developments of outstanding advantage to the allies. The Turkish Government would surrender, be overthrown, or fly to Asia. As Constantinople possessed the only munitions factories in the Ottoman Empire, even if formal surrender was not obtained Turkish military resistance would be broken. The threat to the Suez Canal would disappear and the way towards the exploitation of Palestine and Syria would be open. The Mesopotamian advance from the Persian Gulf would be so much more secure, and Russia could withdraw her troops from the Caucasus in order to stiffen her resistance to the Austrians and Germans. The German eastward expansion, financial, political and military, would be halted and the Berlin–Baghdad railway axed, thus reducing the threat to India.

Even greater possibilities were considered. It was not merely that Russian wheat would be freed to assist her allies and that Russia herself would be aided by war materiel. It was hoped that British sea power, by means of the Danubian waterway, would be brought to bear in central and south-eastern Europe, and Germany forced into bolstering her Austrian ally, who was now threatened by the British Navy and a rejuvenated Russian 'steam roller'. In consequence, Germany would have to withdraw troops from the Western Front, and this would probably facilitate an allied breakthrough.

In the Balkans, it was anticipated that Serbia would be rescued from the danger of Austro-German defeat, and Greece actively influenced to join the allies, Romania likewise, and perhaps Italy too. Certainly Bulgaria would be tempted away from Teutonic enveiglement so that a united Balkan coalition would face Austria. Not surprisingly it was considered that the advent of these conditions would speedily bring a victorious end to the war.

Lord Kitchener had made it clear that there were no troops available for the opening of a new front, but Churchill had stressed that no troops would be needed and old ships would be used. The economy of the whole

5 P.R.O. Cab. 22/1 3623.

scheme went far to securing War Council unanimity.[6] It should be noted that at the crucial War Council of 8 January 1915 it was also resolved that 'if the position in the Western theatre becomes, in the Spring, one of stalemate, British troops should be dispatched to another theatre and objective, and that adequate investigation and preparation would be taken with that purpose'.[7] Kitchener had declared that such an expedition might need 150,000 men, and at the War Council of 9 February he assured members that 'if the Navy required the assistance of the land forces at a later stage, that assistance would be forthcoming'.[8]

Meanwhile a plan was drawn up for the progressive bombardment of the outer forts of the Dardanelles. The French were invited to take part and on 2 February the French Minister of Marine, Augagneur, replied to Churchill that there was nothing in the project to which he had the least objection. The plans seemed to Augagneur to be 'conceived with prudence and foresight, allowing the halting of the operations without any loss of prestige if difficulties were encountered'.[9]

The necessary strengthening of the allied squadrons in the eastern Mediterranean took place in late January and early February 1915. On 25 January the *Inflexible*, fresh from the Falkland Islands victory of 8 December, had relieved the *Indefatigable* as Carden's flagship. The old battleship *Triumph* arrived on 15 February from the successful Tsing-Tau action[10] and further battleships of a similar vintage, the *Vengeance*, the *Cornwallis* and the *Albion*, arrived in time for the beginning of the new operations on 19 February. The French ships had been augmented by the arrival of the battleships *Bouvet*, *Charlemagne* and *Gaulois*.

There are interesting comparisons in the active-service experience of the complements of some of the British ships. Stewart and Peshall, both of whom served in the *Cornwallis*, state in *The Immortal Gamble*[11] that

---

[6] Once serious naval losses were incurred and the necessity for major troop involvement was grudgingly accepted, disenchantment would split this unanimity, with significant influence on the chances of success for what had become an increasingly complex combined operation.

[7] Hankey's notes on the conclusions to the 8 January War Council meeting (P.R.O. Cab. 22/1 3623).

[8] Hankey's notes on the War Council meeting, 9 February (P.R.O. Cab. 22/1 3623).

[9] Chack and Antier, *Histoire maritime*, vol. 2, p. 143.

[10] Tsing-Tau was the port of Kiaochow, the German protectorate on the Chinese Yellow Sea coast. In September 1914 British troops landed near the port and with Japanese forces laid successful siege against it.

[11] p. 11.

their Captain was the only man on board who had been in action, whereas the *Inflexible* had had naval battle experience and the *Triumph* had bombarded forts and assisted in the landing of troops.[12] With regard to the question of morale, the recollections of Pierre Vallet, in 1915 an Ensign on board the *Gaulois*, suggest that the team spirit of his ship was attributable to the fact that so many of the crew were Bretons and that there was a healthy mixture of the experience of older reservists and the devil-may-care approach of those who were much younger.

The plan for 19 February was detailed and involved an initial bombardment at long range of the forts on both sides of the entrance to the Straits, followed by a closer-range bombardment to overwhelm the forts and allow the beginning of mine-sweeping operations. Ships were intended to keep under way when firing and some of the fire was to be indirect, with other ships doing the necessary spotting. In the event it was found that the fire was too inaccurate from the moving ships and all were ordered to anchor for firing.

The activity on board a ship in action is vividly illustrated in *With the Fleet in the Dardanelles*. The author, W. H. Price, who had been a chaplain on H.M.S. *Triumph* in 1914–15, reminds the reader of the battle preparation orders before action: 'Wash clothes as convenient this afternoon. All men are to wear clean clothes and flannels tomorrow.'[13] These instructions were considered essential by the naval surgeons because dirty clothes led to septic wounds. 'Any vulnerable part of the ship had to be protected by sandbags. Hammocks had to be packed here and there to prevent shell splinters striking men who must be exposed . . . decks are speedily cleared at the sounding of "General Quarters". Hoses are rigged to keep a running stream of water over the woodwork and thus minimize the possibility of fire. Watertight doors are shut, but not before the surgeons and their attendants have moved the sick from the "Sick Bay" into a place of safety below armour, and taken their instruments and stretchers to their station. The gun crews are in their turrets and casemates, the control officers have climbed into the foretop, the ammunition supply parties find their way to the magazine, half a dozen men take their places in the Transmission Station. Somewhere hidden in the heart of the ship, the "black squad" are stoking their furnaces. Engineers, electricians, carpenters, and armourers each has his post.'[14] W. H. Price was in the 'fore-

---

[12] It is a point of some interest that these troops, the South Wales Borderers at Tsing-Tau, would later be landed by the *Cornwallis* at S beach on 25 April 1915.

[13] p. 11.

[14] W. H. Price, *With the Fleet in the Dardanelles*, pp. 12–13.

cross passage' with the medical party during the action of 19 February. He described the heated, crowded depths of this area and the dimly lit ammunition passages along which the shells were transported to the hoists by overhead rails. Some of the shells, in the lulls between firing, were chalked with drawings or messages conveying rather vulgar greetings to the Sultan.

The private diary for 19 February of Midshipman William-Powlett, on board the *Vengeance*, replacing the *Cornwallis*, which was ordered out of action at 11.30 a.m. because her damaged capstan prevented her from firing at anchor, records his experience as his ship closed in for shorter-range observation. 'Suddenly No. 1 Fort opened fire on us. We turned round to port and made off westwards, slowly firing on No. 1 with our starboard 6-inch. I did not realize that the shells were falling so close to us. At first they fell short and then over till they picked up our range. A 1 [turret] had a misfire as we were going away. I was rather nervous as I wasn't quite sure what would be the right thing to do. We tried every circuit but none succeeded. So I had it taken out and thrown overboard. I had never had to deal with such a thing before and was terrified it was going to explode. I could hear the shells whistling over us. Just as we were getting out of range one pitched about ten yards off starboard bow. Another splintered the foreyard. All this time Admiral de Robeck had been dodging round the conning tower.' Needless to say the midshipman's official log is a more sober statement of fact, and is less obviously from the pen of a fifteen-year-old lad.

The 19 February bombardment, augmented by the newly arrived *Queen Elizabeth*, achieved disappointing results, and bad weather caused the postponement of further operations till the 25th.

The contemporary notes of a young French officer on board the *Suffren*, René Sagnier, show that he had no illusions about the results of the action. The outer forts appeared to have been silenced, but they had not been seriously damaged. The English were misled as to the effectiveness of their fire, which by its slow deliberation and equally slow plan of progressive destruction of the forts was to lose interminable time. 'Nothing has been gained from the day's action – it will have to be done all over again.' Sagnier goes on to remark that the *Triumph*'s task of indirect firing, first when making way and then at anchor in the current, could not usefully be carried out, and that to attempt such an action showed the ignorance of the British command.

Midshipman Seyeux in the *Gaulois* recorded in his diary on 19 February that he had received his baptism of fire. With evident interest he had noticed a 'ship to shelter aeroplanes' – it must have been the Navy's first seaplane carrier, the *Ark Royal* – and saw one of the aeroplanes rise into the air and circle over the Turkish hills. It was fired on, but the 'large bird' was well away from the exploding shells. The midshipman wrote that the fire of the English *Inflexible* was not well aimed, though some of her shells fell on target. He makes similar criticism of the French *Suffren*, but remarked that the fire of the *Vengeance* was good. A gunnery officer in the *Gaulois*, Jean Deffez, noted in his diary that the day was the 199th of the war but the first day of action for his ship. It was his baptism of fire also. He noted the large number of English ships and the eagerness of the men around him for real action and their disappointment that their ship was used only for support and observation. The solemn silence affected them all before the firing broke out. There was frustration as the noise of the firing increased, but they were not to take part until the end of the day's action when they returned the fire of one of the Turkish forts. Pierre Vallet recalls that, with his gun team entombed in a small am- munition magazine on the same ship, they were not at the time unduly conscious that, in the event of an order to abandon ship, escape would have been a very tricky business as they attempted to scale the ladder leading from their depths.

The diaries of Englishmen and Frenchmen in the allied squadron on 20 February have a clear common concern – impatience and disappoint- ment that the weather had changed and that there were strong winds and quite a high sea. It was not until 25 February that the attack could be resumed, by which time Midshipman William-Powlett had noted in his private diary the German press report that the British Admiral's ship had been sunk in the attack. Nevertheless both the British battleships with admirals aboard (the *Inflexible* with Vice-Admiral Carden and the *Vengeance* with Vice-Admiral de Robeck) were in action again on the 25th. William-Powlett described watching the effect of the *Queen Eliza- beth*'s fire from the *Vengeance*: 'It was beautiful to see the 15-inch [shells] bursting and the damage done . . . At 1 p.m. *Cornwallis* and us prepared for the first run. I felt extremely nervous but I was all right once we got on the move.' In fact the experience was not to be unduly unnerving as there was only desultory fire in reply and by dusk 'it was a fine sight to see all the forts ablaze'.

The general scheme of the bombardment on 25 February was the same as that of the 19th, with long-range shelling followed by short-range destruction of the forts. The *Queen Elizabeth*, the *Agamemnon*, the *Irre- sistible* and the *Gaulois* were the principal ships carrying out the first phase of the work, with the *Vengeance*, the *Cornwallis*, the *Suffren*, the *Charlemagne*, the *Albion* and the *Triumph* tackling the shorter-range work, though there were other ships involved, like the *Dublin*, which was engaged on spotting for the *Queen Elizabeth*. The heavy fire under which the *Gaulois* came and the effect this had on her relatively raw crew are illustrated by the entry for 25 February in the diary of Jean Deffez: 'From where I was sheltering I could see two severely shocked men. Was this to be my last hour and this was the end of *Gaulois*? We certainly didn't fear death but we didn't look on the thought of horrible wounds with any pleasure. When we saw how near the shells were, as fountains of water were thrown up around us, we were without any doubt feeling the strain.'

The *Mitchell Report* states that this bombardment put out of action at least 30 per cent of the guns at Kum Kale and 50 per cent of those in Seddel Bahr. Turkish military authorities interviewed in 1919 by the Dardanelles Committee gave evidence for the *Mitchell Report* which accepted that 'the batteries and ammunition dumps were all destroyed, but none of the magazines touched. The forts were evacuated because the short-range fire had destroyed them entirely. The morale of the defenders was perfect, and there was no shortage of ammunition. The crews of the guns felt natural grief at the loss of their comrades and the destruction of guns and ammunition, but were not in any way shaken in their morale or in their opinion of the strength of the defences.'[15] However exaggerated this Turkish evidence may be, in view of the fact that demolition parties found a lot of work to do, particularly at Kum Kale, it was realized by those on the spot at all levels that short-range bombardment could not be relied on to render a fort completely useless and beyond repair. Demolition by shore party was the next essential preparation for mine-sweeping and in fact the first shore party landed on 26 February.

[15] *Mitchell Report*, p. 37.

3.   Landing Parties and Minesweepers

During the afternoon of 26 February a destroyer towed in cutters from the *Irresistible* to the Seddel Bahr beach. Thirty sailors and forty-five Marines were in this party and their task was to destroy the big guns in the fort and the torpedo tubes. The *Mitchell Report*[1] gives details about the means of destruction and how they were landed: 'It was decided to use 90 lb. of gun-cotton per gun. The wet gun-cotton for these charges was broken up and made into 30-lb. charges in canvas hoses about $9\frac{1}{2}$ inches in diameter (just less than the bore of the guns). These hoses were fitted with canvas straps, so that they could be carried on the shoulders, leaving the hands free for a rifle or other small gear. A tin tube, obtained from the $16\frac{1}{4}$-lb. tins of wet gun-cotton, was fitted in each hose for the ultimate insertion of the dry gun-cotton primer. These latter were carried separately, and to provide for eventualities, fitted with two detonators, one for electrical and one for time-fuse firing.' In the event all six guns were rendered useless, but no torpedo tubes could be found. From H.M.S. *Irresistible* a midshipman, now Captain L. A. K. Boswell, remembers being late on deck when the demolition party was leaving and being called back for reprimand by the Captain, who had spotted him sliding down a life-line into the cutter. Boswell avoided disappointment on the second and third occasions by being well on time to depart for Kum Kale and Seddel Bahr respectively. At Kum Kale the enemy gunners had fled and under a covering guard of the *Irresistible*'s Royal Marines the sailors had gone from gun to gun and taken cover as each one was destroyed by individual charges. Slight opposition at Seddel Bahr allowed the Marines to get in some small arms fire.

On the afternoon of the 26th there was an enormous explosion when the first four guns were detonated simultaneously. From H.M.S. *Cornwallis* it was an impressive sight and sound. 'We had never heard anything like it. There was a sudden crack, as loud and dull as thunder, and an enormous rolling cloud of white smoke that swelled and swelled. Stones and masonry in chunks flew out into the sea for hundreds of yards. When we could distinguish anything, we realized that practically the whole fort had gone – a ruin marked it. The battery had disappeared.'[2]

[1] p. 38.
[2] A. T. Stewart, C. J. E. Peshall, *The Immortal Gamble*, p. 21.

Midshipman William-Powlett recorded in his diary the progress of the demolition party sent from the *Vengeance* to Kum Kale at the same time as the *Irresistible* party left for Seddel Bahr. He begins as if about to give a detached account of some exciting manoeuvre, but the end is rather different. 'They landed by the pier at No. 6 [Fort] and got into scattered formation immediately. "A" Company was left in Kum Kale while the remainder proceeded up to No. 4. They were fired on by Turks in the windmills at Yeni Shehr which were soon brought down by us and the *Dublin*. It was a fine sight to see the windmills crumple up and fall down. When the party got to No. 4 Fort they smashed up a searchlight and several wires connecting mines but did not blow up the guns. On the way back they were cut off by some Turks in a cemetery. We had some difficulty in finding the point of aim owing to the wrong bearing being passed up. The captain got furious and came and trained the gun himself. He cursed me and told me I ought to have turned Mr C— out. It was rather a difficult position. The Turks were driven off and our Marines got back to their boats. I did not expect half of them to come back. Only one was killed and three wounded. The one killed I am afraid was mutilated – the Turks venting their whole wrath on him. His head was smashed in, four bullet holes in his face, one in his wrist, one in shoulder and one in the knee – this was an explosive bullet and had blown his knee cap off. Both his legs were broken and a bayonet wound in his abdomen. One [Marine] was wounded in the eye and subsequently had it taken out, one in the shoulder and one in the chin.'

The midshipman records the naval burial on the 27th of the mutilated Marine, Sergeant Turnbull, and, though he makes no further comment on the incident, that very day two tubes of the *Vengeance*'s boilers burst and five men were burned so seriously that two died. A worse accident had been prevented by one of the men wrapping a sack round his scalded head and dashing in this condition up a ladder to turn off a stop-valve. The fifteen-year-old boy, in this precipitate process of maturing into an experienced officer, shows an understandable readiness to seek a lighter-hearted recollection of the day when he describes with an amusing sketch having seen one of the officers looking 'so funny walking in the latest overall oilskin blown out like a balloon'.

A further landing for demolition purposes was carried out by a party from the *Irresistible* on 27 February and despite stronger opposition six howitzers were destroyed. On 1 March a successful operation was carried out from the *Irresistible* on the Kum Kale Fort 4 to complete work begun by the *Vengeance* party on the 26th, and this assisted the bombardment already begun of the Turkish defences in the Straits. The progressive destruction of these defences was essential to allow the British North Sea trawlers and the French vessels to sweep a safe passage further and further up the Straits. None of the Turkish guns was put out of action in these bombardments and their deceptive silence was the result of both economy of use of ammunition and the temporary evacuation of forts when deemed necessary. The *Mitchell Report* again makes significant observations on the effectiveness of the allied bombardment. Only a direct hit would knock out a gun, and twelve-inch guns at a range of between 10,000 and 12,000 yards had a 2 per cent chance of a direct hit if the firing was done under anchor, in a calm sea, with new guns and perfect observation. What success could be expected with the ships manoeuvring, old guns, a choppy sea and salvo firing impossible because of the need for economy? Even the indirect bombardment of Forts 13 and 17 by the *Queen Elizabeth*'s fifteen-inch shells fired over the Peninsula from near Gaba Tepe on 5 and 6 March, though causing great alarm to the defenders, did little serious damage because the seaplane-spotting was a failure[3] and spotting by other ships proved an inadequate substitute. It is noteworthy that one seaplane pilot, Geoffrey Bromet, acknowledging the difficulty of estimating from the air the damage done to the forts, thought that: 'Shrapnel ought to be used to clear away the personnel before common [shell, i.e. high explosive] is resorted to.'

In the meantime the attempted shore demolition had continued, but on 4 March had met with a considerable check. On the previous day a reconnaissance had been undertaken at the Camber, Seddel Bahr. On the 4th, Marines were landed from the *Scorpion* and the *Wolverine* at Kum Kale, from the *Lord Nelson* to destroy Fort 4, from the *Irresistible* to destroy the bridge over the Mendere, and from the *Inflexible* and the *Ocean* on the northern shore. The Turks were now in greater strength and anticipated this landing. All the disadvantages of landing a small force against stronger forces expecting an attack were illustrated in the failure to make any progress on the Peninsula side. There was a tactical failure at Kum Kale too and it was matched by a high percentage of casualties. A seaman on board the *Lord Nelson*, George Keeler, recorded in his diary:

'Demolishing party from our ship landed at Kum Kale and met half-

---

[3] The first machine crashed through breaking her propeller while in the air, the second was fired on by rifles and the pilot wounded so that he had to return, and the third found that spotting was difficult on Fort 13 because the slope of the Kilid Bahr plateau was too steep.

way by a hail of bullets from enemy concealed in trenches and houses. We continued to bombard heavily doing considerable damage whilst party tried to reach forts and blow up guns etc. – but they found road to fort commanded by enemy well entrenched so eventually had to retire as they were only twenty-seven to hundreds of Turks. Much difficulty was found in the retirement as there was very little cover available and a movement from anyone was a signal for a hail of bullets. The two killed from our ship were P.O. Newlands and Cummings, signalman. It was rotten to see the way that they struggled back fighting all the way along the beach. I could see them through the range-finder, crawling through the water. The Marine Brigade suffered more severely, several killed and wounded, one of which died as they brought him off to the ship. We finished embarking troops at dark but we could not find out where our party had got to until later when they were reported on board the *Irresistible*.'

Captain Boswell, a midshipman in 1915, was with the *Irresistible* party and recalls that the Turks were certainly prepared on this occasion. The Royal Naval Division Marines, according to Boswell, proved less adequate under fire than the *Irresistible*'s own Marines and when 'Lieutenant Sandford and I moved inland to find why we had had no signal to advance on the fort it seemed that there was no properly organized defence for our work. Because of this we had to crawl back and then along the beach, behind a bank of seaweed.' It is perhaps this experience which reinforces Captain Boswell's conviction that the idea that the Army was essential for the successful demolition of the Narrows' forts was a 'hoary old myth'.

Colonel Matthews of the Plymouth Battalion, Royal Marines, later to be concerned in the controversial Y-beach landing on 25 April, went with one of the companies of Marines to Kum Kale. The Brigade Major, C. F. Jerram, observed their progress through binoculars. In a letter to a former Marine, W. J. Parnham, who became orderly to Colonel Matthews, Lieut-Colonel Jerram wrote many years later:

'I spotted Turks breaking away from the windmills and it looked as if they were going to cut off Bewes' Company in the nullah[4] at the foot of the hill. I was sent ashore to tell Col. Matthews to withdraw and to stay and help him. A good deal of bullets and shrapnel going in, which frightened me into fits and I landed at the Fort where I found no one doing anything. All they knew was that Col. Matthews was somewhere out there and that there were snipers in the houses fifty yards away and if I went out there,

[4] A dry river gulley.

they'd get me for sure. I hadn't time to ask why the hell they didn't get the snipers out and they didn't get me anyway. I found Col. Matthews alone – no orderly – he told me (1) to send back the Naval Demolition Party lying out on the spit, (2) get a Platoon up to protect our left flank, (3) go on and tell Maj. Bewes to retire. There were a lot of bullets; however I got to the naval party and lay down beside a seaman until I found that his idea of cover was a box of detonators. Passing the word to their officer led to a "sauve qui peut" – in other words a complete bunk led by the officer. I yelled to him to keep behind to no effect and they left two dead men behind them. Then I went to the Platoon. Their officer was paralysed with funk and wouldn't budge. The Sergeant was wounded in the head and the men took their cue from their officer which was right and proper.'

The letter continues to detail that one young Marine agreed to come with Jerram and thus the others were induced to move. Unfortunately the volunteer was wounded and as Jerram was dressing his wound Colonel Matthews arrived to ask in no uncertain terms why his orders had not been carried out. The real answer was evaded in their agreement that Bewes' Company could escape only with the aid of covering fire and this Jerram would have to get by signal from the fort to the ships. He confessed that his journey, running like a snipe, trying desperately to avoid rifle fire, gave him more sympathy for the platoon than he had felt hitherto. Jerram added a footnote that later, as they were all embarking, the two 'dead sailors' got up and started staggering back. Two officers took a stretcher and went back for them. Colonel Matthews refused to let anyone else go and Jerram was to tell them that a boat would be sent for them. A boat from the destroyer went in after dark but, according to the letter, the crew had to be forcibly persuaded to embark upon this mission and, though each man involved was later awarded the D.C.M., the two officers who had stayed with the wounded sailors got nothing. Jerram concludes his letter with a touching recollection. When as a boy he had had fights with his older brother, he had gained the necessary courage by tightly lacing up his boots. He had found himself doing the same when being rowed into the Kum Kale shore.

It would seem that by ignoring the few occasions when officers and men through the campaign failed to live up to the generally high level of conduct and morale, we fail to put into perspective the splendid overall record. 4 March was a bad day and, as R. R. James points out: 'It was . . . a grim portent. The disembarkation of troops under fire, their deployment when landed, their handling on largely unknown beaches; all these were novel problems, not only for the men of the Plymouth Battalion, but for everyone.'[5]As early as 2 March, Flight Lieutenant Bromet, later to be Air Vice Marshal Sir Geoffrey Bromet, had expressed in his diary a prophetic awareness of the problems which lay ahead. 'The Germans have frightened the Turks out of their lives and brought their wonderful organization and military genius to bear to the extent of making the Dardanelles a very difficult problem for the allies. Up to the present matters have all been our own way, but I think we shall find the narrows somewhat difficult to pass and perhaps by that time the Germans will have produced a submarine to tackle us. They are capable of great things.'

Despite the serious damage and destruction sustained by the forts from bombardments and the landing of demolition parties, they maintained their essential function of protecting the minefields. The losses on 18 March of the *Bouvet*, the *Ocean* and the *Irresistible* and the near loss of the *Inflexible*, each as a result of its hitting a mine, illustrate this clearly. The British North Sea trawlers used for the sweeping and their volunteer crews of fishermen have frequently been blamed for the losses, but the facts would suggest that the obvious unsuitability of the vessels for their appointed task renders criticism of the crews harsh to say the least. Indeed, A. J. Marder has written that the whole idea of using these slow trawlers was a 'basic error'.[6]

Above the Suandere in March there were 324 mines in ten lines, though in fact the allies believed that there were 289 in eight lines. There were five lines of mines in the Narrows, not one, as was reported. The Kephez minefield had two fewer lines – five – than had been reported. In addition it was incorrectly conjectured that there were mines at the entrance. Twenty-one trawlers were available for sweeping, but when working against the strong current some of them could barely make headway and the others achieved a maximum speed of only three and a half knots. When the time necessary for assembling and manoeuvring is considered and the fact that all the work had to be done under point-blank fire, it is difficult to estimate just what could have been achieved. The crews are described in the *Mitchell Report* as 'generally of poor physique with very little discipline',[7] but on 2 March Admiral Carden,

[5] *Gallipoli*, p. 45.
[6] A 'basic error was the conception that slow mine-sweeping trawlers could clear a passage up to and through the Narrows to enable the fleet to reach the Marmara', A. J. Marder, *From the Dardanelles to Oran*, p. 2.
[7] p. 51.

having seen their performance under fire, made a general signal: 'Mine-sweepers are doing fine work. Their perseverance and steadiness are excellent. Much depends on them.'[8] It is scarcely surprising that their morale was eroded by the strain of sweeping at night, when they knew that the very success of their work, that is the finding and exploding of mines, would disclose them to the probing searchlights and leave them open to heavy shell-fire. On 10 March the destroyers which accompanied them failed to silence the batteries, a trawler was sunk by the mine she had exploded and heavy shell-fire resulted in two trawlers being hit while exposed in the glare of the searchlights. On the 11th, when caught by searchlights and shell-fire, the leading trawler turned for home and the rest followed. Admiral de Robeck reported that 'in some cases the crews appear to have no objection to being blown up by mines, though they do not seem to like working under gunfire, which is a new element in their calling'.[9] It is perhaps stating the obvious that the Admiral, who had long Royal Navy service, wrote his report from a well-armoured and armed battleship; nevertheless his frustration was shared by officers and men in the squadron. Some, such as Midshipman William-Powlett, who had themselves felt the strain of unaccustomed danger expressed it simply as a matter beyond the competence of crews and their morale. 'Minesweepers are too slow for sweeping. They can only do one knot against the current with their sweeps out and so they have sent for some fast sweepers.'[10] The seaplane pilot Geoffrey Bromet had no doubt about the task facing the trawlermen. 'Their job is a most arduous and danger-ous one, and up to the present, although little success has rewarded their efforts, they have shown themselves most capable and absolutely chock-a-block with guts.'

By order of Admiral Carden, the trawler crews were accordingly stiffened by three Navy volunteers per ship, but their gallantry on 13–14 March and in the protecting cruiser *Amethyst* only served to prove that the speed of the trawlers was insufficient to enable them to carry out their task.[11] Faster trawlers were requested and the French made brave

---

[8] *Official History: Naval Operations*, vol. 2, p. 169.

[9] *Official History: Naval Operations*, vol. 2, p. 207.

[10] After the bombardment of 5 March he recorded: 'It is simply beastly for the first time to sit there in cold blood to be shot at and not know where from. We were stopped and continually these salvoes would come over eight at a time and every one seemed coming straight for you ... I did not like the idea of going in [to bombard] again. I felt very helpless and longed to go home. It was not the kind of fighting I expected to get.'

[11] R.N. picket boats had been used against the Kephez minefield as early as 8 March.

efforts with their vessels. The only really effective sweeping under the special conditions of the Dardanelles was not however to be possible till after the disasters of 18 March,[12] which will be described in the next chapter, and from soon after this date the Navy was pledged by Vice-Admiral de Robeck to a supporting rather than a leading role.

The damage suffered by the trawlers, whether with mixed crews or entirely Navy crews, was severe. The *Mitchell Report* describes some of the results of the night sweeping on 13 March in which two trawlers collided and came under concentrated fire which killed the Captain and all the upper-deck hands on one. Trawler 49 had her 'mess deck completely wrecked by a large shell, shell right through ship and out at after gallows, bunker flooded by a shell below the water line, small shell through bridge, masts and rigging shot through, boats riddled and various small damage'.[13]

The *Amethyst* herself suffered severely in this action. A member of her crew, E. Weaver, has written: 'We had been ordered to go below and write letters home as well as getting some refreshment. Later at action stations all was going well, with the picket boats pulling the mines away with grappling irons, and suddenly we were the centre of searchlight glare and all hell broke loose. My gun received a direct hit and all but two of us were wounded. In the forepart of the ship, shells killed many men still in their hammocks. A watch of stokers all together in the bathroom were wiped out and the upper deck looked like a ploughed field. We got out past Cape Helles at daybreak and that was the nicest sunrise I'd ever seen.'

Official sources indicate that the sweeping attempts were continued right up to 18 March, even though the plan for the attack was based on the need to reduce the forts and batteries to silence before the minefields could be completely cleared. It is a small point in view of the fact that the critical line of mines laid by the *Nousret*, which accounted for the 18 March losses, was laid on 8 March, but Captain Boswell, serving in the *Irresistible*, positively denies that there was any sweeping on the day before the attack of the area from which the bombardment was to take place.

Fernand Pion, an engineer and a reservist in the crew of the French minesweeper *Pioche*, described his ship as having the appearance of a powerful tug with a high bridge and drawing little water, purpose-built for its work, unlike the English North Sea trawlers, and with a gun capable of destroying the mines surfaced by its operations. The crew was well

---

[12] From 4 April Beagle Class destroyers became operational as minesweepers.
[13] *Mitchell Report*, p. 57.

trained in the handling of the sweep and their boats operated at a far greater speed than the British ones – they were capable of sweeping individually a 200-metre channel to a depth of six metres in a single sweep. Pion recalls that his Captain was summoned to Vice-Admiral de Robeck and officially informed that the English trawlers had failed and it was now up to the French. The Captain had all the machinery and engines checked thoroughly and the crew reduced to essential members to avoid unnecessary casualties. In the French sweeping operations Pion admits that during the strain of fifteen days' work up to 17 March two of their crew proved incapable of disguising the nervous state all must have experienced. They gesticulated wildly, called upon Heaven, their wives and children, banged their heads against the bulkheads, burst into tears and then had to be transferred to the *Bouvet*. There they began to recover their spirits, only, by the sad irony of fate, to succumb with most of the *Bouvet*'s crew to the effect of the minesweepers' failure to detect that vital line of mines off the Asiatic shore of Erenkeui Bay. Pion wrote to his mother on 2 March:

'We had our life belts on all the time and it was an unforgettable experience as the shells from batteries towards Chanak regularly straddled us and the protecting British battleship *Albion* searched for the batteries firing on us, to engage them and attempt to silence them. The French gunnery is marvellous. Don't you believe it if you hear of German telegrams reporting differently. The pigs have had the cheek to send wireless messages (one of which we have intercepted) saying that we have failed and four minesweepers and two cruisers have been sunk, which is obviously false. I hope that soon in Constantinople we shall be able to stuff their lies in their mouths with 380-cm. shells. Such a victory would have considerable influence on the course of the war as it would force Turkey to give in immediately, Russia could free the Bosphorus and the Balkan peoples would all rise up with us to take their share of the oriental cake.'

Beside this letter from a man obviously conscious of wider issues than the safety of his own boat, it is interesting to place the recollections of Chief Petty Officer Cave. He recalls in his memoirs of service in the cruiser *Dublin* that at 'about this time [date uncertain] we took on board a group of city types, dressed to match, armed with brief cases and we left for a port away up north in Bulgaria. I managed to get a glimpse of the chart which indicated by the ship's course that the port must have been Dedeagatch. I didn't know what it was all about but by the appearance of the men's faces on their return it had not been a successful trip.'

In fact the date of the return of the 'city gents' was 17 March and they had been attempting to buy Turkish withdrawal from the war. The British agents involved had been empowered to negotiate up to £4,000,000 for this aim, but the chief stumbling-blocks to successful negotiation proved to be the question of sovereignty over Constantinople and the apparently successful progress of naval operations in the Dardanelles. Evidence had come to light that the Turks were very short of ammunition for their forts. A member of the well-known English trading family in Constantinople, the Whittalls, was involved in the talks and he was accompanied by a former technical adviser to the Foreign Office during the attempt to improve Anglo-Turkish relations in the summer of 1914. His name was C. G. Eady and his son-in-law, Captain G. R. Allen, has written that from the evidence of his father-in-law's diary and from the naval failure of 18 March 'it does seem remarkable that a mission which had carried matters so far successfully should have been allowed to wither ignominiously at such a moment'.[14] Another man who played a small part in the earliest Anglo-Turkish financial haggling was Captain H. N. Lyster,[15] who recently wrote in *The Gallipolian* of a journey made in August 1914 from London to Paris and Marseilles on what was then a secret mission conducted by the Imperial Ottoman Bank, by which he was employed. Only later did he learn that he had been involved in Britain offering 'Turkey a paper loan of £5,000,000 to enter the war with us or remain neutral, but Germany had offered £2,000,000 in gold and the *Goeben* did the rest'. It is tempting but fruitless to speculate on the possible consequences had either the August 1914 or the early March 1915 talks reached a happy settlement, but neither financial negotiations nor active minesweeping were to prevent the launching and failure of the naval attack of 18 March.

[14] Captain C. R. G. Allen, 'A Ghost from Gallipoli', *Royal United Service Institute Journal*, May 1963, p. 138.
[15] *The Gallipolian*, Autumn, 1973, pp. 9–11.

4.   The Naval Assault of 18 March

The failure of the minesweeping operations led to the decision to launch another attack on the forts, but this time a far more concentrated one. Success, it was believed, would allow the clearance of the minefields to proceed without hindrance. Such a belief was, however, considerably to underestimate the threat of the batteries and particularly the mobile batteries. On the Asiatic side of the Straits, water buffalo, like those still to be seen there today, were used to move and re-site howitzer batteries at night. Dummy batteries of smoking cylinders were difficult to distinguish from the real thing in these confined, swiftly flowing waters, with fire being directed from both shores. Gone were the days, amusingly described by E. W. Bullock, a seaman in the *Inflexible*, when camouflage could be painted undisturbed on one side of a vessel while long-range unanswered bombardment was being conducted from the other. Liman von Sanders, the commander of the German forces in Turkey, referring to an allied naval bombardment on 1 March, described the work of the Turkish howitzer batteries on the heights of Erenkeui and Halil Eli: 'The batteries . . . belonged to the 8th Foot Artillery Regiment commanded by Colonel Wehrle and had been detached from the First Army under my command to strengthen temporarily the artillery defences of the Dardanelles Straits. The Regiment, variously grouped on the heights of the Asiatic and European shores, gave splendid support to the artillery of the fortress and with its brave commander earned much praise. The hostile ships directed their fire not only against his batteries but against dummy positions he had constructed and frequently changed.'[1]

The transfer of command of the allied squadron from the sick Admiral Carden to Vice-Admiral de Robeck in no way interfered with the thoroughness of the preparations for the great assault. The plans are dated 15 March and are under Carden's name, though operational orders of the 17th bear de Robeck's name. They provided for the more modern ships, the *Inflexible*, the *Lord Nelson*, the *Agamemnon* and the *Queen Elizabeth*, to prepare the way by long-range bombardment for the older French ships, the *Suffren*, the *Bouvet*, the *Gaulois* and the *Charlemagne*, to bombard at closer range with support from the *Triumph* and the

[1] L. von Sanders, *Five Years in Turkey*, pp. 54–5.

Prince George. It does not come within the scope of this work to describe in detail the alternative plans and the system of reliefs or indeed the events of a day so well documented, but rather to examine the personal experiences of men at the heart of the action.

A very good general impression through the eyes of a midshipman in the *Prince George* is conveyed by the log of A. G. Buchanan for 18 March. 'We were hit once on the mess deck of B2 and once on the shelter deck about twenty-one feet from A1. One of these shells burst and made a mess of everything near but no damage of any consequence was done. About a quarter of an hour after the second shell hit us, the order was passed from the foretop for A1 to stand by to man the sea boat as a Frenchman, the *Bouvet*, had struck a mine; a minute later an order was passed down "Man the lifeboat" and then later "Hurry up with the boat, she's gone." This had all happened in about three minutes. Our picket boat shoved off immediately and picked up thirty-five survivors and the cutter picked up one . . . There were only forty-odd[2] altogether . . . The coxswain of our picket boat said that there were several explosions after she had gone down, apparently caused by the remaining watertight compartments giving way. Her starboard 10.8-inch gun was seen to fall overboard as she heeled over apparently badly damaged by the explosion. The *Inflexible*'s fore bridge was seen to be on fire at one time during the action, but the fire was got under when she drew out of range . . . As we were waiting outside for our picket boat and cutter to come up, we noticed that the *Gaulois* was much down by the head. All the destroyers raced up to her and stood by her. The *Canopus*, *Cornwallis* and a French ship also stood by. It was soon found that she was in no immediate danger of sinking . . . Wireless signals were picked up at about this time, stating that the *Irresistible* had struck a mine and the *Ocean* had been ordered to stand by her.'

In his memoirs E. W. Bullock has written: 'We could hear the thunder of the guns above the engines together with the shuddering and the blast showering dust everywhere, but we had no knowledge of course of how things were going; then there was a thud which shook the ship. It was followed by the silence from our guns. Then we could hear the tread of feet on the deck, meanwhile all electric lights had failed and we lit our secondary oil lamps that gave only a dim light. The engine-room telegraphs rang half ahead and remained at that long enough for us to surmise that we were either through the Narrows or we were retiring. The matter was confirmed by a well-meaning voice shouting down the

[2] In fact there were sixty-six.

lift-shaft "Abandon ship stations". We were still unaware of what had happened until the engineer of the watch received from the bridge a message stating that we had been mined forard, and if possible we would make for Mudros and beach ourselves in shallow water.

'Of the watches down below one should go to his abandon ship station and the other remain down below till the last moment. Each man tossed up with his opposite number. I won against my friend Wiggie Bennett and in my heart I felt a pang, feeling that all or none should remain down below. We were urged to get a move on as the ship was developing a list and the bows were deeper in the water also. Up we went on the various ladders, groping our way as it was total darkness on the way up. We knew our way so the only problem was the watertight door that led to the mess deck. After knocking off the clips we couldn't push it open and no wonder because we should have been pulling it. Once outside we were amazed at the shambles. First of all we could see that the mess tables and chairs had been taken for buoyancy if the men had had to go overboard, then twenty-nine had been killed in the forard torpedo flat by the explosion of the mine and damage by another mine had flooded the food store, thus compensating for the list we were experiencing to starboard. Some of the men were stripped to their underclothes with their lifesaving belts blown up. I noticed that one of the ship's police had a football tied to his waist and as the valve to my lifebelt was missing someone tied the end with string. Wounded were being placed into the boats. I particularly remember the Master of Arms sitting in a cutter smoking his pipe and making light of his injuries, also the Gunnery Commander being carried on a stretcher to a boat. Though he was soon to die, I heard him say "I'm a poor specimen of humanity now".'

The *Inflexible* did reach Mudros, and Stoker Bullock not only had a chance to survey the full extent of the damage to the ship but was one of the funeral party for the sea burial of the dead, who had already been sewn up in canvas shrouds weighted with fire bars. The bodies of those killed in the flooded torpedo flat were recovered later.

A seaman in the *Lord Nelson*, G. E. Keeler, wrote in his diary for 18 March that he had seen the *Bouvet* 'turn turtle in less than two minutes'. He also recorded the difficulty of sighting the Turkish howitzer batteries and taking on board the *Irresistible* survivors. Of the *Lord Nelson* under fire, Keeler wrote, 'It was not very cheerful in the maintop with too many splinters flying around.' Keeler saw the *Inflexible* taking the punishment being suffered while Stoker Bullock was below. 'Her foretop was smashed in and soon she was hit on the forebridge setting it on fire. It was a sight to see her blazing away and firing her 12-inch guns at the same time.' Keeler also saw a 'splendid piece of work' done by the destroyer flotilla as they dashed through the shells to take everyone off the *Ocean*, which was flying distress signals. His final entries for the day were the cheering sight of 'Lizzie[3] doing a bit of good to Chanak and Aggie[4] with a lovely hole in her funnel knocking nearly half of it away'.

Midshipman William-Powlett recorded in his diary for the same day that those who saw the *Bouvet* go down 'were rather cut up. It was not a nice thing to see on our way in.' How honestly this chronicles the natural feelings of someone faced by a tragedy which might soon be shared! The midshipman wrote: 'I am afraid I was not able to take my usual notes as I was too busy but I managed some and I can remember most.' He had observed the excellent Turkish gunfire on the *Albion* and the *Irresistible* and he made a sketch in his diary to show how the splashes sometimes obscured the whole of the ship. Regrettably the photographs he took through the gun port did not come out successfully, but he described vividly the men crowding over the listing *Irresistible* into the destroyer *Wear* and picket boats while under heavy fire. He saw the *Inflexible* letting off great clouds of steam and heard her blowing her siren in distress. Volunteer cutters searched unavailingly during the night for the *Irresistible* and the *Ocean*, both of which had sunk. William-Powlett, as he rested on the gun-room settee, wrote in his diary that 'we were most lucky. If we had carried out the first plan we would have taken the *Ocean*'s place.'

W. L. Berridge, aboard the *Albion*, was greatly impressed by the conduct of the men on board the crippled, sinking *Irresistible*. In a letter now in the Imperial War Museum he wrote to his parents and sister: '. . . and all through [the shell fire] her people were waiting quietly for the destroyers to take them off. One shot fell right in the middle of the quarter deck and must have wrought awful havoc. But there was no panic, none tried to get away before ordered to. And the destroyers were wonderfully handled and saved the situation completely.' The letter concludes: 'Of other damage to the fleet I will not tell but the day was far from a victory for us. Something near our fort exploded and burst violently and I believe most of the forts stopped firing but the guns were probably intact and the Turks merely left temporarily. I hope the next show will be better.' These sentiments would no doubt have been echoed by Edward Grayken, a Marine on board the *Irresistible*, who had climbed up the listing deck of

[3] H.M.S. *Queen Elizabeth*, firing 15-inch shells.
[4] H.M.S. *Agamemnon*.

the ship, slid over the side onto the torpedo nets, disentangled himself and was taken from the water by a picket boat which put him aboard the *Ocean*. Within a very short time a not dissimilar procedure enabled him to escape from the mined *Ocean* and his rescue this time was by a destroyer.

For the French ships and their crews the drama was especially associated with the loss of the *Bouvet* and the severe damage sustained by the *Gaulois*. From the *Vengeance*, the *Bouvet* had been observed by Midshipman William-Powlett to have had, in full view of the deck, all her officers in full dress uniform, a band playing and numbers of sheep and cattle, as the French ship led the attack. Midshipman Seyeux, in the *Gaulois*, describes in his diary for 18 March the tragically swift sinking of the *Bouvet* and the prolonged strain of keeping the *Gaulois* afloat. The explosion of shrapnel shells above the *Queen Elizabeth* was seen as the sudden appearance of little black clouds which seemed to produce rain. When all the forts opened fire they produced an 'astonishing noise'. Blackish smoke was seen rising from the bridge of the *Inflexible* and then the *Gaulois* herself was hit. Men were wounded, among them a friend of the diarist, and shells began falling all around them. They were hit again and a slight shock was felt throughout the ship – a more violent explosion – and they made an effort to retire. The *Bouvet* turned in order to place herself behind the *Suffren* and she hit a mine. A small sheaf of flame and yellowish smoke appeared from a starboard 27-cm. gun turret. 'For a few seconds it continued its course then gently without an explosion it listed to starboard. The Commander clearly had had no time to stop the engines as we saw it sinking lower and lower without losing speed. A minute after seeing the sheaf of flame, before our astonished eyes, the *Bouvet* turned completely over to starboard and disappeared.' Immediately they moved towards the 'large white spot' which marked where the vessel had sunk to see if they could pick up survivors, but English motorboats were there first, followed by a torpedo boat to help to pick up the last ones found.

Over 600 men had drowned or been killed by the explosion in that dreadful minute or so. There were sixty-six survivors. In 1973 Sauveur Payro, who had been traced to Marseilles, gave an account of his escape which differed on no material points from a statement he had made to the senior surviving officer within two days of his being rescued.[5] The statement records that he 'was sent to get spare shells for the 27-cm. port gun turret. I was in the right place for the shells when the blow came. The boat immediately listed to starboard. I was completely covered in

[5] The *Bouvet* file in the French Navy Archives and P.L.

the coal dust which came from the bunkers. I went to the signal ladder and with the second mate we climbed up. I then went up the ladder leading to the upper battery. From the bridge I got myself onto the funnel which was entering the water. Then I climbed onto the hull. I believe the second mate was trapped by the landing keel blocks and that he fell into a hatch way. From the keel I threw myself into the water. I am a very good swimmer.' In 1973 M. Payro spoke of the blood bursting through his ears and nose, as he was carried deeply under. He came to the surface to be rescued by a British picket or motor-boat. The officer who took the depositions in March 1915 ended his report by remarking that not a single survivor had seen any regrettable behaviour by those now living or dead.

The other French battleship, the *Gaulois*, was also beginning to sink. Midshipman Seyeux wrote in his diary that there was no chance of reaching Tenedos. By an irony of fate one of the *Bouvet* survivors brought by an English motor-boat had only recently been transferred from the *Gaulois* to the *Bouvet*. Inside the *Gaulois* the water was rising rapidly, the dynamos had failed and there were only oil lamps giving illumination in the evening darkness as they crept towards the Rabbit Islands. The ship's company were assembled in their disembarking stations and some were taken off. Others collected chairs and tables ready to throw them into the sea if need be, to give support in the water. Some partly undressed so that they would be able to swim more easily. The stokers and engineers went to their jobs below with admirable *sang-froid*. The officers anxiously watched from the bridge to see if the *Gaulois* would reach Mavro Island. Towing offers from *Suffren* and British ships had been refused, but when 'English officers came on board asking what help we needed, we asked for and received an anchor and divers who could examine and repair our holed keel. *Gaulois* only just reached the island in time as the rapidly constructed wooden partition which was designed to cover the hole was giving way under the enormous pressure of the water. Admiral Guépratte had previously come on board to congratulate our Commander on the skilful way he was handling the ship.' The *Gaulois* was gently beached on Mavro Island.

Rear-Admiral Lucas, in 1915 an officer in the *Gaulois*, slightly senior to Midshipman Seyeux, recalls in his memoirs the action of their Captain Biard in taking the *Gaulois* immediately to the rescue of any possible survivors of the *Bouvet* despite the obvious dangers. Later, with half the crew off and the danger of sinking very real, Captain Biard had asked for his best uniform and a glass of port. This was apparently to set an example of *sang-froid*, but Midshipman Seyeux had not apparently understood these orders, which convinced him that his Captain was determined to poison himself rather than survive his ship. When Admiral Guépratte visited the ship in its sad condition and was given the full ceremonial greeting appropriate to his rank, the English sailors present in the boats closely attendant upon the stricken vessel must, considered Lucas, have been puzzled at such formality under these circumstances, but 'everyone on the *Gaulois* on 18 March behaved in accordance with the great traditions of the French Navy'. Lucas himself admitted that he had been very frightened and had taken an experienced sailor with him when ordered below to search for and bring up the ship's code books at a time when it looked as if the *Gaulois* would sink.[6]

The diary account of Jean Deffez, whose reactions to the bombardment of 25 February we have already seen, noted the similarity of the noise of the explosion of a Turkish shell hitting their deck to that of the French shells as they left the ship's guns. He mentions the sour taste in his throat and the poisonous air from the acrid fumes of explosions, and writes bitterly of the '*vilains Turcs*' and the '*criminels Boches*' who fired on the rescue work among the *Bouvet* survivors, an incident also mentioned by Sauveur Payro in his recollections. On 20 March Deffez wrote his ten long pages on the events of 18 March and confirmed his attachment to this record of his service in a revealing entry. On being ordered to prepare to abandon ship, he had gone below and in the shadowy gloom, after several attempts found his locker and brought up to safety his diary, his wallet and a change of clothes.

Among the papers of Admiral Guépratte there is much evidence of his personal interest in the welfare of his men. His very small private diary records for 18 March that 'the honour of the Flag has been fully but dearly maintained. *Bouvet* struck by a mine has sunk – all on board have perished save a fraction.' Then the five surviving senior officers are named.[7] On a scrap of paper is pencilled the service career of one of the able-seamen saved from the *Bouvet*. 'Payro Sauveur. At the Dardanelles since 15 November 1914 has participated in all the actions of the 3rd Division up to 18 March. Had his position in the 27-cm. turret.' When making his recommendations after the attack he mentioned 'Enseigne de

---

[6] These books were handed for safety to an English vessel and among the Guépratte Papers is an acknowledgement for their safe return.

[7] That Guépratte evaluated his officers carefully is indicated by notes he made on 15 October 1914 in which he deplores the nonchalance affected by his officers and reminds them that the men must be inspired by example as well as precept.

Vaisseau de Première Classe Sagnier, a gunnery officer who showed in the action the most intelligent and ingenious zeal which he had displayed in the previous actions – a perfect *sang-froid* and an extremely valuable team spirit for getting his gun into action.' Among the same recommendations to officers and men in the *Suffren* is one for a man who 'conducted himself very cheerfully under fire'. In the *Gaulois* M. E. Seyeux was one of those who 'always showed the greatest courage and calmness under fire'.

The united spirit of the allied officers and crew, despite Guépratte's impatience with the British Admiralty for so strictly insisting upon British overall command, is reflected in the letters received by the Admiral immediately after the action of 18 March. On the day following, the Commander of the *Agamemnon* wrote to express 'our deepest sympathy and sorrow with you and our brother officers and men of your squadron, in the loss and fate of so many gallant comrades'. A Navigating Lieutenant (L. H. Lindner) in the *Indefatigable* wrote his congratulations to the French Admiral on the bombardment and his 'deep regret at the loss of so many of your brave officers and men of the *Bouvet*. My mess mates ask me to say they join in wishing you the best of luck in forthcoming operations.' From Brest, the Admiral was assured by Admiral Vergniaud that 'each day we think of you, of the brave ones who fight on those shores on such a noble mission'. If the Admiral ever doubted the warm respect in which he was held by all ranks of the British squadron, those doubts must have been dispelled by a signal which was scarcely official but is, in retrospect, significant. It reads in full: 'Monsieur, I shall have great pleasure in giving a song (which I have composed) during the interval of the cinema concert if you will kindly permit me to do so. Roberts.' There is no doubt of the popularity of the French naval officers and men with the English naval or R.N.A.S. officers with whom they came into contact. The *Ark Royal* seaplane pilot Geoffrey Bromet wrote in his diary after the 18 March attack: 'One and all were glad to see that the French squadron had been congratulated by the Vice-Admiral and also the Admiralty. Their gallant conduct and high-spirited efforts at all times have made them very popular with our fleet.'

For all the spirit, *élan* and seamanship of the allied squadron, the great attack had been a failure. The unswept line of mines off Erenkeui had rendered valueless the temporary silencing of some Turkish batteries and the damage to the torpedo tube gear at Kilid Bahr. In only one respect was the Turkish defence of the Narrows seriously weakened and that was in their considerable expenditure of ammunition, which was now in short supply.

Of course the significance of the damage cannot be measured solely by casualty statistics; nevertheless it is a point worth making that the number of casualties in the *Bouvet* alone, with 600 drowned, far outweighs the thirty-eight to forty-three Turkish gunners and officers killed by the bombardment. The Turkish officers interviewed in 1919 by the members of the investigating committee which produced the *Mitchell Report* testified to the maintenance of a high morale among the fort and howitzer battery gun crews. The sinking of the ships and the failure to resume the attack were of course materially important in this. The point was made that public morale was similarly influenced by Turkish victory. A Turkish naval officer affirmed that when the attack on the 18th was broken off 'it was commonly said that the English had only gone home to tea and that they would start again as soon as they had had breakfast in the morning'.[8]

General Askir Arkayan, an observation officer with a howitzer battery on the heights above Erenkeui Bay, has recently written his recollections of his experiences on 18 March. 'We saw a mass of ships such as we had never seen before. We were amazed, but realizing that we should be faced that day with an out and out conflict, we completed our supplies and prepared for the attack . . . We knew each ship well from the lists we possessed . . . The battle developed with considerable violence and at noon the French ships in the second line advanced through the first line and opened a tremendous bombardment. The batteries replied effectively. Under this fire the *Bouvet* started to withdraw, but at that moment a cloud of red and black smoke arose from the ship, which may have struck a mine. Immediately after this there was a much more violent explosion. We believed that a shell from Mejidiye had blown up the magazine. The ship heeled over at once and her crew poured into the sea. On both sides fire ceased. The destroyers in the rear hastened to save the crew. We opened fire but again firing ceased . . . towards sunset the battle slackened and the ships withdrew. Just then the *Queen Elizabeth* lying off Hissarlik opened fire on my battery. She was too far away for us to reply and we withdrew the gun crews, without any damage being done. Throughout the night we prepared for the battle to be renewed on the following morning, changing battery positions and bringing up ammunition.'

The well-known on-the-spot description[9] by the American newspaper

<hr />

[8]   *Mitchell Report*, p. 86, evidence of Lieut-Commander Raaf. The *Mitchell Report* considered that this officer's main objective seemed to be to please, and no weight can be attached to his opinions.

[9]   P.R.O. W.O. 106/1465 2099.

correspondent George Shreiner was filed at the War Office with a note: 'a picturesque account of the bombardment of the Dardanelles forts on 19 March [*sic*]. It is evidently the product of a Germanophile brain garnished with great powers of imaginative description. Much of it is however undoubtedly true.' The description relates that 'comparatively little damage had been done to the Turkish positions' and with regard to the morale of the defenders there is some inconsistency as he finds Turks in a 'rather elated frame of mind'. Some were building a sort of monument out of two huge steel pieces which had landed in an adjacent garden, but the 'murderous fire' on Chanak caused the many soldiers and civilians who were leaving the town to scatter hurriedly for shelter. 'But shelter there really was none. Shells were falling on the water front, and on the next street in front and behind.'

An observer of more consequence than the American was General Sir Ian Hamilton, the Commander in Chief of the newly constituted Mediterranean Expeditionary Force. On 16 February it had been agreed in the War Council that the 29th Division should be dispatched to Lemnos, the island which seemed most likely to serve as a base for Gallipoli operations. Kitchener had second thoughts about the dispatch of this division of regular troops, and Churchill's changed emphasis was dramatically illustrated when he complained at the War Council meeting on 19 February that 'insufficient military support at the critical moment' might lead to failure.[10] He even announced that he would 'disclaim all responsibility if a disaster occurs in Turkey owing to insufficiency of troops'.[11] The official documentary evidence certainly invites the conclusion that the original conception was unrealistic, or, if viewed more tolerantly, was organic and subject to change.

On 10 March Lord Kitchener had finally agreed to the dispatch of the 29th Division. Three days later General Sir Ian Hamilton was summoned to the War Office to be informed that he was to command the force which was to concentrate in the eastern Mediterranean to support the Navy in securing their gains. Hamilton arrived in the Aegean the day before the great assault and was able to view from within the Straits the latter half of the action. On the new battleship *Queen Elizabeth*, Vice-Admiral de Robeck conferred with the General on 22 March. They agreed on the need for a combined operation which would enable the Narrows to be commanded from the European side, the waters swept and thus the

[10] Hankey's notes to the War Council meeting of 19 February (P.R.O. Cab. 22/1 262).
[11] ibid.

larger ships enabled to move through to the Marmara. Again contention
has arisen over the real authorship of the fundamental change in policy
which was now to relegate the Navy to a supporting role in the launching
of a combined operation to land allied forces to capture the Gallipoli
Peninsula.

From 19 March to the day of the landing, the undamaged allied ships,
together with the replacements for those sunk or seriously damaged,
patrolled the entrance to the Straits and the Gulf of Saros, and carried out
the necessary reconnaissance of the Peninsula to prepare for the landing.
The mine-sweeping flotilla was reorganized to enable fast sweeping to
be undertaken by the Beagle Class destroyers. In addition, the bombardment of forts and howitzer batteries continued with the assistance of
aeroplane observation. On one occasion the *Prince of Wales*, with two
rounds of 12-inch shrapnel and from a mere 1,500 yards, completely
obliterated a string of camels in full career with armed riders. Vice-
Admiral Longley-Cook remembered his sadness at witnessing such
wholesale slaughter of man and beast.

The usefulness of aerial observation is exemplified by a report from
H.M.S. *Ark Royal* of a flight on 11 March by Seaplane 172 (Flight
Lieutenant Bromet and Lieutenant Torrington, R.N.V.R.) at an average
height of 3,000 feet, with very good visibility. 'Road round Eastern
end of Gulf [of Saros] has on either side of it an impassable swamp . . .
Between Kavak River and Bulair village are four lines of traversed
trenches. About one mile east of Bulair is a large camp of forty-six large
square tents and six bell tents. There are two large newly dug earth-
works in the neighbourhood of this camp between it and Bulair, each
to hold four guns, but none were seen in place. There are numerous
trenches round these two works . . . Forts Sultan and Napoleon did not
appear to be seriously damaged. Roads all in good repair but no movement was seen on them or on anywhere else. Gun emplacement for one
gun on cliff facing seaward (2 F.31). Gun emplacement for two guns in
2 D.33 flanking landing place.'[12]

In considering whether to land at the Gulf of Saros, Sir Ian Hamilton
must have been impressed by this sort of report, together with Vice-
Admiral de Robeck's concern for his communications at the rear should
his squadron be able to break into the Narrows. He had, it must be
accepted, contrary reports on the state of defensive preparation at Bulair.
They came, for example, from the *Gaulois*, as is recorded in M. E.
Seyeux's diary before 18 March, and from the Royal Naval Division

[12] Original Flight Report (P.L.).

subsequently. The thoroughness with which the Gulf was examined should not be underestimated. The *Mitchell Report*[13] indicates that 'from 31 March to 8 April *Henri IV*, with *Agamemnon*, *Lord Nelson* and *Talbot*, was operating in the Gulf of Zeros [Saros]; sketches were made of all possible landing places and a few rounds were fired at Turkish works; *Agamemnon* examined Enos on the 31st and landed a party at Zeros island which brought off three Greek fishermen; boats were also sent in close to the Bulair trenches which were fired into and found unoccupied.' The use of a kite balloon by H.M.S. *Talbot* and later both a kite balloon and a spherical observation balloon from H.M.S. *Manica* assisted the aerial reconnaissance. From 24 March this reconnaissance was stepped up when No. 3 Squadron Royal Naval Air Service,[14] with eighteen planes, arrived at Tenedos to establish an air base to supplement the work carried out to this date by the six seaplanes attached to the *Ark Royal* and the two attached to the French ship *Rabenfels*.[15] By this means and by direct naval observation the Turkish defensive preparations, both on the Asiatic shore and on the Peninsula, were closely watched during the weeks of preparation for the combined operation.

Both contemporary evidence as well as the recollections of survivors leave no doubt that the ordinary soldiers and the junior officers, as well as those in higher command, expected no easy landing. That the naval command still had every intention of getting into the Marmara is indicated by de Robeck's orders from the *Queen Elizabeth* on 2 April, in which he says that 'until the Military have stated their demands it is impossible to give detailed proposals of the naval co-operation . . . during disembarkation the Vice-Admiral will be on board *Queen Elizabeth* [and] on the fleet proceeding through the Narrows, the Vice-Admiral will hoist his flag in *Lord Nelson* and take command of the Squadron in the Marmara.'

In his memoirs Liman von Sanders describes the thoroughness of the Turkish preparations.[16] He had been appointed to organize the defence of the Dardanelles on 24 March, and so had a month for preparations,

---

[13] p. 93. Similar details recorded for 8, 10, 11 and 16 April.

[14] Of this squadron the Director of Military Aeronautics in the War Office, Lieut-Colonel Brancker, had written to Hamilton in March: 'For offensive work and bomb dropping you will find them excellent but if you want to get efficient results from their reconnaissance you will have to keep a tight hand on them as they have very few ideas on the subject' (King's College, London, Centre for Military Archives, Hamilton papers).

[15] The *Mitchell Report* gives a figure of 80 bombs dropped by allied aeroplanes between 19 March and 24 April (p. 94). But see also footnote 21, p. 243, of this book.

[16] L. von Sanders, *Five Years in Turkey*, pp. 57–62.

during which he strengthened the three areas which he considered possible landing places: the Gulf of Saros, the southern end of the Peninsula and the Asiatic side of the Narrows. Of great significance was his development of the mobility of his battle groups. Roads were constructed or improved, training marches insisted upon and, as far as possible, all movement took place by night. Field fortifications were constructed or strengthened, barbed wire stretched under water, landmines laid. Kannengiesser Pasha[17] acknowledges the co-operation in these preparations of Admiral von Usedom, whose base in command of the Straits themselves was at Chanak. There is in Kannengiesser's book a menacingly apt reference to the siting of 'flanking fire by machine and other guns' of the potential landing places together with wire entanglements, pit and mines and the commencement of a new road from the town of Gallipoli. This road was sheltered under the shoulder of the hilly plateau which stretches down the Straits' coast of the Peninsula to Cape Helles. When Kannengiesser writes that 'all of us who took part in the war know how, after weeks of high tension and expectation, the final commencement of the attack was welcome as a kind of relief', he writes in the knowledge that the time for preparation had been sufficient. Nevertheless the tension and frustration had been hard to bear. It had been no less hard for the allied troops assembling in the eastern Mediterranean.

[17] *The Campaign in Gallipoli*, p. 94 ff. Colonel Kannengiesser had been in command of the Turkish XVI Army Corps in 1915.

5.   The Mediterranean Expeditionary Force

Though united in a common enterprise, the allied force which gradually assembled in Egypt was heterogeneous in composition and character. With the English, Welsh and Irish troops, there were Australians and New Zealanders, some of whom were just recently out of Britain, as well as Indians, Russians, Palestinians, Senegalese, North Africans and soldiers of metropolitan France. There was however further diversity in the British troops. There were regulars in the battalions of Lancashire Fusiliers, Essex and Worcester Regiments, Dublin Fusiliers, Munster Fusiliers, Royal Fusiliers, Border Regiment, Hampshire Regiment, Royal Marines, Inniskillings, King's Own Scottish Borderers, and South Wales Borderers, and in the batteries of the Royal Field and Royal Horse Artillery. There were territorials like the West Riding Engineers, some of the Field Ambulance Units and the 1/5 Royal Scots. Indeed many of the rank and file of the Royal Naval Division were in effect Kitchener Volunteers of August, September and October 1914, though there was a Brigade of regular Royal Marines within the Division. The French troops were mainly conscripts[1] and a large percentage of the Australian and New Zealand troops had had some experience of voluntary or compulsory military training before the war.

The consequence of this was that the active-service experience of the men involved varied from Boer War campaigning, service in India and elsewhere on imperial duty to pre-war part-time training. A few gunners had experienced the first weeks of the Western Front fighting in 1914, for some in the Royal Naval Division there had been active service at Antwerp, and for South Wales Borderers the combined operation of Tsing-Tau in China, but for others previously occupied at the coal face or office desk there had been only a few short months of accelerated training. Not only were there differences in service experience and differences in physique consequent upon conditions of work and living, but there were differences in outlook, again bred by different values held in communities widely separated either by geography or by social distinctions. The situation was made still more complicated when Gurkha and Sikh troops reinforced the men on the Peninsula, and from this

[1] See p. 65.

point of view it might be added that the Greeks too were represented, but by labourers, contractors and interpreters and not by a military force. Differences of language, religious observance and sometimes food must also be considered, and those who concentrate solely on the differences in the Australian and British attitudes towards military discipline considerably over-simplify the problems of a force working in daily co-operation under a single commander, who was himself dependent on so many considerations beyond his control. An examination of the background of a number of the English troops who may be taken as representative of their units will show clearly the varied material within even the 29th Division and the Royal Naval Division.

Trumpeter Lissenburg (R.F.A.), with a family tradition of army service in India, had been at the Delhi Durbar in December 1911. In the same year B. A. McConnell had joined the Royal Inniskilling Fusiliers at Armagh depot and had served at Aldershot and in India. With approximately three years' full military service behind them, these men were among the experienced regular soldiers forming the backbone of the 29th Division which landed at Cape Helles on 25 April. Even Lissenburg and McConnell however could not match the experience of W. G. Wood, who had been in the famous L Battery R.H.A. action at Néry on the retirement from Mons in August 1914 which earned the battery three V.C.s.

With part-time 'Saturday-night' soldiering in the Territorial Force, G. B. Smith was mobilized from his Sheffield steel-works on 4 August to serve in the West Riding Engineers Field Company, which involved him in the *River Clyde* landing eight months later. Nevertheless his experience – once-weekly training and an annual camp – was more than that of A. E. Wilson, from a Stockton shipbuilding firm. He had joined the Royal Naval Division Nelson Battalion as a Kitchener Volunteer in August 1914 and found himself in action at Antwerp in the first week in October. Even Wilson's preparation for action in Gallipoli was more thorough than that of Joseph Murray (R.N.D. *Hood*), a Durham miner early in October 1914, who was seen off to the war in mid-October by a sobbing mother and a concertina-led station-platform sing-song from relatives and friends. 'Something had told me I should [go] and as I wished to see the world, this was my great opportunity.'[2]

Eric Wettern, who was in a family granite business, had received, as a member of the Institutions of Civil, Mechanical and Electrical Engineers, a letter dated 14 September 1914 from A. G. Lyster, the President of the Institution of Civil Engineers. The letter, having drawn attention to the

[2] J. Murray, *Gallipoli As I Saw It*, p. 19.

desire of members 'to serve in the army now being raised', announced that an opportunity was now afforded for members to serve together in the Divisional Engineer Units of the Royal Naval Division. 'The terms of enlistment will be for the duration of the war but not in any case exceeding three years . . . Pay is under consideration but will not be less than the Army rates.' Wettern responded to the letter and his paybook records that he was paid 2s. 6d. a day, of which 1s. 4d. was the special rate for Engineers. His first letter home from the R.N.D. Engineer camp at Oxney Bottom, Ringwould, near Dover, on 1 October 1914 gives brief first impressions. 'Under canvas, don't know anything about our duties yet – shall find out tomorrow. Shall have blue jackets uniform pro tem.' In approximately seven months he would be in a dugout under shell-fire, would have definite and dangerous duties to perform and would not be clad in the much-sought-after sailor's uniform.

In contrast to the British, the French soldiers who saw service at Gallipoli had nearly all been conscripted by an annual system of class registration. By a law passed in 1913, the age of call-up was reduced from twenty-one to twenty. Of course there were regular officers for whom the Army was a career. Their task was to train the conscripts. There were also the volunteers of the Foreign Legion, and a battalion of the Legion in fact served on the Peninsula from May 1915. It should not be forgotten that there was a percentage of volunteers in the French Army as well as the older men, reservists who had been recalled to the colours. With the outbreak of war in August 1914, of three men who were to serve on the Peninsula and to whom reference will be made later, Raymond Weil, an artillery officer, would grasp the opportunity for accelerated advancement in his chosen profession, but for conscripts like Charles Thierry in the infantry and M. A. Sylvestre in the artillery, however enthusiastically they were to play their part, their Army service was an interruption of the development of their civilian careers. Conscription secured for the French a general degree of national and individual preparation for the Army well in advance of her ally, but to achieve a quality of experience to match the quantity was obviously a difficult matter. A deeper study of the varying background of the British and French troops who landed at Cape Helles and Kum Kale on 25 April would have to be carried out before valid comparisons of quality could be made, but if the 29th Division was a more homogeneous and professionally trained body of men than for example the French Colonial and Metropolitan Brigades, the experience of the latter as units was considerably more than that of the Royal Naval Division.

3

The social background and the degree of pre-war military training of the Australian and New Zealand soldiers in their respective expeditionary forces were richly varied, but certainly there was a unity in their spirit of loyalty to the Empire, anticipation of adventure and eagerness to prove themselves more than capable of justifying their individual and collective confidence in fulfilling any task set before them. They were proud of their identity as Australians and New Zealanders but they felt strongly the pull of imperial unity and the needs of the mother country. It is interesting to compare the differing ways in which these sentiments were viewed retrospectively in 1919 and 1974. Immediately after the war Major Waite wrote concerning New Zealand that 'the musterer and station owner alike forsook their flock; the bushman put away his crosscut and axe; the flax-mill hand left swamp and mill and hurried to the nearest railway station. Quiet men up on the hillside watched the train coming across country with the eagerly awaited newspapers. The strain of waiting was unendurable. With the call of Old England throbbing in their ears, they left their stock unattended in the paddocks and swelled the procession to the railway station.'[3]

Certainly more analytically but with a cynicism which itself requires evaluation, Bill Gammage wrote in 1974 of pre-war young Australians being deliberately taught 'the virtues of patriotism and glories of race and Empire. In New South Wales State and Catholic schools, every educational influence – policy, the syllabus, text books, the school magazine, school ceremonies, and recreation – was designed to awaken in children a patriotic affection for both nation and Empire . . . By 1914 most young Australians had thoroughly learnt an adherence to war, race and glory, and to two nations separated by the world.'[4]

As a direct result of Kitchener's visit to Australasia in 1910 both countries had by Parliamentary Defence Acts brought in compulsory military service for home defence, so that a large percentage of those who volunteered from August 1914 for overseas service had had experience of part-time training. These men had been to military camps, had drilled, experienced military discipline, often under the stern eye of British N.C.O.s, and had 'fired their course'. However, among those fulfilling the enlistment requirements, who in Australia for example would have to be between nineteen and thirty-five years of age, of a minimum height of five feet six inches and a minimum chest measurement of thirty-four inches, and satisfy strict demands concerning the condition

[3]   *The New Zealanders at Gallipoli*, p. 2.
[4]   *The Broken Years: Australian Soldiers in the Great War*, pp. 2–3.

of their teeth and feet and their general fitness, there were some men who had had no experience at all of military training, and others who had been regular soldiers in the British Army. Men beyond the age of eligibility for compulsory military service, which in Australia was twenty-six, had not done any training unless in the Australian equivalent of the British Territorial Force. For various reasons usually connected with remoteness from any recognized centre of military training, but also for reasons of independent objection to a coercive enlistment for which they could see no need, there were many who had done no military training. Recent immigrants from the British Isles, unless they were ex-regulars or territorials, were in a similar position.

With this variable factor in the recruitment and training of the 1st A.I.F. (Australian Imperial Force) and 1st N.Z.E.F. (New Zealand Expeditionary Force) there was a more unifying factor in the considerable percentage of recent British immigrants in both forces. Bill Gammage states that 22.25 per cent of those Australians who embarked in the A.I.F. during the war were born overseas and mainly in the British Isles,[5] and naturally the figure for those whose parents had been born in Britain would be dramatically higher. Generalizations about the background of the 200 Australian and New Zealander Gallipoli veterans interviewed by the present writer in 1974 would be fruitless, but it can be said that many seemed to have proved their manhood against vicissitude and challenge at a very early age. Clearly they had developed a sturdy independence and confidence which could be an outstanding asset in battle but which could also prove, perhaps particularly in training and in the confinement of military inactivity, a potential problem. Among those interviewed was one who had been a teenager disillusioned with life at a Staffordshire coalface, another who had had pre-1914 experience as a deep-sea deck hand. A timber 'bullockie' in Western Australia, a bush clearer, a kauri-gum digger in Northland, a former gamekeeper in County Durham, a New South Wales sheep-station roustabout, and an opal digger were also represented. There were men who ran away to sea and 'found themselves' in New Zealand or Australia, men whose youthful independence and determination to carve out a future for themselves were backed by their parents, men who pioneered the road, rail and telegraph system and the mapping of remote areas, men who prospected in gold and other minerals, together with those whose training and experience lay in the expanding, challenging fields of business and commerce. As they met at camps like those at

[5] *The Broken Years*, Appendix 1, p. 281.

Blackboy Hill, Perth, at Tahuna Park, Dunedin, Addington near Christ-church, Broadmeadows at Melbourne, Claremont near Hobart, at Randwick racecourse, Sydney, or Awapuni racecourse near Palmerston North, the equipping and training of fighting units began.

For some, like those in the Medical Corps, the training was specialized. E. Moore, in the Australian Army Medical Corps, wrote in his diary: '18 September 1914. Biked into Concentration Camp at Brighton and was drafted into Clearing Hospital and recommended a dresser on 25 September. Wednesday 30 September. Moved camp to Claremont. Started to go into Hobart Hospital every other day for training during which time saw several operations.' More mundane is the diary of C. L. Comyns for 13 August: 'Enlisted today and proceeded to Palmerston North on 14th. Sent to camp at Trentham, Wellington. Mother was very sad at the thought but when I explained my reasons she seemed proud to understand and before we parted gave me many words of comfort and advice. In camp it is curious to see the squads in Mufti and uniform drilling. Allotted a tent, served out with equipment, belt, rifle etc. Kept very busy all day and finished very tired – I think with excitement. At the close of this eventful day I laid down to rest – a one day old British Soldier.'

Not all the training was enjoyed and a New Zealander, A. Currey, wrote in 1915 that he 'learned very little at Palmerston North as most of my time was spent on fatigues, in fact I was on fatigues every Sunday I was there and have even done three days' fatigues right off ... Our N.C.O.s coming from different parts of N.Z. tried to show off their good points by shouting loud and long at their men; this used to grate on the ears, especially when we were doing our best ... Some of them (the N.C.O.s) could not name off the part of their gun without the aid of their hand book. When instructing their men they would bluff their way through by standing off and shouting a lot of quick commands at new men and then bully their men because they had made no progress.'

While officers and men were involved at different ends of the training programme there were elementary lessons for N.C.O.s to learn too. R. H. Harris describes how 'one day we had rowed ashore and were having a picnic. One of the men came to me when the officer was tem-porarily absent and asked if he might go for a few minutes with his brother to see their mother who lived just up the road. On their promise to be back in ten minutes at most I let them go. We found them finally at the Three Lamps Hotel and were to regret many times thereafter that we had not left them there.'

Of course for the British troops the nature of their work in England on arrival from overseas or on assembly after enlistment, was conditioned by whether or not they were regulars. A young Anglican chaplain, Oswald Creighton, who had joined the new or Kitchener army, has written[6] of his somewhat unrewarding task in the 29th Division at Leamington and Nuneaton. The Division had just returned from India, and Creighton was quickly informed that 'the men are not at all religious and I would have a lot of disappointments but would always find them very civil. They did not like going to church.' However Creighton found the men 'exceedingly smart and seasoned troops [who] have an air that there is nothing they don't know about soldiering'. Route marches with the music of their bands were regular occurrences from the end of January 1915. Creighton had some girls ejected from the gallery of Stockingford Church on Sunday, 1 January. He had asked that no ladies should be present as he wished to direct his sermon towards the importance of good behaviour towards the ladies of the locality, who 'had never had military in the place before and were naturally very excited'. On hearing ugly rumours of the conduct of troops in the late evening in the town, Creighton was one of the chaplains who carried out an inquiry patrol; it failed to disclose anything untoward. He found that most of the few who came to his voluntary services were Catholics and 'they did not sing hymns and were very loath to stand'. This attitude towards religion was not confined to the rankers. 'Many of the officers are very pleasant, but I don't feel they very much care whether one exists or not. After all, why should they?'

An illustration of the extent of the involvement of the 29th Division in their local environment is provided by Admiral Oliver, who, in early 1915 was at Rugby School. 'I remember the K.O.S.B. playing the School XV at rugger with a huge crowd of fans from the school and from the regiment. The School was leading at half-time, then the K.O.S.B. brought their Pipers on to the touchline marching up and down and playing, with the result that they scored heavily during the second half and won.'

There was some trench-digging, marksmanship contests, lectures and concerts. Creighton himself secured the support of a 'coy and buxom woman who sang patriotic songs in her dressing gown and a blind man who played the concertina'. They had both been accorded a rousing reception. On 11 March a sham battle was fought involving cyclists holding a line on one side of the River Avon, and on the following day they were reviewed by the King. From Coventry station the 12,000 men

[6] In *With the 29th Division in Gallipoli*, Chapter 1.

in the Division departed for Avonmouth docks. There was scarcely a dry female eye in Leamington, according to a lady who had witnessed a departure which for her remained an abidingly poignant occasion. She knew how anxiously the 29th Division casualty lists would soon be scanned by those women who had, as friends, sweethearts or warm-hearted landladies, come to know the soldiers so well.

The training of the Royal Naval Division had at once to be more basic and more intensive than this. This division was formed at the outbreak of war at the specific request of Winston Churchill. Incorporated in it were Royal Marines, Royal Naval Volunteer Reservists and Royal Navy officers, as well as a flood of recruits with no naval or military training. As there were insufficient ships for the men available to crew them, Churchill wished to prepare for active service a new unit which would be trained as infantry but retain naval elements in rank, uniform and procedure. He intended that 'All the men, whether sailors or marines . . . will be available if required for service afloat, and it must be distinctly understood that this is the paramount claim upon them; but in the meantime they will be left to be organized for land service.'[7]

The diary and letters of Eric Wettern, an engineer in the R.N.D., show a thoroughness and practicability which would be invaluable on the Peninsula. Fitness and infantry drill were the first requirements. A letter of 7 October 1914 describes a run before breakfast, parade, rifle drill, signalling, a route march and skirmishing, all in one day. 'Tonight I have just been on a night attack – twenty-five men forming an attacking party to try to get into the camp singly without being caught. Twenty-five of us were defending and we caught twenty of the attackers, five getting in.' In mid-November he moved to Walmer from Ringwould, where he had been 'cultivating a beautiful ocean wave walk which is requisite and necessary in order to avoid treading on your trousers'. The bell trousers had been issued with little more respect to the wearer's dimensions than the round blue hat with a bow which had been handed out in identical sizes to men laboriously lined up in size order. Wettern's diary for January 1915 records the setting-up of wire entanglements on Kingsdown cliff and the blasting of portions of cliff to make them unscalable. His photographs indicate the increasingly technical side of their work in demolition, digging wells and building bridges. There was still time to arrange a special dance on 5 February at the Masonic Hall, Deal, for which he pencilled in the name of Miss Dunn for the 16th and last dance, 'Valse . . .

7   Memorandum of 16 August to the First and Second Sea Lords (quoted in M. Gilbert, *Winston S. Churchill*, vol. 3, p. 47–8).

Un peu d'Amour'. He left Walmer on 1 March to embark on S.S. *Somali*, which left Avonmouth docks the same day.

Sub-Lieutenant A. W. Tisdall (R.N.D. *Anson* Battalion), who was to win the V.C. at the landing, wrote from the large camp at Blandford in Dorset on 22 February 1915 that on Wednesday 'we parade before Winston Churchill and on Thursday march off to some seaport and ship for the Mediterranean.[8] We have been promised a six-week or two-month

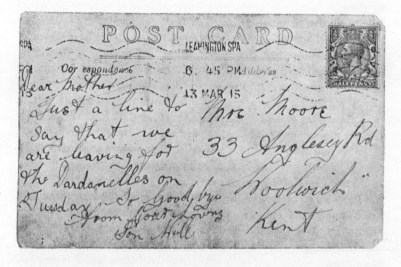

Army Secrecy. A 29th Division soldier informs his mother that he is 'leaving for the Dardanelles on Tuesday'. The postmark date is 13.3.15.

campaign, probably fairly exciting.' Clearly Tisdall shared the common feeling of depression at Blandford because he wrote that 'the mud gets deeper and softer and the work less and less interesting, the officers get into quarrels with each other' and his observation on leading personalities still requires censorship. His last sentence makes the point, 'if we do anything you will see it in the papers probably with big headlines to

[8] A 29th Division N.C.O., W. C. Moore, posted a card on 13 March with the plain unvarnished message: 'We are leaving for the Dardanelles on Tuesday.' Five days later the Governor General of Malta wrote to Vice-Admiral Limpus at the Malta dockyard: 'My daughter and a Miss Baring suggest raising a fund for the sailors and soldiers in the Dardanelles. – I personally don't think such a fund necessary but if you and Mrs Limpus think otherwise then nothing easier.'

please Winston.' It was incidentally at Blandford that the naval uniforms were handed in for khaki, with the sole concession of a round cap with black cap ribbon and gold lettering. But even this cap was in khaki.

The Crystal Palace was the divisional depot at which new and reserve R.N.D. battalions were trained. In addition to this, officers, N.C.O.s and various specialists were trained for constructional work. Douglas Jerrold has written: 'The atmosphere at the Crystal Palace was rather different: the officer's time of training there was emphatically not a period in which he learnt how to carry out orders, but what orders to give, and how to get them executed, not a period in which he learnt his drill and musketry but how to teach drill and musketry; not a period in which he was taught elementary tactics, but rather the underlying principles, knowing which he could not only solve minor tactical problems himself, but could face with a certain measure of confidence the practical business of training troops.'[9] Though this is a fair assessment of one side of the work undertaken at the Crystal Palace, Brigadier B. B. Rackham (R.N.D. *Hawke*) remembers the discomforts of the cold, draughty, stone-floored buildings and the spread of a serious and mysterious epidemic, which was finally traced to the prevalent habit of spitting, common to so many of the men. H. C. Kerr remembers it as the 'Glass Frigate' or 'H.M.S. *Never Float*', and recalls in particular the tremendous efforts to create a naval atmosphere there. A ship's bell rang, no clock chimed; sentry duty was not kept, but Port and Starboard Watch were; men got shore leave and if late were reported 'adrift', though whether the fire drill of climbing down ropes from upper storeys was intended to follow 'naval' practice or was due to the absence of more efficient safety measures was not clear.

There were other R.N.D. training camps at Chatham, Betteshanger, Portsmouth, Plymouth, Portland, Gravesend, Browndown, Tavistock, Deal and Alnwick. The Royal Scots and the West Riding Engineers had had similar training to that of the R.N.D., but their territorial experience was sufficient to make much of the work familiar.

The diary of Second Lieutenant R. B. Gillett of the 2nd Battalion the Hampshire Regiment amply illustrates the less intensive pressure upon the regular during these months in England. '1 January: When we got to the range a gale was blowing and soon afterwards it started raining in torrents. Of course we did not fire and started home. 3 January: It is raining hard so I cancelled church parade. 12 January: We did two hours' squad drill and one of physical drill, only rifle inspection in the afternoon. 17 January: I did not go to Church Parade today so did not get up till late. I wrote a few letters in the morning. Telephoned through to Hobbs and arranged to go and have tea with him this afternoon.' It must be noted however that the diary laconically records that one element was not neglected by this battalion – regular musketry drill.

6

The M.E.F. Arrives in Egypt

The Australian and New Zealand troops were the first to leave their homeland. The New Zealanders in fact had one false start occasioned by the fear of there being insufficient naval protection for the troopships which were to join those from Australian ports. The scene for some was set by fine march-pasts through the city centre to the docks, final quayside farewells and then a rousing, flag-waving, stirring but tear-stained departure.

A New Zealander, E. H. Honnor, admitted in his letter home on 1 January that 'a thought of home had come over him' as he left Wellington and that he realized that the parting was particularly hard on his mother, but 'after the horrors of Hartlepool and Scarborough I am proud that I will have a chance of getting a little back on them'. Less moved by the imminence of his departure was Second Lieutenant Carrington, a former Duntroon cadet. From Wellington he wrote, 'It's blowing a howling gale and is raining hard this morning [and as for farewell] there were seven speeches. Each one started by saying he wouldn't keep us long and each one kept us longer than the one before . . . after the speeches about five different sorts of parsons said different sorts of prayers; at least I suppose they were different but I couldn't hear them.'

For the overwhelming majority the voyage was to be an entirely new experience and something of the excitement is shown in many diaries. Sergeant A. G. Jennings of the Wellington Battalion wrote: '16 October 1914 Left Wellington harbour this morning at 6 a.m. It was a grand sight steaming out in line. The weather is perfect and there is hardly any movement on our ship. After clearing the Heads the *Minotaur* and a Japanese battleship[1] steamed ahead clearing the way while the *Psyche* and *Philomel* each led a line of five transports. We are leading our line. Had no idea the South Island was so large. The whole day we steamed through the Straits.' This diarist was interested by the 'old-fashioned style of houses' he was to see in Hobart, though he thought that 'the girls do not come up to the N.Z. standard as regards good looks . . . We had great fun in giving Hakas [war cries] and talking in Maori.'

A West Australian, E. C. Skinner, had a less satisfactory farewell from

[1] Battleship is an error. The *Ibuki* was a cruiser.

Fremantle. His letter to his sister inquired whether she had been down at the port or not. 'Clarke and your humble both had good possies but we saw not a single soul we knew – the only thing I can see for it is you must have arrived at Fremantle just too late. You can imagine what a disappointment it was, especially after expecting to see you there – a very unfortunate start off, but it couldn't be helped as we knew next to nothing about the time of embarkation and if we had told friends to be there earlier nine times out of ten the boat wouldn't have sailed till late. From what the South Australian boys say (they manage things better in the East – of course that is understood) they tell us they were allowed to mix with their friends for two hours on the wharf before sailing and we were penned up like a lot of sheep.'[2]

The troops leaving Brisbane received a message, 'Queensland expects every man will do his duty,' and when they temporarily disembarked at Albany in Western Australia the Queenslanders 'returned decorated with flowers', according to A. E. Joyce's diary. Some of the New Zealand troopships left Wellington on 14 October and Captain A. B. Morton, who was to leave on the 16th, watched the departure. 'It was a fine sight to see the troopships slowly draw away from the wharves, the decks and rigging crowded with khaki figures cheering and waving their farewell with bands playing good old airs ... The streets of Wellington seem deserted tonight in the absence of the hundreds of soldiers who have been in town on leave every night during the past fortnight.'

Lieutenant C. S. Algie, who remembered the Boer War send-off from Auckland, noted in his diary entry for 23 September that 'there did not seem to be the same wild state of enthusiasm', but that 'there was a much more business-like air about everything. The public were considered very little on this occasion, the troops being marched aboard and kept there without the presence of any but a few civilians.'

Whether the farewells had been well organized or not, the last sight of their homeland was an emotional moment. C. L. Comyns noted that: 'Just at sunset we passed Farewell Spit and I silently said goodbye my own, my native land. Goodbye Mother, Eilley, Doll, Friends and Wanganui. Goodbye New Zealand.'

The novelty of the experience and the sense of excitement faded during the weeks afloat. Despite attempts to hold deck sports, with boxing and greasy-pole pillow fighting, and endless card-playing and gambling, the monotony and the heat of the Indian Ocean took their toll. There was some seasickness at first, and later sunstroke and sore

[2] Skinner was in fact with later reinforcements.

throats made for well-attended sick parades as diary after diary records that the sea was 'perfectly calm and that on board it is very very hot'.

'I am still reading Emerson and find him a little difficult – there are very few places in which he speaks in simple terms,' wrote J. R. T. Keast, who later complained that the gamblers occupied so much space that there was scarcely room to write a letter.

There was excitement and pride at the defeat of the German raider *Emden* in the Cocos Islands by the Australian cruiser *Sydney*. Many men record the *Sydney* steaming off at high speed and the Japanese cruiser *Ibuki* attempting to follow but being clearly ordered back to guard the troopships. At Colombo several of the troopships took on board the prisoners from the *Emden*, and one German sailor, a champion wrestler, took part in a match with the best Australian wrestler. The bout was enjoyed by as large a crowd as those which assembled at the court of King Neptune for the crossing-the-line ceremonies. Cobden Parkes, according to his diary for 13 November, had 'got ready to go before Father Neptune but only the officers went through the performance. Most of the men ran amok and water was thrown everywhere.'

Even if a transport was not carrying horses there were likely to be bullocks and sheep on board to provide fresh meat. The smell and mess of these animals, the overcrowded canteen, the vaccinations, the physical exercises and for some the lectures and training in, for example, signalling were experiences to which they became accustomed. J. R. T. Keast recorded that they 'had a lecture by Dr McWay on pox. Told us what a dreadful disease it was and it is especially in Egypt. He warned all the men and gave them the best cures and preventatives he knew.' W. Thyer, a South Australian signals officer, mentioned in a letter on 24 February the argument against a regular pay allowance. 'There is money aboard but owing to the heavy gambling that is continually in progress I am in accord with the policy of holding it back until prior to the landing so that some of the men will have some cash to go on with.' He may perhaps also have been in a minority in recording the excellence of a service and an address by their chaplain, Captain Jenkins. 'Had a nice service last night at which we sang Sankey's hymns. Was sorry when it was over.' On the S.S. *Arawa* Second Lieutenant Carrington recorded in a letter of 21 October that the impressive solemnity of one of their services was not increased by the Salvation Army padre being seasick during the sermon.

Thyer also wrote of the improvised unofficial games on board. 'The last night or two we have been like a mob of kids [playing trains], particularly in the section where I sleep. Get into our hammocks at the stated hour 9 p.m. and as we hang from the roof so close together that we rub sides, one case (a hard case too) acts as the engine and gets the rest of us swaying from side to side; during this performance another nut crawls along the top of us as a ticket collector at the peril of smashing his head on the ceiling. Needless to say we get into a great perspiration on the job; during the procedure we stop with a bump at various stations and yell like heathens.'

Cecil Malthus[3] describes how the sheer monotony of the shipboard diet of bread, stew and cheese, despite its adequacy, led to the cultivation of skill in theft by mechanical contrivance, for example by hook and line, or by diversionary tactics. Malthus also gives an account of a potentially dangerous situation involving protest over food. A similar incident on another ship bringing Australian reinforcements in May was to result in a mutiny. The whole affair is recorded in the diary of a young soldier, already a journalist and later to become a newspaper editor.

The problem, which may have originated in the refusal in April 1915 of any leave to men in Broadmeadows Camp, Victoria, developed on board the troopship *Ulysses* with grievances over the cook's illicit sale of tea. It is clear from I. T. Birtwistle's diary that there was discontent over the prices in the Soldiers' Institute canteen ('1s. 6d. for tin of fig jam'), the regular rigour of picket inspections which involved transit through both officers' and sergeants' messes, and the strictness and occasional stupidity of petty regulations. Even Empire Day celebrations involving the singing of the National Anthem, three cheers for the King and Empire and boos for the Kaiser failed to quench the fires of discontent. At Colombo the men were prevented from buying fresh fruit or anything else from the local vendors. A march through Colombo's steaming heat proved nearly the last straw. Leave was granted only to privileged persons – two sergeants from each company and the officers. 'Spent the day looking at Colombo from the ship, hot, perspiring, irritated. Those who have taken illegal leave were heavily fined (privates fined £5 as well as ten days C.B. and no leave till conclusion of voyage).' With this judgement by Colonel Crouch the storm broke on the evening of 27 May.

A petition for modification of the fines attracted a large crowd of willing signatories. A jeering chant broke out parodying the Colonel's motto of 'Wipe out the Bloody Germans', which now appeared as 'Chuck the Bastard overboard'. When the officers remonstrated the retort was, 'You treat us like dogs, won't you let us bark?' Although Crouch's presence persuaded the men to disperse, the chanting continued

[3] *Anzac: A Retrospect*, pp. 19–21.

and efforts by the Adjutant failed to avert further trouble. A pair of Colonel Crouch's boots were taken and hidden. The canteen was closed by force by an officer and military police, who were roughly handled. One of the police was nearly thrown overboard but at the last minute hauled back and beaten up instead. The Colonel, sitting by himself in the officers' mess, became increasingly isolated. Finally the canteen was broken open and the goods looted. The guard was called out but refused to leave the guard room, and the chaplain's well-meaning diversion of having the organ played proved fruitless. The detention cells were forced open and the inmates released, the doors being flung overboard.

As the evening wore on, the second in command, Major Smith, moved among the men and another senior officer promised attention to their grievances. The tension eased and the crisis was past. It would, however, be difficult for the 22nd Battalion to embark upon their Gallipoli service with their morale unaffected by such a prolonged experience of bad relations.

The normal grouses of life aboard a troopship received legitimate outlet in the form of newsheets. The *Clan McGillivray* had one such paper, the *Clan News*, and on board the transport *Tahiti*, bringing reinforcements from New Zealand, the *Tahitian Tatler*[4] would have needed humour no more sophisticated than the following two examples to be sure of knowing nods from its readers.

Orderly Officer (at door of Messroom): 'What Mess is this?'
Trooper McAwfull: 'I don't know, Sir, but the cook said it was stew.'

Orderly Officer: 'Any complaints, men?'
Private: 'Yessir. Taste this, Sir.'
Officer: 'H'm, rather thin and greasy, otherwise not bad soup.'
Private: 'Yessir, that is what we thought, but the cook says it's tea.'

Egypt, after a voyage of such frustrating length, seemed very attractive at first, even though the Australasian troops had expected and hoped that their destination would be England and then France. The delights of Zeitoun were similar to those of nearby Cairo, and at Mena, a few miles away, there was the stimulus even to the most philistine of being beneath the pyramids. In Cairo itself there were the crowded bazaars and the varied entertainment, which ranged from the Zoological Gardens and Luna Park to the bawdy-houses in the notorious 'Wasser'. The eastern scents and the smells, the tram rides between the sand dunes, the

4 Issue of 17 July (P.L.).

gharries and the veiled women, presented an excitingly unfamiliar picture. There were so many contrasts like that between the well-dressed, wealthy Egyptian and the appalling poverty of the deformed, dirty, ulcerated, elderly or boy beggars. Above all there was a new sense of the colossal span of history where the edifice of six thousand summers looked down on their tented encampment.

The journey in a troop train from Alexandria to Cairo enabled Lieutenant C. S. Algie, in the Auckland Battalion, to see something of a country 'as flat as a pancake and under cultivation. The bullock, donkey, mule and camel are the beasts of burden and hundreds of each were to be seen throughout – the ploughs are just as the ancients used, I should think. It is very hard to realize that we are in a country of such antiquity.'

The great art of bartering had to be learned, and while it was possible to jump off a gharry into the sand to avoid paying, and by force of numbers or strength to escape the cheap tram fares or guide-fees to ancient monuments, payment for camel rides or photographs on camel back in front of the pyramids was difficult to avoid even if the amount was negotiable. C. L. Comyns indicated in his diary that the delicacies of barter were double-sided. 'Some of the boys obtained oranges for their identification discs, but the balance was frequently adjusted by the natives getting the cash and disappearing without giving the fruit.'

Cobden Parkes, with the 1st Battalion A.I.F., arrived at Mena Camp after midnight, following the train journey from Alexandria and the tram to the camp. 'Slept in coats only, on the sand. Cold as blazes. Pyramids looming over sandhills seem to overshadow everything. 9 December: Woke up at Reveille terribly stiff and cold. Went up pyramids and shown round by guide.' He climbed the pyramids on the next two days as well and one of his party fell 'from about 100 yards from the top. Terribly injured about head but no bones broken.'

During the lengthy and increasingly tedious period spent by the men in Egypt before they moved to the island of Lemnos, the rigour of their desert training, the involvement of New Zealanders in the February defence of the canal and the famous Battle of the Wasser stand out as deserving recall. After the long sea voyage the men needed retraining for active service. The bitterly cold nights and intensely hot days had taken their toll with influenza and pneumonia. In addition to marksmanship at the Heliopolis rifle range, desert manoeuvres and sham fights, lengthy route marches had regularly to be endured, as well as full-scale military parades and a march through the native quarter of Cairo to impress the populace with the massive strength of the British Empire under arms.

The training was exhausting and not everyone appreciated its necessity. The fact that the Commander of the Australian and New Zealand Division, General Godley, had his wife with him and that she was often in attendance when the troops were working makes it scarcely surprising that her supposed remark at one review, that she wished to see the men 'do it again, Alex', spread like wildfire. It may be one of the earliest celebrated 'furphies', or latrine rumours, the truth of which can seldom be definitely established. Cobden Parkes's diary records his personal regret at having been caught up in a collective refusal to obey an order after a very tiring route march, but for the New Zealanders, at least, there was a break in the monotony as they helped Indian troops repel a brave but futile Turkish attempt to cross the Suez Canal in strength.

Advance intelligence had warned of the approach of the Turks, and when their pontoons had been launched for the crossing during the early morning of 3 February they had been met by concentrated small-arms fire from No. 10 Platoon of the Nelson Company of the Canterbury Battalion. Morning light revealed bodies of Turks on the east side of the canal, and more New Zealand and Indian troops became involved in the action as the Turks shelled their entrenched positions with shrapnel. The warship *Swiftsure* raced up the canal, sending a great surge of water up the sloping banks as it shelled the Turks. Several New Zealand diaries actually record seeing the masthead lookout on the *Swiftsure* being shot, and in fact the first New Zealander to die as a result of a wound in action was hit in the neck during the night fighting. H. G. Hunter unconsciously illustrated the small-scale threat which had been presented when he wrote on 4 February that, having been ordered in the early morning to the canal to dig trenches and having seen the *Swiftsure* dispose of the Turkish trenches, 'we left and caught the train at 9 a.m. arriving in camp at 11 a.m.'. Nevertheless some of the New Zealanders had been in action. They had suffered some casualties and inflicted far more, though those who wrote home to the Nelson area describing heroic deeds in an epic encounter were the source of much derision when their letters, printed in local newspapers, found their way back to Egypt.

But for the other New Zealand and Australian troops there was nothing much to excite their pride or interest. Tensions were beginning to be felt. The root problem lay in their remoteness from both their homeland and what they considered to be the real seat of the war, France and Belgium. Their frustration is well expressed in a rhyme then popular among the New Zealanders and recorded in H. P. Rasmussen's memoirs, which, after making uncomplimentary reference to Egypt, continues:

Half the world we crossed to reach you;
Hearts were light and hopes were high,
Thinking that we came for fighting,
But we're only 'standing by'.

Sea-sickness, inoculation,
Tropic heat and horsey smell,
All the incidents of travel
(Though we stood them rather well),
Trains and transports, field manœuvres,
Bivouac beneath the sky,
Fitting us for Active Service,
Also perhaps for 'standing by'.

Jealousies between and within units were raising their heads. C. L. Comyns wrote home that if the 'constant energy expended in injuring others were concentrated in heroic efforts to better themselves, the results would be vastly different both for themselves, the world and our camp'. His diary describes fifty men leaving camp under strong escort to be sent home to New Zealand for refusing to be inoculated, for bad behaviour or for having contracted V.D. Australians and New Zealanders, soon to serve in such complete harmony under the grim Peninsula conditions, were increasingly involved in street brawls amongst themselves as well as in trouble with the Egyptians. For some their upbringing and the constant exhortations of the Army chaplains were sufficient to ward off temptation. A. E. Joyce reported that there was a 'Church parade at 9 a.m. Address by Archdeacon Richard, his text being "Be not deceived". He spoke remarkably well. Everyone I think thought him good. We did not get the conclusion of his theory until he had finished, which was "Be not deceived. God is not mocked, for whatsoever a man soweth that shall he also reap!" '

As the encamped troops eyed each other through this period of frustration, mutual disparagement was to be expected and can be seen in a letter from New Zealander, E. H. Honnor. 'The English Territorials here have made complaints about not getting their food parcels; there are nearly twenty thousand of these fellows here, and you never saw such a miserable-looking crowd in all your life. Of course a lot of them are (on the whole) boys but the best of them look miserable; that could easily be overlooked if they behaved themselves; but there is not much between them and the Australians, and the way they go on here it is a wonder there is not a riot every night. The boys get a bit rowdy at times, and it is a good thing the blacks are either good-natured, good-tempered or afraid.'

There had been a degree of trouble in Colombo during the brief stay of some of the troopships, and more rioting and looting at Christmas had led General Birdwood to write anxiously to General Bridges on 27 December about the conduct of the men: 'Unless . . . [each man] is doing his best to keep himself efficient he is swindling the Government which has sent him to represent it and fight for it.'[5] The Australian Minister of Defence, Senator Pearce, was to receive a letter from a sergeant in the A.I.F. who attempted to put the matter into perspective. Pearce, a friend of the Collins family, was informed by Sergeant Collins that 'as one who knocked about with the next and saw all that was worst and best in Cairo (which at the particular time might be called a cesspool) I can conscientiously say that the conduct throughout was admirable. Events that did occur were caused and carried out by an element of undesirables who no matter when or where they happened to be would be up against law and order.'[6]

General Bridges himself made an illuminating remark in a letter to the Governor-General of Australia written on 5 April. 'Our men are in capital spirit – their discipline has greatly improved – orders are now given and obeyed that officers would hardly have ventured to give five months ago.'[7] Colonel D. Marks, an officer in the 13th Battalion, noted in his diary that on 16 March 'C.O. withheld the men's pay, whereupon a deputation of the whole battalion marched in an orderly manner to Brigade H.Q. and laid its case before the Brigadier'.[8]

Certainly the behaviour of some of the bored troops in Cairo was bound to arouse antagonism. Egyptians had been thrown off trams into the sand, gharries had been commandeered, goods taken without payment, and Cecil Malthus, on the very morning of the Good Friday Battle of the Wasser, had been shocked to see 'a poor Arab boy run over by a car full of mad Australians and instantly killed'.[9]

Neither original documents at high or low level nor the recollections of witnesses make it clear who was responsible for the riot in the Wasser. Private T. S. Smith of the 2nd Battalion A.I.F. has described in detail

5 Australia War Memorial, Canberra.
6 La Trobe Library, Melbourne.
7 National Archives, Canberra, Papers of Lord Novar (Sir James Fergusson), Governor-General of Australia.
8 Mitchell Library, Sydney.
9 C. Malthus, *Anzac: A Retrospect*, p. 33.

how a visit to a brothel in the area (ironically a Turkish establishment) led to his being drugged, robbed and dumped in a water conduit. A flushing of cold water had revived him and he had successfully searched for the house of his hostesses, with their large Nubian bodyguard. By the unorthodox method of butting the stomach of the Nubian with his head, so that the latter crashed through a balustrade into the courtyard below, he was able to depart with the day's takings, including presumably his own.

It seems that men fleeced as Smith had been, or possibly infected by V.D., had banded together to wreak vengeance on a certain brothel in the main street. They had broken the doors and windows, and then thrown the furnishing of the rooms from upstairs windows into the street below. As the contents of one room included a piano, the determination of the men concerned can be clearly estimated, and the crowd of interested sightseers grew larger. A bonfire was made of the beds, mattresses and other goods piled in the street. The blaze spread to a Greek drinking-shop or café, and the native fire brigade arrived. In the ensuing mêlée some soldiers cut the hoses, the civil police seemed or were unwilling seriously to intervene, and the area was not quietened even when Military Police, having been pelted with various missiles, actually fired into the crowd, killing a man and wounding others. The riot spread to Heliopolis, some miles to the north-east of Cairo, where a café, two shops and the camp cinema were wrecked or burned, but Lancashire Territorials with fixed bayonets, in front of Shepheard's Hotel, had prevented the trouble spreading further in Cairo itself.

Troops with long-pent-up frustrations, which had been aggravated since their eager enlistment by the major trial of a long voyage, the heat, training for 'standing-by' in Egypt and the restrictive regulations of Army camp life, had at last blown off steam. An example of the regulations which might be taken to symbolize the source of their impatience, however few in fact were affected by it, was a General Routine Order N.Z. Division of 28 December 1914: 'The engines of motor-cycles are not now to be started within a hundred yards of Divisional H.Q.'[10] Whether or not rumour laid this order at Lady Godley's door we do not know, nor do we know whether General Godley was correct in writing to the New Zealand Minister of Defence, Sir James Allan, on that Good Friday that a 'some-what serious riot' had taken place – 'some men in the venereal hospital – it is said that they were Australians, but of this we have no proof – deter-mined that they would get their revenge on the houses of ill fame where

[10] New Zealand National Archives.

they had contracted the disease – demanded a refund of their money and on this being refused, the riot took place.'[11] In any case the time for 'standing-by' was almost over. The Australian Division and the Australian and New Zealand Division, to be put to the test on 25 April, had been efficiently and rigorously trained. If it is maintained that they were not trained for what they would experience on Gallipoli, it might reasonably be contended that this was not possible in Egypt or indeed anywhere else in early 1915.

On the evening of 3 April, with their equipment stacked ready for tram transport, the Mena Camp incinerators burning their rubbish and one battalion enjoying a farewell sing-song, the men awaited their route march to Cairo and train to Alexandria for embarkation. On Monday, 5 April, Gunner Brownell helped to unpitch tents and pack the wagons, but a 'terrible sand storm started early in the morning and kept on all day hampering our work. Left Mena at 8 p.m. fully packed and equipped. Route marched to Cairo and reached station at 11 p.m. Loaded horses, guns and equipment on the troop trains and left station at 1.30 a.m. for Alexandria. While waiting to get away some of us ducked away and had supper in Cairo. Tuesday, 6 April. After travelling in train all night arrived at Alexandria Quay at 7 a.m. alongside troopship *A 17*. We unloaded the train and led the horses straight onto the boat, having them all aboard in three quarters of an hour. Some of our guns are also loaded on. Nicked off into town for a time both in morning and in afternoon. Changed into English coin *all* my money which was 6 P.T. = about 1s. 3d. Was told off for guard on the ship at 6.30 p.m.' The ship, the *Atlantian*, sailed for Lemnos on Thursday, 8 April. Two New Zealand officers had selected their shipboard reading for the journey on their troopship. At Ismailia station bookstall, a professor at Canterbury College had chosen Ovid and a young lawyer, now Sir Kenneth Gresson, an eminent judge, had secured *La Vie Parisienne*.

The great expanse of Mudros harbour was crowded by naval vessels of all sizes. They ranged from the huge *Queen Elizabeth* to the little pinnaces and picket boats. The lines of troopships were the clearest evidence to the ordinary soldier that he was involved in a great enterprise. C. L. Comyns echoed the thoughts and indeed foreshadowed the recollections of many in writing that the sight 'gave a feeling of awe and helped to show me how great was the mission we were on'.

Within one day of his arrival Comyns, in the Wellington Battalion, had had bayonet-fighting and musketry drill on board in the morning, and

[11] ibid.

later he could see the Australians disembarking for a route march while 'our company practised landing in life boats and climbing ladders'. On the following day rowing exercises were made more stimulating by being organized into a race. Practice in unloading horses, route marches and a severe gale on the 20th and 21st were balanced by bathing, the distribution of a big mail and shipboard concerts.

Now they were so near to their destination, despite a bad-weather postponement, and with official information and orders taking the place of rumour and conjecture, the tension increased. It was held in control by the confidence felt by all units. When General Godley wrote to New Zealand on 21 April that 'there is no doubt that we have a very tough job before us'[12] he was expressing a sentiment shared by many in the ranks.

An Australian, G. C. Grove, diligently copied into his diary the essence of Birdwood's order, which was displayed on the ship's notice-board, that the men were not to think themselves forgotten if they had to go without food for a few days because supply would be difficult, but were above all to remember the importance of 'concealment, covering fire, control of fire and communications'. Four days later, on the 23rd, he noted the details of a proclamation issued that the 'persons, property and religion of the villages of the Gallipoli Peninsula are to be scrupulously respected by all ranks of the Division'.

On the *Annaberg* a New Zealander, L. H. Latimer, was struck by the irony of a religious address being interrupted by the appearance on deck of four grinding-stones to sharpen bayonets, and C. R. Rawlings recorded in his diary for the 24th, 'Inspection of identity discs and field dressing. Heavy marching-order parade during the afternoon.' During this last tense day of waiting, Corporal Hawke of the Canterbury Battalion 'crimed Signaller Ashley for insolence to N.C.O. one days' C.B.', but we are not informed whether Ashley missed the historic 25th.

A typical New Zealander's reaction to the information that the Australians were to make the initial landing was given in a letter written on the 24th by Cecil Malthus. 'We reacted to this news with mixed feelings, in which relief was the main ingredient.'[13] From the 3rd Brigade A.I.F. transports, during that same afternoon, destroyers took about 500 men of the 9th Battalion to the *Queen*, 500 of the 10th to the *Prince of Wales* and 500 of the 11th to the *London*, and these ships, led by the *Queen Elizabeth*, with the *Triumph*, the *Majestic*, six destroyers and the 3rd Brigade

[12] Alexander Turnbull Library, Wellington, Sir James A. Wilson Papers.
[13] *Anzac: A Retrospect*, p. 43.

transports, slowly threaded their way through ships ringing with cheers and so out of the harbour. With the exception of the *Queen Elizabeth*, bound for the Dardanelles, this force was to rendezvous off Imbros for the Anzac landing. The 2nd and 1st Brigades A.I.F. and the troops of the Australian and New Zealand Division, who were to reinforce the initial assault, were making ready for their scheduled departure even as a religious service was being held under the guns of the *Prince of Wales* as she made for Imbros. Taking a Communion Service later in the evening on one of the ships, the celebrant was relieved that the darkness prevented the men from seeing the tears drawn from him by the emotion of the momentous occasion.[14]

The French troops began leaving Marseilles on 4 March. The *Provence*, the *Savoie*, the *Lorraine*, the *Charles Roux*, the *Armand Behic*, the *Italie* and other transports were given a heroic send-off. Father Charles Roux, on board the *Provence*, one of the finest French transatlantic liners, could not help but be struck by the sight of the promenade deck being transformed into stables with horses' heads thrusting through the windows of the luxury cabins occupied by the officers.[15] The men would have gladly exchanged some of the splendid columns and gilt decoration for a mattress in the great dining-room where they slept. Everywhere on deck there was the strong smell of dung; below deck, the smell of horses and of men was equally mixed. With a stop at Bizerta in Tunis, the *Provence* reached Lemnos on the 15th. The troops moved later in the month to Alexandria, arriving on the 30th, three days later than the British Royal Naval Division, which had remained at Port Said. Since the beginning of December the Australians and New Zealanders had been encamped near Cairo, but the French troops, like the British 29th Division, stayed at Alexandria. Their contact with British troops led to numerous English diary references to the impression made by the colourful and somewhat unusual appearance of the tall black Senegalese troops, the Zouaves, the Chasseurs d'Afrique and the troops of metropolitan France. When the French troops were reviewed by Hamilton and the French Commander of the Corps Expéditionnaire d'Orient, Father Roux wrote that bandsmen from all the different units were at forty-eight hours' notice called together to prepare a programme which included 'La Marseillaise, le God Save, et l'hymne Russe et La Marche Sultanieh'. 'The two generals, good horsemen, with a youthful aspect, had a degree of elegant smartness which

[14] Canon M. Andrews. See his *Canon's Folly* and P.L.
[15] C. Roux, *L'Expédition des Dardanelles*, p. 90.

produced a great impression.'[16] With regard to the necessary repacking of stores at Alexandria, he enigmatically wrote that 'this time nothing is lacking and the place of each object is known'. Each ship was designated by a letter and a number printed on the bridge and replacing the ship's name. One rather amusing confusion remained. Hamilton's proclamation of 22 April, which was couched in moving as well as suitably martial phrases, began 'Soldiers of France and of the King'. The French translators were perturbed in case among the French troops *'quelques imbéciles'* feared for the health of the French Republic when they read that apparently they were soldiers of the King – which king? The formula was tactfully made more explicit in the French translation, *'Soldats de France et soldats du Roi'*.

The French artillery officer Raymond Weil, whose scientific ingenuity was to be demonstrated in the campaign and in a lifetime of concern with experimentation,[17] found time on the day his battery awaited embarkation in Marseilles to buy 'pince-nez, china ink and a pocket Kodak'. He watched with concern his horse, slung by the stomach, winched on board their steamer, the *Italie*. He was later to superintend the placement of two of the guns of the battery in position on deck for defence against submarine surface attack. His diary describes how at a slide-show and concert in Alexandria, when a portrait of George V was shown and the British National Anthem played, the English soldiers had stood and the French from politeness also rose from their seats. The English however had not returned the compliment for Poincaré and 'La Marseillaise'. He noted that above the Staff H.Q. at Victoria College, Alexandria, there flew the English flag flanked by 'a little French flag'. Weil's meticulous habits are indicated by the fact that from the time he left France he always carried a bag containing a small, flat spirit stove, methylated spirits, some medical ointments, his diary and a sketch pad. The first three articles performed admirable service on the Peninsula and the latter two provided posterity with a splendid record of personal service *'pour la Patrie'*.

Some of the French transports left Alexandria on 16 April, others remained till the 22nd. The rendezvous for the French was off the island

[16] Father Charles Roux adds a footnote concerning the piquancy of French troops being reviewed by the English officer commanding a joint expeditionary force against the Turks so near to Aboukir Bay, where Nelson had beaten the French in 1798 and on the shores of which Napoleon had beaten the Sultan's army in 1799.

[17] Commandant Weil had been concerned in early wireless experiments and in 1917 designed and put into practice a system of co-ordinated anti-aircraft defence for Paris. This system was later introduced into other towns facing German air attack.

of Skyros, but from here they sailed to Lemnos. After further rowing and disembarkation practice, the troops and stores for the Kum Kale assault were accommodated in the *Savoie*, the *Carthage*, the *Vinh-Long*, the *Th. Mante* and the *Ceylan*, these ships leaving the outer harbour of Mudros at 10 p.m. on 24 April.

Ships from England, carrying the 29th Division and the Royal Naval Division, began to leave Avonmouth on 1 March. On 2 March, Sapper A. Gillott (R.N.D. Engineers) was obviously rather sorry that his transport, the *Somali*, was no longer being escorted by her guardian angels, in the form of two submarines. Already his diary shows that 'about half troops sick and myself feeling as though I may become a friend of the fishes'. The following day he 'fed the fishes'. His diary and that of Arthur Douglas[18] chronicle the collision drills, the impressive snowy Sierra Nevadas, Gibraltar, the North African coast and Malta, where the first contact was made with their French allies: 'A large French battleship is coming in harbour. Ah! here she comes, *Leon Gambetta*. Oh what a rush we made for the ship's side! As the battleship neared us, their band played a nice selection, eventually turning on to "It's a long way to Tipperary". We cheered and cheered, and then joined in the song. The French crew lined their deck rails and stood to attention as they passed us, then they removed their caps and waved and cheered us.'[19] When the French troopship *Charles Roux* arrived in Malta the next day, more warm courtesies were exchanged. The *Somali* reached Lemnos on 13 March and Sapper Gillott was predictably impressed by the sight of a 'good collection of battleships etc., *Queen Lizzie*, *Lord Nelson*, *Triumph*, *Majestic*, *Agamemnon*'. He noted 'Asia Minor's snow-capped mountains which could be seen quite clearly looking very fine', but from the day of arrival the serious business of preparation for the landing began as 'several boats went out for practice rowing'.

An experienced regular, Second Lieutenant Huttenbach, R.H.A., could not understand why the rifles were stored inaccessibly and wondered if the authorities feared that the men would sell them in Egypt in anticipation of easy replacements. For a territorial like Henry Harris in the 87th Field Ambulance Brigade, the main problem of the unfamiliar life on a troopship was sleeping. 'When one got in at one side of a hammock the likelihood was that you came out the other side. When everyone was in, the hammocks were so close together that no one could get out until

[18] *My Diary 1915: Walmer to the Dardanelles.*
[19] ibid., p. 8.

in the morning; a few of the hefty ones managed it. In a swell the hammocks all moved together with the ship's movement.' Another new experience for Harris was the issue of pith helmets and the length of cloth known as the puggaree to be wound round them. The King's Own Scottish Borderers, on board S.S. *Dongola*, were able to demonstrate their recent long service in India by assisting in this tricky task.

Enough has already been written, in the official history and in other accounts, of the futile hope of secrecy and surprise once the allied troops began their concentration in Egypt and were for example reviewed publicly at both Alexandria and Cairo. Other well-recorded features of this period before the landing were the widespread efforts to buy landing craft and the thoughtless packing of stores and equipment on the boats which, with the unsuitability of Mudros as a port[20] as opposed to its excellence as a harbour, necessitated the return of the advanced units from the island of Lemnos to Alexandria for unloading and re-stowing.

Whatever confusion there may have been at top level and however much the difficulty of their task was being made more severe by the unilateral naval attempt, failure and consequent delay allowing intensive defensive preparations, these were matters quite beyond their control and indeed quite beyond the conscious concern of the majority of the men, who are our main concern, until just before the landing. Nevertheless the point might be made that there were enormous and unprecedented logistical problems involved in such an enterprise. It is a sobering fact that Sir Ian Hamilton was informed of his appointment on 12 March and in under six weeks his French, Australian, New Zealand and British troops were landed according to plans the thoroughness of which, except in one aspect, is apparent to all but those using the distorting spectacles of hindsight.

Sapper Wettern's diary illustrates the activities of the R.N.D. Engineers before the landing. There was rowing, not always successful, in Mudros harbour, a demonstration cruise off the northern shores of the Gallipoli Peninsula on 18 March, Morse practice, and a sail from Lemnos to Egypt, arriving on 25 March in Port Said. He found Port Said 'quite an interesting place. Ramshackle with some good shops. Very mixed lot of people.' After review practice there was an impressive inspection by

---

[20] Because of lack of available fresh water in large quantities and a complete absence of piers and jetties. The *Official History: Gallipoli*, vol. 2, p. 95, makes the point that the harbour was so huge that 'even in a moderate breeze the sea rapidly became too rough for small boats'. This is supported in many diary accounts of men who had spent long exhausting hours attempting to row back to their ships after having been ashore.

General Sir Ian Hamilton on 3 April. There was entertainment by the
Hood Battalion band, sorting and arranging mobilization stores, filling
and sealing four-gallon cans with fresh water and loading them into
lighters. They left Port Said in the S.S. *Ayrshire*, a much dirtier ship than
the S.S. *Somali*, and again there was a wait in Mudros harbour. For the
R.N.D. Engineers the waiting was to be slightly extended. '24 April:
Steamers leaving every few minutes throughout the day. No orders for
us. 25 April: Harbour almost empty. Still no orders for us. Landing
supposed to have started at dawn. Church parade at 10 on boat deck.'

For Second Lieutenant Gillett (2nd Hampshire Battalion) it was fortunate that he was to transfer from the troopship *Manitou* to the troopship
Aragon for the journey to Lemnos. The *Manitou* was to have a narrow
escape, described below. In Mudros harbour Gillett regularly practised
rowing with the eight selected rowers of his platoon, who even received a
special word of praise from the General for their oarsmanship. They also
practised getting down into the boats from the troopship by rope ladders
and marching on the deck in full pack order.[21] He was greatly taken with
a dummy battleship in the harbour. 'Large anchors painted on her side,
a great number of guns on her all made of wood and two sham funnels.'
It is recorded that a German submarine sank such a disguised warship –
there must at least have been a measure of disappointment for the submarine commander as he saw the wooden superstructure float away. The
skill with which these dummy ships had been prepared is indicated by
the fact that the range-finder, Cave, in the *Dublin* notified his puzzled
captain that H.M.S. *Lion* and other ships believed to be in Scapa were
off their port bow in these warm Aegean waters. Gillett was also intrigued
by an airship on a tramp steamer. The 2nd Battalion Hampshire Regiment
was transferred on 21 April to H.M.T. *Alaunia*, which sailed for the
island of Tenedos, off which the men were moved to S.S. *River Clyde* on
the evening of Saturday the 24th.

The *Manitou* incident on 16 April is one of the small number of
occasions when it is clear that a high standard of conduct and morale was
not maintained. Captain D. N. Meneaud Lissenburg was the trumpeter
of the 97th Battery and was on duty at the time on the *Manitou*. He had
seen a small boat approaching rapidly and noticed that his boat had
stopped. The object, now obviously a gunboat flying the Greek flag,

---

[21] See also O. Creighton, *With the 29th Division in Gallipoli*, p. 38: 'All kinds of boat
drill has been going on. The men are not much good at rowing, and the boats are
very heavy and cumbersome. But they are as a rule towed in strings of five or six by a
steam pinnace.'

drew alongside the port side and the crew of a torpedo projector hurried to train it on the *Manitou*. An officer on the gun boat, using a megaphone, challenged the *Manitou*, shouting in what Lissenburg describes as a German accent. A White Ensign was spread over the side of the boat and immediately the Turkish crescent replaced the Greek flag on the gunboat. The voice shouted, 'Three minutes to clear your decks.'

'All the guns, machine guns and ammunition were stored in the hold[22] and we were totally unprepared for what was happening. I don't know how long we were in fact given but certainly I did not move. I saw the first torpedo plop into the sea and begin its journey directly under me as the gunboat was only twenty or thirty yards away. Nothing happened. We raced to look over the starboard side and there it was skimming away with its bow well out of the water like a speedboat. I hurried to the orderly room and asked the R.S.M. what I was to do. I expected to have to sound the "Stand-to" but instead I was told that the order was every man for himself, scuttle away and find a boat. I was going below to get my lifebelt when at the stairs I was astonished to see the panic-stricken crush of men trying to get up, fighting against those trying to get down. There was chaos on the boat deck too. We had never had boat drill nor been alloted to a particular boat. Lt Beckett was however using his formidable figure to secure calm as he grasped the muzzle end of a rifle and threatened anyone who rushed at the particular boat he was supervising. I removed my boots and puttees, got into an overcrowded boat which, badly handled by our own men, capsized as it was lowered and we were all thrown into the water. Fortunately I was a good swimmer and got away from the side of the ship. The crew of the Turkish gunboat were laughing at us. Our ginger-haired doctor organized us into providing help for the non-swimmers, as did the steward, who had already survived the *Titanic* disaster. We were quite a while in the water before a warship, the *Prince George*, approached us and lowered her lifeboats to pick us up.'

Three torpedoes had been fired at the *Manitou* and all had plunged too deeply to strike her at such close range. The gunboat was chased off and beached herself, which allowed the crew to escape. Lieutenant Gillett was told by an R.F.A. officer the following day that some of the men from the *Manitou* had been killed by hatches and other material which would float being thrown on top of them. Some officers had retired to the saloon to drink; others, like the Colonel, had led the rush overboard and had been quickly picked up. Some of the men, according to the R.F.A. officer, had looted the officers' cabins, but others, Lissenburg

[22] Note the precautions of Lieutenant Weil on board the French troopship.

was informed, had been led by a Second Lieutenant to release the horses and mules from their stalls where, sensing danger, they were struggling to get free. Fifty-one lives had been lost, but the official military history relegates the affair to a footnote. There is some variation between the official naval account and that in R. R. James's *Gallipoli*, but whichever version is the correct one the affair brings little credit to anyone. It is in fact one of those rare incidents throughout the demanding campaign of a failure of leadership by officers in immediate command.[23]

Of an altogether different character was the final dramatic naval event before the landing itself. On 17 April one of the new class of submarines, the *E 15*, under the command of Lieut-Commander T. S. Brodie, in attempting to get through the Straits, ran aground just south of Kephez light. Brodie himself was killed by Turkish artillery fire, probably from the near-by Fort Dardanos. A Turkish artillery officer, now Colonel Adel Savasman, was in the battery which fired on the *E 15*, having first sighted its periscope and then hitting the conning-tower. Savasman found Brodie dead over his maps from a stomach wound. The Turkish officer helped to bury Brodie and the other dead on the beach, though the official naval history records that a more honourable burial was given later on higher Turkish authority.

In *Forlorn Hope 1915*[24] C. G. Brodie, brother of T. S., who was also Commander of a submarine in these waters, wrote of his looking over the *E 15* at the start of her endeavour to be the first allied submarine into the Marmara. He found *E 15* all 'cluttered up with gear and food for three weeks patrol . . . The men had been working all night, and were tired and unkempt but eager, and to my eyes very young. A few key ratings had been with T. S. [Brodie] in *D 8* [an earlier submarine] and I knew his reliance upon them. I could sense their confidence and affection for him.' Leaving *E 15* at Tenedos, C. G. Brodie fought to balance his brother's serenity and confidence against his own forebodings. The R.N.A.S. were to play their part by time-synchronized bombing to divert attention from *E 15*'s attempt and C. G. Brodie was to fly in one of the planes. When Brodie saw 'a slim grey straw at right angles to the line of the shore and a smaller black straw at an acute angle beside it . . . I realized it was failure and for *E 15* final. I was conscious of disappointment but oddly no surprise.' The black straw was a Turkish torpedo boat attempting to salvage the submarine, in which some members of the crew had been

[23] *Official History: Gallipoli*, vol. 1, p. 140 n.; *Official History: Naval Operations*, vol. 2, pp. 300–301; R. R. James, *Gallipoli*, p. 91.
[24] pp. 37 ff.

asphyxiated. The others, having taken to the water, were to be picked up by the Turks.

De Robeck was determined that the Turks and Germans must not learn the secrets of this latest submarine and ordered her destruction. Two submarines, two destroyers and the old battleships *Majestic* and *Triumph* failed in their efforts to accomplish this, the Turks being fully alerted and greeting the battleships 'with such a shower of shell that it was impossible to get within 12,000 yards of their target'.[25] The fearful task was finally accomplished by a boat from each of the battleships daringly dodging the searchlights until, in being caught, they also found *E 15*, which they destroyed by torpedo. Lieut-Commander Robinson of the *Vengeance* was in command of the volunteer crew of the *Triumph* boat while a similar crew from the *Majestic* was under the command of Lieutenant C. H. Godwin. Godwin's boat was hit and sank just after all the men were taken off by Robinson's boat. Only one man had been lost under a storm of fire and the official naval history, not given to exaggeration, quite reasonably maintains that 'it was a gallant feat, finely executed, and one which it is pleasant to know extorted the highest admiration from the enemy'.[26]

The period spent by the 29th Division in Egypt is well chronicled in the Reverend O. Creighton's book,[27] and several diaries pay tribute to his organization of refreshment and leisure facilities at Mex, near Alexandria. Creighton persuaded the Brigade Major to part with funds sufficient to buy a large native tent, 'beautifully decorated inside and lit with a large arc lamp'. He borrowed tables and benches and then, with a sergeant and a transport wagon, regularly bought pastries, oranges, cigarettes, magazines, games and writing paper, thus providing a well-equipped recreation centre. His services were now far better attended, even by troops tired out after 'a long tiring day practising landing from boats'. Forty-six men applied for confirmation classes, which were arranged despite the difficulties of training schedules and the short time available. 'We sat in a circle on the sand just outside the big tent. The only light was the new moon and an electric torch I had to help me write the men's names down. I was greatly surprised at the regularity with which they came and the quietness with which they listened.' The published diary of a 29th Division R.A.M.C. officer makes a contrast with Creighton's personal humility and

[25] *Official History: Naval Operations*, vol. 2, p. 302.
[26] ibid., p. 304.
[27] *With the 29th Division in Gallipoli*, Chapter 3.

sense of humour which must have been to a considerable extent responsible
for the latter's popularity. In writing of Hamilton's inspection at
Mex, Creighton describes an unintended entertainment for which he was
also responsible. 'It was a wonderful sight seeing them all massed together
with plenty of room to manoeuvre on the stretches of smooth sand. I rode
to a small hill at a distance and dismounted as I watched them. My groom
had not tightened my saddle and girths and when I tried to mount again
the saddle slipped round and I rolled off. The regiments at the moment
were marching off in column. Imagine my dismay as I saw my horse take
fright and tear off right past the Commander in Chief and his staff, and
then all among the men, nearly upsetting the column.'

During the last few days before the landing, the details of Mediterranean
Expeditionary Force H.Q. planning and administration filtered through
to junior officers and men. By now a booklet on the Turkish Army had
been produced which gave detailed notes on organization, uniform,
weapons, badges, etc. Soldiers were enjoined to recognize a 'country
Turk of the village class to a certain extent by his dress. He wears as a
rule a red fez, with a small coloured turban, a pair of very baggy bloomers
of bluish cotton stuff, which are girt above the knee; a leather belt with
a large pouch in front; white woollen stockings and large thick slippers . . .
In Constantinople itself soldiers must beware of the Europeans inhabiting
the low-class districts near the docks, cinematograph-show keepers,
grog-shop keepers and the hangers-on of disorderly houses.'[28] Of course
before either the Turk of the village class or the hangers-on of a disorderly
house had to be faced, there were the Turkish soldiers on the Peninsula.
An Army leaflet[29] gave information for this eventuality. 'Turkish soldiers
as a rule manifest their desire to surrender by holding their rifle butt
upwards and by waving clothes or rags of any colour. An actual white
flag should be regarded with the utmost suspicion as a Turkish soldier
is unlikely to possess anything of that colour.' There followed a list
of Turkish language equivalents to 'Surrender', 'You will be well
treated', 'Throw down your rifles', 'Hold up your hands', 'Higher than
that', etc.

It is difficult to make sound general observations on the briefings which
were received by, for example, Second Lieutenants, N.C.O.s and men
because they were so varied. Captain R. B. Gillett has affirmed categorically to me that he received his map of the Cape Helles end of the
Peninsula in March and that he marked in ink on the map further

[28] *Notes on the Turkish Army 1915*, p. 18.
[29] A.A.C. Intelligence Staff, *Surrender of Turkish Troops*, Imperial War Museum.

information on the defences as it was given to him.[30] The men engaged
upon the feint landing demonstration in the Gulf of Saros knew their
task too. According to Creighton, the officers and men of the 29th
Division knew of the increasing strength of the Peninsula defences.
'Thursday, 22 April. It seems a perfectly desperate undertaking . . . The
aerial reconnaissance reports acres of barbed wire, labyrinths of trenches,
concealed guns, maxims and howitzers everywhere. The ground is
mined. In fact everything conceivable has been done. Our men have to
be towed in little open boats to land in the face of all this.'[31] Major
Davidson of the R.A.M.C. 89th Field Ambulance, in his published
diary,[32] entered for 21 April, 'Marching orders were received this morning.
They run as follows . . .' In his summary of the plans he gives full
details of the objectives, with map references to be gained by the first
landings and the instruction that 'a hot meal is to be taken before leaving
the ship'. The official military history records the somewhat alarming
note which every man in the 29th Division received from Hunter
Weston, the Divisional Commander, that there would be 'heavy losses by
bullets, by shells . . . by mines and by drowning'. The conclusion is
drawn that this may have been responsible for the degree of hesitancy
shown on some beaches in the afternoon. 'As an example of the state of
mind which this order induced, a man on X beach went up to Brig-Gen.
Marshall with a dead tortoise which he had found and said, "I've found
one of these here landmines, Sir".'[33] Nevertheless, it is likely, and
perhaps it was also proper, that for many rankers the briefing was
minimal. Certainly General Hunter Weston's printed address to his
division was issued and there must have been many small unit instructions
on equipment and on anticipated deployment from the beaches as well as
morale-boosting pep talks. In a letter dated 24 April 1915 Cecil Malthus,
with the New Zealanders, wrote that he had 'spent most of the week
duplicating maps of the Peninsula with Fougère the Scout Corporal.
It was slow, tedious work, all done by hand, but we have learnt to know
the ground thoroughly and the knowledge will be invaluable if we are
advancing over fresh country every day.'[34] He was not to know of course
that the maps were of the wrong area and inaccurate and that in any
case they would not be advancing over fresh ground every day.

[30] This map is now in Peter Liddle's collection.
[31] op. cit., p. 42.
[32] G. Davidson, *The Incomparable 29th and the River Clyde*.
[33] *Official History: Gallipoli*, vol. 2, n. 1, p. 254.
[34] *Anzac: A Retrospect*, p. 42.

That no one expected an easy landing was abundantly evident as the naval and transport vessels moved towards their appointed stations, off the island of Tenedos in the case of the 29th Division and off the island of Imbros in the case of the Australian and New Zealand Army Corps. H. W. Nevinson summed up the emotions which roused men to tumultuous cheering as the ships left Mudros in their 'excitement, comradeship, the infectious joy of confronting a dangerous enterprise side by side'.[35] Many men must silently have been asking themselves whether they would let themselves and their friends down when faced by wounding and death. On 19 April the Reverend O. Creighton had been saddened by seeing the midshipmen at a ship's concert, some only sixteen, drinking a good deal of whisky and smoking many cigarettes during the evening. One such midshipman, G. L. Drewry, in a letter of 12 May (in the Imperial War Museum) described to his father how he had felt burdened by his responsibilities towards the soldiers cooped below decks on the *River Clyde*. 'I found myself on the bridge very sleepy with only the helmsman, steering towards the Turkish searchlights on a calm night just making headway against the current, shadowy forms of destroyers and battleships slipping past me. Visions of mines and submarines rose before me as I thought of the $2\frac{1}{2}$ thousand men in the holds and I felt very young.' Drewry was to show a courage within a few hours which earned him the Victoria Cross. Whisky and cigarettes may well have been the nervous signs of boys playing at being men, but when the moment came this recently feigned maturity more than stood the test.

A consideration of the choice of landing places will conclude this work and it is not appropriate at this point to do more than record the dispersal of the landing areas. The French troops were to make a diversionary attack on the Asian side of the entrance to the Straits at Kum Kale, the Australian and New Zealand Army Corps was to be landed north of the Kilid Bahr plateau near the prominent Gaba Tepe headland, in a bay which was to be named after the initials of the corps, and where flatter land invited the prospect of a successful dash across the Peninsula, and the 29th Division was to make five separate landings at beaches labelled Y, X, W, V, and S around Cape Helles. In addition there was to be a demonstration offshore near the Turkish lines at Bulair, which, it was hoped, would convince the Turks that the main attack was to be launched here, from the Gulf of Saros, against the narrow isthmus of the Peninsula. (See Map. 2, pp. 16–17.)

[35] *The Dardanelles Campaign*, p. 90.

From 12 April naval orders were issued by de Robeck, Rear-Admiral Wemyss and Rear-Admiral Thursby to deal with the organization of the combined operation of landing the troops.[36] From 13 April military orders for the landing were issued by the Mediterranean Expeditionary Force H.Q. staff. These plans have been seriously criticized in R. R. James's book[37] and there is no doubt that the separation of the naval and army planning staffs was a blunder. Hamilton was unfortunately unwilling to see the vital nature of planning, which could only be carried out by a large, experienced administrative staff, and this imposed a heavy and badly placed burden on the back of his small General Staff. Despite the soundness of the criticism, it may perhaps give an unbalanced picture. In detail the plans compel a degree of admiration which need not be lessened by doubts concerning the 'grand strategy' of the campaign or indeed by knowledge of some organizational mistakes. If we examine merely one or two small items concerned with the well-being of the lower ranks involved in the landing, it can scarcely be maintained that men were launched lightly into an operation which it was realized would be hazardous. For base and flanking stations established ashore, sailors were to wear 'working suits and solar helmets dyed khaki colour by day. Night clothing, spare socks and one blanket are to be taken. Pistol, belt and fifty rounds ammunition, canteens and water bottles, two days' iron rations and first-aid dressings are to be carried.' In an order issued on 18 April concerning visual signalling, it is stated that every transport officer is to be supplied with six haversacks for correspondence, marked with the letter of the beach. A final example might be taken from Force Order No. 1 issued on 13 April which instructed that 'a hot meal will be issued to all troops before leaving their transports, and troops will land in marching order with pack and one day's rations and two iron rations (or three iron rations in the case of units for which this number is available on their ships).'[38]

It is only in the provision for wounded at the landing that we see an obvious indication of an underestimation of the task ahead. In an order dated 22 April Wemyss instructs that at the landing 'one surgeon and two sick berth ratings are to be held in readiness to proceed to the beach at any time they may be required after 2 p.m. to attend and embark any wounded in the launches. The surgeons should carry their pocket instrument cases. The launches will, if possible, be taken to an empty

[36] Given in full in the *Mitchell Report*, pp. 107 ff.
[37] *Gallipoli*, pp. 77 ff.
[38] *Mitchell Report*, p. 134.

4

transport, which will be called up for the purpose, or to a hospital ship, if ordered. Attendant ships will have to provide the towage.'[39] Hindsight is the historian's dubiously valid weapon, but one cannot but call to mind the near impossibility of obtaining medical aid for the dying and wounded in the early hours of V and W beaches and the pathetic sight of unmanned cutters or whalers drifting helplessly from the shore with their complement of dead and wounded. Indeed the inadequacy of these preparations left the late-arriving Adjutant-General, Brigadier General Woodward, and the Director of Medical Services, Surgeon-General Birrell, aghast. With less than a week to go, there was insufficient time to make material improvements and in any case the need to get soldiers and necessary stores and equipment ashore as quickly as possible, rather than use the ships' boats to bring the wounded off the beaches, was something on which Sir Ian Hamilton had insisted.[40]

This work is not attempting a continuous assessment of the administrative and executive planning of the M.E.F. H.Q. staff, but it is important to point out that a picture of unrelieved incompetence by Hamilton and by his staff at every level cannot be maintained. However easy it may be to draw attention to blunders made or problems left unconsidered – and insufficient preparations to attend to casualties is an obvious example – it should be recognized that the scale of the task was unprecedented. When R. R. James makes a comparison with the tragic failure of the 1809 Walcheren expedition, he surely does not stress sufficiently the enlarged scale of every single aspect of the 1915 combined operation.

[39] ibid., p. 121.
[40] See *Official History: Gallipoli*, vol. 1, pp. 145–6.

7

25 April: The Landing at Anzac

The intended landing area for the Anzac force was just north of the Gaba Tepe headland. The relatively flat terrain here[1] offered few natural difficulties opposing swift progress inland in an attempt to cross the Peninsula and secure Maidos on the Dardanelles side. As the assault in fact took place a full mile further north, in exceptionally broken country, the defences opposing a Gaba Tepe landing were to be untested and the physical obstacles to the actual landing were to be totally unexpected. Subsequent information has suggested that the difficulty of overcoming the defences at Gaba Tepe would certainly have counter-balanced the fact that easier terrain awaited the assault. The explanation of the inadequacy of the north-eastern sectors of the prepared maps was that this area, forbidding enough from sea level and bewildering from the air, was so broken by precipitous ridges, sudden washaways and twisting narrow valleys themselves entered by narrower, steep, contorted side-gullies that accurate mapping in detail would have been difficult even under peace-time conditions.

Except where the bare sand and gravel clay had been exposed on steep slopes, and the thin layer of earth had been eroded, dense, scrubby vegetation with closely growing thorns still further hid the nature of the difficulties of moving inland from the Anzac shore. Low but abrupt slopes rise immediately above the cove itself, and then to the north castellated, gaunt canyons are set back slightly further from the beach. Even today, as afforestation is changing the sheer severity of much of the terrain, it remains a physical shock to visit the area for the first time. There is a newly made road leading off the Anzac-to-Eceabat (Maidos) route and it scales the spiny Sari Bair Ridge (see Map 2, pp. 16–17), giving access by side tracks to the various cemeteries, but to leave this road is to risk at best having one's clothing torn and at worst getting lost and having a serious fall. Viewing the area from the top of this main ridge, one is aware that in winning this little horseshoe of broken beach-head the Australians and New Zealanders had gained a mighty achievement.

North of the long straight beach from Gaba Tepe is a slight headland which became known as Hell Spit. From this headland a small

[1] Both north and south of this area the terrain was higher and more broken.

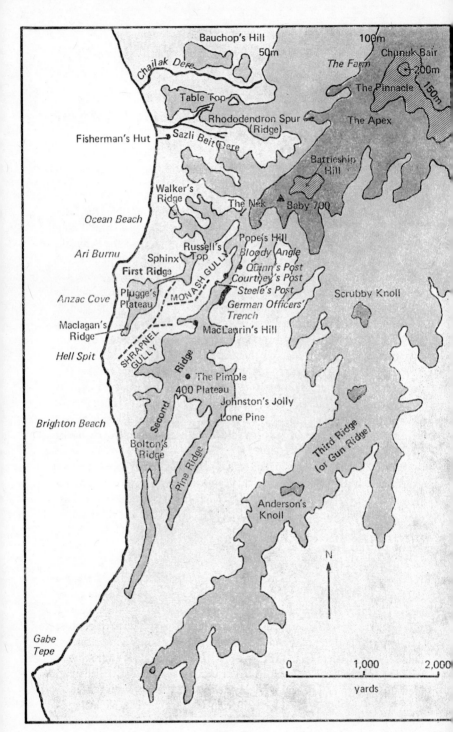

Map 3: Anzac

crescent-curved beach of about 1,000 yards in length (Anzac Cove) ends in a further headland, Ari Burnu.

From a distance the immediately significant geographical objective is the Sari Bair Ridge. As it runs diagonally south-westwards towards Ari Burnu, its most significant heights separated by sudden depressions, the ridge splits into three subsidiary ridges. The first one to be faced from Anzac Cove was Maclagan's Ridge, which leads to Plugge's Plateau (below which lies the Ari Burnu headland). From this plateau an unscalable razor ridge leads to the southern end of Russell's Top, from which the distinctive Sphinx juts out precipitously. Russell's Top, further inland, had a seaward-side extension known as Walker's Ridge, before it reaches the saddle of the Nek and the main ridge at Baby 700. The height of none of these features is extraordinary; it is their steepness and abrupt changes of direction and slope which make this such difficult country for advancing infantry and scarcely practicable for artillery despite the achievement of the Anzac gunners.[2]

The significance of the inadequate mapping and therefore the need for improvisation during the assault is well demonstrated in the official history concerning the description of First Ridge. 'It is important to note that whereas the original map indicated that troops could advance straight up First Ridge from its Southern extremity to Baby 700, in point of fact the Razor Edge made this impossible, and to get from Plugge's Plateau to Russell's Top it was necessary to climb down into the gully and up the steep slope on the other side.'[3]

The Second Ridge runs from Baby 700 to Pope's Hill, Quinn's Post, Courtney's Post, Steele's Post, to 400 Plateau, Lone Pine and Pine Ridge. Third Ridge, which became known as Gun Ridge, leads from Chunuk Bair to Scrubby Knoll and Anderson's Knoll and has a seaward spur which in fact forms the Gaba Tepe headland.

To secure the main heights of the Sari Bair Ridge, which at approximately 970 feet commanded the land on both the Aegean and the Dardanelles side, was to be the critical objective from the start to the finish of the campaign, and though a few Anzacs and indeed a few British soldiers briefly glimpsed the gleaming Narrows from these heights, the intervening distance to Maidos, so mockingly insignificant in being less than

[2] Naturally the names used to describe this and the other ridges were acquired during the campaign, but to write more accurately of 'First Ridge', for instance, is to convey so much less than to use the names of the well-remembered and well-recorded individuality of the land.

[3] *Official History: Gallipoli*, vol. 1, p. 168.

two miles, was not to be covered by successfully advancing allied troops.[4]

The strongest Turkish defences commanded by enfilade fire the intended landing area just north of Gaba Tepe leading to Brighton Beach. These defences on and near the Gaba Tepe headland consisted of trenches, wire entanglements, two 12-cm. guns and several Nordenfelt guns. There was in addition a mountain battery on Lone Pine directly to the rear of the beach. Actually in position in the Anzac Cove area, where the landing was to take place as a result of navigational error in the dark, the defences were much less significant and amounted to a few defended posts on the low hills commanding the beach north of Ari Burnu and a trench on Plugge's Plateau. There was but one battalion to guard the Gaba Tepe coastline, but in reserve there were five further battalions which awaited information concerning the precise location of the intending invaders' real threat. Further reserves at Maidos itself were available to bolster the defence of Gaba Tepe, Helles or even of the Asiatic side of the Dardanelles.

The instructions received by General Birdwood were explicit. 'By the time the Second Division begins to land, sufficient troops should be available to admit of a further advance. Leaving the covering force to protect the northern flank of the landing place and line of communication, an effort will be made to storm Mal Tepe, which is the centre and key to the ridge over which the Gallipoli–Maidos and Boghali–Kojadere roads run. Should the A. and N.Z. Army Corps succeed in securing the ridge the results should be more vital and valuable than the capture of the Kilid Bahr plateau itself.'[5] It was the task of the troops on the warships stealing through the darkness towards Imbros and then Gaba Tepe to effect a landing and secure the beach-head. They were the covering force preparing the way for the main body to land and strike for the heights with the vital road and Dardanelles shore beneath.

'I don't know my own feelings. I don't think I am afraid at any rate. It is just a mixture of excitement and wondering what it would all be like' is the diary entry of C. J. Lawless. It was written a few hours before the landing, but with the covering force was an unidentified soldier who did not survive the campaign but who recorded on the Peninsula a very fine

---

[4] Had Mal Tepe itself been taken, the distance was a mere 1¼ miles to the Dardanelles, and directly beneath this height lay the sole land supply route to the Turks defending Helles.

[5] Instructions for G.O.C. Australian and New Zealand Army Corps from General Headquarters, 13 April 1915, quoted in the *Mitchell Report*, p. 137.

account of what he experienced.[6] He was on board H.M.S. *London*. After a service at midnight they had all tried to get some rest. 'We were called upon to fall in at 2.30 a.m., each man was given a very liberal supply of rum, and then stood by to await landing. Time 3.30. The moon just going down behind the horizon, the cliffs ashore just looming up like large grey clouds. The war boats had all stopped steaming. Sailors were everywhere, moving about very silently. Not a noise of any kind could be heard. The sea was as smooth as glass. The boats were being lowered into the water. The order came to get into the boats. Every man was in a short time seated in his respective boat, and everything was done in such a quiet manner that one would not realize that such a movement in the dark had been carried out. Each man had on his person a full pack consisting of one towel, one shirt, socks, greatcoat, cap, comforter, a change of under-clothing, three sandbags rolled up and tied into the belt of the equipment at the back, three days' rations, consisting of from two to three tins pre-served meat, three pounds of hard biscuits, and one emergency ration consisting of half an ounce of tea, two of sugar and an extract of beef. They also had from two to three hundred rounds of ammunition.

'The boats were in four lines and a pinnace was in front of each line. They towed us [to] within a certain distance from shore, and then let us pull the rest of the way ourselves. Everything was going well, and one can marvel at the way it was carried out for quietness. But an accident happened as we were nearing shore, one of the pinnaces' funnels caught fire and sent up a flare that could be seen miles off. Then a voice rang out in the quietness "You are going the wrong way, bear over," but our man would not move out of his course. The voice rang out again, and then they tried to force us over by coming close alongside us. Still our man would not move out of his course so they towed us in and made the landing in the place where our boat was making for . . . On nearing the shore the first thing that came to our notice was the flash of a huge searchlight. It appeared to come from Cape Helles and shortly afterwards there came a second flash from farther round the Cape. Then everything remained quiet and still again. We were fast approaching the shore and the steam pinnaces had cast us loose. Then a shot rang out in the cliff in front of us and the echo in the still of the morning travelled right along the hills. There was a pause and the battle commenced to rage . . .

'Our boys had to jump over the side of the boats into the water, in some places up to our armpits, our rifles were not loaded and we had to

---

[6] The soldier, mortally wounded in August, had handed this account to R. A. Nicholas, a private in the Hospital Transport Corps.

fix bayonets on getting ashore. Now we had received orders that as soon as we had all got ashore, every man was to fix bayonet and get into line, each man taking hold of the sleeve of the man next to him with his disengaged hand. But one can imagine to oneself why that was not carried out. Some men were shot getting out of the boats, others in the water and sank to rise no more, and a great number on the shore, so that the orders laid down for the line of advance could not, under the conditions that then existed, be carried out . . . Men of all units were mixed up, command as far as orders were concerned was lost, i.e., what to do and how to do it. There was one yell and a rush towards the cliff . . . shouting like demons. The value of our severe training in Egypt standing us in good stead.'

The strength of the current and the difficulty of discerning accurately the coastline ahead had led to an error of navigation. Subsequent rumours of the Turks having moved the navigation buoy supposedly set by *Triumph* have not been satisfactorily substantiated. Commander Dix, on the left of the landing flotilla over which he held command, was aware of the drifting and bunching northwards. He was frustrated in his efforts to correct this, and the error was further compounded by Lieutenant Waterlow, who was responsible for guiding the tows. Waterlow, sighting Ari Burnu, identified it as Gaba Tepe and altered his course accordingly. Commander Dix took his tow across the stern of those crossing his desired correction course ahead and the sailors in his boats brought them in around Ari Burnu while the three left-hand tows were some 200 yards north. Altogether the landing was about a mile further north than had been intended.[7]

Despite the naval responsibility for the error, seen both in contemporary evidence and in retrospect, the bearing of the young midshipmen – one, Eric Bush, being not yet sixteen years of age – made a tremendous impression. G. A. Radnell is just one of many Australians who have paid tribute to them. Their composure under fire, their businesslike command and authority were what those responsible for their training at Osborne and Dartmouth, the junior and senior departments of the Royal Naval College, would have expected but would nevertheless have been intensely proud to see so amply demonstrated. A New Zealander remembers the general amusement which eased the tension when a rosy-cheeked midshipman dealt with a querulous remonstration by replying

[7] It seems unreasonable to attach any weight to the theory that Admiral Thursby, the naval officer in command of the Anzac landing, had at the last moment given different orders to Lieutenant Waterlow which instructed him to set course for Hell Spit. See R. R. James, *Gallipoli*, pp. 105–6.

that he expected to be addressed as 'Sir'. The midshipman was of course in command of his boat. Midshipman Eric Longley-Cook had spoken similarly to an Australian officer and then, as his picket boat came under fire, a three-pounder shell came through the thin steel screen in front of his wheel, through his straddled legs and the cabin immediately behind him, to wound two sailors in the stern of his boat. On a second trip to the landing beach he was somewhat dismayed to see dark khaki bundles above the shoreline and then relieved to find that they were not bodies but merely the discarded packs of the Australians as they stormed up the beach to the higher ground. Longley-Cook wrote to his father: 'The extraordinary thing is that I didn't feel a bit funky.'

Eric Bush's gallantry was recorded in the *Bacchante*'s 'Report of Proceedings' that is the Captain's report. 'I would especially wish to bring to your notice the two Midshipmen of this ship who were in our steamboats: Mr Eric Wheeler Bush, Royal Navy, and Mr Charles Douglas Herbert Horsfall Dixon R.N. who came to us as *only first-term cadets from Dartmouth* and who I saw repeatedly doing good work.' The father of another very young Midshipman, Aubrey Mansergh, had been so annoyed at still having to contribute to his son's Dartmouth fees that he had written to the First Lord of the Admiralty about it. Churchill promised to look into this injustice but was 'happy to inform my father that his son had been awarded the Distinguished Cross for service at the Dardanelles'.

Bacchante's young ship's writer, A. H. K. Cobb, denied the privilege of taking the troops ashore, was in command of the fore transmitting room with twelve hands under him. He watched the landing and was able to describe it immediately in his log. 'We closed to within 800 yards of the shore and commenced firing at 4.30 . . . on the farther ridge a splendid Turkish battery was concealed and they burst shrapnel over the landing troops absolutely unmercifully. By our heavy firing we were able to stop the battery considerably and by night we had landed some thousands who had taken the first ridge and were entrenching themselves rapidly. You could see them silhouetted on the skyline digging like sin.'

Another officer on board *Bacchante*, W. O'Neill, watched the Australian effort and recorded in his log the murderous fire of the Turks 'causing many casualties, but nothing could stop these undaunted troops who simply had their bayonets fixed and made a gallant charge up the hill'.

The sudden cliffs and valleys and unexpected precipitous rises led to the development of completely unconnected fighting incidents. Men

deliberately jumped feet first to slide down the gravelly sides of a minia-
ture canyon and, with a free hand to grasp at roots, used bayonet or entrenching tool to clamber up the other side in pursuit of shadowy figures
who were often using paths of escape quite unknown to the Australians.
How far to advance where there seemed little or no opposition was a
question many had to answer, but, as the morning wore on, when to
retire if opposition increased and one's own party was small became the
critical issue.

Following quickly upon the landing of the covering force came the
main body, to be landed by destroyers and troopships. G. C. Grove
found the beach 'littered all over with bits of web equipment, bags of iron
rations, caps, hats, rifles, ammunition lying in amongst the dead and
wounded . . . packs and equipment had been left all over the place in the
scrub and on the side of the gully.' Grove, with the 2nd Field Company
of Engineers, was soon involved in carrying stores up the gully behind
the first ridge and there they bored successfully for water. 'Troops on the
way to the firing line were stopping all day to get a drink so we were
working pretty hard with the pumps, having to fall flat on the ground
every minute or so on account of the shrapnel shells and bullets bursting
over and amongst us all the time. There were a lot of snipers about on the
ridges, so when passing backwards and forwards to the beach we had to
keep under cover as much as possible. Stretcher-bearers and A.M.C.
passing unceasingly backwards and forwards between the beach and the
firing line doing magnificent work. Guard mounted over water reserve
during the night. I had the 12 to 2 a.m. shift, very dark when moon went
down. Had to keep our eyes very wide open in spite of our tiredness. Did
not get any rest all night on account of having to man the pumps to supply
the mules and water carts with water.'

Corporal J. Sinclair of the 10th Battalion, wounded at the landing,
wrote from his hospital in Malta on 4 May that right up to their landing
it was impossible to exaggerate 'the hospitality and kindness' of the
sailors of the *Prince of Wales*. '. . . If I ever have the chance to help any
British sailor I shall do so.'[8] Sinclair admitted in his letter that from the
top of the first hill 'we went after [the Turks] without much system, all
the different companies mixed up . . . I think the lack of system was why
we missed so many snipers who lay in the bushes and were passed by our
men.' Though he did not mention that their orders at every level had
been to press on with all attention to speed, he was critical of Australian
conduct later in this confused day. 'Then they came running in. One

8 Letter in the South Australia State Library.

fellow stood up and started to explain why he had come in, with bullets falling around us thick as peas. He ought to have got down as quickly as possible. He did get down when he was ordered to. This is typical of the way the Australians acted throughout. I do not think we fully appreciated the danger we were in, any of us.'

Another letter, dated from 4 May, from a 10th Battalion man, W. J. Welch, wounded at the landing and apparently anxious to get back to the Peninsula to 'find the bloke who got in on me when I wasn't looking', wrote of the landing: 'My word, what a mix-up it was,' and Captain G. D. Shaw in the same battalion conceded in a letter to his wife that he felt 'years older and I don't think I want to laugh very much any more'. Private Knight, more elated despite his wound, wrote of the Turks, who were of course greatly outnumbered, 'You should have seen the cowardly curs run. They scuttled out of the trenches like rabbits and we were the whippets giving chase.'[9]

The special tasks to be performed by the engineers at the landing or during the next few days were many and varied, and at least one for which they were well prepared was never accomplished: one man, D. S. M. Oakes, staggering ashore in the shallows laden with gun-cotton and demolition equipment, was with a party briefed to destroy the gun emplacement at Gaba Tepe! Harold Bachtold was in command of the beaching and arrangement of the first pontoon for the assistance of un-loading stores from lighters. The officer on the beach required so many minor adjustments to the course of the pontoon as it neared the shore that Bachtold cut short any further frustrating delay by running the joined sections ashore as he saw fit. 'It was a raft built up of barrels – the raft with us on it was towed by a destroyer about a mile, arriving at the beach about 2 o'clock in the afternoon. Directly we left our transport we had to run the gauntlet of shrapnel fire directed at us . . . on arrival at the beach we connected up with shore in about fifteen minutes and then handed it over to the A.M.C. who immediately commenced to use it for embarking the wounded.'

Particularly tragic had been the fate of men of the 7th Battalion in four of the boats on the left of the landing.[10] With all the rowers killed, oars lost or smashed and many of the soldiers killed or disabled, the boats had drifted helplessly just off shore, an easy target for accurate fire from

[9] Letters from the South Australia State Library. Captain Shaw's and Private Knight's letters are undated.

[10] For the sad story of these men of the 7th Battalion and the brave efforts to rescue survivors see the *Official History of Australia in the War of 1914–18*, vol. 1, pp. 325 ff.

the direction of Fisherman's Hut. Among the most unforgettable of the early impressions of those who survived their first days on the Peninsula was the sight of these 7th Battalion casualties lying for several days un-buried on the shoreline or in the stranded, waterlogged boats.

The work of the Australian and New Zealand Engineers won an unconscious but deserved tribute in the diary of Eric Wettern who, with the 2nd Field Company R.N.D. Engineers, landed at Anzac on the 29th and found 'several landing piers in bay at foot of cliff – crowded with stores etc. – quite a small town'. The R.N.D. Engineers were to be engaged in 'making road up shore hillside for guns – record time – got it finished by dark [on 30th] and got one gun up. Congratulated by Australians.'

Wettern had little idea of the difficulties encountered at Anzac and the splendid recovery from the dangerous situation of the first twenty-four hours. The brigade and battalion War Diaries of the A.I.F. in the South Australian State Library provide an indication of the disintegration of the meticulous planning and the consequent strain upon the men. In official orders beforehand it is specifically stated: 'No rifle fire is to be employed until broad daylight. The bayonet only is to be used. No bugle calls to be sounded after leaving Lemnos. No bugle calls are to be sounded during the charge.' For 5 a.m. on the 25th the War Diary for the H.Q. of the 3rd Infantry Brigade reads, 'Bde considerably mixed but roughly in order', and by the 29th, 'Our men were thoroughly exhausted and their nerves shattered after ninety-six hours' continuous fighting in the trenches with little or no sleep.' The strain was not limited to the rankers – one senior Australian officer was sent back to Alexandria by Bridges as he was 'quite dangerous, thinking everyone was a spy'.[11]

The capacity of the Turks, aided by the terrain, to infiltrate the newly established positions of the Australians and New Zealanders was the source of a good deal of the morale-sapping confusion. There are numerous stories of Turks and indeed Germans in the uniforms of dead Australians or merely unseen in the scrub or the darkness of night, shouting confusing orders to the Anzacs such as 'Don't shoot – Indian troops.' Not always was there a Captain Croly quickly to make up men's minds with, 'Shoot the bloody buggers, they're Turks.'[12] Colonel Marks,

[11] Australian National Library, Canberra, Lord Novar Papers, Bridges, letter to Mrs Bridges, 5 May 1915.
[12] See W. C. Belford, *Legs Eleven*. The Australian official history discounts the theory of the Turks cunningly adopting such ruses by the actual use of spies and attributes the reality of the situation to rumour, mistakes and confusion. See vol. 1, p. 470.

who landed with his 13th Battalion on the 26th and fed that night on 'dead men's rations', recorded in his diary for the 27th that 'during the afternoon we were repeatedly ordered to cease fire as the British and French were coming up'.[13] Signalled messages to the same effect were received but they were found to emanate 'from spies actually in our trenches'. Then, 'the Turks heavily attacked, blowing weird calls on a bugle'. General Bridges wrote to his wife from Anzac Cove, 'Troops had to be shoved in just as they landed which mixed units up and we never got straight for days.'[14] In the same letter Bridges wrote that 'the Brigadiers thought that they could not hold on for another day', and there is ample evidence for this dangerous situation in Birdwood's diary and correspondence.[15] On the 29th Birdwood wrote that his men went forward with 'too much dash for they took on more than they could manage, dashing away to the extreme spurs of the hills which were much too extended to hold . . . but then the most awful reaction followed', and he described how near the beach he had met small groups of Australians returning from the firing line convinced that they were the last of their units and had narrowly escaped being cut off. From a different level Cecil Malthus's book gives similar evidence when he writes of a state of muddle and utter exhaustion existing everywhere and the defence of their beach-head being terribly weak. On the 26th there was an incursion into a trench held by the Canterbury Battalion by a party of Australians who had been cut off ahead of the coalescing front line. 'Now they had suddenly lost their nerve, though not immediately threatened, and working their way along the cliff top came dashing in without warning over the top of our trench . . . They were in a bad state with exhaustion and thirst.'[16]

Naturally only the men on the beach and near the Brigade H.Q.s had any inkling of the seriousness of the overall tactical situation on the evening of the landing, but those involved in reversing the parapets of trenches near the beach were aware that the fearful possibility of a withdrawal under fire was being actively considered. This beach defence activity is well remembered by D. S. M. Oakes of the 1st Field Company Engineers, who had stumbled ashore with the demolition equipment for the Gaba Tepe gun emplacement, but it is right that note should be taken of C. W. Bean's advice that the situation on the beach, with its

[13] Mitchell Library, Sydney.
[14] See n. 11 above.
[15] Australian War Memorial, Canberra.
[16] *Anzac: A Retrospect*, pp. 49–50.

stragglers and its wounded, should not be taken to reflect the state of morale in the firing line.

In the diary of C.Q.M.S. A. L. Guppy[17] of the 14th Battalion there is a revealing entry for 25 April, written while his transport *A 31* (*Seang Choon*) stood off shore. 'At about 11 p.m. a picket boat came round and a Naval Officer shouted up to us to get boats' crews told off ready to man all boats ready to go ashore as it was expected that all troops ashore would be re-embarked. This got our blood up a bit to think that so many lives had been thrown away and the thing a failure. However about midnight the order was cancelled.'

Awaiting his time to land like Guppy was A. L. Hellman, and his diary, in the Mitchell Library, Sidney, illustrates the strain of inaction further heightened by what he could see and what he was told. '25 April 1915: Our boys are getting a terrible time. Boat after boat of wounded are being brought alongside. What an awful sight to see our boys cut about. 27 April 1915: The sooner we get ashore the better. Let us avenge the death of our comrades. Thank God I was born a man and not a woman. I would not be out of this for anything. 28 April 1915: A lot of our men have had their tongues cut out by the Turks! We have eight prisoners on board. They are being treated as well as we are.'

From 4.15 a.m. according to the 3rd Infantry Brigade War Diary,[18] the first troops were being landed from the battleships and the men from the destroyers were only ten minutes behind, except for those drowned in the sad accident to a boat swamped as it drifted in too closely to the destroyer *Foxhound* when still well off shore. From 5.30 a.m. to 7.30 a.m. Australians from the 2nd and 1st Brigades were landed; there is a photograph of the H.Q. of the 1st Australian Division landing at 10 a.m.[19] The first New Zealanders in the Australian and New Zealand Division were landed by 10.30 and they were from the Auckland Battalion.

From the N.Z. Divisional Signal Company, C. R. G. Bassett, who was in August to earn the V.C., remembers being concerned at the landing when he saw lines of Australian dead, whether he would be able to 'maintain his honour' in action. A. E. Robinson in the Auckland Battalion, far in advance of what was to be Quinn's Post, saw the waters of the Dardanelles, but when his companion Private Crum was hit and they seemed alone against heavy machine-gun fire, they made their way back.

[17] Australian War Memorial, Canberra.
[18] The Australian official history, vol. 1, p. 267, gives the time of landing at 4.30, with the men from the destroyers 20 minutes later.
[19] Australian War Memorial, Canberra (G905).

D. E. Stacey, in the same battalion, recalled that Colonel Plugge formed them up on the beach in fours to march along to the left, but before long this order was reversed, and avoiding the folly of making such a target for Turkish fire they made a much less formal move to positions on the right. Colonel W. I. K. Jennings, then an officer in the Otago Battalion, had suffered the indignity of jumping into the water far too soon and having to be hauled back, while W. H. Foord, in the N.Z. Engineers, remembers that on their transport a good deal of time was used in extracting the stretchers from beneath the barbed wire under which they had been stowed.

The original documentary evidence of the personal experience of New Zealanders at the landing consistently records the dual impact of the sight of death and, amidst death, of Australian achievement. Lieutenant Algie recorded in his diary: 'We landed on an open beach and were greeted with a sight to try the nerves of the strongest – dead, dying and wounded in all directions. The Australians who had landed at dawn had suffered heavily but performed a feat of which we were all proud in driving the enemy out of his positions at all.'

Captain A. B. Morton, with the Staff of the Australian and New Zealand Division, having mentioned in his diary for the 24th that he had 'put the finishing touch on the edge of my sword which I have decided to take with me in case it may come in useful', grimly lists over the next several pages, the New Zealand killed, wounded and missing between the 25th and 30th.[20] He himself was to be killed on 3 May.

C. J. Walsh, in the Auckland Battalion, sought no disguise to his feelings. 'The Turks have got the range of this place and they pepper it. Dozens coming back wounded. Singie got shot in thigh. Lots dead . . . Latest news is that nearly all officers shot and extreme left wing retreating. No reinforcements and no artillery . . . Rifle fire continued all through night. On duty most of night. I feel very frightened. Raining slightly during night.' H. G. Hunter, in the Canterbury Battalion, having landed in the evening of the 25th, had by the 27th 'not fired a shot yet, neither have any of the rest of my platoon'. The relatively small numbers of the Turks present during the first days and their skill at concealment meant that Hunter's experience in failing so far even to have seen the enemy was common.

[20] The breakdown of these figures into killed, wounded and missing is not given because there are some inaccuracies: 661 names from the Auckland, Canterbury and Wellington Battalions are listed, and for example H. V. Palmer of the *Nelson* Company, Canterbury Battalion, is listed as killed. He was still alive in June 1974.

A sergeant in the Wellington Battalion, A. G. Jennings, wrote pencilled snatches in his diary at any opportunity. '25 April: This is going
to be serious. Boatloads of wounded Australians are coming aboard.
27 April: Took a box of ammunition to our left flank and nearly got
potted twice. Coming back lost my way and came across three New
Zealanders lying down. Thought they were wounded and offered to help
them but found they were dead.' Quite a number of men understandably
recorded their distress at being unable to bring help or water to the
piteously crying wounded just ahead of hurriedly makeshift entrenchments.

With far more wounded than had been estimated there were harrowing
scenes, both on the beach and on the transports, of untended men lying
either in the sun or on overcrowded decks. For men unable to help themselves, the heat, the flies, the pain and effect of their wounds, as well as
the sight of them, made the days from 25 April a nightmare. The diary of
Lieut-Colonel P. C. Fenwick, the New Zealand Assistant Director
Medical Services, shows that, 'at one time over 400 were lying on the
stones [of the beach] waiting to be moved . . . Violent burst of shrapnel
swept over us and many wounded were hit a second time. Col. Howse
was packing boats and lighters with these poor chaps as fast as possible,
but the beach kept filling up again with appalling quickness . . . I dressed
as many as I could but it was a dreadful time . . . At midnight I got four
big horse boats which held twelve stretchers on the bottom and I packed
in less severe cases along the sides, sitting, kneeling, lying – anyhow,
about 120 all told.' Also on the beach, Edney Moore, in the Australian
Medical Corps, noted that 'owing to boats being busy landing troops,
they were unable to take the wounded off. God wasn't it an awful mix-up
stooping over the men trying to help them as they lay in the scorching
sun.'

Vice-Admiral Longley-Cook remembered his midshipman's work that
day taking wounded on a huge flat-topped Greek lighter lashed to his
picket boat. One wounded Australian had a red and black shoulder flash
immediately above what was left of his arm, which was burnt black where it
was not red with blood. 'I took this load of wounded to ship after ship, only
to be waved away as they were full. Finally I took them to my own ship,
Prince of Wales, and risking a beating for insolence secured alongside and
went up to the officer of the watch, told him what had happened and that
he must take them. All was well, the wounded were taken on board and I
returned to the beach.'

On board H.M.S. *Prince of Wales* the Australian wounded received attention, and one of the R.N. medical orderlies, G. F. Moseley, has never forgotten a soldier holding his eye in place until a naval surgeon cut the shreds which still held it. A New Zealander, Major Furby, himself wounded, saw amputations of fingers carried out with a table knife on board the transport *Itonus*, and another New Zealander, J. A. Fagan, who lay on a hard iron deck for his return to Alexandria, remembered not only the impossible task for two doctors on board, but the bandaged bodies washed ashore near Alexandria because of inefficient sea burials from this transport. Not all the wounded suffered from small arms or shrapnel fire. Some had spinal injuries like H. V. Hitch, who had had to make a dramatic jump down a precipice to avoid being an easy target on the skyline where he had been spotted. But surely no account of the sufferings of the variously injured men could be more horrifying than that contained in a letter in the Mitchell Library written by Peter Hall, in the 2nd Stationary Hospital, on 2 May from the S.S. *Seang Choon* in Alexandria harbour:

'I shall not easily forget that first feeling of awe that came over me as I looked over the side of the ship, down on these boatloads of mangled human beings. As [our] infantry had not left the ship the blankets had not been sterilized – three English doctors and fifteen men none of whom had been trained for anything but general duties in a hospital trying to attend 659 wounded men, the majority of them in an awful state – it was a matter of difficulty to walk anywhere on the decks so closely were they packed. Some of these men with arms and legs all smashed up lay squeezed up against others with half their faces blown away. Men sat all night and well into the next day with congealed blood hanging from mouths unable to speak, but with an awful appeal in their eyes imploring you to bring the doctor. The doctors were doing their best but it was an impossible task to attend to so many. One man begged of me to take five sovereigns he had, just to bring the doctor to him for one minute. [One] man sat there while the doctor cut away the loose pieces of flesh and removed the shattered teeth and bone. Men [were] going for days without having broken limbs set – [there were] no proper splints.

'For the first two days it was a common sight to find men sewn in their blankets laying about the deck – sewn up by men who yet had themelves to go out and face what these fellows had done.' Looking at the expression on the faces of the dead, Hall wrote that it was heartbreaking to think of those who were waiting at home for news of their menfolk. Having described the crowded mess-deck, he concluded: 'All this was someone's fault but God knows it was not ours who already had a superhuman task before us. Some day it may be fixed to somebody holding a much higher position than any of ours. Surely a want of preparation and foresight on somebody's part.'[21]

For the Turks the exact location of the Anzac landing had come as a surprise. Major Zeki, in command of the 1st/57th Regiment, informed the post-1918 Armistice Dardanelles investigators that no special dispositions of troops had been made there because it was thought that the ground was too broken and that naval gunfire could not adequately support a landing.[22] Once it was realized that this landing was a serious threat, the readily available reinforcements were hurried up into position, but with the exhaustion of this reserve Major Zeki affirmed that the 26th had been a very critical day for the defenders.

An indication of the critical nature of the balance between defeat and the avoidance of defeat is given in the memoirs of Liman von Sanders, Kannengiesser Pasha and Mustapha Kemal himself.[23] But at a lower level there is evidence too. Sureya Dilmen, a civilian, happened to be visiting his uncle, a captain in the 27th Infantry Regiment stationed in the Olive Grove, when news of the landing was brought to the regiment. Dilmen was given a rifle and told to come along to help fight for his fatherland and this, he recalls today, he was proud to do. Captain Ozgen informed the writer of the Turkish shortage of ammunition during the first days of the landing and their use of both rocks and explosive charges thrown or rolled down gullies on to troops attempting to scale them.

A remarkably interesting letter, dated 7 May, describing the landing as seen by the Turks has survived and was given to me by its writer, General Fahrettin Altay.[24] 'Naturally we moved up to Maidos on the afternoon of the first day of the battle, and for three or four days what anxieties we endured God alone knows! All actions devolved upon myself . . . above Ari Burnu there is a fairly high hill called Koja Chemen Dagh that completely overlooks the Straits. The enemy's intention was to seize this hill suddenly, but on my timely insistence, the force held in this neighbourhood arrived in time to occupy the hill before the enemy, and to force the latter into a steep, very rough and rather narrow ravine between the hill

<hr />

[21] For further details of the clearing of the wounded see the Australian official history, vol. 1, Chapter 25.

[22] *Mitchell Report*, pp. 167–9.

[23] L. von Sanders, *Five Years in Turkey*, p. 57; Kannengiesser Pasha, *The Campaign of Gallipoli*, p. 98; *Gallipoli Memoirs of Mustapha Kemal*, translated typescript, Imperial War Museum; *Ataturk Memoirs of the Anafarta Battles*, pp. 4–10.

[24] The translation of this letter was made by Major T. Verschoyle, an oriental scholar as well as a Gallipoli veteran.

and the sea. Although three attacks were made to throw the enemy into the sea, they were foiled again by naval and machine-gun fire and by the ruggedness of the land and the enemy's defences. We suffered great losses, but those of the enemy were even greater, and he had not achieved his purpose. That he has a few troops on land is of no importance. He can land troops whenever he likes, but his main purpose is to seize the Straits and for that great self-sacrifice is required. Of this, however, there is no sign, for the morale of his troops has sunk so low as to be beyond description, as we can see for ourselves and learn from prisoners . . . These fellows will eventually have to embark their troops at Ari Burnu and re-move them one of these nights. They cannot advance one step further but it will be a bit harder to chase them from Seddel Bahr . . .

'Thanks be to the Almighty our officers and men rushed forward with a self-sacrifice beyond description. The Germans are astonished at the bravery and self-sacrifice of our soldiers . . . Only the crew of the *Nuseyri* who had been posted to some of the Arab battalions threatened to flee: but they were brought to their senses when three of them were shot.

'A wounded private was being carried from the front line to the rear. I walked with him for a little, holding him by the hand. When I un-covered his face and smoothed his bloody cheeks, he sighed: "Ah Sir, I am not grieving over my wounds, but because I cannot now see those fellows chased into the sea I am grieving. Perhaps if I could have stayed a little longer, I should have seen them."

'On the second night of the battle four thousand wounded were collected around us. The landing stages [at Maidos] were under fire from the fleet. Maidos was in flames, and shells fell on the hospital; but all the wounded were rescued except for ten or so. There were three severely wounded British prisoners, and these were burned. That a hospital should be shelled was something unheard of up till then. Later on Chanakkale was bombarded and it too was set on fire. The towns have been virtually evacuated. Gelibolu was shelled from the Gulf of Saros and a few houses burned down: later it too was evacuated. Aeroplanes twice dropped bombs near our H.Q. but only one bomb scored a hit, on the telephone tent, four unfortunate men being killed and one wounded. A splinter from a naval shell pierced my tent whilst I was away, and destroyed a basket in it . . .

'With the orderly who is bringing this letter we have sent as a present to the Vice-Commander in Chief a British machine-gun, two rifles and a map. If you look at the machine-gun, which will probably be placed in a museum, you will see that I have written on it and Pasha has also signed it . . . I haven't any present to send you. Will you make up a small parcel of four batteries for electric torches (they are three or four piastres each), a bottle of eau de cologne, soap and a box of biscuits and send it by the orderly who brings this letter ... violent days are past and the rest is easy.'

Altay's letter to his father does something to balance the picture of the Anzac landing given in allied personal documentation. With an eye towards the morale of the recipient, the morale of the Anzac soldiers is described as having sunk so low as to be beyond description. The reader in Constantinople is informed of the shelling of a hospital and can draw the invited conclusion whether this had been deliberate or not. Similarly from Brisbane to Bolton and Bar le Duc, parents, relatives and friends would read of the Turks running away 'like cowardly curs' and of their mutilation of allied prisoners. In spite of the fact that morale at home and at the front was to be as significant later in 1915 as in May, respect and even scarcely begrudged admiration of the foe, earned by both sides, were in future to exercise their own censorship of news which, if stimulating to the distant recipient, was remote from the reality of the situation.

Nevertheless Lieut-Colonel Altay's letter contained an accurate appraisal of the general tactical and strategic situation within a fortnight of the landing, which was, in view of his seniority, far beyond the capability of the ranker or junior officer. Even if his concluding comment that 'violent days are past and the rest is easy' was obviously to reassure his father, his forecast that no further allied advance at Anzac was possible and that the force would have to be re-embarked was an accurate prediction which would only be briefly challenged in August before being vindicated in December. Von Sanders, now satisfied that no serious attack was intended at the Bulair lines, had committed all his reserves to Anzac and Helles. The counter-attack launched by Kemal Pasha with his 19th Division was decisively to wrest victory away from the allies at Anzac.

Not even the whole of First Ridge had been taken by the brave Australian and New Zealand assault. Its northern starting-point, Baby 700, a vital key, was not to be held after its early capture despite the fact that much of Second Ridge had been won. This Second Ridge, with the northern section of First Ridge, was to form throughout the campaign the front-line zone. Isolated parties, like that led by Lieutenant Loutit of the 10th Battalion, had reached vantage-points on Third Ridge like Scrubby Knoll which enabled them to see the Dardanelles only three and a half miles away, but they had been forced to retire as the general confusion fatally delayed the sending of reinforcements to hold the vital heights gained.

On Battleship Hill and on Baby 700, similarly small parties had either been forced to retire or had been overwhelmed. The latter was the fate of Captain Peter Lalor of the 12th Battalion, while Tulloch of the 11th, having been outflanked after his successful ascent of Battleship Hill, had to withdraw when his small group was opposed by increasingly strong resistance. Lieutenant Margetts, of the 12th Battalion, twice reached the summit of Baby 700 and, 'further to the left, near the summit of the hill, where Gordon's company of the 2nd Battalion was mixed with remnants of the 11th and 12th, the line swept backwards and forwards over the summit of Baby 700 no less than five times. Each time after holding for a while, it was driven back. Almost every officer was killed or wounded, but Margetts still remained.'[25] The heroism of these men, of Major Kindon and of the Auckland and Canterbury Battalions who came up to their support on Baby 700, is superbly told in the Australian official history; but the hill was lost. Without artillery support, as the Indian Mountain battery had been counter-batteried out of action, and with no Australian or New Zealand eighteen-pounder gun in action before 6 p.m. that day,[26] the unconnected parties holding Baby 700 broke and retired at about 4.30 in the afternoon against a strong Turkish assault. The Nek was to fall in the evening, and by morning Bloody Angle too, but what was to become Quinn's Post held, and on the right the Australian line, after bitter fighting, was forced to retire to Bolton's Ridge, a position seaward of Lone Pine, Johnston's Jolly and the crest of McLaurin's Hill. Even without Hamilton's celebrated order, the entrenching tool was to be every Anzac's closest ally.

Earlier in the day the Anzacs had shown their confident dash, their physical stamina and their athleticism. As the day wore on they would demonstrate their capacity to endure, grimly to hold on when faced by that most dangerously gnawing erosion of individual and collective confidence, a severe check to a consciousness of superiority. They had found that they were not, on this historic day, to stride across the Peninsula, but the Turk would learn that to check their invasion was one thing, to throw them into the sea was another. As at Helles, the scene was set for another Flanders.

The achievement at Anzac had fallen far short of what had been necessary to secure a tactical victory which would have influenced the events at Helles now to be described and perhaps the whole enterprise.

[25] *Official History of Australia in the War of 1914–18*, vol. 1, p. 299.
[26] The *Bacchante* concentrated on attempting to silence the Turkish enfilading fire from Gaba Tepe.

There is ample evidence that, though few of the men involved had
expected easy success, the frustration of their efforts was a sobering
experience. Fortunately the effect of this experience was counter-balanced
by an astonishing resilience and capacity to endure the grim conditions.
It is, as at Helles, quite reasonable to speak of a collective achievement
and of individual achievement. Against increasingly strong defences and
obvious geographical disadvantages the Australian and New Zealand
troops had stormed, then defended, a beach-head and inland area which,
though small, was to be so securely held that no massed Turkish counter-
attack from the end of April to the evacuation in December would
seriously threaten their control. No one familiar with the Anzac landscape
would deny that a victory had been gained even if not quite the victory
which was necessary for overall success.[27]

---

[27] For a graphic description of the evacuation issue during the night of 25/26 April, see
the Australian official history, vol. 1, pp. 457–63.

8. 25 April: The Landing at Cape Helles

Y beach

Of the forces assigned to launch the attack on the five chosen beaches of
Cape Helles, that which landed at Y beach included the 1st King's Own
Scottish Borderers, one company of the South Wales Borderers and the
Plymouth Marine Battalion. The significance of this action is indicated
by the account in the official history.[1] Sir Ian Hamilton had hoped that
landing at a point just west of Krithia would both threaten Turkish communications to the toe of the Peninsula and safeguard the flank of the
Helles landings by providing for the establishment of a link with X beach
which would considerably threaten Turkish defence against the V and W
beach landings. An examination of the landing-site confirms the reasonable witticism published in the M.E.F. newspaper, *Peninsula Press*, later
in the campaign: 'Y beach? – it's nothing but a bloody cliff.' The almost
sheer cliffs, approaching 200 feet high, with only two narrow defiles
allowing an approach to the top, had been left undefended by the Turks.
Led by the Scottish Borderers, the landing was completely unopposed.
For the subsequent failure to exploit this lack of opposition, the official
history indicts firstly Colonel Matthews of the Marines, the question of
whose overall command was sadly decided for the most senior officer who
doubted it, Colonel Koe of the Scottish Borderers, by the latter's mortal
wound. Colonel Matthews, in the absence of orders confirming that he
was to exploit the unopposed landing either towards X beach or towards
the apparently undefended Krithia, delayed making any decision until
mid-afternoon on the 25th, when he ordered defensive entrenchment of
the cliff-top 'beach-head', and furthermore failed to convey this decision
to the watching ships, whose observation was hindered by the spoon-like
depression of the land behind the cliff edge. The official account also
indicts the lack of initiative by Sir Ian Hamilton, who had taken a special
interest in the plan for an attack at Y and had invited Hunter-Weston, the
Divisional Commander, to exploit it when the first indications of an
unopposed landing were received. Finally Hunter-Weston's preoccupation with V and W and his lack of both tactical awareness and responsibility towards Y are also quite reasonably censured.

[1] *Official History: Gallipoli*, vol. 1, pp. 204–15.

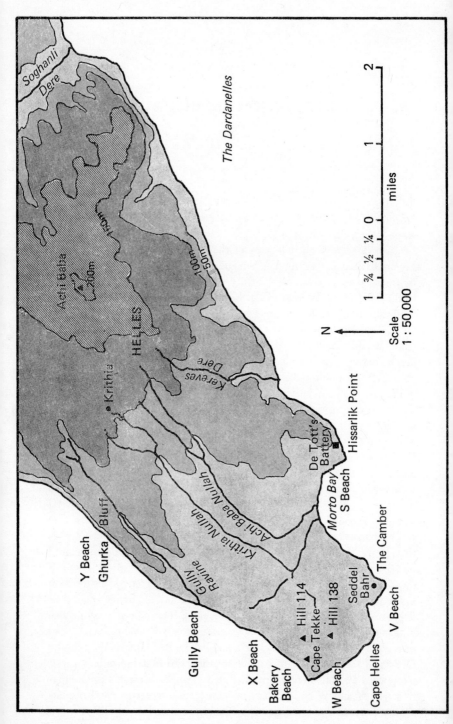

Map 4: Helles

The war diary of the 1st Battalion King's Own Scottish Borderers illustrates how the closeness of the fighting led to some of the confusion. 'In one place a German officer walked up to our trench and said, "You English surrender. We ten to one." He was thereupon hit on the head with a spade.' The Turks had even brought up a machine-gun on a pony. The diary frankly admits that confusion had been caused by an order from Colonel Matthews at approximately 9.30 a.m. on the 26th that 'the whole force would move down the coast by prolonging its right. There was some misunderstanding and this order was taken to be a command to retire.'[2]

The previously unpublished recollections of two men not only convey some sense of the confusion and bitterness of the fighting in the late afternoon of the 25th when the Turks came up in strength,[3] but shed some personal light on the burning issues of responsibility for the lost opportunity, an opportunity which seems still more tantalizing in the light of the adamant assertion by a third man, J. M. Johnson (Royal Marines), that in the early hours of the landing he and others had 'strolled through Krithia and on the left shoulder of Achi Baba'.

W. J. Parnham, a Plymouth Marine, was Colonel Matthews's orderly and was throughout the action in personal attendance on the Colonel. 'From the trawlers we got into open boats. Before dawn the ships opened up a violent bombardment and, as dawn came, our boats crept in and we were ashore. We were unexpected, surmounted the cliffs and made an advance inland, our only casualties resulting from shells dropped short by the ships. We captured some Turkish scouts and withdrew to the cliffs to take up a position. We commenced digging in when suddenly bullets from goodness knows where whizzed over us. The fire increased and we returned it but had no targets at which to fire. Then the harsher reports of hand grenades falling among us made it clear just how near the Turks were. After dark the Turks attacked in greater strength and we were driven back to the cliff edge. We were blazing away, using ammunition brought up the cliff to us. The darkness was broken by the flashes of rifles and exploding grenades, and there was a constant crackle of small arms fire. All we had for signalling purposes was the Colonel's torch. There were awful shouts and cries. In the confusion furious complaints of "You're firing into our backs" were mixed with the Turkish appeals to

[2] P.R.O. W.O. 95 4311 XK 976.
[3] Shortly after 4 p.m. a Turkish field gun was brought into action between Krithia and Gully Ravine, and at 5.40 p.m. there developed the first of a series of attacks which continued through the night' (*Official History: Gallipoli*, vol. 2, p. 207).

Allah. When daylight came, the ships were able to reopen fire and the Turkish attack petered out. At about dinner time we had orders to retire to the boats. It was very difficult getting the wounded down the cliffs, and the wounds from the grenades in particular were terrible. The sailors helped to get many of the wounded away using waterproof sheets. With regard to Colonel Matthews, I was with him on his quick trip round the perimeter to convey his decision about entrenchment to the C.O.s of the other units. This was at about 3 p.m. on the 25th. Next morning when we reached Colonel Koe he was being held up by two other men. The Colonel was coughing blood and was quite unable to speak. He had a dreadful stomach wound. Distressed and overcome, Colonel Matthews, without a word to the others, laid his hand gently on his shoulder and said, "My poor fellow," and then he hurried back to our own Battalion.'

Chief Petty Officer Cave, using a range-finder on H.M.S. *Dublin*, noticed some flashing from a dip in the cliffs and had a signalman take what was obviously a message. The message was that their C.O. had been wounded the day before and needed medical attention urgently. 'Capt. Kelly ordered a sick berth attendant, a whaler's crew of five, two spare hands and myself to go ashore. It took us some time to select a place to climb the cliff. The wounded man was a heavily built officer and he was in a very bad way with a stomach wound. With our patient groaning, at times delirious and only occasionally able to speak rational words, betraying by accent he was a Scot, and accompanied by another slightly wounded Scot, we made our way down, but it was exceptionally difficult with such a heavy man on such a boulder-strewn steep route. At the bottom there were boats and pinnaces ferrying wounded and unwounded off to the *Goliath* and our wounded man, who I believe died within a short time, was taken off to the old battleship.' The wounded man must surely have been Colonel Koe.

There is still dispute over whose orders had actually begun the Y beach withdrawal. At the Dardanelles Commission inquiry Colonel Matthews was to accept responsibility, seeing no other course but evacuation open to a force running short of ammunition and without reinforcements. A. W. Clarke, who assisted in the evacuation, remembers seeing the Colonel striding down the cliff path, swishing with his cane at the gorse which impeded him. Clarke feels sure that there was no one else to bring away from the beach.

By 11.30 a.m. on the 26th the last men had been evacuated from Y beach. A landing begun with such promise had ended in disappointment and consequential controversy. The question whether victory at Y beach was within the grasp of Hamilton, Hunter-Weston and Colonel Matthews himself remains today as tantalizing as the other 'might-have-beens' of the campaign.

X beach

For the X-beach landing both the experience of the men concerned and the tactical outcome were to be more satisfactory, but not without a hint that the best advantage of initial success had not been taken. Staff planning had not allowed for the fact that the geography of the Peninsula favoured early visual communication between X and S beaches (only two miles apart) and the joining-up of the landing forces from the two beaches, thus cutting off from Krithia the Turkish forces holding up the V and W beach landings. As at Y beach, the Turks did not anticipate an attack at the steep though lower cliffs just a few yards from the sandy X beach. At this spot the 2nd Battalion Royal Fusiliers and a platoon of the Anson Battalion R.N.D. were to land. Their assault was to be supported by the 1st Battalion Border Regiment and the 1st Battalion Inniskilling Fusiliers. The *Implacable* was to land the men and provide the covering bombardment. On landing, the troops were to move southwards to link up with the Lancashire Fusiliers at W beach. The *Dublin* was also to assist in the bombardment during the day.

The *Implacable* was stationed only 500 yards off shore and the closeness of her involvement is indicated by the death, from a Turkish rifle bullet, of a surgeon on deck. Midshipman A. W. Clarke of the *Implacable* recorded in his log for 24 April:

'Entered Tenedos in the forenoon. Drew our boats from transport and also four picket boats from other ships. Prepared the boats and provisioned them. In the evening the 700 troops, the covering force, came aboard from the trawlers who had fetched them from the transports. The crews manned the transport boats and secured astern of the ship. About 10 p.m. the ship proceeded to sea for the Dardanelles, towing us in the boats astern. All the fleet followed.

'25 April: As soon as daylight the boats came alongside the ship and we took the 700 aboard and in company with the ship we closed into the beach, the ship firing hard to cover us. Then the boats made a dash and we landed the first 700 men with hardly a casualty owing to the good firing of the ship[4] . . . We landed troops all the forenoon with the support

---

[4] The official history gives a figure of only twelve Turkish defenders in the entrenchment near the top of the cliff, and this is the figure given in the *Mitchell Report*.

of the fleet. The remainder of the transports came up during the day. About 4 p.m. after we had landed the complete covering force we started to take the wounded off again.'[5]

Major Jebens, then a second lieutenant in the 2nd Battalion Royal Fusiliers, remembered the intensity of the *Implacable*'s pre-landing bombardment, and the lack of any opposition as they landed and climbed the cliffs. Only when they moved off inland were they fired on from both a field battery near Krithia and the Turkish troops commanding the slight rise towards the right flank, where resistance was continuing to the W-beach Lancashire Fusilier landing. It was the sight of the dead Fusiliers laid out on top of the cliffs which greeted the Inniskillings when they landed. B. A. McConnell has written of the strong impression this made on him when he was asked by his Inniskilling machine-gun officer to find the range of the battery firing on the Border Regiment on their left. The range he had taken was signalled to the *Implacable* and McConnell saw the battery blown to the sky almost immediately. Before he was wounded in late May and put permanently out of action, this was the sole occasion on which it was possible to set up and use his range-finder. McConnell had the exhausting task of bringing from the beach the machine-gun ammunition boxes during a night of constant firing. With their gun capable of firing 600 rounds to the minute there were many journeys for the boxes, which contained 250 rounds. X beach was secured and, furthermore, a bayonet attack took the important Hill 114 which commanded W beach. Nevinson[6] and other authors record that this attack was watched and cheered by sailors on the deck of the *Implacable*. The significance of the success concerned not only W beach itself; it also enabled Lancashire and Royal Fusiliers to outflank the Turkish defence against the V-beach assault.

But X beach had been a searing experience for Tom Sye in the 87th Field Ambulance: 'We landed at X beach on Sunday last under fire and in one ghastly moment for me the war had begun. I have been unable to write anything up to now, having been busy and also perhaps too horror-struck to write . . . I have never known it was possible to fear so acutely – I was terrified . . . God! When will it stop? I pray for the end with every minute that passes.'

---

[5] Midshipman Clarke records for the 26th that 'soon after 8 a.m. all our boats were ordered to Y beach to re-embark all the troops from there as they had to evacuate the place . . . we spent the night landing French troops on V beach without any opposition.'

[6] *The Dardanelles Campaign*, pp. 105–6.

S beach

Of the five Cape Helles landings only X and S could be claimed as successes in other than Pyrrhic terms. At S beach the *Cornwallis* landed the 2nd Battalion South Wales Borderers and the 2nd London Field Company of the Royal Engineers. S beach, with the shallow waters of Morto Bay, is dominated by the abrupt heights of the disused de Tott's battery and the beach was openly exposed to fire from Asiatic batteries. The landing was successfully made and maintained, but resistance was such that there was no possibility of any breakout from the heights which surrounded the bay. The diary of Private T. S. Rees of the South Wales Borderers gives a terse description of the attack up the beach. 'Troops ready to land. Forced a landing about 7 a.m. Made a charge and took a trench. Took a hill about an hour after landing. Captured some Turks. Heavy firing all night. 26th: Enemy retiring about middle of the day and shelled by our fleet. Cannot move on, waiting for our left to come up in line.' Rees later recalled the excitement among the troops as the trawlers took them into the Straits before they were transferred to rowing boats which were soon under small-arms fire. Some of the wounded had to be dragged through the water from the boats to the beach and it was some time before there was sufficient organization on the beach to enable them to make a charge. Even when they had taken their immediate objectives they were constantly in danger from snipers. The snipers even troubled the covering ships. Midshipman William-Powlett on the *Vengeance* recorded in his private diary that on deck they were troubled all day by their 'pet sniper who hides in the cliffs and takes pot shots at people on board. We call him Rupert.'

Air Vice-Marshal Traill, a midshipman in 1915, had towed boatloads of South Wales Borderers during the organizational preparations for the 25th. He has written in his unpublished memoirs, 'I wish I could hear them sing again . . . it was a horrid thing to see those same men under fire as the small boats took them inshore at the landing.'

A particularly graphic account of the S-beach landing is contained in *The Immortal Gamble*, which might be termed an unofficial biography of the battleship *Cornwallis*.[7] The Captain of the *Cornwallis* and a number of his men, together with Marines, actually landed and became engaged in stiff fighting to protect the left flank of the assault. The South Wales Borderers however were the first to be observed from the ship. 'It was an unforgettable experience to watch this well-trained battalion working its

[7] A. T. Stewart and C. J. E. Peshall, *The Immortal Gamble*, pp. 75 ff.

way methodically and without confusion to the top of the battery from both sides . . . The Marines ascending the hill watched the South Wales Borderers literally fly on ahead, line a wall at the top, place Maxim guns in position, run telephone communications down the hill and station snipers on a wall running at right angles to their position.' The Marines then joined up with the soldiers. Sailors from the *Cornwallis*, having accomplished various beach tasks, joined in the attack from the beach and a trench was taken by bayonet charge. The sailors rather resented having to give up the opportunity of taking prisoners as this was properly the work of the troops. 'And all the time a battery on the Asiatic side fired on the beach below, never getting a shell inland, fairly plastering the water's edge . . . Some of the shells fell in shallow water, hit the bottom and rebounded again, coming out like a trout jumping.' The landing-area thus made good here was to be taken over by the French, who, with their Kum Kale diversionary landing force and the remainder of their troops, were to be landed at V beach. From here they were to move up to hold the right-hand sector of the line which was to be created out of the landing operations, until from S beach across the Kereves Dere,[8] Achi Baba Nullah, Krithia Nullah and Gully Ravine to the Aegean a trench-embattled no-man's land had been forged which, though different in detail, bore a distressing resemblance to that from Nieuport to the Swiss frontier. So much for the hopes of politicians, the plans of generals and the gallantry of men.

V beach

Of all the landings, that at V beach was to hold the strongest elements of tragedy, prolonged into a grimly sustained frustration of collective and individual heroism. In the suicidal dash along the *River Clyde*'s gangways, the grim waiting for others cooped in her holds, the strain and danger of holding the bridging lighters together, the helpless hours of sheltering behind a life-preserving sandbank and the later brave rushes up past the castle to the village, all these isolated and linked dramas have combined to leave an imperishable record and ineffaceable impressions on all who survived. The most vivid and frightful overall impression was that of Commander Samson, of the R.N.A.S. He was flying over the beach and was later to record in his memoirs that for half a mile off shore the sea was a crescent of red.

The beach itself, situated just to the west of the village of Seddel Bahr,

[8] 'Dere' is a Turkish word meaning the same as 'nullah', that is a dry river gully.

is crescent-shaped, and the gentle slope of the enclosing land is more abrupt to the west, on the heights of which was the fort seriously damaged as early as 3 November 1914. Behind the eastern or Straits side of the crescent lay the ancient castle. The whole beach and approaches to the surrounding higher ground provided an absolutely clear field for defensive fire, with the single exception of a raised beach escarpment, the height of which the official history estimates at about five feet. Photographic evidence and recent examination would suggest that this may be a generous exaggeration. There were strong barbed-wire entanglements along the beach and again higher up the slope, and barbed wire linked the two. There was a strong redoubt and a connected fire trench which, with the ruined castle walls, provided excellent all-round defensive fire cover for small arms, the two 37-cm. Nordenfelts (pom-poms) and at least four machine-guns.[9]

There were three distinct features of the landing plan. Two platoons of the Royal Dublin Fusiliers were to land on the Straits side of the village at what had become known as the Camber. Then by five tows of four small boats each, the 1st Battalion of the Royal Dublin Fusiliers, less one and a half companies, and one platoon of the *Anson* Battalion R.N.D. were to be landed on the main beach. From the *River Clyde* about 2,000 men consisting of the 1st Battalion Royal Munster Fusiliers, the 2nd Battalion Hampshire Regiment (less two companies), one company of the Royal Dublin Fusiliers, one platoon *Anson* Battalion R.N.D., G.H.Q. Signal Section, the West Riding Field Company R.E. and three bearer sub-divisions of a field ambulance were to debouch from specially cut holes in the side of the ship and then pass along gangways leading to lighters making a bridge to the shore. The supporting bombardment was to come from H.M.S. *Cornwallis* and H.M.S. *Albion*.

Both the official history[10] and R. R. James's book[11] give vivid accounts of 25 April at Seddel Bahr. The latter mentions the Turkish use of incendiary shells which set one of the boats on fire, burning the men inside her, as well as the well-documented and dreadful details of those wounded, drowning or suffocating at the bottom of a crush of wounded and dead in boats filling with water.

The experience of the young midshipmen involved is well illustrated

[9] *Official History: Gallipoli*, vol. 1, p. 231. It should be noted that the Turkish sources denied having machine-guns in their defences at W beach and assert that two of the four machine-guns at V beach had been destroyed by the preliminary naval bombardment. See *Official History: Gallipoli*, vol. 1, p. 221 n.

[10] pp. 232 ff.

[11] *Gallipoli*, pp. 121 ff.

by the letters in the Imperial War Museum of G. L. Drewry and of W. L. Berridge. On 12 May Drewry, ordered to take over the hopper accompanying the *Clyde* for use as part of the landing bridge, wrote to his father about his task: 'So I climbed over the side across the lighters into the hopper and then came an anxious time. We steered straight towards Cape Helles and in a few minutes the bombardment commenced. Dad, it was glorious! Dozens of ships, battleships, cruisers, destroyers and transports. The morning mist lay on the land which seemed to be a mass of fire and smoke as the ships raked it with shell. Straight into the sun past battleships roaring with their 12-inch, the noise was awful and the air full of powder. Shells began to fall around us thick but did not hit us. We were half a mile from the beach and we were told not yet, so we took a turn round two ships, at last we had the signal at 6 a.m. and in we dashed – Unwin on the bridge and I at the helm of the hopper with my crew of six Greeks and one sailor, Sampson. At 6.10 the ship struck, very easily – she brought up and I shot ahead and grounded on her port bow. Then the fun began, picket boats towed lifeboats full of soldiers inshore and slipped them as the water shoaled and they rowed the rest of the way. The soldiers jumped out as the boats beached and they died almost all of them, wiped out with the boats' crews. We had a line from the stern of the hopper to the lighters and this we tried to haul in, the hardest haul I've ever tried. Then the Capt. appeared on the lighters and the steam pinnace took hold of the lighters and plucked them in until she could go no closer. Instead of joining up to the hopper the Captain decided to make the connection with a spit of rock on the other bow. Seeing this we let go our rope, and Sampson and I tried to put a brow out over the bow, the Greeks had run below and two of us could not do it, so I told him also to get out of the rain, and I jumped over the bow and waded ashore, meeting a soldier wounded in the water, we (I and another soldier from a boat) tried to carry him ashore but he was again shot in our arms, his neck in two pieces nearly, so we left him and I ran along the beach towards the spit, I threw away my revolver, coat and hat and waded out to the Captain. He was in the water with a man named Williams wading and towing the lighters towards the spit. I gave a pull for a few minutes and then climbed aboard the lighters and got the brows lowered onto the lighters. The Captain, still in the water, sang out for more rope so I went on board and brought a rope down with the help of a man called Ellard. As we reached the end of the lighters the Capt. was wading towards us carrying Williams, pulled him into the lighter and Ellard carried him on board the ship on his shoulders . . . Williams was dead . . .

1. *Above* A 14-pounder gun on the foreshelter deck of H.M.S. *Triumph* after being hit by a Turkish shell, 18 March 1915
2. An officer's bathroom after a shell had pierced H.M.S. *Triumph*'s quarter deck and burst inside during the bombardment of Chanak, 18 March 1915

3. *Above* A picnic at Mudros: Midshipman Lowry, Malleson and the Hon. Guy Russell of H.M.S. *Lord Nelson*, May 1915
4. The French wine store, in the background the French Hospital at Mudros

5. *Above* Australians embarking on the S.S. *Omrah* at Brisbane,
   24 September 1914
6. *Below left* The horse of a French artillery officer, Raymond Weil, being
   disembarked at Alexandria, 30 March 1915
7. *Below right* New Zealanders searching for their kitbags on arrival at
   Alexandria, December 1914

8. *Below* The splendour of Australian physique against a pyramid
9. *Above right* Officers in charge of beach parties at Anzac, 25 April 1915.
   Left to right Midshipman Marriott, Gunner Gamblen and Midshipman Haes

10. *Centre below* New Zealanders landing at Anzac, 25 April 1915
11. *Bottom* H.M.S. *Implacable*'s landing at X beach, Cape Helles

12. *Above* V beach taken from the bridge of the *River Clyde*, May 1915

13. The bakery at Cape Helles (Bakery Beach) from which bread was first issued on 21 May 1915. Above Bakery Beach was the best place to 'win' wood, a very scarce commodity

14. *Above* The French 176th Infantry Regiment make the best of Helles: wine, camp furniture and the shade of a tree
15. A trench periscope in use in the front line at Helles

16. *Above* On 21 May a Turkish staff officer mounts a horse and leaves the Allied beach area having negotiated the terms of the truce to bury the dead in the Anzac no-man's land
17. Making bombs from empty jam tins, filled with old nails, bits of shell, barbed wire, and an explosive charge. These bombs were first issued in very small quantities about an hour before the third battle for Krithia, 4 June 1915

18. A burial at Helles and a cremation at Anzac. *Above* one of the first funerals at the later named Skew Bridge Cemetery, Helles. Padre Bewill Close officiating. *Below* men of the 14th Sikhs preparing a funeral pyre for a comrade killed by a bomb, Anzac

19. *Below* Newly landed horses in the northern base area at Suvla. Kiretch Tepe Ridge in the background
20. *Above right* Suvla Bay: Yeomanry on the beach behind Lala Baba, August 1915

21. *Centre below* Commander Nasmith and Lieutenant D'Oyley Hughes on the bridge of submarine *E11* just before she proceeded up the Dardanelles
22. *Bottom* A Sopwith seaplane on board H.M.S. *Ark Royal*

23. *Above* Quinn's Post with its separated bomb-proof shelters. This was the scene of some of the fiercest and closest fighting of the whole campaign

24. Mudros: Loading up a lighter with sick men for conveyance to a hospital ship. In the background are the hospital ship and an airship, the latter was known as the 'submarine catcher' or the 'Silver Baby'

25. *Above* Ocean Beach, Anzac, looking towards Suvla. In the foreground is
    No 1 Australian Stationary Hospital; in the centre are the Ordnance and Supply
    Stores and the Y.M.C.A. Tent. No. 13 Casualty Clearing Station is in the distance
26. New Zealand machine-gunner, Errol Rudd, with a captured Turkish machine-
    gun at Hill 60, a vital point linking the Suvla and Anzac sectors, 21 August 1915

27. Isolation.
    Above left Sapper Wettern in
    his Gallipoli dugout 'The Pigsty'.
    Below left the misery of the
    weather in November 1915 at
    Anzac and Suvla
28. Deception.
    Opposite above a camouflaged
    Turkish sniper photographed
    immediately after capture, and
    while he was being brought in
    under guard.
    Below left a New Zealander and
    the dummy he made to deceive
    the Turks at the evacuation of
    Anzac on 20 December 1915.
    Below right the French
    interrogate a Turk, at Eski
    Hissarlik

29. *Above* Evacuating guns and personnel from Suvla Point on rafts in daylight, December 1915
30. Farewell to Gallipoli. Allied troops aboard H.M.S. *Hibernia*, January 1916

'Got a rope from the lighter to the spit and then with difficulty I hauled the Captain onto the lighter – he was nearly done and I was alone . . .

'I stayed on the lighters and tried to keep the men going ashore but it was murder and soon the first lighter was covered with dead and wounded and the spit was awful, the sea round it for some yards was red. When they got ashore they were little better off for they were picked off, many of them before they could dig themselves in. They stopped coming and I ran on board into No. 1 [hold] and saw an awful sight, dead and dying lay around the ports where their curiosity had led them. I went up to the saloon and saw the Capt. being rubbed down. He murmured something about the third lighter so I went down again and in a few minutes a picket boat came along the starboard side and gave the reserve lighter a push that sent it as far as the hopper . . . with Lieut. Morse and myself on it. Just as we hit the hopper a piece of shrapnel hit me on the head knocking me down for a second or two and covering me with blood . . . I took a rope and swam towards the other lighters but the rope was not long enough and I was stuck in the middle. I sang out to Mid. Malleson . . . in the picket boat to throw me a line but he had no line except the one that had originally kept the lighters to the spit. He stood up and hauled this line in and then as I had drifted away he swam towards the lighter I had left and made it all right. Then I made for home but had a job climbing up the lighters as I was rather played out. When I got on board the Doctor dressed my head and rubbed me down. I was awfully cold. He would not let me get up and I had to lay down and listen to the din.'

Midshipman Drewry was awarded the V.C. for the services which he recorded with such boyish interest and excitement. He was certainly not insensitive to the suffering of the men he saw so seriously wounded, and the newness of it all was a stronger emotion than any fears he seems to have had for his own safety. 'While the troops were going out (eight o'clock in the evening) I had a party getting wounded from the hopper and lighters and putting them on board a trawler laying under our quarter. An awful job, they had not been dressed at all and some of the poor souls were in an awful state. I never knew blood smelt so strong before.'

W. L. Berridge was a midshipman on the covering ship *Albion* and his letter of 22 May to his father and sister shows that he had a good view of events at Seddel Bahr. 'The slaughter was awful and you could see them falling on the beach and in the water. They got into dead ground under a bank however and there remained for the whole day . . . How the Turks stood our fire I don't know. I don't mind admitting I'd have hopped it

5

full speed . . . The morrow came and with it a splendid sight which very few have witnessed. The troops advanced bit by bit up the hill until near the top. It was wonderfully done and I didn't see a man fall, all the way. They advanced from cover to cover in rushes . . . They reached the top and took an old fort which gave them a splendid position to hold. Just as the final rush was made the main body of our troops landed on our beach came out of the village of Seddel Bahr, miraculously found a way through barbed-wire entanglements and joined hands with the rest at the top. Of course all this up to the final rush had been under cover of our fire which was of a very rapid and exact nature.'

With the 2nd Battalion Hampshire Regiment in a hold within the *River Clyde* was Second Lieutenant R. B. Gillett. His diary does not tell us much about his service on the Peninsula. It reads: '25 April – landed. 26 April – wounded. *Caledonia* 6 p.m.' His recollections however fill in the picture of the coldness within the holds even though they were crowded with men, and of the scarcely perceptible slide of the boat into the sand, though they had been told to brace themselves. After complete silence, Gillett recalls the firing breaking out in a deafening roar as the bullets hit the sides of the *River Clyde*. They were also being shelled from the Asiatic shore, and one shell killed men in No. 4 hold next to the one in which Gillett was incarcerated. In the afternoon some of the officers were allowed up onto the afterdeck of the *River Clyde*, where they were sheltered from fire from the beach by the ship's superstructure. From here the French troops were seen attacking Kum Kale, and in the sky Samson's dropping of coloured flares as a guide for the naval bombardment was also observed. Late in the afternoon they had to return to the holds and they were ordered to land just before dusk. Gillett led his platoon out along the catwalk and the sight, he recalled, was horrifying. 'The barges were piled high with dead and wounded and where the barges did not quite reach the shore, there was literally a pile of dead bodies on which you simply had to walk. The sea was red. To protect the beach against night attack we advanced through the barbed wire and took up a defensive position on the Turkish side of the wire.'

During the cold night Turkish searchlights swept the slope from the beach but the traversing machine-gun fire failed to find them. With no sleep Gillett tried to keep his men awake by passing a stream of messages along their line. He was wounded the following day in reconnoitring for an attack on the redoubt, after they had cleared the Turks out of the village. He and another officer had first climbed round the low cliffs below the Straits side of the castle in order to get into the village from the flank. A rock thrown down from the castle wall, along the line of where they were believed to be climbing, had narrowly missed them and only one of their men had been hit in the dangerous job of clearing the village house by house.

Some awkward objects had to be carried out of the *River Clyde* and down the gangways, which had taken on the aspect of a moving target at a shooting gallery. A West Riding Royal Engineer, G. B. Smith, saw their bugler with a rifle and fixed bayonet in one hand and the cookhouse dixie in the other. He himself had detonators, explosives and a shovel. The shovel he lost in his dash down the gangway and onto the barges, with their awful cargo of dead and wounded, through and over which he had to crawl before sliding over the gunwale into the sea and finally reaching the sandbank.

Just one of the many acts of gallantry on V beach that morning, performed in the heat of battle and without thought of reward or recognition, was that of Private Hennessy. Captain Wilson, the Adjutant of the Royal Munster Fusiliers, made a report that Hennessy had displayed conspicuous gallantry in carrying three wounded men, one after the other, from the lighters where they were being fired on by snipers and machine-guns, to the *River Clyde*; and then with Lance-Corporal Quinalt and another man he had crawled along two lighters under heavy fire, endeavouring to throw planks across to connect them to the shore. He and Quinalt were wounded and the third man was killed.[12]

In the Reverend H. C. Foster's book there is an account by Sub-Lieutenant Perring which describes the burial on 28 April in one large grave of 213 men whose bodies had been strewn about the beach.[13] French troops who had landed on V beach after the Kum Kale landing have an indelible recollection of the red sand and the lines or clumps of the dead. Indeed it is this picture with the *River Clyde* in the background which they have chosen to symbolize the allied Gallipoli experience.[14] A company commander's report attached to the Royal Munster Fusiliers' War Diary states that 'there is no doubt that men were drowned owing chiefly I think to the great weight of equipment they were carrying – a full pack, 250 rounds of ammunition, and three days' rations. I know I felt it. All the officers were dressed and equipped like the men.'[15]

[12] War Diary and Reports of the Royal Munster Fusiliers (P.R.O. W.O. 95 4310 XK 976).
[13] *At Antwerp and in the Dardanelles*, pp. 85, 86, 87.
[14] On the cover of the Triennial bulletin of the French Dardanelles Veterans Association.
[15] War Diary and Reports of Royal Munster Fusiliers (P.R.O. W.O. 95 4310 XK 976).

Among the deaths on that day was that of the Catholic Padre of the Dublins, Father Finn. He had given his Anglican colleague, the Reverend H. C. Foster, the same medal of 'Our Lady of Mount Carmel' as he had given to his men and hoped that it would bring him good fortune. Father Finn, badly wounded, had reached the sheltering sandbank but ran back to the dead and dying on the water-line to administer Extreme Unction. He was further wounded by a shrapnel shell but carried on his work until he collapsed and died from exhaustion and loss of blood. The Anglican wrote that Father Finn's 'death was a great grief to me, as we had become firm friends on the transport, and a great blow to his men who well-nigh worshipped him'.[16] In the service of the predominantly Catholic Dublins and Munsters at Helles and mainly Protestant 10th Irish Division at Suvla there is apparently no contemporary or recollected evidence of sectarian issues in this year before the Easter Rebellion. Initially the British and French were suspicious of each other and there was a good deal of jealousy from the British towards the Anzacs for the publicity attendant upon their exploits, but apparently among the serving soldiers the Irish problem had been as temporarily submerged as the other dominant pre-war concerns of British public life, industrial disputes and social issues.

W beach

The slope on W beach is appreciably greater than at V and examination discloses quite a disconcerting undertow within feet of the water-line. The implication of this may be added to the problems of burdened men, soaked and in many cases wounded, encountering the concealed barbed wire in the shallows. There were also wire entanglements and landmines above the shore-line. The encircling low cliffs, sufficiently high at either end of the little beach to dominate the shore, were strongly fortified with trenches, some evidence of which remains today. Behind the cliffs at either end of the beach, ground slightly higher than the cliffs provided the sites for further strongly defended redoubts. Barbed-wire entanglements not only protected these redoubts, but effectively cut off communication with V beach.

The 1st Battalion of the Lancashire Fusiliers and one platoon of the *Anson* Battalion R.N.D. were to be landed in tows from the cruiser H.M.S. *Euryalus*, which provided covering fire in addition to that of H.M.S. *Swiftsure*. One company of the Lancashire Fusiliers was brought to the beach in tows from H.M.S. *Implacable*. From the *Euryalus*, six

[16] op. cit., p. 84.

picket boats each towed four cutters. Under a mile from the beach, these six were joined by two picket boats, each towing four cutters from the *Implacable*. Later in the morning men of the Worcester, Essex and Hampshire Regiments originally intended for the 'main-body' V-beach landing were to be diverted to W beach.

One of the picket boats was under the command of Midshipman H. Wilson, whose letter to his mother on 4 May gives a precise account of what he saw of the landing. He was in the left-hand boat, No. 6, of the picket boats leaving the *Euryalus*. 'We got going about 4.30 and steamed slowly for the shore in line abreast gradually wheeling round to get opposite W beach . . . *Swiftsure* did a lot of firing at this time at the cliffs each side of W beach but as it afterwards turned out she hadn't put them in the right place or at least not half enough of them. It was just getting daylight while this was going on and as it was misty it was very hard to say what W beach was like and where exactly it was. We had only rough maps of the place and as we approached it from a totally different direction we expected, you couldn't predict what sort of reception you were going to get. We slipped about 30 yards from the beach but my boat was closer as we had come round the corner. We were nearly on the rocks and only just slipped in time. All the tows slipped alright and pulled in without fouling each other. There were two rows of barbed wire the whole length of the beach. The Turks opened fire with maxims, pompoms, rifles, just as we slipped. You could see them standing up in the trenches, which obviously had not been properly shelled. They were pouring a terrific fire down on us and it is a most extraordinary thing how any of the cutters which were open and absolutely unprotected and crammed with men survived it. The soldiers had to jump out into three feet of water and it was a most awful sight seeing them being shot down as soon as they got into the water and the wounded men must have drowned. When they got onto the beach they were held up by the barbed wire and got a tremendous lot more casualties as the Turks practically mowed them down as they moved through the gaps in the wire which they had cut.'

The cliffs were successfully stormed, but Wilson had been shocked by the losses and he considered that three mistakes had been made. '1. Not shelling enough. 2. Not mounting Maxims and Q.F. guns in the picket boats. If these had had proper shields we could have fired them and done a lot of damage as we could see them plainly. It would also have encouraged the troops and drawn the fire off the soldiers onto the picket boats. 3. The men landed with their heavy equipment which got frightfully in the way while they were disembarking.'

It is interesting that the young Wilson lists mistakes he considered that the Turks had made. He did not believe that they had put landmines and barbed wire in the water, as they ought to have done, and he was sure that British troops would have been able to prevent any landing at all. From this conjecture the midshipman moved on to rumour and here he was on much less sure ground: 'The Australians at Gaba Tepe got an awful hot time and saw red. They are giving no quarter and taking no prisoners. We are taking as few as possible and the French shoot everybody.'

Wilson's picket boat was later in the day used to bring the wounded off the *River Clyde* and the open lighters and cutters beside her. 'There was an awful rush and some of the wounded got hit getting into the boat and squashed as well. We got about twenty in the boat and then cleared out as we were the only boat there.' R. W. Moore, who had watched the landing from the masthead lookout on the *Euryalus*, was to be sickened by the bloody water dripping through the holes in one of the cutters when it was winched aboard.

Another midshipman, now Commander A. M. Williams, in command of a towing boat from the *Euryalus*, recalled trying not to waken the Lancashire Fusiliers when rising, lashing up and stowing his hammock in the early hours of the morning. He was to be in a steam pinnace on the right and it was, he said, a tremendous job to keep up with the other picket boats. The steel shields on the picket boats and the pinnaces protected the crews who sheltered behind them and few casualties were suffered. Later in the day he had to leave his picket boat to help in the work of landing stores. This resulted in his coxswain reporting him missing and presumed killed. The fact that in his work he had fallen on a big round cheese and 'stank to high heaven' as a result did not affect the warmth of his welcome when he did report back to the *Euryalus*.

Able Seaman Measures, on board the *Euryalus*, remembers not merely helping aboard wounded from the returning cutters and sorting them out on stretchers and blankets, but taking the particulars of the dead and sewing the bodies into fire-bar-weighted hammocks for sea burial. The Reverend H. C. Foster, later in the morning of the 25th, was landed in one of the cutters which had brought back wounded. He had the grim experience of noticing that the bottom of the boat was 'running with blood; there was blood on the oars, blood on the seats, blood all over and bits of skin here and there'.[17]

---

[17] *At Antwerp and in the Dardanelles*, p. 90.

One of the six Lancashire Fusiliers later to be awarded the V.C. for gallantry at the landing, J. E. Grimshaw, recollects that the men were so crowded on the boats that in his boat 'it was impossible to tell who had been hit as they were prevented from falling inboard or overboard by the crush. The firing broke out all at once and the water seemed to be boiling all around us. I managed to get over the barbed wire which was in the water and then through the stuff on the beach but later when some of us got to the base of the cliff I found that my cap badge had been hit by a bullet, and my pack and water bottle riddled.'

Three accounts given by Lancashire Fusilier officers subsequently killed on Gallipoli are given in the Reverend O. Creighton's book[18] and together exemplify all that officers and men had to endure in driving the Turks from their well-sited trenches. An extract from Captain H. R. Clayton's letter home may be used as an example. 'Men were being hit in the boats and as they splashed ashore. I got up to my waist in water, tripped over a rock and went under, got up and made for the shore and lay down by the barbed wire. There was a man there before me shouting for wire cutters. I got mine out but could not make the slightest impression. The front of the wire by now was a thick mass of men the majority of whom never moved again. The trenches on the right raked us and those above us raked our right, while trenches and machine-guns fired straight down the valley. The noise was ghastly and the sights terrible.'

On such exposed beaches as V and W, British training, discipline, loyalty and sheer courage were put to the most searching test, as indeed was the renowned Turkish quality of dogged determination against adversity as the defenders faced the heavy preliminary bombardment. It was a searing experience for all those involved. The British at great topographical and tactical odds, the Turks against far heavier shell-fire and many more men, performed with a heroism which has left an imperishable record. Lancashire Landing Cemetery and the Turkish memorial to their machine-gunner above V beach are eloquent witnesses to the cost of such service, as indeed is the grim brevity and under-statement of the Lancashire Fusiliers' War Diary entry for 5.30 a.m. on the 25th. 'Landed under heavy fire from machine guns and rifles from cliffs. Heavy casualties. Several men hit in boats and in water before getting ashore.'[19]

[18] *With the 29th Division in Gallipoli*, pp. 57 ff.
[19] Lancashire Fusiliers' War Diary, 25 April 1915 (P.R.O. W.O. 95 4310 XK 976).

The Diversion in the Gulf of Saros

After naval bombardment of the Bulair lines by H.M.S. *Doris* and H.M.S. *Dartmouth*, minesweeping activities and aeroplane reconnaissance early on the morning of the 25th, and a naval reconnaissance by H.M.S. *Kent*, close to Karachali village, and by H.M.S. *Canopus* towards the Bulair lines, the Royal Naval Division on the ten or eleven transports was kept waiting until dusk, when 1,200 men were embarked in the transport ships' boats. They were towed towards the shore, but according to the *Mitchell Report* the only man to land was the officer (Freyburg), who swam ashore to light flares intended to simulate the bivouac fires of encamped troops. Of course the inactivity throughout the day must have lessened the reality of the exercise, and the Mitchell inquirers found after the war that the Turkish officers on shore had not been deceived because the transports had not been handled as if they 'really meant to land troops'.[20]

In the *Hood* Battalion, Joseph Murray wrote in his diary for the 25 April: '10 p.m. Volunteers from R.N.D. C Coy, manned boats and we were towed into 800 yards from Turkish shore to make the Turks concentrate some of their troops to oppose us. While we were cruising about Sub-Lieut. Freyburg[21] swam ashore and ignited some fire bombs.' A. E. Wilson, of D Company *Nelson* Battalion, recorded similar details in his diary. 'Proceeded to within 200 yards of shore and returned to shore without drawing any fire. Left Gulf of Saros and steamed to end of Peninsula.' Murray recorded in his book[22] that before the night operations on 25–26 April they were all issued with a new pair of canvas slippers, cardigan, a woollen cap-comforter and two bandoliers each having fifty rounds of ammunition, and plenty of hot cocoa. With regard to the amount of time spent in the boats – 'were we lost? If it was the intention to land, why didn't we? If we were to attract attention only, why not a few rounds of rapid fire? If [the rifles] were not to be used, why on earth did we bring them with us?' The official history explains that the *Hood* Platoon was merely covering Freyburg's swim.[23]

Similarly ineffective seems to have been the influence of the French diversionary demonstration off Besika Bay, south of Kum Kale. The strength of the Turkish forces at Bulair, where a landing was expected, and the difficulties experienced at the Helles landings against numerically

[20] *Mitchell Report*, p. 178.
[21] Freyburg was in fact a Lieut-Commander.
[22] *Gallipoli As I Saw It*, pp. 54–5.
[23] *Official History: Gallipoli*, p. 164.

weaker opposition would suggest that those who consider inexpensive success was invited here are dwelling in the realms of fantasy.[24]

Kum Kale

The purpose of the French landing at Kum Kale was to confuse the Turks as to the area of the main landing and to protect the V-beach landing from the fire of the Kum Kale battery. The 6th Colonial Regiment and a battery of 75-mm. guns and necessary landing stores were brought towards the Asiatic shores in the *Savoie*, the *Carthage*, the *Vinh Long*, the *Théodore Mante* and the *Ceylan*. The French warships and the British *Prince George* covered the landing, and the five-funnelled Russian cruiser *Askold* added her bombardment. The *Askold* had already been nicknamed by the British 'the packet of Woodbines', but the chivalrous Guépratte took care that officers and men on board were given due personal recognition in his reports and recommendations. More French transports were ready to follow up the initial assault, which was largely, though not entirely, being made by Senegalese troops together with French metropolitan field-ambulance men, engineers, machine-gunners, signallers, and of course the artillerymen.

There were towing delays in the strong current, so that the supporting ships maintained their covering bombardment over a longer period. The earliest objectives were quickly taken, as the flat land provided little cover for defenders. The fort, the village and Achilles tomb were soon in French hands, but in the area around the village cemetery resistance stiffened. As more French and Turkish troops were sent into this area, confusion increased. Maître Gondard has described what happened to him: 'Throughout the night of the 25th we had alerts but we were able to repel the Turkish attacks. In the morning the Turks waved white rags. We stopped firing and the Turks came forward. We took them prisoner and I was collecting their arms and ammunition. But in fact more and more Turks were coming up and they had not given up their arms. We found ourselves surrounded, at least those of us not in a group. I was grabbed by both arms and with a third man thrusting a gun into my back I was marched off.' Colonel Ruef's official report, quoted in the British official history,[25] indicates that this confusion led to unofficial French reprisals. The French executed an officer and eight men of a group of

[24] ibid., vol. 1, pp. 255–6.
[25] *Official History: Gallipoli*, vol. 1, pp. 261–2; taken from the French official account, vol. 8, Annexes i, No. 99.

about eighty who, apparently giving themselves up as prisoners, had been encouraged to escape during negotiations and recommence the fighting when reinforced by Turks who had not given up their arms. Colonel Ruef blamed the inadequacy of the French interpreters for the confusion which had led to this 'deplorable incident'.

The French troops had had landing-practices within the harbour at Mudros, and d'Amade's official report stresses that he and Admiral Guépratte had ordered such an exercise for all troops involved. There does not seem to be general agreement among survivors of the landing on the question whether they had been told in their briefing that their landing was to be a diversion and that they were to be re-embarked, and yet Hamilton's orders to d'Amade leave no doubt about this.[26] François Bollon, in the single European battalion of the 6th Colonial Regiment, remembers that they had practised landings in rubber or canvas boats at Lemnos but some of these boats had sunk and they were not used again. There was certainly no briefing for the men with whom Bollon landed. They did not know it was to be a diversion. He recalled, in fact, that a good many of the officers did not even land with them. They had to carry a sort of wire which could be pulled out by two men like an accordion. It was not barbed wire but could be used as an obstruction against a counter-attack. In his knapsack there were twenty biscuits, two container tins, brand new boots and a body-belt, and they were wearing their capes over their '*horizon bleu*' uniforms. They were in tows of three cutters and not only did they make slow progress against the current but the rope towing their boat snapped and they drifted away, which caused more delay before they were rescued. Bollon remembered quite categorically being told in the boat by a sergeant that it would be better to commit suicide than be captured.

'We landed after the Senegalese troops and saw some of their dead as we advanced towards the fort. We had to dig individual holes for cover and from them we made two fifty-metre dashes forward. In my section of fifteen men, the captain was killed and two men either side were both hit in the stomach and during the night asked piteously for water. They were both dead in the morning, and I seemed to be the only one alive in my section. Earlier I had heard Capt. Blanchard call out, "*Sauve qui peut!*" It was very difficult to see the Turks, and during the second day the Turks received reinforcements which enabled them to get through

---

[26] French Military Archives C.E.O. 2QN 27, Ordre de L'Armée No. 1: 'Le débarquement près de Koum Kaleh est considéré comme une diversion.'

to within thirty metres or so of us. Then their officers were shot and soon a large number of them were surrendering but we ourselves were soon to be pulled off the shore. By the time I realized what was happening, the boats had left but fortunately I was spotted and one came back for me.'

Jean Pierre Bory, on one of the troopships, has written of the first wounded Senegalese troops being brought on board, and then of the prisoners. 'There were about four hundred I think, with five officers, two of whom were Germans. The officer prisoners were well accommodated in cabins but the ordinary soldiers were put in the hold under double sentries. They were given a large barrel of water from which to drink and dress their wounds. Some had really bad bayonet wounds.'

Perhaps over-reacting to Moorehead's complimentary summary of the action,[27] R. R. James considered that 'it had been something less than the glittering triumph sometimes claimed for it',[28] but despite the lateness of the landing and the confused nature of some of the action, the French soldier had captured and held his objectives. A large body of Turks had been ultimately engaged after the initial landing, but there is no evidence that any of these Turks was able to serve on the Peninsula before 29 April. The V-beach landing would have been still more hard-pressed had the landing at Kum Kale not been successful, though admittedly the delay at Kum Kale was regrettable. The French had taken 500 prisoners and the severity of their engagement is indicated by their losses of 6 officers and 166 men killed, 10 officers and 471 men wounded and 4 officers and 125 men missing.

A veteran of the 6th Colonial Regiment, M. Jomain, remembers not only d'Amade's stirring preliminary address but more particularly the congratulations on the successful landing and the promise of a long leave. The leave lasted a day, and was spent on board ship. On the 28th he landed with other French troops, 'to go to help the English in difficulties at Seddel Bahr'.

---

[27] A. Moorehead, *Gallipoli*, p. 150.
[28] *Gallipoli*, p. 126.

9.   Helles in April and May

The Turks had been forced to retreat by the initial determination and greater strength of the allied assault upon Helles. They had been unable to bring reinforcements quickly from the Asiatic shore because of the Kum Kale landings and they were heavily committed to the defence of Anzac. It is clear today that at several levels of command and indeed among the men themselves there was a regrettable incapacity to profit from the Turkish withdrawal after the heroic endeavours of the 29th Division on the 25th and 26th. The X-beach landing was linked to W beach on the 25th and after fierce fighting Seddel Bahr village was won on the following day. It was not however until the afternoon of the 26th that the forces on V and W had made effective contact, and their positions were not linked to the S-beach troops until 5.30 p.m. on the 27th. At this stage a continuous allied line across the Peninsula from X to S beaches had been established, but the Turks had been allowed to retire to organize the defence of the village of Krithia, an essential position on the approach to Achi Baba. At the point of closest penetration towards Krithia, the allied line was a mere $2\frac{1}{4}$ miles from V beach itself.

The official history leaves no doubt about the tired condition of the allied troops attempting on 28 April the task of capturing this shelled Turkish village, which nestled at the foot of the brooding dominance of Achi Baba, the 700-foot hill from which was conducted effective Turkish observation of all the enemy operations.[1] With the ground sloping into a saucer-like bowl rimmed by the seaward cliffs and isolated knolls near the cliffs, allied advance was completely exposed. The only natural cover lay in the gullies or nullahs which ran like the spokes of a wheel-hub from the slopes of Achi Baba to the sea. The depth, steepness and tortuous bends of the four main gullies, particularly Gully Ravine and the Kereves Dere, should not be underestimated. They form just as significant a feature of the Helles fighting as the more dramatically contorted Anzac terrain. This flat land, offering no natural cover from Turkish observation, was to be criss-crossed from gully to gully and longitudinally linked for communication with the base areas near the beaches by a webbed network of trenches. This is now obliterated, but

[1] *Official History: Gallipoli*, vol. 1, pp. 288 ff.

the evidence is perpetuated in the trench maps, which are no less complex than those for the Western Front, despite the significant differences. The trenches of the Peninsula were perhaps less deep, less professionally constructed and equipped, and they were certainly separated by a far narrower no-man's land than those of the Western Front. It is often stressed that at Anzac the trenches were in parts only five or seven yards apart. This was indeed the case, but, as the gullies themselves at Helles became fortified, there were occasions when only a sandbagged barricade or an abrupt bend in a gully separated forces able, by machine-gun fire or sniper, murderously to enfilade the enemy trench, or use the short intervening distance to lob various types of army issue or home-made bombs into the opposing trenches.

Of course this trench system was a creation of weeks and months of virtually static warfare and it was constantly being improved or elaborated, but that a form of trench fighting was conducted almost from the first day of the campaign is indicated in the official history account of the opening of the attack on Krithia on 28 April. 'About 8 a.m. . . . the weary troops of the 29th Division climbed out of their trenches and plodded forward in the general direction of Krithia.'[2] The armoured cars of the R.N.A.S., one or two of which were at least landed, though uselessly, at Cape Helles, the bicycles of some 29th Division Units[3] and the horses of the Australian reinforcements which were to get no further than Egypt, as the optimistic façade of the hopes of a swiftly successful campaign, were to be forgotten in the grim attrition of trench warfare. On 20 December 1915, with the Anzac and Suvla troops safely away, the ordinary ranker and the young officer in 8th Army Corps at Helles received a copy of a special order of the day by Lieut-General Sir Francis Davies in which it was stressed that 'in front of this position division after division of the Turkish army has been worn down, and so many Turks have been killed that this part of the Peninsula is known among them as "the slaughter house". We can only hope that the Germans will force the Turks, already heartily sick of the war, to attack us again and again, being

[22] *Official History: Gallipoli*, vol. 1, p. 288.
[23] Major-General T. Jameson of the cyclist company Royal Marines (Portsmouth) has written that some cycles were loaded onto two barges for the landing. One drifted away never to be seen again, the other beached at Cape Helles. Captain A. W. Clarke of the *Implacable* has recalled seeing bicycles strapped to the backs of some of the French troops he saw landing at V beach on the night of 26/27th and J. D. Crighton proudly recalls that he did much of his 87th Field Ambulance wounded and sick report deliveries by bicycle. The *Official History* (vol. 2, p. 50) records that an attempt to use armoured cars in the third battle for Krithia was a complete failure.

confident that the same fate will befall all fresh troops brought against us as befell their predecessors.'[4] The later tragic parallels of costly frustration on the Somme and in the Ypres salient scarcely efface the irony of the fate of the Gallipoli endeavour, historically described by its chief author as an 'immortal gamble'.

On 28 April the troops were indeed worn out after their unprecedented physical and nervous exertion since the landing. The lassitude which descends after the last reserves of physical and nervous energy have been called upon was increased by the sun and acute shortage of water. Diary entries and more descriptive letters escaping the scrutiny of the censor indicate the strain. On the 28th T. Rees merely has time to record: 'French force took over our position at 2 a.m. Joined the Brigade at dawn and entrenched. General advance started after breakfast under heavy shell and rifle fire. Reinforced the Border Regiment. Got repulsed twice and then took the position again at 6 p.m. and entrenched. Joined the Battalion at 12 midnight and entrenched.'

Stretcher-bearer work at X beach had been exhausting. Private Tomkinson of the 87th Field Ambulance snatched time to make a diary entry describing how on the night of the landing he had 'tried to sleep in a sitting position, the room being scarce. Rained slightly. Turks made a desperate struggle to clear us off. Sgt Johnson killed. The Navy opened a terrific bombardment. A terrible night. 26 April, 3.30 a.m.: Went out to Inniskilling trenches and brought back a wounded man. Beach covered with wounded. Firing ceased about 4.30 a.m. Things quieter till evening, when Turks began a fresh attack, got a little sleep, but was terribly cold about the feet . . . 28 April: About 1.30 p.m. the wounded started pouring in from the action, a general advance having been made. About 2 p.m. went along the cliffs to assist the walking cases, got some back in a rowing boat, then brought in a stretcher-case overland. Made another journey to an old farm used as an aid post. Volunteered to go to firing line and bring in Major MacAllister of the K.O.S.B. Shrapnel was bursting all about us. He was wounded in right pelvis and had to hold his leg all the way. Capt. gave morphia. Brought in another case after a little tea. Got wringing wet, having put my jacket over wounded man. It came on to pour with rain . . . Shall never forget the scene when I got back to beach. Pouring with rain! Beach littered with corpses and many very serious and were groaning. Very cold and lack of groundsheets to cover the wounded. Rain stopped about 9.30 p.m. Changed my shirt, had a cup of tea and went out about 10.30 . . . Got a case, a man of the

[4] Official Papers, M.E.F. (P.L.).

Border Regt. Must have weighed fifteen stone. Got back about 2.45 a.m.
... Roused about 5.30 a.m., having got into a place that was wanted.
Made a new and bigger dugout.'

A letter in the Imperial War Museum written on 4 May by Captain
Warneford Nightingale of the 1st Royal Munster Fusiliers gives a
picture of the strain undergone by men who had survived the V-beach
landing. 'We have got a good bit of the old Peninsula now but the last
fortnight has been absolute hell! It is the only word for it. There is
hardly anybody left in the Regiment – only four officers and all the best
men gone too. We're no worse off than any other regiment either and
of course it was all expected.' The house-to-house fighting on the 26th,
the arrival of the French on the 27th and the advance on the 28th are
described. 'We have been in the firing line (continuously) and are all
very exhausted. We never get any sleep at night as the Turks know we
are waiting for more troops, and they attack us every night to try to get
a victory over us before we can get help. On the night of the 1st of May
we had a tremendous attack. They crept up in the dark and were in our
trenches and bayonetting our men before we knew the attack had begun.
We lost some trenches but recovered them all in half an hour. The attack
lasted from 10.30 till dawn. The Turks attacked again and again shouting
Allah! Allah! It was most exciting hearing them collecting in a dip in the
hill about forty yards away waiting for their next charge. We mowed them
down and only once did they get so close that we were able to bayonet
them. When dawn broke, we saw them in hundreds retiring and simply
mowed them down. We took 300 prisoners and could have taken 3,000
but we preferred shooting them. All the streams were running blood
and the heaps of dead were a grand sight. We lost four more officers and
200 men. We now total four officers and 430 men out of our original 1,000.'

The experience of the French troops on the right flank had been very
nearly disastrous. In their blue uniforms, and with some in white cork
hats, as soon as they were observed approaching the entrance to the
Kereves Dere they were decimated by shell-fire. When the Turkish
counter-attacks were hammered home from the night of 1 May, there
was a real danger of their being driven into the sea at Morto Bay.
Raymond Weil, the French artillery officer, sent 'desperate signals to the
transport *Provence* asking urgently for tugs and barges to bring our
ammunition ashore because we are needing it'. The terrible confusion
in the darkness at V beach among the wounded and the stores on lighters
ready for unloading made it impossible that night for the ammunition
to be brought up to the French position, but somehow the infantry held

on. Weil's captain was so exhausted after being without sleep for two days that he could scarcely speak. The ferocity of these counter-attacks was due in no small measure to the German commander of the Turkish troops exhorting them to destroy their enemy, for retirement would be the death of their religion, country and nation. There were other factors related by Turkish veterans, as for example their bitterness against the black Senegalese soldier with his dreadful knife (*coupe-coupe*) and the 'unfair' use by the British of flêchettes, the metal darts dropped from planes on any concentration of troops.

Australian and New Zealand troops were transferred from Anzac to take part in the second attempt to seize Krithia, which had been scarcely defended, according to the official history, on 25 April.[5] It had not been strongly defended when the allies had attacked on 28 April and had not been outflanked in a battle which had merely straightened the British line by removing the indentation in its left flank. The Turks had now been considerably reinforced and were strongly entrenched in front of the village in a state of readiness to receive a further assault. This assault began on 6 May. The Australians were not used until the 8 May and an Australian sapper, now Colonel McKinlay, who was wounded early in a brave charge which resulted in fearful losses, remembers a young English stretcher-bearer pleading successfully to come over the top with the Australians to bring in the wounded. He also saw the Australian war correspondent Dr Bean striding along with his walking-stick, disdainfully refusing to take cover. McKinlay and others remember the repeated calls of their Colonel, 'Come along Australians', but for many veteran New Zealanders the memory of the attack across the Helles Daisy Patch is as bitter as any recollection of their service on the Peninsula.[6] J. G. Gasparich remembered that: 'the men had to make zigzag dashes across an open area wholly exposed to enemy rifle and machine-gun fire. I watched every single man in one party fall as he was hit so that none reached the spot where we had dug shallow cover. The grassy daisy-covered space was now a pathetic field of dead. Other lines followed and except for three men who swiftly returned to their cover the same fate awaited all who tried to reach us. I was aghast at the utterly useless and wanton waste of valuable lives.'

The French, still in their red and blue uniforms, suffered cruelly in this second battle for Krithia, but already the famous French 75s were winning praise at all levels for their accuracy and rapidity of fire. Raymond

---

[5] *Official History: Gallipoli*, vol. 1, p. 291.
[6] C. Malthus, *Anzac: A Retrospect*, p. 70.

Weil, who was in one of these batteries, in turn paid a tribute in his diary to the supporting naval gun-fire on the morning of the attack and recorded how their spirits had been raised by the arrival of both troops and munitions on the troopship *France*. At 7 p.m. on the 8th just after watching a magnificent attack by French troops, he sadly saw the French falling like flies before a Turkish counter-attack. There were signs of panic, as the French were not protected by artillery fire during this counter-attack, but later in the evening the positions lost were regained.

British, Commonwealth and French troops had advanced against withering fire and had suffered dreadful losses. Their gains by the end of 8 May were still far short of their objective for 6 May. An ominous resemblance to Western Front conditions was appearing, though there was still one source of encouragement amidst the gloom. At this stage of the campaign the British naval support of their troops was an ever-present source of strength in materiel and in morale. On 28 April a splendid single shot of the *Queen Elizabeth*'s fifteen-inch shrapnel shell with 24,000 bullets entirely wiped out a Turkish company charging British troops whose morale appeared to be broken, and the sinking of a Turkish transport by *Queen Elizabeth*'s indirect fire across the Peninsula are incidents described in the official history.[7] Without telescope or field-glasses the progress of the fighting could be observed from the ships. Midshipman Clarke of the *Implacable* scribbled a note on 7 May for later transfer into his log: 'The troops made a determined attack all the forenoon and succeeding in gaining a mile or so although up to date they did not capture Achi Baba as was intended. The resistance was terrific and the air was full of shells. We assisted where we could by firing.'

Two letters written within two days of each other by newly arrived reinforcements on the Peninsula and a letter by a naval officer in the same week provide us with significant first impressions. On 17 May, Charles Thierry, of the 176th Infantry Regiment, assured his parents that at that moment his unit was in the rear suffering few casualties. They were however always under shell-fire and that evening were moving up through the second line to the front line, so would his parents not expect any letters for a week. 'We hope to push the Turks back and then the base area will be a little quieter.' The concept of a quiet base area, as on the Western Front, was never to exist on the Peninsula. Dugouts or strongly built shelters were as necessary for the Divisional Commanding Officer as the trench dugout was for his men. As far as documentary

[7] pp. 292 and 282-3 respectively.

research and fieldwork can establish, the sole base area on the Peninsula entirely free from Turkish shell-fire was by reason of geographical eccentricity the narrow beach at the foot of the almost overhanging cliffs at Suvla where the Kiretch Tepe ridge juts into the sea. Such security was unfortunately three months away and on a sector where the French were not to serve.

The second letter was written on 15 May by an English officer in a territorial regiment, Second Lieutenant E. Duckworth, 6th Battalion Lancashire Fusiliers. 'Well, we have had two days experience in the front trenches and they are not full of the joy we anticipated when we were so bored in Cairo! In fact they were distinctly otherwise. I myself was lucky enough to come out unhurt but my platoon . . . [crossed out by censor] suffered somewhat through having to advance about 100 yards over open ground. I cannot go into details as regards numbers of casualties but 12 per cent only are killed out of the total of killed, wounded and missing. The enemy are very heavily entrenched on a hill which is at present our main objective to capture. They have an enormous number of machine-guns and their fire is very well controlled. Their artillery is not as heavy as we had expected and shell-fire has not cost us above a few men. However we have had our fill of war and shall not mind when it ends. I have just censored an article by the *Times* correspondent which gives you full detail and a bit more. But I expect he has to enlarge a bit in order to make a story . . . The men stick it quite well on the whole, though amongst the younger there was a tendency perhaps natural to hang back a bit. The fire we went through was inconceivable, like a wall of bullets. The old South African people say they never struck anything like it in the whole war.'

On board H.M.S. *Minerva* a young naval officer, H. K. L. Shaw, had written to his family on the 10 May: 'Things have quietened down a lot for us on board the ships; but not so on shore where, as Harry Lauder says, "the cannon's death rattle" goes on day and night, by Gad! Things are fairly humming on the land and from all accounts the casualties on both sides are tremendous. The Turks and Huns having had plenty of time to prepare, have taken full advantage of all the natural advantage of their hilly country and have fairly dug themselves in; also they seem to have an enormous number of guns etc. in concealed gullies so it's going to be some job to shift them. I can assure you that all of us out here are pretty fed up with the breezy manner in which a lot of the newspaper rags have been spouting about getting to Constantinople etc. as if it was a mere walk-over.'

The allied failure in the first two battles for Krithia was not only significant in terms of the final result of the campaign but also by circumscribing the area of the Peninsula held at Cape Helles, it determined the nature of the fighting. At this stage and for the rest of the campaign the land won from the Turks was scarcely more than an enlarged beach-head. When Helles was evacuated in January 1916 the British front line was approximately four miles inland from V and W beaches, and still another mile beyond lay battered Krithia. In May, despite the shelling, the Krithia plain was still green, carpeted with flowers, rimmed by the deep blue of the sea which glistened in the morning and turned to molten gold against the rays of the setting sun. Under a clear azure sky, in the quietness between shelling, and with the air as yet not strongly poisoned either by cordite fumes or decaying corpses, the scene still retained much of its surpassing beauty. 'Later, except for the trees and shrubs, the Peninsula, worn down by the passing of thousands of men, and the endless coming and going of transport from the beaches to the camps, became a bare sandy waste. In time it was worse than that . . . The army was indeed caught between the hill and sea; it could go neither backward nor forward. The plain, for all its openness, was a prison which became a tomb.'[8]

[8] D. Jerrold, *With the Royal Naval Division*, p. 113.

10. May and Early Summer at Anzac

While the prime task for the troops at Anzac during the month of May was to ensure that the area won at such cost was maintained against mass frontal attack, and that the flanks were secure, there was at no level a passive acquiescence in the stalemate. At the very beginning of the month raids on either flank indicated the aggressive spirit which remained for so long a characteristic of the defence of Anzac.

In a reconnaissance far out to the left by New Zealanders during the last days of April, a Turk had stumbled down a gully and landed helplessly in the arms of some Canterbury men. J. A. Anderson records that, in the tangled vegetation and difficult ground, the New Zealanders had got behind the Turkish defences and secured information from their prisoner of an enemy outpost near the Salt Lake. This post was attacked by fifty men of the Canterbury Battalion, who had been transported to Suvla during the night of the 1–2 May, and the signed report by Captain Waite and Captain Cribb shows how completely successful was this well-conceived raid.[1] 'We came on a trench which was occupied by a party of Turks asleep. One Turk grasped his rifle and wakened the others, whereupon some of our men fired, killing three and wounding four others. We covered the rest of the party and disarmed them . . . All arms, equipment and papers were collected and taken to the torpedo boat *Colne*. The papers were handed to General Godley on our return.' An officer and twelve Turkish soldiers had been captured, but on the right flank a raid still more dangerous, in view of the known strength of the defences, had been unsuccessful.

At dawn on 4 May, a hundred men of the 11th Battalion A.I.F., together with some engineers, were landed just north of the Gaba Tepe headland with the task of raiding and dismantling the fort, the main gun of which was such a danger to the Anzac beach-head. The four ship's boats, making the landing from the destroyer *Colne*, were fired on as they were just off the beach and, as the men landed, machine-guns and a one-inch quick-firing gun convinced Captain Leane, who was in command of the party, that despite the naval shell-fire from supporting ships there was

[1] New Zealand National Archives, Wellington, War Diary of Canterbury Battalion, Report of Raid on Nibrunesi Point Observation Station.

no hope of success for their mission. Under heavy fire the party was re-embarked – the originally planned escape route along the beach to Anzac, through gaps cut in the wire by a support party, was clearly too dangerous.

R. L. Jones, who was on this raid, remembers that single men had been invited to volunteer and that on the beach under cover from the fort they had gathered round Captain Leane like a troop of scouts round a scout-master. A man had been sent to reconnoitre and he came back with the report that they had no chance of taking the fort, so a signaller flagged a message to that effect towards Anzac. The only reply was, 'Regret cannot assist. Goodbye and good luck.' The plight of the small force was then signalled to the ships off shore and their reply was that they would assist by taking the wounded off. Under a Red Cross flag this was done and the Turks did not fire. Following the successful embarkation of the wounded, the Navy, under the cover of a very heavy bombardment, sent boats in to get the Australians. 'A middle-aged sailor bearded like the one on the back of the cigarette packet was rowing in our boat towards the ship with his head erect like those of the other sailors while we were only too anxious to take cover from the fire. He called out to one and all, "The Good Lord had us in the hollow of His hand this day." ' Certainly, with only six killed and eighteen wounded, the survivors had reason to feel fortunate.

The main Turkish effort to throw the invaders into the sea came on 19 May. On the 18th, R.N.A.S. reconnaissance had reported large con-centrations of Turkish troops assembling behind their front line and still more reinforcements being landed on the Dardanelles shore. The massed forward movement into the attack was sighted from the Anzac positions just before 3.30 in the morning. The Turkish veteran, Captain Ozgen, asked by the writer how morale had been maintained as the successive assaults were murderously dealt with by artillery fire from Plugge's Plateau[2] and by machine-gun and rifle fire all along the Anzac position, admitted that military discipline, patriotism and religious fervour had all played their part in this, but he emphasized the influence of a military band concealed in a forward position which had played martial music throughout the action.

W. W. Paterson, in the 3rd Infantry Brigade, writing to his brother on 12 July, describes how he was lying out in front of his trench on outpost guard when 'I heard a murmuring and rustling ahead of me. I woke up my mates and we got ready. Presently about fifty yards in front over a

[2] See report by Brig.-General C. M. Wagstaff of action on the night of 18–19 May, Mitchell Library, Sydney.

sky line I saw moving figures coming towards me. We sent back word to
the firing line . . . In another minute a form rose up out of the low scrub
about fifteen yards in front of me and started giving orders. I had him
covered as he rose and although pretty nervy I do not think I missed. It
seemed as if my shot was the signal, for immediately the machine-guns
opened with a roar and with another roar the Turks rushed forward. We
darted back for our lines and got in just as they came up in dense masses
about fifty yards behind.' Paterson went to assist the short-handed
machine-gunners and shared the work of firing, feeding and bringing up
water, oil and ammunition. With traversing bursts they swept the front,
also wiping out a party of men and mules moving to the front. Then in
broad daylight their gun, assisted by naval shrapnel fire, caught the
Turks in an open space and mercilessly destroyed their retreat.

The attack provided the first opportunity to inflict heavy casualties
among the Turks from positions of relative safety. 'Then they rushed to
within twenty or thirty yards of our position but our lads mowed them
down like grass . . . our lads were as cool as if they were shooting ducks
. . . one poor chap died on his knees not thirty yards from our trenches
and is still in the same position.'[3] A. L. Guppy wrote his diary account[4]
that night of a particularly celebrated incident during the attack. 'At the
entrance to the sector of our trench captured by the Turks . . . L/Cpl
Jacka leapt over [two dead Australians] and got in among the Turks. He
quickly shot three and bayonetted four more and cleared the sector.'

In the Australian Medical Corps, Edney Moore must have been
sufficiently aware, even during a heavy day of tending to wounded, that
an outstandingly brave man had been lost when he wrote on the 19 May:
'Poor Simpson of 3rd F.A. was killed early in morning while still doing
good work with the donkey.' The imperturbable manner in which this
man, born in South Shields, County Durham, but enlisting in a West
Australian unit, had brought wounded men down to the beach with the aid
of his donkey was already growing into a legend which in doing due
honour to Simpson was to symbolize the brave work done by men of all
the field ambulance units. In 1916 Colonel Fergusson, in command of the
21st Kohat Mountain battery, wrote of Simpson, 'One Australian
stretcher bearer in particular attached himself to us permanently from
the very first. We called him Murphy because that is what he called all
his donkeys. He always had a donkey with him which he used to work

<hr>

[3] C. L. Lock, *The Fighting 10th*, p. 45, quoting a letter dated 20 May by Lieut-Colonel
S. P. Weir.

[4] Australian War Memorial, Canberra.

Shrapnel Valley, bringing down men wounded in the legs or any cases which could ride but not walk. He had many donkeys and men killed beside him but led a charmed life himself till 19 May. We treasured his last donkey and evacuated it safely at the end with a view to presenting it to Australia but it was stolen from our mule lines in Mudros.'

Simpson was not to receive the anxious letter from his sister in England which would have told him that 'Mother has not had any word from you since she read of the landing of the Australians in the Dardanelles – of course I expect you will have had your hands full . . . Oh to have you home again. Home will not be complete again until you come back.'[5] By an interesting irony of fate one of the New Zealanders who did similar work to Simpson's but whose name was never well known has been commemorated in an unusual manner. Sapper Moore-Jones, the New Zealand soldier artist, was handed a photograph which was said to be of Simpson. He used it to assist in the painting of the fine work which he inscribed 'To the memory of our comrade Murphy (Simpson) killed May 1915'. The photograph was in fact of a New Zealander, Henderson, and so the features of the stalwart Simpson are those of Henderson, who had been, unknown to the photographer, the subject of his print.

The war diary of one of the New Zealand reinforcement regiments, the Auckland Mounted Rifles, which had landed at Anzac on the 12 May, shows that the cost to the Turks of their great offensive had been high.[6] '19 May: Walker's Ridge . . . at about 3.30 the enemy assault our trenches in superior force but are driven off at 4.30 a.m. by gallant counter-attacks by a troop of 4th commanded by Lieut-Col James and also by a troop of 11th Squadron commanded by Lieut P. Logan. The enemy leave the ground strewn with dead and wounded.' The Australian Light Horse regiments and the New Zealand Mounted Rifle regiments, though disappointed at leaving their horses behind in Egypt and thus changing their role in accordance with their Peninsula destination, were to provide infantry reinforcement at a vital time after the frustration of the first Anzac assault and with the growing threat of reinforced Turkish counter-attacks.

Sapper G. C. Grove's diary for the day of the attack describes how 'some of the Turks had managed to get even onto the parapet of our firing trench but were driven off at the point of the bayonet and point-blank rifle fire. Several Turks taken prisoner and hundreds killed and wounded. In front of No. 4 Sap they were literally piled up in heaps.'

The problem of burying the dead of no-man's land was not new but

[5] Australian War Memorial, Canberra, letters of John Simpson Kirkpatrick (749/80/7).
[6] Copy supplied by K. Stevens.

was now made far more serious. A young New Zealand Staff Officer, J. L. Anderson, who had aptly written in his diary[7] on 5 May that 'the whole place beggars description', was to add two days later that from a battery commanded by a Major Sykes he had seen 'dead men which neither we nor the Turks can get at. There will have to be an armistice soon for identifying and burying.'

Both the Australian and the British official histories[8] describe in detail the first moves towards a truce to bury the dead, and the whole story is recorded in General Birdwood's diary. Local commander initiative on the Australian side, in sympathy with Turkish wounded in no-man's land, had been taken even before General Birdwood's request to Sir Ian Hamilton for a truce had been refused because the Turks might have used the request as propaganda. The unofficial truce, arranged locally on the evening of the 20th, had been terminated by fears that approaching darkness would enable a surprise attack to be launched by the large numbers of armed troops who appeared to be concentrating in the Turkish forward trenches. On one sector, Turkish stretcher-bearers were fired on as they moved forward in the gathering gloom without the Australians knowing of the informal negotiations. A resumption of firing effectively prevented the Turks taking advantage of General Walker's verbal invitation for a parley to discuss a cease-fire, but a written invitattion to send an officer to conduct negotiations led to the Turks taking up this offer.

Many troops who were on the beach or had a view of the beach saw this officer coming along the shore from Gaba Tepe. He was helped into the sea and round the barbed wire which closed the extreme right flank of the Anzac position, blindfolded and led on a horse into the lines. Negotiations for a truce on the following day, the 24th, were successfully concluded and at least one copy survives, in the La Trobe Library, Melbourne, of the Australian orders issued for the truce. The suspension of arms was to last nine hours, from 7.30 a.m. to 4.30 p.m. Parties of not more than two hundred unarmed men of each side, equipped with water bottles, stretchers and picks and shovels, were to work in 1,000-metre-long areas designated after the Staff officers of either side had worked on delimiting no-man's land. Arms and equipment of dead and wounded officers were to be handed over without restriction, but the bolts of the rifles of all rankers were to be removed first. No work was to be done on

[7] Christchurch Public Library.
[8] Australian: vol. 2, p. 164 ff. British: vol. 2, pp. 20 ff. The Birdwood diaries are held at Canberra in the Australian War Memorial.

trenches, saps or communication trenches or gun emplacements. A dividing line was to be marked by two hundred white flag-bearers from either side and to this line the bodies were to be taken and laid respectfully in line, not in heaps, for removal and burial by men of the respective sides. To avoid any misinterpretation, rifles were to be carried to this line on stretchers and not by hand. Strict observation was to be maintained throughout, to see that there was no breach of the agreed terms by preparations for an attack under the guise of truce activities.

Naturally advantage was taken during the nine hours to survey as much as possible of enemy positions. According to the Turkish Captain Ozgen's memoirs, the famous Lieut-Colonel Mustafa Kemal, who was commanding the 19th Division, had dressed as a medical orderly and by this means succeeded in viewing the Australian positions. Certainly notes and sketches containing much useful information were made by Australian officers. Whether particularly tall troops were selected for the work is difficult to establish, as indeed it is to know whether there was a serious attempt to leave equipment like bayonets sticking up in order to be used as sighting marks on particular positions. Although two Australians were shot by a sniper[9] who knew nothing of the agreement and, according to the Australian official history, a Turkish howitzer on Gaba Tepe was fired, there was no incident which seriously endangered the continuation of the truce.

Major Butcher remembered that those concerned with the no-man's land activity had been ordered to be shaved and particularly smart in their appearance to impress the Turks, and he also recalls the fraternization which took place and a Turk declaring loudly, 'We are bloody silly.' Colonel D. Marks noted in his diary that he had 'exchanged coins with Turkish and German officers',[10] and indeed the period of the truce was to provide a quite extraordinary experience. G. C. Grove observed the work of the burial parties. 'Seemed very queer all day with everything so quiet, no firing or anything all the time. Our men and Turks were exchanging cigarettes and tobacco while some were burying the dead. The smell was something cruel, most of the bodies being almost totally decomposed.'

The work of moving and burying bodies in an advanced state of decomposition was difficult as well as particularly unpleasant. The New Zealander Lieut-Col. Fenwick wrote that: 'Everywhere one looked lay

[9] New Zealand and Australian Division War Diary (New Zealand National Archives). This war diary shows that during the truce both sides levelled accusations against the other of illegal activities.

[10] Mitchell Library, Sydney.

dead, swollen, black, hideous and over all a nauseating stench that nearly made one vomit. We exchanged cigarettes with the other officers frequently and the senior Turkish medico gave me two pieces of scented wool to put in my nostrils . . . there was a narrow path absolutely blocked with dead, also a swathe of men who had fallen face down as if on parade . . . The Turkish officers were charming. The Germans were rude and dictatorial and accused us of digging trenches. I lost my temper (and my German) and told them the corpses were so decomposed that they could not be lifted and our men were merely digging pits to put the awful things into.' An Australian Salvation Army Padre, McKenzie, wrote to his wife on 29 May that it had been, 'the most dreadful experience even I have had, burying people who had been dead a month. I retched and have been sleepless since . . . No words can describe the ghastliness.'

Of the strain of service at Quinn's Post in the Anzac front line during this period, Cecil Malthus has written particularly well.[11] The post, at the top of a steep cliff, was reached by a straight staircase with the steps cut out of the cliff and reinforced with brushwood. Divided into no less than six separate commands at the head and on either side of the ladder, the position was in parts only seven yards from the Turkish parapet, with a listening post even closer, and was as ridiculously insecure as it was vital in preventing Turkish domination of the valley below the cliff. Australians and then New Zealanders had won, defended and improved these hazardous positions under constant bombing attacks, rifle fire and the threat of enemy mining explosions. The listening post was a 'little timbered passage, practically below ground level, though heavily roofed with sandbags. A tiny loophole enabled us to watch the Turk's parapet a few feet away and through a manhole at the side we could crawl or lean out to throw bombs. I spent two nights in this place and both times the roof was more or less blown in and some of my companions were badly wounded . . . To lie cowering in the darkness of the cramped and evil-smelling pit and watch a big bomb sputtering among the corpses just against our loophole while waiting for the burst was an experience that no man could endure unmoved.'

Major Chambers noted that even when the men became expert in throwing bombs back before they burst, speed of reaction and agility of movement were hampered by two important factors. 'The trouble was that the explosions deafened us so much that after a time we could not hear where the bombs were falling and then the strain was pretty bad. The trenches were very narrow and a man had to be careful not to get

[11] *Anzac: A Retrospect*, Chapter 5.

stuck when either reaching for a bomb or getting away. Wounded men lying in the bottom of the trenches were really the worst sufferers from bombs.'

To defend against mining, advanced underground galleries were dug, linked so that in front of the Anzac position ran a forward subterranean line which could be used to launch counter-mining activities as well as to defend the Anzac position. 'We are continually sapping towards the Australian trenches in our front and have now only a few feet to go. The Australians are sapping towards the Turks' trenches and are now only ten yards away. The Turks have only to put their rifles over their trenches and shoot straight down onto our trenches. Hand bombs are being hurled every few minutes.'[12] This diary entry by the New Zealander A. E. Gascoigne indicates the conditions in those front-line posts where the opposing troops were so close.

Courtney's Post and Johnston's Jolly were further examples of positions involving exceptional problems of intercommunication and supply as well as active defence. A consideration of the problem of food, water and sanitation makes one aware of the debilitating effect of service in these sectors. As the summer heat increased, the flies massed in strength and the maggots waxed in numbers and girth. Among the men retaining vivid recollections of these singularly unpleasant conditions was J. G. Gasparich. 'The flies flew in their thousands from swollen, rotten bodies lying in the scrub. From this oozing matter where they bred so promiscuously they would move to the open latrines and so to the men themselves. They sought moisture from our ears, our noses, our eyes, our mouths. Men wrapped their heads in hessian in an endeavour to escape them until they were nearly suffocated in the heat but still the flies managed to get in. Liquid spilled on the floor was soon covered by layers of furiously struggling flies fighting to reach the dampness. You had to keep a moving hand over any morsel of food and drink in a forlorn attempt to keep the flies from entering your mouth.' Inadequate latrine facilities and unvaried and perhaps unsuitable food were to make men already weakened in nerve and body a ready prey to enteric fever and dysentery, but the full effects of this were to be kept at bay until the supreme effort to break out of the Anzac position in August.

It should not be assumed that Australasians alone were enduring these trials at Anzac. At the landing there had been the 150 young Englishmen of the Ceylon Planters' Rifle Corps attached to the Australian and New

[12] For 18 May 1915 (Alexander Turnbull Library, Wellington). He was killed two days later.

Zealand Army Corps. In a letter of 17 May, Birdwood wrote, 'I have an excellent guard of Ceylon Planters who are such a nice lot of fellows.'[13] Also in the Indian Army there was the 7th Mountain Artillery Brigade,[14] which had been in action since 25 April. Colonel Fergusson, of the 21st Kohat Battery, wrote an account in 1916 of the astonishing heroism of Karm Singh, one of his gunners, who continued at his post despite being blinded in both eyes by shrapnel pellets. He had kept on saying, "Bilkul taqrah (quite fit), Sahib" to all anxious inquiries.'

From August, the 1/5, 1/6 and 2/10 Gurkhas and the 14th Sikhs, all from the 29th Indian Brigade, were to serve with distinction at Anzac, as of course were English units,[15] but the Indian Mule Cart Corps with two officers and 227 other ranks had been at the original landing. Together with the Second Indian Field Ambulance, the Indian Mule Corps, with their little carts or winding trains of mules, were to carry out a large part of the difficult, dangerous and essential work of the movement of supplies from the beach. Although an attempt was made to set up a small-gauge railway or tramway line, it was never of real operational value, and the Anzac supply line was largely maintained by the Indians and the six officers and 240 men of the Zion Mule Corps which also landed on 25 April.

This Jewish unit suffered eight killed and fifty-five wounded during their Gallipoli service. They were of Russian nationality and were refugees from Palestine. Their unit had been formed as recently as 23 March in Egypt, when these earnest volunteers had sworn an oath of obedience to their English Commander, Lieut-Colonel Patterson, and their appointed officers. A feature of the Zionists' work was that at every opportunity, whether at Helles or at Anzac, they rode their mules and it was not long before they were known either as the 'allies cavalry' or 'Ally Sloper's cavalry'. Though to the majority of the corps, Russian and Hebrew were their natural tongues, they were commanded in English, and Lieut-Colonel Parker remembers the influence the Peninsula had on one of the tenets of their faith. Parker was in charge of a supply dump and the Zionists refused on principle to carry the sides of bacon from the jetty to this store. On the arrival of a special dispensation from the Chief Rabbi allowing them to eat bacon, and of course carry it, the unit applied unsuccessfully for their previously rejected rations.

[13] Lord Birdwood Papers, Australian War Memorial.
[14] 21st and 26th Batteries.
[15] Units of the R.N.D. also landed at Anzac on 25 April 1915 and during the next few days before being transferred to Helles. See Australian official history, vol. 1, p. 281.

Parker also has recollection of a very special, indeed perhaps unique, 'unit'. It was the task of a man named Wilson, who had been a butcher, to row from shore armed with a sort of lance (or later with a butcher's knife lashed to a pole), clad in waterproof clothing, and lance or slash the gaseous bloated carcasses of mules killed ashore and unsuccessfully dumped in the sea for burial, to make them sink. On return from these missions, Wilson's smell was abominable and his nickname unprintable.

Similarly unusual but completely diverse in their nature were two experiences recollected by A. L. Rutter. Weakened by dysentery, he had fallen from the perching poles into a latrine. Helpless in the filthy material, as he was too ill even to attempt to climb the steep sides of the pit, his faint cries had after some time been heard. He was dragged out and thrown into the sea to get clean. Rutter was in fact a keen and not un-skilled violinist. Somehow he had managed to bring his precious violin to the Peninsula and on quiet evenings before dysentery had begun to take hold of him he had played in his trench the popular airs of the day. Not surprisingly 'Turkish Patrol' was one of the most popular and on several evenings, as the notes rose into the still air, the applause of Australian troops was distinctly joined by acclaim from the Turkish trenches.

Entertainment of a different kind was provided on 18 June, when A. S. Hutton saw 'two of our chaps had a real good stand-up fight at the supports of Courtney's Post yesterday. It lasted about half an hour. There was much cheering going on.'[16]

Besides the news which arrived in out-of-date Australian and New Zealand papers, officially approved information was issued in the form of the *Peninsula Press* news sheet which was displayed on various boards at Anzac as at Helles. Propaganda was naturally a factor in this M.E.F. H.Q. publication. In a report published on 11 June, readers were informed that a Turkish prisoner had on him a copy of army orders which stated that a great deal of ammunition is being expended and 'this is proof that while the enemy is losing the terror we at first instilled in him, we our-selves are afraid'.[17] It seems little wonder that an Australian wrote on the back of a copy he sent home of the *Peninsula Press* for 22 May, 'We don't get the bad news. This is our only source of information.' Despite the attempt to censor information coming to the troops at Anzac, and of course the Australasian newspapers themselves contained only approved news, there is little evidence that censorship was any more strict at Anzac than at Helles. While many of the letter writers were intentionally or

[16] South Australian State Archives (D 4975).
[17] *Peninsula Press*, 11 June 1915 (P.L.).

otherwise their own censor and some seem to show their awareness of the censor by warning the recipient that they could not give details, few of the large number of letters which remain in archival or personal preservation show traces of the blue pencil. There is no doubt of the identity of the censor most feared by B. Savage, writing from the Peninsula to his former headmaster. 'The censor will gaze with suspicion at my bulky letter, visions of stolen plans and designs may rise before his eyes, so I had better close. I hope you won't correct my letter as an essay and return it for me to rewrite as a reminder of the days when my corrections exceeded my homework in quantity.'

Both June and July saw costly diversionary attacks launched with little time for considered planning, as M.E.F. H.Q. considered the secrecy of the date of the main offensives being launched at Helles must take precedence over all other factors. The losses suffered without any apparent local or overall benefit, together with the problems already mentioned, gnawed away at the physique and morale of the troops. As early as 16 June, Lieut-Colonel Fenwick, the Assistant Director of Medical Services, was moved to write in his journal: 'The flies are a dreadful nuisance. You have to brush them off just as you put each bit of food into your mouth, otherwise you eat flies, because they decline to leave the food, even when inside your mouth. We have no means of killing these pests.' Fenwick was in fact soon to leave the Peninsula to work in a general field hospital at Heliopolis, near Cairo, but still earlier in June a young staff officer, J. L. Anderson, noted that 'diarrhoea is getting pretty serious here and in the congested way we are at present is likely to remain. Things may become serious. It is hard to find latrines sufficiently far enough away not to interfere with things in general and to keep them away from the wells.'[18] Anderson proceeded to criticize the lack of preparations for offsetting these problems and blamed Fenwick for this inaction.

On 7 June, Private H. V. Palmer in the Canterbury Battalion escaped the rigours of Quinn's Post for a swim, even though it was under shellfire. 'I took shelter under an old wharf and finished my wash, being the first wash I've had for a week after laying in very dirty trenches and getting smothered with maggots from dead lying under our rifle points . . . after dinner we rested but was annoyed by small flies. We took our shirts off and had what we call a count of lice to see if there were any cowards among them [who had] left while we were under fire but they seemed to be all there. We gave them something to do in our trousers by turning them inside out to get next to the skin again.' Even under these conditions,

[18] Diary for 9 June, Christchurch Library.

on the evening of 15 June Palmer's *Nelson* Company managed a concert, with their new Colonel giving a song and other men obliging, despite the rifle fire, with songs or recitations. By the 22nd, however, Palmer was finding sleep very difficult to come by anywhere near Quinn's. 'If you laid down in the dust you got full of lice and annoyed by flies and men walking over you and when on duty [you are] getting blown to pieces by bombs or the Turks tunnelling towards us and blowing up the trenches.' Away from the front line, fatigues on a shift basis were extremely exhausting for men whose nerves had been strained and who lacked sleep. Well might another New Zealander, Sergeant Cardno, write for the 26 June, 'A big sick parade today. It's high time the men were given a spell.' On 8 July the same diarist wrote that 'the health of the troops is very bad. A rest is badly needed.'

The manner in which officers below Staff level like F. M. Twisleton made critical appraisal in their letters of the conditions under which the campaign was being conducted is interesting. 'The men dress as they please and as they can, slacks, riding pants or shorts, anything does, and anything does as far as language goes . . . the men will risk anything for a swim, the days are hot, there is little water and unless you get into the sea you can't wash . . . there ought to be a first-rate canteen ship where men could get what they need in order to vary the diet. If they could get milk and rice there would be fewer men getting sick. It is a pity the powers that be stopped the daily issues of rum. A large proportion of the men have been used to a certain amount of alcohol every day, and to have it stopped means making them unstable, though they might not think so themselves . . . I have not yet seen a forge for sharpening picks and they should be everywhere, nor yet a grindstone. It would make things much easier if all tools were sharp.' In the same letter this Otago Mounted Rifles officer made shrewd general observations on the strategy of the campaign. 'If the Army and Navy had stuck together Gallipoli would have fallen easily. But the Navy came and went several times and gave the Turks two months to prepare defences.'

Despite the fact that July saw no major offensive at Anzac it proved a depressingly costly month, with an alarming decline in the condition of the troops. Uncovered latrines and unburied corpses provided such a breeding ground for the large green flies that diarrhoea and dysentery caused the necessary departure from the Peninsula of many men and the weakening of almost all. Unappetizing and unsuitable food, persistently under the assault of swarms of flies, was an aid to neither health nor morale. Bully beef which could be almost poured like treacle from its tin and rock-hard biscuits flavoured with well-nigh liquid plum or apricot jam proved memorably indigestible in their unvarying repetition. A significantly additional discomfort was the widespread dental decay, for the treatment of which there were completely inadequate facilities. The loss of five teeth through eating hard biscuits was recorded by G. C. Kilner. These factors, together with delayed mail, parcels with spoiled contents and a growing sense of purposelessness, eroded the spirit of men who were to be called to make one more supreme effort.

So many diaries record their daily near-by tragedy. One records men excitedly rushing for the newly arrived mail and being hit by a shrapnel shell burst, others the loss of a personal friend. Gruesome details like those recorded by Sergeant Cardno are phrased in an unemotional, mechanical yet detailed way: 'Lawrie was killed, blown to bits.' A. S. Hutton was still more explicit: 'One of our fellows had his brains blown out just in front of me, some of which went on his cap, some on my trousers and some on the ground.'[19] The troops at Anzac could hardly be expected to display the confident aggression of the early weeks of the campaign, but they knew that something was afoot and that it might enable them successfully to break out of their embattled position. Their wary readiness and parsimoniously conceded optimism is expressed in Cardno's diary entry for 5 August: 'We are ready for the big move on the left. I don't know what's in store for us but I hope we pull it off.'

[19] Diary, 29 May 1915, South Australian State Archives (D 4975).

11.   At Sea: Defeat on the Surface, Achievement Below

Though the naval officer on board the *Minerva* (H. K. L. Shaw) had quite reasonably observed on 10 May that 'things have quietened down a lot for us on board the ships', this state of affairs was to change rapidly and significantly within the next fortnight. On 12 May the security and confidence of naval personnel was further demonstrated by a well-conceived co-operative operation with an attack by the 6th Gurkhas. The attack secured the bluff overlooking Y beach which had been such a thorn in the allied left flank as Turkish snipers in concealed dugouts with bullet-proof shields effectively prevented any outflanking of Krithia. A Gurkha scout officer on board the cruiser *Talbot* assisted in the direction of heavy fire which enabled the soldiers, almost without loss, to take a position previously defended in strength. Not surprisingly the success of the attack also owed much to the special quality of the troops involved – the silent traversing of Y beach and the climb up the steep cliffs to wait concealed in the darkness for the moment of attack were peculiarly suited to these splendid soldiers. This 'Gurkha Bluff' success however was to be balanced on the following night by a loss of major importance.

The Turkish torpedo-boat destroyer *Muavenet-i-Miliet*, with a German commander and a German reinforced crew, had used the dense banks of fog as she approached from Chanak to escape detection until the very last moment as she fired three torpedoes at the *Goliath* in Morto Bay, where the old battleship was supporting the French at the Kereves Dere. The *Goliath* quickly turned turtle, trapping hundreds of men below decks. She sank in about two minutes and approximately five hundred and seventy of her crew were lost, some escaping the ship's plunge only to be carried away in the darkness by the swift current. The night-time isolation of troops from the supporting ships is well illustrated by the fact that several detailed diaries of French officers and men within easy day-time sight of *Goliath* make no mention of the tragedy. An account by a surviving midshipman was published in 1916, significantly without the ship being named:[1]

[1] *From Dartmouth to the Dardanelles*, A Midshipman's Log Edited by his Mother, pp. 152 ff.

'Some of the midshipmen were already standing on the deck in their pyjamas . . . the ship was now heeling about five degrees to starboard and I climbed up the port side. It was nearly pitch dark . . . a crowd gathered along the port side "Boat ahoy! Boat ahoy!" they yelled, but as the ship listed more and more and there was no sign or sound of any approaching vessel, the men's voices seemed to get hopeless. Inside the ship everything which was not secured was sliding about and bringing up against the bulkheads with a series of crashes . . . She had heeled over to about 20 degrees, then she stopped and remained steady for a few seconds. In the momentary lull the voice of one of our officers rang out steady and clear as at "divisions":[2] "Keep calm men. Be British!" Then the ship started to heel rapidly again and I felt sure there was no chance of saving her. I turned to jump overboard . . . Raising my arms above my head I sprang well out-board and dived. Just before I struck the water my face hit the side of the ship. It was a horrid feeling sliding on my face down the slimy side and a second later I splashed in with tremendous force, having dived about thirty feet. Just as I was rising to the surface again, a heavy body came down on top of me. I fought clear and rose rather breathless and bruised.'

The midshipman swam to get clear of the suction of the sinking ship and watched her going down. He could hear objects being smashed inside the ship and saw the final 'mass of bubbles' where she had disappeared. He tried to swim towards the *Cornwallis* but failed to reach her. 'Soon the shrieks of the drowning grew faint in the distance and I swam on with three others near me . . . The current was very strong and of course this was a great help to those of us who were swimming.' Finally he was caught in the beam of the searchlights of H.M.S. *Lord Nelson* and picked up by another ship's boat. Another survivor on board had been badly bruised by drifting wreckage. Similar impressions are given by a number of men.

The log of George Keeler on board the *Nelson* provides an interesting indication not only of the depression caused by the loss and of the great efforts to save as many of the crew as possible, but of the acceptance that the ship's work was still to be done. 'A very bad start for the day. At 1.25 this morning we lost the *Goliath*. I woke up hearing the lifeboats' crew called away. I ran up on deck but was not soon enough to catch up the lifeboat. We were soon having some of the lads aboard and were dishing out blankets or anything for them to put on . . . We got about eleven officers and 100 men aboard. Three died soon after . . . After saving all we could we got under way and stayed at sea all night and got

[2] Inspection on board ship.

into Mudros in the following afternoon. We buried the dead on the way. When we arrived in Mudros we coaled 550 tons.'

Amongst the Limpus papers in the National Maritime Museum is a letter which Vice Admiral de Robeck wrote on the 16th to Vice Admiral Limpus at Malta dockyard. 'My most important requirements are nets and lighters to which to hang the nets and place them round these ships; when that is done we can feel some confidence that the ship will not be done down by a submarine.' Six days later he wrote to Limpus regarding the loss of the *Goliath*: 'I fear poor Shelford had no sort of arrangements to meet a torpedo attack: it is all quite incomprehensible to me and am recommending a Court of Enquiry later on.'

The state of tension induced by the loss and the rumour of the arrival of German U-boats was felt no less by officers and men of the Mediterranean Squadron than by the Admiralty in London. Geoffrey Bromet, the R.N.A.S. seaplane pilot, entered in his diary on 10 May: 'There is now a genuine submarine flap and *Ark Royal* has been ordered to reduce her draught to fifteen feet and find a comfortable secluded spot in Kephalo Bay where she is to remain until further orders.' The crisis was brought to a head by the sinking of the battleships *Triumph* on 25 May and *Majestic* on 27 May. The *Queen Elizabeth* had already been ordered home and left on 14 May. She was to begin an undignified withdrawal of the major vessels from close Peninsula support which, while tactically and strategically justified, nevertheless is recorded and recollected by countless soldiers of Helles and Anzac in terms indicating that they had been forsaken. In retrospect many not unnaturally view the period as that in which the whole fate of the expedition was decided. In a diary account written in December 1915 an unknown petty officer on a trawler acknowledged the changed situation: '. . . trawlers and minesweepers should never be forgotten by the troops since the sub-marines drove our battleships to shelter. It was then that the Turks took advantage and brought heavy guns and bombarded the troops with such fearful loss; for six weeks from sinking H.M.S. *Triumph* the situation changed completely; all that was on the sea was trawlers and fleet sweepers to feed the Peninsula. T.B. destroyers were kept at it and must have covered many a mile, drawing the enemy's fire etc.'[3] It goes without saying that those on the Peninsula in 1915 were quite unconscious of the titanic struggle of will and of words being waged in London while they faced and fought with weapons more destructive of bodies than reputations.

The Commander of the German submarine which produced such a

[3] 'The Work of a Trawler in the Aegean Sea', *Naval Review*, vol. 6, 1918.

fateful development was Otto Hersing. His account of the exploits of
U 21 was published in 1932.[4] He had left Wilhelmshaven on the date of
the Gallipoli landings and had safely navigated his way round Scotland
and through the Straits of Gibraltar. He had eluded French and British
patrolling destroyers and smaller craft and at about noon on 25 May
approached Gaba Tepe, where the *Triumph* was sighted. Hersing writes
that 'the English ship had been shooting into the Turkish trenches and
was now having a mid-day rest. It was steaming up and down the coast
at about five or six knots with torpedo nets out. All the crew were on
deck and sunning themselves; only the look-outs with their binoculars
were watching for a U-boat.' The *Triumph* was however also being
protected by the encircling sweeps of a destroyer, which made Hersing's
task more difficult. He went to a depth of sixteen metres to avoid the
risk of being rammed and, though the destroyer's screws were heard
overhead, the submarine remained undetected. The *Triumph* was
torpedoed and sank according to Hersing in nine minutes, but he had to
remain below the surface for twenty-nine hours in all before he could
surface to recharge his batteries.

The recollections of Percy May on board the *Triumph* belie any
atmosphere of mid-day relaxation. They were at action stations, watertight doors shut and the light guns manned. Calmness on board together
with the admirable seamanship of the patrolling destroyer *Chelmer*
ensured the rescue of all but seventy-three of her complement of more
than 600. Of course the rescued men were in a shocked state despite the
brave cheer which the official history records their giving to the *Triumph*
in her last plunge, but the damaging blow to May's own physical and
emotional well-being came from an unexpected source. The rescued
men were crowded onto the decks of *Chelmer*. May was on the fo'castle
immediately below the muzzle of a four-inch gun when it blasted off at
the supposed sighting of the submarine. Both his ear drums were perfora-
ted and bleeding, his hair and eyebrows were singed off and, though he was
not to be invalided out of the service, the searing shock of this incident
was to disturb him for many years and even in 1972 caused him pain.[5]

---

[4] O. Hersing, *U 21 Rettet die Dardanellen*, pp. 46 ff.
[5] Captain J. Savile Metcalf has written to the author that later in 1915 Commander
Egerton of the *Triumph* had told him of the sinking as follows: 'I shouted for my
bugler and there was no reply. "Where's the bloody bugler?" I called again. At that
moment the bugler jumped through the door from the Shelter Deck dressed only in
the lanyard of his bugle. At my order he sounded the charge, threw his bugle as far as
he could into the sea and dived after it. Commander Egerton also recorded seeing a
Chinese steward clinging to a slowly turning propeller when the ship had turned turtle.'

The whole drama had been played out in full view of the Anzac trench system. The Turks cheered, and Hersing received congratulatory letters from Germans who were prisoners of the Japanese after the successful Anglo-Japanese taking of Tsing-Tau in which the *Triumph* played a notable part. A New Zealand officer, C. R. Rawlings, wrote in his diary, 'H.M.S. *Triumph* sunk out in the roadstead by Turkish submarine about 12 o'clock. All the other warships and transports are clearing out as well.' Sapper Colin Grove of the 1st Australian Division was in a dressing station having a septic arm and leg seen to when 'I was astonished to see all the vessels near, hospital ships, destroyers, battleships and transports moving about turning round and round. I began to wonder what was on. Some time later I was looking out to sea and I caught sight of a flash on the water. I called some of the chaps and they agreed with me that they could see it the second time it appeared. We watched carefully and to our astonishment at 12.7 p.m. we saw the [periscope] of a submarine appear out of the water. Almost immediately there was a splash, a report and then to our alarm and disgust a terrific explosion occurred on board the H.M.S. *Triumph*. At once a column of water shot up into the air as high as the masthead. She listed to starboard almost immediately and gradually began to lean over more and more. I at once got my telescope on her and could see the sailors all lining the decks. A large puff of black smoke came from the funnels and then everything was clear and we knew that the fires had been drawn to avoid an explosion. Already destroyers were hurrying at full speed to the scene. From the beach could be heard the order 'four steam pinnaces make at full speed for *Triumph*'. Within a few minutes they were there, but by this time the doomed vessel had heeled right over on her side and turned turtle, her propellors being seen easily sticking up clear of the water. Through the telescope men could be seen floating in the water, climbing up onto the pinnaces and destroyers and lining the decks of the latter. Within a few minutes other destroyers were racing off in all directions to search for the submarine. One destroyer fired four shots at something in the water but it could not be seen whether they had hit anything. At 12.19 *Triumph* sank below the water having taken twelve minutes from the time she was hit.'

U 21's work was not yet completed. Hersing's published account shows that he was off Cape Helles early on the 27th and saw a great number of small craft 'going to and fro in front of the beach like wasps around their nest', and then the masts of a battleship lying at anchor close to the shore. He found a small gap in the defensive screen and was thus able to torpedo the *Majestic*, which sank quickly with the upturned keel of the bow half remaining above water. He searched unavailingly for other major vessels and proclaims in his memoirs that 'the whole strong English and French fleet had taken refuge in the well-protected harbour of the Isle of Lemnos'.[6]

The midshipmen's logs reflect a consistent picture of alarm and security precautions. Buchanan, on the *Prince George*, noted that 'We left the harbour [Mudros] at midnight [26/27 May] for Cape Helles. We were about four miles off Cape Helles at 5 a.m. when we received a signal sending us back to Mudros. We could see the *Majestic* lying off W beach surrounded on the seaward side by colliers to prevent a torpedo attack on her.' On the torpedoing of the *Majestic* Buchanan's ship was ordered back to search for the U-boat but finished the day at Mudros. As a way of relaxing he 'went for a picnic in the whaler in the afternoon, found a very good sandy beach for bathing from'. Ship's writer Cobb in the *Bacchante* was at Mudros on the 25th when news arrived of the loss of the *Triumph*. 'It is a very sad show . . . all the ships are coming in here helter-skelter to escape the German submarines.' He adds an interesting note on the significance of which it is profitless to speculate. 'Had a court of inquiry on board on the suicide of a seaman in the *Carmania* yesterday. I took shorthand notes which ought to get me 10 bob.'

A further point of ironic significance in the light of later knowledge is that on the 27th, after the sinking of the *Majestic*, the *Bacchante*, steering a fast zig-zag course, sailed to Bodrum in search of the submarine. Several small craft and schooners were sunk in the harbour at Bodrum and on the 29th, the *Bacchante*, having failed to find *U 21*, was back in Mudros. Hersing's memoirs show us that he arrived in the neighbourhood of Bodrum on 30 May. In fact the German submarine base had been secretly prepared on the north side of the Gulf of Cos by Hans von Mohl,[7] acting on Admiral Souchon's instruction to find and establish such a base. At first fuel and other stores came to the base by camel train. The weakness of this supply link was just one of von Mohl's problems, the most serious of which was to escape detection from prowling British and French reconnaissance patrols. The two German officers, three German sailors, a Turkish naval officer and twenty-five gendarmes

[6] O. Hersing, *U 21 Rettet die Dardanellen*. Nothing is mentioned of his sinking the dummy battleship H.M.S. *Tiger*. It was after this sinking that de Robeck wrote of the elderly skipper: 'Old Willy Forbes who is now nearly seventy behaved splendidly and the old man wants another job out here but thinks he had better go home and see his wife and get some new clothes.'

[7] Hans von Mohl, article in *Deutsch-Africaner* (Pretoria, 1930), and memoirs.

lived in the ruins of an old stone tower which they shared with scorpions and snakes, but they had the satisfaction of hearing a personal account from Hersing of his successes and from another U-boat captain whose prey was probably the *Royal Edward*. The base, which was useful to the larger U-boats and indispensable to the small ones with only one motor, remained operational till October, when it only just escaped detection.

An interesting sidelight on the attempt to find this base is provided by G. W. Heath. 'I was on H.M. yacht *Beryl*. This boat had belonged to the Prince of Monaco and then to Lord Inverclyde. The Admiralty was now using it for secret service work. We had to dress in civilian clothes in all ports and as we claimed to be from the New York Yachting Squadron we flew the Stars and Stripes in or near port. We had a concealed gun for self-defence during our work of searching the Aegean for oil stores which would have given an indication of a submarine base.'

There had very nearly been a further allied disaster to add to the three British battleship sinkings – the running-aground of the *Albion* off Gaba Tepe on 22 May. In a letter in the Imperial War Museum written on the 26th, Midshipman Berridge informed his parents that it was 'perhaps the most trying time of our existence here'. They were well within rifle range and yet everyone went aft and they were made to 'jump about', while the engines were full astern. The *Canopus* and destroyers, 'beautifully handled', made repeated efforts under fire to pull the *Albion* clear. The Turks 'soon began to burst shrapnel over the quarter deck but there was no one there. They tired of this and at 8.15 started to hit us with cannon shell. Almost every shot hit and every few seconds there was an explosion and the clattering of falling splinters. One shell set the twelve-pounder cordite on fire on the port side of shelter deck. It didn't last long but we ditched all the rest outside, though it was dangerous work. At 9.11 we got off . . . our total casualties were one killed and nine or ten wounded. Cheap, wasn't it?' It is scarcely surprising that Berridge follows his account with a well-calculated plea to his mother. 'Mother dear! I hope you don't mind, but I smoke in moderation. You will understand what a trying life this is with submarines to add to the charms. So please forgive me. It is very soothing.'[8]

That some young officers were deeply concerned at the overall significance of the naval losses is shown in Geoffrey Bromet's diary comments on the reporting of Winston Churchill's celebrated Dundee speech, in

[8] The private diary of Midshipman William-Powlett records a narrow miss by a torpedo fired at the *Vengeance* on the morning of the attack on the *Triumph*, but Hersing makes no mention of this unsuccessful attack in his book.

which the First Lord had commented on the sinkings. 'It is stupid to say that ships like the *Triumph*, *Majestic* and *Goliath* can easily be spared. They cannot. It is equally false to say that our losses are necessarily great but that they were expected to be and "when looking at the losses involved, we must not forget the prize for which we are contending". If these statements were made in all good faith nobody would complain, but when they come from the mouth of a man who fully expected . . . the navy alone to force the Dardanelles and in about three months, it is scandalous. . . It is wrong to tell the good people of Dundee that the Dardanelles is as good as forced when the greatest difficulties have yet to be tackled and it is grossly unfair and discouraging to Mr Tommy Atkins to suggest that his job is easy and ought any day to be accomplished.'

The whale-like keel of the *Majestic* off W beach was a grim sight for soldiers wending down to the beach for stores, and the stronger swimmers were easily able to reach it. There was however naval news of different character which did something to counterbalance the gloom caused by the departure of the big ships and the remaining evidence of one of the three disasters. On 30 May Second Lieutenant Duckworth wrote home that he had 'just heard of a fine exploit by two of our submarines in the Sea of Marmara; the Commander has got the V.C. Also reported the *Goeben* sunk'. His information on the *Goeben* was wrong but the Marmara achievement was nevertheless considerable.

The *Mitchell Report* carefully examined the relative effect of attacks on Turkish communications from Constantinople by submarines, aircraft and naval bombardment, and with the help of information supplied after the war by the Turks the Mitchell investigators had no hesitation in declaring that 'the limitations imposed upon the Turkish communications by the operations of the submarines nearly proved decisive'. The Turks admitted that at one period in June they had only 160 rounds of small arms ammunition per man left. 'This was due to the ships sunk by the submarines and to the fact that the land route was not yet equal to the call made upon it.'[9] The whole question of how critical was the Turkish shortage of ammunition is a difficult one. Examination of a report by the German officer in command of Turkish ordnance production and supply, General Pieper, which does not appear to have been published or referred to in any publication,[10] casts some light on this matter. It indicates the tremendous efforts made to increase production from existing factories and to convert others for munitions purposes, the introduction

[9] *Mitchell Report*, p. 211.
[10] The *Pieper Report* (P.L.).

of skilled German labour and the use of military conscript labour, the specialization of weapons and ammunition for the particular geography of the Peninsula and the successful production, just too late for use at the Dardanelles, of flame-throwers and gas shells. It was the allied submarines which most seriously reduced the effectiveness of the vigorous attempts by the Germans to increase Turkish munitions and arms production. Between 25 April 1915 and 3 January 1916, with the single exception of the period 8 to 12 June, there was always at least one British submarine in the Marmara. There had been losses: *A E 11* was sunk on the 30 April, *E 7* was sunk at the Nagara net on the 4 September, the French *Turquoise* captured on the 30 October and *E 11* sunk on the 6 November, but Nagara Point had been passed on twenty-seven occasions and troopships had been driven from the sea by the second half of May. By that date the Turkish troops on the Peninsula were entirely dependent for reinforcements on a five-day march from Usun Köprü after a day's train journey from Constantinople. Ammunition and similar supplies had to come by bullock cart or camel train from Usun Köprü. As the submarines also attacked railways, bridges, harbours, viaducts, and all food supply vessels as well as preventing Turkish naval reply to British indirect bombardment, their work was of the utmost significance.

The nature of submarine work and living conditions at this period and the constant attempts by the Turks to strengthen their defences, as for example by the Nagara net, made the strain on submariners one that should not be forgotten in recording the striking achievements of, for example, *E 20*, in her twenty-day cruise.

Diesel engines powered the submarine on the surface and worked the dynamos which produced the electricity for undersea travel. When submerged, the problem of air, fouled through over-use, was made more serious by the pollution of acid fumes from the batteries, and there was also a constant and overpowering smell of oil. These were critical factors in physical and mental endurance, which was continuously being tested by the ever-present threat of the current, shore batteries, patrolling torpedo boats, mines and nets. Small wonder that there was frustrated disappointment when at first 'blood money' to the tune of about £1,000 per man was not paid to the crew of Commander Boyle's *E 14*, which had sunk a Turkish troopship and in consequence was able to claim from the Admiralty £5 per head for every member of the enemy they had put out of action.[11]

[11] W. G. Carr, *By Guess and by God*, p. 28. The claim was at first denied by the Admiralty Prize Court on the grounds that the troopship was only defensively armed, but was carried on appeal to the Privy Council and the full amount awarded to officers and men.

Some of the mundane problems of submarine life are described in W. G. Carr's book *By Guess and by God*.[12] 'All boats carried soap which would lather in salt water. Bathing consisted of stripping and jumping into the water while the watch kept a sharp look-out . . . clothes were laundered using the steel decks as a washboard, and hung up on the jumping wires to dry . . . Some cooking could be done on the little electric stoves but it was impossible to keep good anything that was not hermetically sealed. Canned goods, hard tack and the blessedly ubiquitous rum were the chief items on a submarine menu. Drinking water was a luxury indulged in only when one was really thirsty.' Of course food and drink were not the only things demanding economy. The Nasmith method of recovering an expensive torpedo which had missed its target was to use swimmers to manhandle it carefully and ease it back into the firing tube.

Boyle, Nasmith and other submarine commanders led their crews to staggering achievements and won renown for such voyages as the one in which Nasmith sank the Turkish battleship *Barbarousse Haireddine*, destroyed the Berlin–Baghdad railway line near the viaduct at Eskihissar, and sank four ships off the Golden Horn at Constantinople and others in the Marmara.[13] On one of these trips Nasmith's *E 11* saved her batteries and increased excitement on board by cruising lashed to a sailing vessel to hide her from the closer shore; on another they had to proceed submerged with a mine caught on their port hydroplane. In his official report on his passage through the Nagara net on the 11 August the Commander of *E 14* gave a description which shows that, while those in command bore the added burden of responsibility, none of the crew could remain unaware of their danger.[14] 'I missed the gate and hit the net. It is possible the net now extends nearly the whole way across . . . There was a tremendous noise, scraping, banging, tearing and rumbling and it sounded as if there were two distinct obstructions as the noise nearly ceased and then came on again and we were apparently checked twice. It took about twenty seconds to get through. I was fired at on rounding Kilid Bahr and a torpedo was fired at me from Chanak, breaking surface a few yards astern of me. A mile south-west of Chanak I scraped past a mine, but it did not check me. After I got out I found some twin electric wire round my propellers and the jumping wire; also the tops of the periscope standards, the bow and various parts of the boat were scraped and scored by wires.'

[12] ibid., p. 40.
[13] These four sinkings are still (1972) marked by buoys off Istanbul.
[14] *Mitchell Report*, p. 201.

The achievement of Lieutenant D'Oyley Hughes who, from *E 11* on the night of 20/21 August, swam ashore in the Gulf of Ismid, pushing a tiny raft with the necessary equipment for his demolition work on the Eskihissar railway, would be difficult to surpass in the most imaginative boys' adventure story. The official history[15] describes how he found the best place to scale the cliffs, which he did armed with revolver, bayonet, torch and whistle, dragging the 16-lb. gun-cotton charge up with him. There was too much activity on the railway viaduct itself, as the submarine's shells had previously damaged it, and so the officer had to place his charge on the approach. His use of the fuse pistol alerted the men working on the line and with an exchange of shots he made for the coast chased by Turks. He had reached the sea when he was rewarded by a huge explosion. His urgent whistle from about five hundred yards out to sea failed to disclose his whereabouts to the submarine and he had to return to shore for a rest. He swam out again as dawn was breaking, and though the submarine now came under rifle fire from the cliffs and D'Oyley Hughes returned to shore, failing to recognize her in the mist, he realized his mistake, entered the sea again and was picked up utterly exhausted. It was this August exploit of *E 11* which the official history[16] shows had sunk or destroyed in twenty-nine days a 'battleship, a gunboat, six transports and an armed steamer, as well as twenty-three sailing vessels, from whose cargoes of fresh victuals and fruit [Nasmith] had been able to keep his men in good health'.

The variety of submarine activity in the Marmara is recorded in the diary of Petty Officer Stephens of *E 2*. On the 13 August *E 2* had proceeded through the Straits, getting caught in the nets but freeing herself in ten minutes, despite the firing of a mine above them. She was pursued by a destroyer but eluded her, and at 5 a.m. on the 14th a gunboat was sighted. 'Dived and attacked her and soon disposed of her with a torpedo from our starboard beam tube. Proceeded under engines and picked up a dhow which we burned, taking six Turks out of her. Carried on till a seaplane made us a visit. This sent us under quick enough to dodge the bomb she dropped for we heard it explode when we were under.' Meeting *E 11*, they gave Nasmith's submarine ammunition and in return received a 'bag of apples'. Another dhow was caught and burned after its crew, with the crew of the previous one, were put in the dhow's small boat. More dhows were burned and their cargoes thrown overboard.

On the 18th a steamer was sighted and a torpedo prepared until she

[15] *Official History: Naval Operations*, vol. 3, pp. 115 ff.
[16] *Official History: Naval Operations*, vol. 3, p. 118.

turned out to be 'a hospital ship so we had to let her off'. On the 20th
they sank a gunboat, on the 22nd a transport, and on the 24th they shelled
forts and damaged other shipping in a harbour by torpedo. Munition
works at Mudania were shelled on the 27th and a railway line on the 28th.
Over the next few days more dhows were burned, an aeroplane was
dodged, the bottom of the sea was hit and, it will be realized, the boat
had to be regularly ventilated and the batteries recharged on the surface.
On 6 September E 2 made her way over 'to the islands which we had not
visited for a few days. They must have got bold as they had not seen us
lately for we got our best bag of any day up there.' Sixteen dhows were
sunk on that day. However, there was to be a setback on the 7th. 'Came
up at 7.40 and proceeded under engines towards Constantinople.' In the
evening, with their nose into the beach, they settled down at sixty feet
for the night. 'Prepared a gun-cotton charge for our 1st Lieutenant in
an endeavour to damage the railway. We got on our way at 2 a.m. and
made our way nearer in shore till we reached twenty feet. 1st Lieutenant
went off with his charge about 3 a.m. Since then we haven't seen him.
Should very much like to see him back again for he was too good to lose.
We waited on the beach till well after daybreak with our conning tower
awash but we had to clear out as there were destroyers about . . .' They
went back at night to try to pick up the 1st Lieutenant but he did not
turn up.

Shortage of fuel, a poor trim and water leaks were signs that the E 2's
trip was approaching its end. The E 7 had failed to make its rendezvous
with her and they heard on their wireless of the loss of that submarine.
Stephens records, 'Think we must have scared pretty well everything
out of the Sea of Marmara as there is nothing to get hold of anywhere.'
On the 14th they went straight through the nets without difficulty and,
though E 2 was shelled by the guns of Kum Kale, they were then safely
on their way to their Imbros base.

Unhappily, the general record of French submarines was not so good.
Chack and Antier[17] list the weakness of the French boats in both endurance and offensive capacity and the melancholy account is not disguised.
'In these conditions, it is not surprising that four of the five French
submarines which tried to force the Dardanelles, – *Saphir, Turquoise,
Mariotte* and *Joule* – perished there.' The *Bernouilli*, the fifth, failed
to find any target, but the most regrettable incident concerned the *Turquoise*. This vessel had arranged a rendezvous near Rodosto with the

[17] *Histoire maritime de la Première Guerre Mondiale*, vol. 2, p. 242 ff.

British submarine *E 20*, but was caught in the Nagara net, ran aground and was disabled by gunfire from the near-by battery. In the interior of the boat there was complete confusion. The lighting failed and before the officers could open the sea cocks to sink the boat the Turks were on board and the crew captured. Of course the submarine made a fine prize at Constantinople, though neither the Turks nor the Germans considered her sufficiently serviceable to be used in active operations. The most significant fact however was that the Commander of the *Turquoise* had failed to destroy a vital book which disclosed to the Germans examining it the rendezvous with *E 20*. The *U 14* was hurriedly made ready to keep the rendezvous and the unsuspecting British submarine was sunk. Nevertheless the British victory beneath the sea was undeniable and, while it is impossible accurately to estimate how near to success the submarine had brought the land campaign, the record of leadership and of the service of the undersea sailors is superb.

With the exception of the Gurkha Bluff operation, the territorial gains achieved since the second battle for Krithia (6–8 May) had been negligible. Sir Ian Hamilton, frustrated by the unwillingness of the War Office to despatch reinforcements and concerned at the increasing strength of the Turks, was tempted to believe that success in a new major attack might convince Lord Kitchener of the value of sending effective numbers of reinforcements without delay.

The meticulous plans for the great attack of 4 June at Helles command admiration for the detail with which they were prepared, but show a sad lack of understanding of the reality of the situation. There were insufficient troops for the attack, but nevertheless such an attack was undertaken. There was insufficient heavy artillery and insufficient high explosive. It was unrealistic to expect the armoured cars to make any progress at all and none was made. Inadequate reserves were available to exploit a success, yet when a breakthrough seemed possible the reserves were incorrectly handled. The ruse of the cheering and bayonet-waving, combined with an artillery lull to lure the Turks from their trenches, completely failed and for a gain in the centre of the line of between 250 and 500 yards there were 6,500 allied killed and wounded in the morning alone. As the French troops were to play a critical part in both the failure of the overall offensive and the qualified success in the centre, it would seem reasonable to deal with them first.

On 2 June they had received an impassioned leaflet appeal by their Commander, General Gouraud:[1] 'The moment has arrived to join with our English comrades in an assault by bayonet to capture the line of Turkish trenches which faces you and hold them against every counter-attack. Not an inch of captured land must be given up.' The soldiers were exhorted to remember that, in fighting the Turks, the hated Germans were the real enemy, and that mercy was to be granted to Turks who surrendered. The troops were encouraged to fight like their brave comrades in France, who were up against far heavier artillery than they were.

On 3 June the French orders[2] were issued. 'At 11.15 there will be a

[1] French Military Archives, Vincennes (C.E.O. 20N 27 and 28, Ordre Général No. 43).
[2] French Military Archives, Vincennes (C.E.O. 20N 27 and 28).

general interruption of the firing. During this interruption, which is designed to give the enemy the idea that they must man their parapets, the infantry without getting out of their trenches will show their bayonets and start cheering. At 11.30 the bombardment will restart. The infantry attack will be made at mid-day precisely.' The second part of the orders provided for the first aid post nearest to Morto Bay to be used to supervise the evacuation of the wounded to hospital ships, obviously so that the more dangerous and tiring journey down to V or W beach would not have to be undertaken.

In the attack the next day, the French infantry were unable to make any progress on their sector. The British official history makes a point which would probably have to be couched more carefully today. 'It must be admitted, indeed, that though the French corps was brilliantly staffed and commanded, the proportion of French infantrymen was insufficient to "leaven the lump" of coloured troops who formed the bulk of the infantry rank and file, and whose conduct under heavy artillery fire again proved unreliable.'[3]

The report of General Simonin,[4] the Commander of the 4th Colonial Mixed Brigade, describes how the *élan* of the French troops was destroyed by the crowding of the trenches with returned wounded, by the high parapet over which they had to climb when they were far too encumbered with heavy equipment, and finally by the totally inadequate artillery preparation.

Ironically the French 75-mm. bombardment did much to aid the British in their attack, even though they had not been successful in their preparation for their own troops. Charles Thierry recorded in his diary: '11 a.m. The bombardment intensifies. It is terrible. Never have I heard anything like it and we are in the reserve trenches. What a terrible noise. The ships in the Straits also join in.'

Raymond Weil, with the 75-mms., wrote of the frustrating need to economize in the use of ammunition. His diary is written in snatches during the day. His fear that 'in these conditions it is not going to be sufficient – but we shall see' is ominously recorded before the bombardment even starts. During the bombardment and before the infantry attack he makes no effort to hide his concern. 'I am very afraid – the fusillade of small arms and machine-gun bullets is still raging,' and 'we are literally inundated with bullets'. Towards the middle of the afternoon he heard

---

[3] *Official History: Gallipoli*, vol. 2, p. 47.
[4] French Military Archives, Vincennes (C.E.O. 20 N 27 and 28), Compte-Rendu du Général Simonin du Combat le 4 Juin (6 June 1915).

by field telephone that 'on the English front a slight advance towards Krithia had been made, but on our front it is a disaster . . . our poor infantry have been scythed down by the machine-guns'. Another artillery-man, Marcel Pegard, recorded in his diary the tremendous noise of the bombardment, the constant work of feeding the guns and the frustrated waiting for an order to move forward.

On the British front, in the sector held by the 42nd Division, the attack was initially successful. The official history[5] notes that the 'Turks were on the run; and the Manchester Territorials, fighting like veterans, were all in high fettle.' On 8 June Second Lieutenant Duckworth wrote of the attack that it was preceded by 'an absolutely terrific bombardment by our artillery. Fifty yards of the enemy trenches kept going into the air at a time with half a dozen lyddite shells fired in a volley, and when we got into their trenches the dead bodies were as thick as flies round a jam pot. I tell you I've seen some sights that would make you physically sick if I told you and I don't mind how soon I'm back in Rochdale . . . I have had two men in my platoon killed called Smith and Mudd. The latter is a particularly sad case – three little kids, eldest six and has never seen the youngest. Have written his wife and told her that if there is anything you can do for her she has only got to go [and ask] and also Mrs Smith. Smith was an awfully nice fellow.' The handwriting then makes a purposeless heavy diagonal line across the page before continuing, 'Excuse that mess but I must get my neck down. Half the parapet of my dug-out has just collapsed and a large shell-case landed in the trench two feet away. It is quite hot. Luck again.'

In the *Hood* Battalion, R.N.D., Joseph Murray had taken part in what he considered a 'plucky bayonet charge. Some went for the second line but never returned. After holding the line for about an hour we were forced to retire to our firing line owing to us being under enfilade fire.' Eric Wettern, R.N.D. Engineers, once his section had got up to the firing line, saw the dreadful decimation of the re-formed *Collingwood* Battalion R.N.D. 'Whole Brig. had to retire. Rotten sight to see the retreat. Nearly a panic.'

Lieutenant Savory, of the 14th Sikhs, was concerned in a personal drama on 4 June, which was to involve his parents in that most harrowing of experiences, the receipt of the buff-coloured telegram of War Office notification of and condolence on the loss of a son. The first letter Savory had written after the battle was on 8 June. In this he reported that they had had some hard fighting and that the regiment had done 'awfully well'. 'It is hard to say what happened on account of the censor; but I am now Adjutant, as well as a Double Company Commander, and our mess is four strong including the doctor . . . so you can draw your own conclusions as to casualties etc. . . . May I have some tooth powder? *Not* paste, as my orderly was killed the other day with my tin of powder on him, consequently I am now reduced to borrowing.' In a second letter, written on 11 June, Savory wrote that as Ashmead Bartlett, the war correspondent, had got away with 'exaggerated yarns of this place', he himself was going to go into more details in his account of the 4 June.

'Our methods here seem to be based on a theory that all tactics are rot, and that the only way to do anything at all is to rush forward bald-headed minus supports, minus reserves and in the end probably minus a limb or two. We had our own special task to advance up a nullah (a thing one has always learned should never be done, until all the ground commanding it is first seized) against the Turks who were in a wired trench at the end and also on both sides and at the top, and their machine-guns took us in front and rear and from practically every side.' Savory then describes the suicidal attack and his own good fortune in merely getting a bayonet wound in the forehead. 'Those damned Turks mutilated some of our wounded, and fired on our stretcher-bearers and wounded, when they were trying to get back to cover . . . I had the extreme satisfaction of bayonetting three Turks, only in the excitement of the moment I left it sticking in the third and ran on with only a revolver . . . They are dirty, unwashed looking devils and nobody loves them: but from all accounts they are getting fed up with the war in general and the Germans in particular: one prisoner I saw volunteered the information that he hated the Germans by spitting and saying "Allemong" in quick succession.'

Before this letter, with its mixture of frustrated cynical criticism and cheerful bloodthirstiness, reached home, Mr and Mrs Savory had been officially notified that their son had been killed in action. Mr Savory wrote to the officer in command of the battalion for further details, and this letter, by a further irony, was dealt with by the son, who was now acting in command. Further telegrams and a field postcard had however by this time corrected the misinformation, and his mother had optimistically written to her son that 'they say it is very lucky to have your death announced and to live'. Savory senior wrote with understandable feeling, 'I shall laugh about it some day. At present I am only filled with a sort of exhilaration that you live – though wounded – and a thankfulness that beats expression . . . Good luck to you, my dear boy. I curse the Germans and in a lesser degree the Turks! and I only hope you killed a few of *both* before they winged you. I wish I was young enough to kill one or more of each. Nothing would help me more in my present frame of mind.'

Though it would be quite wrong to make general observations from this correspondence, it is nevertheless as well to be aware of the extent to which the Gallipoli experience affected the Home Front. Somehow, unlike Salonika or even Mesopotamia, the scenes in 1915 and 1916 of events of considerable moment which failed to dominate the news, the public's consciousness of Gallipoli was alert and concerned. Both Hansard and the national daily papers may be cited as evidence that at Helles, Anzac and later at Suvla there was no 'forgotten army'. It was scarcely surprising that Gallipoli was to figure prominently on Australian recruitment posters, and that the main attraction at 'war meetings' was a 'soldier from the Dardanelles, wounded'.[6] An English schoolgirl's diary provides an interesting illustration of the varied time lag for the release of Peninsula news. The diary is clearly influenced by the direction of her parents, but on 2 November 1915 young Miss Alexander wrote that 'Mummie has heard what happened at Suvla Bay,' on 6 November, that Kitchener had gone out to the Dardanelles, 'where they are doing so badly,' and, as early as 9 January, that Helles had been evacuated and the 'whole expedition has been a fearful waste of men's lives, ships and money'.

Recollections of the third battle of Krithia and of the later fighting in June and July at Helles support the documentary evidence. Major G. Cripps was a lieutenant attached to the Royal Dublin Fusiliers and his battalion, the combined remnants of the Royal Munster and Royal Dublin Fusiliers, attacked in support of the 14th Sikhs. Cripps was in command of four Vickers machine-guns, despite his protest of ignorance of the gun. He recalled the excellent target his men made as they were herded into the narrow defile of the gully. When the Sikhs could get no further, his men were ordered up through them and he was sent in front to search for a position for his machine-guns to give covering fire. He clambered up the side of the nullah towards the Turkish wire, the posts of which he could see. Surrounded by dead and dying Sikhs, he himself came under fire. Crawling along like a snake in front of the wire he saw that it was unbroken and immensely strong. He slithered down into the gully again, watched by the men below, and tried climbing the other side, but once more soon came under fire and found the Turks above that side too. Cripps's good fortune was that he was now separated from his men and

[6] See the poster held in the Mitchell Library, Sydney, for the meeting at the Roseville Hall on 23 September 1915.

freed from the responsibility of leading them, as the major in command now instructed, round the S-bend of the gully straight into a hail of fire. The major had decided that the men could not remain where they were. The officer who led the platoon had reached the Peninsular only the night before. 'With a yell and a roar from us all he charged round the corner' into an uproar of fire. Later in the afternoon a single mortally wounded man crawled back, the only man in that platoon to be seen alive again.

R. M. Gale (R.N.D.E. Signals Company), a sapper attached on 4 June to the French troops, saw the Senegalese troops, urged on by their officers, waving their rifles with bayonets fixed. 'The rifle fire from the Turks rose to an unbelievable intensity. There was no sound of individual shots; it was a sustained roar. Looking up one expected to see a curtain of bullets and one had the feeling that even a finger above the parapet would get hit. Then the men began to scramble over the parapet. My heart ached for them as it looked like certain death to be in the open. Almost immediately the first casualty dropped back into the trench. He was a large black man and both hands were clapped to his left thigh and the blood was spurting through his fingers. My dominant feeling was one of surprise that his blood should look exactly like mine; what colour I expected it to be I cannot say. More and more wounded came in and made their way either alone or assisted to the rear. The medical arrangements were probably situated in the support line but I can only say that I saw none at all. More casualties tumbled back. Some died as they fell; some just lay where they fell and died soon; I cannot recall any able-bodied men returning. The heat and the flies beat down.'

Gale was seeing war for the first time. Later in the afternoon white French troops were moved up for an attack, and Gale caught the eye of one fixing his bayonet, patting it and smiling at the young Englishman. 'I managed to smile back.' The vividness of his impressions remains ineffaceable. Later in the day he took a wrong turning in the trench system which led him into a different sector. 'It was difficult to make progress because the floor was covered in wounded and one of them winced fearing that he was going to be trodden on.' Gale risked a look over the parapet and saw scores of khaki-clad bodies in the burned-up grass and barbed wire. 'They lay about like dead leaves in autumn. These were the men who had travelled out on *Ivernia* with me; the rough-talking Tynesiders who had been vaccinated on board and, as I had seen for myself, had arms black and swollen. I have no doubt that many died with one arm more or less incapacitated.'

It should not be presumed that preparations for and the experience of a major offensive dominated every week in June and July. Indeed some troops were given a respite from the privations. Gale himself was to enjoy a spell at the rest camp on Imbros. Semaphore and helio practice on sun-baked hills, walks in flower-covered glens with clear streams, undisturbed sea-bathing, villages and beaches where Turkish delight, fruit and nuts could be bought, biblical scenes of water jars being filled by veiled women at wells – these were refreshing experiences, even though the thudding of the guns at Anzac could still be heard over the twelve miles of intervening water. Back on the Peninsula, though nowhere was free from shell-fire, improvised recreation was taking place. From the first, sea-bathers had stoically ignored the desultory shell-fire and A. Sylvestre has recalled the fascination of the French at the English preoccupation with games of football even under such fire. *The 7th Manchester Sentry* trench news-sheet recorded the progress of the battalion football team in the Dardanelles Cup. The 7th Manchesters had beaten the 8th and 6th Manchesters and the R.A.M.C., and none of the team had been wounded when the battalion had taken its turn in the line before the next round on the 'artillery ground' against the 10th Manchesters. This game was delayed as 'shells actually dropped right into the centre of the playing pitch and even through the goals'. The delay proved an unfortunate omen for the 7th because, 'although much better than our opponents', they were defeated 1–0.[7] On 10 July the Royal Naval Division held a sports meeting. Gale himself was unplaced in the cycle race and prevented from improving on this in the sack race, which was indefinitely postponed because of 'unsporting' Turkish shelling. That weekend also saw a church service held at dusk. Undenominational, and accompanied by rifle and machine-gun fire, the quite emotional service closed with 'Abide with me'. Gale enumerates in his memoirs the conspicious absentees in the Gallipoli experience – Y.M.C.A.,[8] proper canteens, shops, concerts, civilians and females. There were not even any female nurses ashore, but he did remember a single occasion when the padre lectured on the antiquity of the land in which they were serving.

The victory of trench warfare over any outflanking movement or successful breakthrough naturally led to the development or improvisation of weapons and equipment suited to these conditions. The trench periscope and the rifle similarly adapted are obvious examples of this,

---

[7]   *The 7th Manchester Sentry*, 1 March 1916 (P.L.).
[8]   There was a Y.M.C.A. tent at Anzac in the late autumn and there is some evidence that a Congregationalist padre provided piano entertainment there.

but the close proximity of the opposing trenches led to makeshift 'factories' for jam-tin bombs and the construction of catapults, some of which, from their three-legged stance, were capable of hurling these bombs two hundred yards.[9] The jam-tin bombs were made of gelignite, detonators and slow-burning fuse supplied from the R.E. stores on W beach. The tin was filled to the correct weight with bullets and odd pieces of metal – usually fragments of Turkish shells, according to Major-General T. Jameson, whose Royal Marine Company had been employed as divisional bombers. The catapults were fitted with ten or twelve lengths of rubber fixed to the top end of each arm and the other ends were fixed to a wire and canvas container suitable for holding a bomb. There was quite an intricate firing mechanism – one which would have been recognized by Roman or medieval throwing-engine experts. The fuse had of course to be lit before the release rachet was struck and it would burn for seven seconds. Slight delay before release would ensure an explosion over a shorter range or in the air above a trench.

The jam-tin bombs could also be thrown by hand. Where the trenches were particularly close, chicken wire covered them in, as a protection against such missiles. Previously, men had been killed or severely wounded attempting to throw the bombs back or shield their comrades from one about to explode. Lord Rowallan has written that he found that 'by taking the red cover off the instantaneous fuse, it looked very like the five-second fuse and this proved a temporarily effective deterrent to the Turks' willingness to throw back the bombs'.

Three documents in the French Military Archives at Vincennes[10] indicate the concern with which new technical developments were viewed. On 9 August a letter to the French War Office, complete with accidentally authenticating squashed and dried Gallipoli flies, was dispatched folded round a bullet. The sender, Captain Bidoz, reported in the letter that the bullet had completely torn off the arm of a soldier and he wished to know if it was an explosive one. Earlier than this the Société d'Optique et de Méchanique de Haute Précision had sent out a trench periscope for trial. Anticipating the curious soldier, the accompanying instructions were precise. 'Never attempt to take one to pieces. You will ruin it. Hold the periscope by the body with the left hand, put your eye to the eye piece and adjust the focusing ring with the right hand.'

[9] This estimate given by Captain Corbett Williamson of the range of the catapults is a good deal less than that of Major-General Jameson. In addition to the catapults there were 3.7-inch trench mortars, Garland mortars and Hales grenades.

[10] C.E.O., Premier Bureau 20 N 15.

On 18 June information was found on a dead Turk that mines were being dug under the English and Australian positions. An official order declared that mine activity could seriously affect morale and the men should be made aware of the fact that once the mines had exploded the danger had passed. This seems peculiar advice, as the explosion of a mine was likely to be followed up immediately by an attack for the purpose of taking and commanding the crater, but there is no doubt that to be aware of a subterranean tunnel being dug and packed with explosives beneath one's position was unnerving.

For the tunnellers, whether for mines or for communication purposes, the work could be still more unnerving. Joseph Murray gives a good account in his book[11] of the dangers of the tunnels caving in, of an underground hand-to-hand engagement with counter-miners and of a tunnel being exploded by the Turkish counter-miners.

With 4 June as an oppressive memory and with the increasing 'refinement' and hopelessness of trench warfare it is little wonder that a French Secret Situation report[12] on 31 July, lamenting the loss of 500 mules in a single day from shell-fire, the fact that there was danger everywhere, no possibility of rest and a general 'diminution of military valour', counselled the immediate abandonment of Gaba Tepe and instead an attempt to be made on the Asiatic shore.

In fact further major attacks were launched in front of Krithia on 21 June by the French and by the British on 28 June and 12 July. The French, attacking on the Kereves Dere sector, planned meticulously for their assault and used their adequate supplies of ammunition to good effect for the preliminary bombardment. Father Charles Roux[13] has written that they were all filled with confidence and felt sure that this time worthwhile gains would be made. Gains were made and held, but they could not be exploited. Charles Thierry was to be slightly wounded in this attack, and his diary for 21 June, though scribbled, is detailed and explicit. 'Reveille at 4 a.m. Lot of alcohol in the coffee. I didn't take it as I wanted to be calm. We left our haversacks and made our way to the reserve of the first line. At 6 a.m. an intense bombardment began. Trench mortars. It is terrible. They are replying very heavily and shells are falling less than five metres from me. At 7 a.m. we see the first bayonet attack. It is the 176th Regiment. I see them, heads down running into the smoke. They have got off quickly because of the specially placed

[11] *Gallipoli As I Saw It.*
[12] French Military Archives, Vincennes (T.O.E. 16 N 1940).
[13] *L'Expédition des Dardanelles*, p. 154.

ladders. Then a second line leaves with bayonets fixed. On the left we can see the first wounded coming back. They appear to have taken two lines of trenches. Our work consists in making a sap – a shot has hit my ladder. We get our equipment ready to make the sap. It is 3 p.m.' Later in the day the diary is recommenced. They had advanced to the Turkish first line and everywhere there were dead, dying and wounded. They were now short of ammunition. Thierry helped a wounded Turk, who kissed his hand in thanks. The shelling began again at 6 p.m. Shrapnel balls were 'falling like rain', and some seconds after the nearest man is hit, 'I was hit in my left hand.' In a letter to his parents he drew a diagram of his wounded hand to assure them that, despite his departure from the Peninsula for hospital treatment at Alexandria, he had been only slightly wounded.

It was about this time that Claudius Viricel wrote in an almost contemporary personal account that on arrival at the Peninsula he had been considerably disconcerted by two sights. The first was, perhaps predictably, a corpse. The second was, the hot-tempered action of an officer, beating with his baton a soldier who had accidentally snagged and broken a field telephone wire with his rifle. First impressions of the Peninsula were all too frequently unfortunate from the time the French troops, landing at V beach, had had to move past the lines of dead Dublins and Munsters. A later reinforcement, Lieutenant Woodworth in the Manchesters, arriving without full kit, was curtly informed, 'Get something out of that bloody lot', and he unwillingly selected from a pile of blood-soaked equipment a bullet-holed haversack.[14] One diary – that of a young draft replacement officer in the Royal Munster Fusiliers, B. S. Aitcheson – manages to summarize on a single day the essence of the Peninsula. 'Saturday, 31st July: Left the beach 6 a.m. Through nullah to reserve trenches. Awfully hot. No grub. Long march. Done up. Snipers and big guns. Flies!'

The British attack from Gully Ravine on 28 June suffered from lack of supporting artillery, ammunition and bombs and the Turks were able to counter-attack with 'showers of bombs'.[15] Though Gully Spur was captured the British casualties were heavy, and the profitless expenditure of men in attacks against strongly held positions insufficiently destroyed by artillery was demonstrated both by the Turkish counter-attacks in the first week of July, when their losses near Gully Ravine amounted to 14,000 men, and by the allied attack on 12 July.

[14] The haversack is in the author's collection.
[15] *Official History: Gallipoli*, vol. 2, p. 90.

The history of the 5th Gurkhas[16] describes the intensity of the Turkish counter-attack on the night of the 2/3 July. 'At 3.50 a.m. the Turks were seen to debouch from the ravine opposite the positions held by the 5th and 6th Gurkhas . . . Supports were rushed up and a withering fire was opened on the densely packed mass which showed as a darker shadow against the dimly lighted background. Almost at once the guns too began to take their part in the work of destruction, and, posted as they were to a flank, did vast execution by means of enfilade fire magnificently directed. Further to add to the utter hopelessness of their task, the attackers were raked from the other side by the quick-firers belonging to one of the two destroyers which had already proved of great assistance in repelling hostile counter-attacks.' Despite their losses the Turks massed more and more men into these attacks: 'As though determined on self-immolation, even larger and more densely packed became the columns which now swarmed into the open. They were mown down in heaps; annihilated . . . Extraordinary scenes occurred in our own trenches, now so congested by the presence of the supports that many men were unable to find standing room at the parapet. Some of these overcame the difficulty by climbing onto the parados and shooting from there over the heads of their comrades in front. Others were seen to hand their rifles to their more fortunately placed friends, whose own weapons had become too hot to hold.'

Before the attack of 12 July the Turks were subjected to the heaviest allied bombardment they had suffered. On the 11th, Major General Egerton informed the 52nd Lowland Division that 'G.O.C. 8th Corps does not anticipate that there will be many Turks alive in the trenches when you enter them.' On the morning of the 12th the men were informed by the Corps Commander that 'if every man goes straight for the part of the enemy's line which is the object of his unit, the capture of the trenches is assured.'

In the event the Turkish trenches were shallow or half completed or even non-existent and the artillery bombardment had further reduced their protective cover. The Scottish troops, caught in the open by machine-gun fire, suffered terrible casualties. James Barnet (2nd Lowland Field Ambulance), in an unforgettable baptism of 'active service', helped to carry the wounded back from the advanced dressing station at Backhouse Post – ceaseless work for almost three days, two men to a stretcher. In their utter weariness it was as well that they were not reminded of training at St Ninian's, Stirling: six men to a stretcher, raising and lowering of stretchers by number.

The 52nd Division took the brunt of the fighting on 12 and 13 June

[16] *History of the 5th Royal Gurkha Rifles*, pp. 242–3.

in the attack known as the action of Achi Baba Nullah and these troops had only just arrived on the Peninsula. One of the Scottish Battalions, the 6th Highland Light Infantry, was, with the 1/4 Royal Scots and the 1/4 King's Own Scottish Borderers, to lose many men in July. Major C. S. Black wrote in the Battalion commemorative booklet[17] after the war that 12 July 'had been awful but the days that followed were hideous. On Gallipoli there were no reserves. The troops that stormed and carried a position had to consolidate and hold on to the captured ground for days or it might be weeks afterwards. And what ground it was to hold on to during those sweltering July days! All around in the open lay our own dead, whom no one could approach to bury by day or by night, for to climb out of the trench even in the dark was to court disaster. The trenches themselves were littered with the Turkish victims of our shell-fire, in places piled on top of one another to the depth of several feet. The stench was indescribable. In one communication trench that had to be used for days until another could be cut, it was necessary to crawl on hands and knees for many yards over the reeking bodies in order to keep within shelter of the parapet. The heat was stifling both day and night; water was almost unobtainable. Turkish snipers could fire direct on to the floor of some of the trenches. It was hell!'

Leaflets dropped by a German aeroplane over the French lines on 26 June made the most of the miserable conditions under which the invading troops were living. Attention was drawn to the all too obvious fact that victory seemed no nearer. The losses to German submarines and the allied dependence upon sea-borne supplies was pointed out. 'You are exposed to certain loss from hunger and thirst.' Above all, it was claimed, 'The English, insatiable in their desire to dominate, have assured themselves of your services by expenditure from which you will not profit.' However even under these plausible blandishments the French troops did not respond to the Turkish invitation. 'Don't hesitate any longer . . . Come . . . Our arms are open.' Some French troops did indeed, like Marcel Pegard, blame the English, 'always with their pride', for the miserable frustration being endured, particularly as the English in individual French consideration were on occasion 'fighting like rabbits', but the end of July was to see the prospect of an attack to change their fortunes and raise morale.

Reinforcements were at last to be available in considerable numbers and a new offensive was to bring fresh troops buoyant with optimism, eager to tip the scales towards an allied victory.

[17] *The Book of the Sixth Highland Light Infantry.*

'The big move on the left' mentioned by Sergeant Cardno in his diary for 5 August[1] was an attempt to co-ordinate a new landing at Suvla with a breakout on the left of Anzac to seize the heights which commanded both sides of the Peninsula.

There had been serious French protests about any move which concentrated on Anzac and ignored the Asiatic shore, even though it was clear to all concerned that a landing on the southern shores of the Dardanelles, by capturing the gun batteries there, could only be for the defence of Helles, and in particular the right-wing sector occupied by the French, rather than of material assistance to any plan for a swift victory on the Peninsula. But Hamilton did not allow the French pressure to deflect him from what he considered the right position for the decisive blow.

The Sari Bair ridge had withstood frontal attack. The limited area held at Anzac was unsuitable as a base for the landing and deployment of large reinforcements for a further frontal attack. To the left of the Anzac position there were however three gullies which would allow a new approach up the sides of the ridge leading directly to the vital objectives of Chunuk Bair and Hill 971. If, with a limited diversionary attack by the tired troops at Helles and a major diversionary attack on the right of the Anzac position, reinforcements were secretly moved in at Anzac to be used in a night attack up these gullies, an attack which itself would coincide with a landing of new troops further north at Suvla Bay, then the campaign might still be won.

The plan had much to commend it, but clearly, and in the event decisively, it made exceptionally high demands on the leadership at both Anzac and Suvla, on administrative co-ordination and supply and on the troops to be involved. During the four nights before 6 August the British 13th Division was to be landed and concealed at Anzac. This in itself was a huge problem, but it was successfully accomplished. At 5.30 in the afternoon of 6 August the Australians were to attempt a more dubious part of the plan, a concentrated and maintained attack on the right flank opposite Lone Pine to draw the Turkish reserves into this area. Immediately after dusk the New Zealanders, including Maoris,

[1] See page 160.

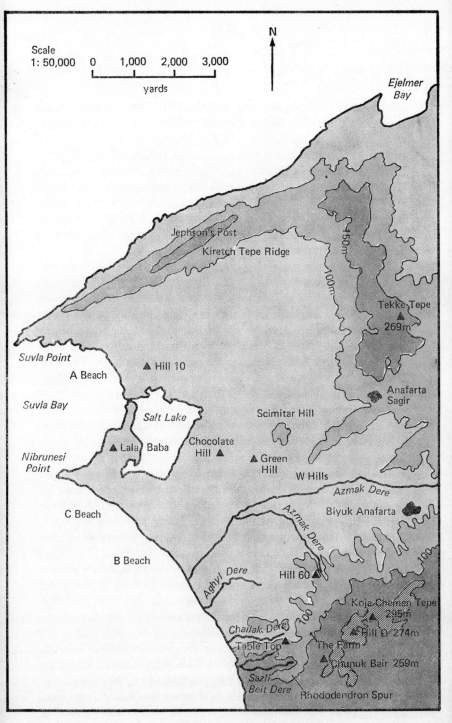

Map 5: Suvla

were to clear the low ground on the left of the Anzac position for the advance of three columns up the gullies. The columns which were to move up the right-hand gullies, the Chailak Dere and the Sazli Beit Dere, consisted of New Zealand troops and the 26th Indian Mountain Battery. They were to meet on Rhododendron Spur for a joint attack on Chunuk Bair. This attack was to coincide with frontal attacks at the Nek, Pope's and Quinn's. The left-hand column of Australians, the 29th Indian Brigade, the 21st Indian Mountain Battery and New Zealand engineers, was to move up the Aghyl Dere to win Hill Q and Koja Chemen Tepe.

The Suvla landing was of course to be precisely synchronized with the Anzac movement. At 9 p.m. on the evening of the 6th, the 11th Division was to land at Nibrunesi Point, take the two isolated hillocks in the face of their attack, cross the open plain ahead of them together with the seaward ridge to the left and, if possible, the three further hillocks and the foot-hills below the main encircling ridge, in the clefts of which lay their later objectives, the two Anafarta villages. The 11th Division would be reinforced at dawn on the 7th by the 10th Division and two further divisions would be landed within a few days.

The planning stage of each attack held certain imponderable and perhaps critical factors. At Anzac, in the broken scrub-covered terrain, was it going to be possible to maintain both surprise and co-ordination? To move by night large bodies of men up three scarcely reconnoitred gullies and deploy them into co-ordinated surprise attacks was a severe challenge. Concerning Suvla there was doubt over the accuracy of reconnaissance reports which discounted the presence of effective opposition. Furthermore, if the main encircling ridge was not taken, the newly landed troops would be under constant observation as they suffered in the heat of the Suvla plain. At least one senior Staff officer was convinced that their IX Corps had completely inadequate artillery support to deal with any serious opposition, and for both the Anzac and the Suvla attack water was a major problem. If lines of supply were disrupted by heavy fighting, or if fresh water could not be made available, the troops would be in considerable difficulty.

From Nibrunesi Point the coastline forms a semicircular bay, the northern horn of which is Suvla Point. This point is the seaward entry of the Kiretch Tepe ridge which falls precipitously to the sea and rim quite steeply the plain it encloses as it meets the Tekke Tepe ridge, itself linked to the Sari Bair ridge. Isolated hillocks and the shining, white expanse of the Salt Lake were the features of the flat Suvla plain, with its low scrub, coarse grass, few trees and some cultivated fields. The more northerly landing beach, with its soft sand and grass-tussocked dunes, was faced by Hill 10, and Nibrunesi Point itself was commanded by a hill called Lala Baba. Immediately inland of Lala Baba lay the summer-dry Salt Lake. The planners were insufficiently sure that it was dry enough to allow a direct crossing to assault the next tactical objective, which was Chocolate Hill, before Green Hill, Scimitar Hill, and the W Hills, foot-hills to the main encircling ridge, had to be taken. The villages of Anafarta Sagir to the north and Biyuk Anafarta to the south nestled into depressions in the rising ground towards the heights above. It would be difficult to imagine a more natural amphitheatre for the enactment of the decisive drama. Certainly the still-preserved dugout from which Kemal would observe the events from the seaward top shoulder of Chunuk Bair gave him superb observation of every allied troop movement. Concealment was at first impossible during the day-time and indeed remained so until the most determined and deep spadework had been completed.

This work is not designed to attempt any chronological evaluation in depth of the planning and military leadership, but for the August attack some exception has to be made, because, in contrast to historical assessment of the April landings, criticism has been levelled at the troops who reinforced the Anzac breakout and who made the Suvla landing.[2] Obviously leadership at Anzac involved Australian and New Zealand troops as much as their British reinforcements and, with regard to the Australians, Birdwood's insistence on the Lone Pine attack was bitterly resented by the Divisional Commander concerned, General Walker. Similarly the attack at the Nek was predictably to result in nothing short of merciless slaughter. It should not be forgotten that the Australian war correspondent Murdoch, who so roundly condemned British leadership and the British reinforcement troops in his celebrated letter, was, in a less well-known letter, as critical of Australian leadership in August. On 13 September he wrote to George Pearce, the Australian Minister of Defence, 'Monash and Hughes dashed their men against a high post here – Baby 700 and they should have known after the first line went out that the job was hopeless. It was pitiful – fine Australian

[2] 'They are merely a lot of childlike youths without strength to endure or brains to improve their condition' was the opinion of the Australian war correspondent K. A. Murdoch, writing to the Australian Prime Minister (Fisher) in a letter of 23 September (typescript copy in the K. A. Murdoch papers, Australian National Archives, Canberra, M5 2823 42.7).

heart and soul and muscle wiped out in an impossible task. Oh, there is a lot of murder through incapacity.'[3]

The first British troops used at Suvla and at Anzac in August, apart from the Indian Army Gurkhas and Sikhs, were largely Kitchener volunteers.[4] Ill-informed criticism has implied that they were therefore raw inexperienced troops, mostly of poor physique and many of them 'mere boys'. The imbalanced and inaccurate judgement of these troops in both contemporary evidence and in historical works seems to have a double source. Firstly it was clearly observed from Anzac that the landing at Suvla was not being vigorously pursued towards a successful conclusion, and secondly this led to the bitterly vented frustration of the Australians and New Zealanders, who felt that their great efforts in April, in May and now above all in August had been let down. This factor remains an abiding memory for many of them, and the Suvla veterans are left philosophically to nurse their resentment at what they consider the cruel injustice of the verdict.

The sympathetic but patronizing charge has been that men, pale and stunted by years in mills, factories and coalmines, or stooped by office work, could hardly be expected to cope with Gallipoli.[5] In fact a complete cross-section of society had volunteered in Britain in August and the autumn months of 1914. If the miner dominated some units, units which incidentally were to distinguish themselves with the utmost gallantry in the terrible battle of the Somme, the farmer and farm-worker dominated others. A generally smaller stature in regiments largely drawn from mining areas does not seem to have been a handicap to the building of a tradition like that earned for example by the Northumberland Fusiliers, but to follow the argument on size, a search among the Dorsetshire, Wiltshire and Border Regiment troops would not have revealed many pale-faced, unhealthy, bent men. The new divisions had had ten months of training and were in fact distinguished by enthusiasm, high morale and a sense of purposeful optimism, even though it cannot be maintained that their military knowledge was sufficiently deep to cope instinctively with terrain vastly different from what they had experienced in training. They were convinced that they could complete the job, so bravely begun

[3]   K. A. Murdoch Papers, M5 2823 42.17.
[4]   The 53rd and 54th Divisions were Territorial Force units and a brigade of the Regular Army, 29th Division, was moved to Suvla from Helles on 17 August.
[5]   This charge was made by a number of Australian veterans interviewed and there was abundant evidence in letters and diaries of the Australian troops of judgement made along similar lines.

and just awaiting the tipping of the scales. The charges that they were reluctant to land,[6] were unsteady under fire and had neither the physical adequacy nor the mental readiness for the fighting will not stand serious examination. Two points require consideration. Firstly, at Anzac in particular, the terrain was perhaps even more difficult and the fighting more savage than it had been in April. Secondly, the recent troopship voyage had left all the new arrivals except the 11th Division with little time for proper acclimatization. Units which spent their time at Mudros before the landing must have been particularly depressed by the low morale and poor administration there, which in no way prepared them cheerfully to accept the scorching sun, dust-laden wind and prevalent diarrhoea. Furthermore, the long, dark, cold, cooped-up six to eight hours which the Suvla troops spent in the landing 'beetles'[7] was hardly an ideal preparation for the launching of a vigorous drive inland.

One of the main reasons for the failure of Suvla lay in the overwhelming priority placed by Hamilton and his staff on secrecy, which led to the absence of adequate briefing and informed preparedness at almost all levels of command. The vital factor, however, was the incapacity of the Corps Commander, the sixty-one-year-old General Stopford, and of some of his Regular Army Brigade and Divisional Commanders and their staffs to maintain an active purposeful control over the advance from the beaches. The work of subordinate commanders at battalion level was also bedevilled on occasions by their excessive age for military campaigning and by their innocent ignorance of what they had to do. Of course it might be said that a lack of independent initiative was shown, but who was to be expected to show it? Initiative which involved taking independent action in the tightly planned organization of a major military undertaking was not to be lightly undertaken by a Regular Army officer all too conscious of the rigid chain of command. Similarly, though there were exceptions, junior officers and N.C.O.s in command of companies or platoons could scarcely, on the wide open plain of Suvla, take independent action with a hundred or less men in an action involving

[6] See E. Bush, *Bless Our Ship*, and the same author's *Gallipoli*, pp. 243 and 246: 'They made a poor showing – no dash and a certain amount of talking. Indeed a handful who obviously had the wind up looked as if they were afraid to land.' Captain Bush's judgement of the men he landed is made clear by the remarkable tone of a further comment: 'they trickled out [of the lighters]. As there appeared to be no opposition they formed up on the foreshore and then had the shock of their lives, for a whole string of mines exploded right and left of them and there were many casualties.'

[7] The landing craft were known as 'beetles' because the hoists of the landing ramp stuck up from the general squat outline like antennae.

thousands. Furthermore the lack of precision or any emphasis on speed in both Corps and 11th Divisional orders reflected an influential indecision as to what could be gained by the morning of the first day.

The British official history explains the situation succinctly.[8] Most of the brigade and battalion commanders were well over fifty years of age and had been brought out of retirement to command this Kitchener New Army of volunteers. 'Some were men who would never have attained command in times of peace, and they lacked the power of inspiring the well-educated and enthusiastic young civilians who had flocked to the Army at the first call to arms.' The irony of this enthusiasm and dash remaining untapped because of ineffectual leadership is increased by our knowledge that the German Commander of the Turkish defence of the Suvla area was aware that his force was too small to prevent a landing. He concentrated his efforts merely to delay the forward movement of the enemy troops. His troops were instructed under no account to become cut off. He had insufficient troops to maintain a forward defensive line above the shore and had to rely on independent posts on the hills, hillocks and headlands, with some short lines of entrenchments in the gaps between the strong points. Without machine-guns or barbed wire, beach defence was by contact mines and trip wires, but the trench digging and troop movements had been done at night and with careful concealment from allied daylight observation. The Turkish delaying capacity at Suvla was greater than was anticipated. Stopford persuaded Hamilton to sanction IX Corps orders requiring a main concentration on securing their base, and the whole essence of the initial bold plan and its vital link with the Anzac flank attack had dissolved almost before the first troops landed at Nibrunesi Point. Anzac and Suvla were to be separate undertakings and it is the reasonable assessment of R. R. James that 'the Suvla landing, by itself, was an irrelevancy'.[9]

Towed in the dark by destroyers to within 500 yards from the shore the new large motor lighters took the first troops, 500 to a lighter, from Imbros to their Suvla landing. Fred Bradford was the A Company signaller in the 6th Green Howards, which was to have the distinction of being the first New Army unit to go into an attack. It was just after 9.30 p.m. 'Getting ashore was not too bad. We lined up on the beach and got our orders. No firing – bayonet only. I saw Captain Morgan look at his wrist compass and point in the direction of the hill ahead

[8] *Official History: Gallipoli*, vol. 2, p. 140.
[9] *Gallipoli*, p. 246.

[Lala Baba]. As we went towards the hill firing broke out and I heard Turks screaming "Allah, Allah". A lot of our men were killed, including Captain Morgan. The wounded were crying out and in the darkness it was all confusion.' Nevertheless, in bitter fighting, the hill was captured by troops tired from morning training as well as from the demands of the trip from Imbros and the strain of operating in darkness. Troops being landed further to the left were however delayed by the incorrect approach of their lighters. They brought the boats up on reefs, forcing the men in the pitch blackness to take to water up to their necks in order to get ashore. There was further confusion as the troops, in consequence, went ashore in the wrong place.[10] Delays from hitting reefs and failing to find bearings once ashore were affecting the movement inland of other units too, and the wide-open expanse of the area was proving in the dark as confusing as the narrower confines of Anzac had been in April. Hill 10 could not even be located, let alone taken.

At daylight, 'the position at Suvla was verging on chaos . . . little of the situation was as yet known at 11th Division headquarters and nothing of it by the Corps Commander.'[11] On the question of events at Suvla being outside the knowledge, let alone control, of the higher command, it is interesting to note the personal diary of a ship's writer on the *Triad*, the armed yacht at Imbros used as de Robeck's H.Q. James Luck, who was constantly engaged upon naval H.Q. secretarial work for the Staff, wrote on 6 August, 'if everything comes off as we expect, we ought to be well on the road to Constantinople before long. We have wonderful organization but it seems to take an awful time to set it going.' On 7 August: 'Admiral [de Robeck] has not returned from the *Chatham* as expected, therefore I conclude we are doing well and he is going to follow up.' On 8 August: 'Evidently everything is progressing swimmingly. From the signals I see we have taken Chocolate Hill.' It is little wonder that on 12 August Luck wrote, 'The Admiral seems to be anxious with regard to the situation. I wonder what is the matter?'

Something certainly had been the matter! The 10th Irish Division had landed on the morning of the 7th after yet more delays and found neither progress nor orders to encourage them. The dash and enthusiasm of the keenest troops can scarcely have remained unaffected by the

---

[10] The Navy had not wished to land troops inside Suvla Bay because of the shallowness of the water, but it was requested by IX Corps in order that Chocolate and Green Hills could be approached from the north-west, where they were believed to be less strongly defended than from the south-west.

[11] *Official History: Gallipoli*, vol. 2, pp. 244–5.

experience recorded in the diary of Lieutenant T. Verschoyle of the 5th Royal Inniskillings. '7 August: Arrived off Suvla Bay at 9 a.m. Watched bombardment by naval guns all morning. Landed via lighter at 4 p.m. Took up position on hills north side of bay. Pretty cold night. 8 August: Glorious day. Wandered to and fro along hillside all day, not firing a shot and only occasional sniping against us. Took up another line at night. 9 August: Beautiful day. Remained on hill all day moving forward about 200 yards at night and dug in. 10 August. In same position all day; a good deal of sniping going on. Kirk and self nearly strafed through excessive curiosity. 11 August: Glorious day. Still on hill. A fair amount of sniping causing odd casualties. Bathed in morning – most refreshing. A trip wire put up in front by R.E.s.' In this fashion the diarist proceeds until he is involved in an attack on the 15th. Thus the inaction, viewed with dismay by the troops on the left at Anzac, was graphically recorded by one of the men concerned. For other troops, like Corporal J. H. Tansley in the York and Lancaster Regiment, there was of course abundant physical exertion as well as fighting, but his diary shows that confusion abounded. '7th: Early morning landed on Peninsula under fire. Dawn – made charge under fierce shrapnel and rifle fire. Had many narrow escapes. 8th: Made an attack. Marching all night. 9th: Made an attack then retired. 10th: Made an attack under severe rifle fire. Came back to support trench. 11th: Went to beach to reorganize. Under shrapnel fire.'

British and French aerial reconnaissance, in flights on the 7th and 8th, had reported on the absence of any strong opposition in front of the landing and indeed those units which had pressed forward had demonstrated the accuracy of this intelligence. The delay in pressing forward had however been too much. In the early morning of the 9th, the 6th Battalion of the East Yorkshire Regiment, after delays through lack of support, attacked up the slopes of Tekke Tepe. They were finally surrounded, after losing heavy casualties to the fire of Turkish reinforcements, which had just reached the ridge in time.[12] The wasted days at Suvla had been disastrously decisive. If the men had been denied the opportunity of securing victory, they were now to be provided with the privilege of advancing, with inadequate artillery support, across the Suvla plain against an enemy well emplaced and with artillery able to fire directly upon a target in full observation. All the advantages of surprise and great superiority in numbers had been frittered away

[12] Their unfortunate capture and the unsavoury consequences are described in E. Wyrall, *The East Yorkshire Regiment in the Great War*, pp. 102ff.

and no one would pay more dearly for this than the troops who had been allowed to remain in their early positions. From 7 August they had been affected with problems which were at one and the same time the cause and the result of their inaction.

A really desperate shortage of water developed quite inexcusably at Suvla, and in addition the general uncertainty as to what to do, and when a further move would be ordered, led to a sleeplessness which worsened the exhaustion produced by the heat and lack of water, the digging, marching and counter-marching. It is well established that men made irresponsible by their acute thirst cut the hoses filling the newly established tanks. There had been, however, a complete failure to transport and distribute the necessary water swiftly, or to dig for water with sufficient urgency, or to locate, test and defend the known wells. This resulted in dreadful privations. Verschoyle recalls that on the left flank none of them would ever forget the water supply maintained by the destroyer *Grampus* during their scorching experience on the Kiretch Tepe ridge. General Stopford wrote somewhat ingenuously to Hamilton on the 10th that the lack of water was one of the main reasons for the failure of his men to make the anticipated advance inland, thus rightly condemning the administrative planning of his own Staff as well as the inaction of the divisional and brigade Staffs. Though the lack of an adequate supply was felt most cruelly in the central area inland of the beach, there is abundant contemporary and recollected evidence that real thirst had been a new and savage experience for almost all the men in the first days of the landing.

The 53rd Division had landed on the 9th and the 54th on the following day, but the Turkish reinforcements had also arrived, and with their artillery sited in their incomparably commanding position the prospects of a general advance across the Suvla plain had been dramatically changed. Furthermore even this attack would lack the necessary essential planning for success. E. D. Wolton, an officer with the 1/5 Battalion of the Suffolk Regiment (54th Division), has written of their advance at 4 p.m. on the 12th: 'the enemy were not surprised but we were, as no battle orders had been given and we were literally flung into action unprepared at a minute's notice. Our own colonel, Colonel Armes, told us verbally at the commencement of the action that we were to advance a mile to drive out snipers! No physical objective was given, so in consequence our line of attack was disjointed and irregular depending upon the character of the terrain and the measure of the local opposition. It was for this reason that whole detachments of our brigade were wiped out piecemeal.'

As early as the 9th the increasing intensity of the firing through the dry scrub had started bush fires which sent aloft billowing clouds of black smoke, hiding the awful tragedies contained within the heart of the swift-spreading fire. Of the attack on the 21st, C. W. Brand wrote six days later: 'We trudged forward for over two and a half miles, over a mile of which was swept by shrapnel fire, the shells falling all round us and men falling in every direction. The hills in the distance were just huge crackling mounds of rifle fire while here and there the sharp insistent rapping of the machine-guns was heard. The ground was covered in places with dry gorse and stunted trees which caught fire and crackled fiercely. Many of the wounded had crawled under these bushes, thinking in a frenzy of pain that they would afford protection, instead of which the fires spread and they were found burnt to death, sometimes past all recognition by the stretcher-bearers.' A surgeon-lieutenant with these stretcher-bearers (C. F. Mayne) remembers the frantic efforts to beat out with spades the flames threatening to engulf men still alive. Unburied, blackened, charred corpses and the loathsome, swelling decomposition of the bodies of men in clearly recognizable units have left ineffaceable recollections for many.

Of the attack on the 21st, J. C. Dart, a signaller in the 10th Irish Division, wrote: 'Mounted Brigades walked across plain in most orderly fashion but suffered severely.' He was easily able to distinguish them because of the shining metal patches[13] cut from biscuit tins and strung round the men's necks to dangle on their backs as assistance to naval observation for supporting fire. H. F. Prynne has described how, advancing at a steady pace in artillery formation, they had broken into the double as they passed through the fire, and E. L. Hutchings of the 10th Battalion Middlesex Regiment, which took part in the attack on the 10th, recalls the 'wall' of high explosive and shrapnel fire as they crossed the Salt Lake, which seemed endless, before the final dash to the foot of Chocolate Hill. Impeded by his entrenching tool as he scrambled up the hill, foolishly he threw it away and frequently during the next few days regretted his impatient jettisoning of equipment which would have provided him with the shallow cover for which he desperately scraped with hands and bayonet.

Snipers seemed able to inflict losses as disturbing as those inflicted

[13] These metal patches were also worn for the diversionary attack at Helles on the 6th and 7th and led to the grimly inaccurate report that the Turkish front line must be captured as British troops were there. The patches were shining but the men were dead.

during the early weeks at Helles and Anzac. There were some trees at Suvla and they provided good cover for the snipers, who were painted green and black to represent foliage and branches. A woman sniper had been caught at Helles, but a still more extraordinary sight is recorded in the Suvla diary of Lieutenant Lindberg of the 8th Northumberland Fusiliers: 'Sniping in trees hard at work again. We brought down three. Another was painted to represent a pig.' Casualties in Lindberg's company included more than half the officers, but not all were from enemy action – dysentery and sunstroke claimed Lindberg himself by the 16th.

The attacks made with great courage on 9, 10, 12, 15 and 21 August had failed to secure the local and perhaps overall victory possible on 7 and 8 August but decreasingly so thereafter. The Corps Commander, Stopford, was superseded on the 15th and the failure of the Anzac and Suvla assault led to the termination of Hamilton's command of the M.E.F., though his removal was not effected until October. For the surviving junior officers and men of the 11th, 10th, 53rd and 54th Divisions, their punishment for failure was to remain in the stagnation and discomfort of the late summer heat at Suvla and, with the exception of the 10th Division, drafted to Salonika in October, to await winter conditions.

Before considering what happened to those taking part in the attacks from Anzac, three further aspects of the August offensive must be mentioned. The least significant was the profitless and indeed nearly disastrous landing by the destroyers *Minerva* and *Jed* in the Gulf of Saros of 350 undisciplined Greek irregular troops under two French officers. It seems scarcely likely that so small a number of untrained troops could have carried out any useful diversionary activity. According to the *Mitchell Report*[14] it was difficult to get the men into the boats, still more to persuade them to leave them, and quite impossible to control them in the face of strong opposition ashore. With forty-six killed, wounded and missing, they were withdrawn after an operation which seemed unfairly taxing on both the Navy and the unsuitable troops.

The naval support for the Suvla landing and Anzac attack was provided by cruisers, destroyers and monitors. It is perhaps worth noting that no battleships were used and, at Suvla certainly, their guns might have made up for the deficiency in field artillery. Nevertheless troops crossing the Suvla plain testify to the encouragement they received from the naval

[14] p. 260.

gunfire. It was far less easy to give naval support to the Anzac attack, though consistently determined efforts were undertaken by the *Bacchante*, the *Grafton*, the *Endymion* and other ships. The searchlight work and shelling of the old No. 3 Post by the *Colne* was certainly a vital factor in assisting the clearance of the foot-hills before the night attack could be launched.

The third aspect of the August offensive which deserves mention, but in view of its sad similarity to previous events in the same area will be dealt with briefly, is the diversionary attack at Helles. This attack, which was meant to draw away from Anzac the potential Turkish reserves, was to begin on the evening of the 6th and continue in a second stage on the 7th, in order that the maximum benefit could be obtained by the available garrison and field artillery working with the support of the Navy. The supply of high-explosive shells was still far below what was necessary, and the Turkish counter-bombardment caused many casualties in the crowded assault trenches, where the attacking troops waited a full seven hours before zero hour of 3.50 p.m. The small gains initially made were lost in counter-attacks and the renewed British attack the following day had a similar result. Casualties had been heavy, with over 3,300 men killed, wounded and missing for little if any material effect on the Turkish defence of Anzac. The 29th Division on the 6th and the 42nd Division on the 7th had greatly distinguished themselves in the Battle of the Vineyard in front of Krithia but, as the history of the 42nd Division records[15] of the Manchesters, 'losses were grievous, the attacking lines being mown down by the enemy's machine-guns'.

15 F. P. Gibbon, *The 42nd East Lancashire Division 1914–18*, p. 44.

On the evening of 6 August, Australian troops opposite the Lone Pine position opened the offensive from the Anzac lines. Across open ground, they were to attack deep entrenchments, most of which were roofed with heavy pine logs. So solidly constructed was the roofing that only in isolated sectors was it possible for the Australians to pull it sufficiently clear to allow themselves to drop into the darkness below and engage in the fierce hand-to-hand bayonet fighting which distinguished this terrible attack. Most of the troops who succeeded in getting into the Turkish trenches were in fact to do so by overrunning the trench and returning along the communication saps to bomb their way into the position from the rear.

Tunnels dug from the Australian front-line trenches enabled some troops to avoid the full exposure of no-man's-land and break out within forty yards of the Turkish line. Attempts had been made by the artillery to destroy the wire which defended this line. The troops taking part in the attack had white calico patches stitched or pinned to their backs and wore white armlets for artillery identification. It would not be possible to rival the comprehensive detailed account in the Australian official history,[1] but the experiences of a few men will indicate something of the ferocity, skill and courage displayed in the attack.

'The noise was unbearable and as it was my first experience in a battle you can imagine my feelings and thoughts, with no time to look around but look straight and fire straight. When I swung round to get some more ammunition I caught sight of my mate George falling back with blood squirting from a large hole in his head.'[2] B. M. Johnson, suddenly faced by a Turk in the confines of a trench and unable to fire, as the rifle's safety catch was on, instinctively hurled the rifle like a harpoon at his enemy. In the intensity of the bombing to defend the newly gained position, heavy casualties were suffered and inflicted. Padre McKenzie wrote on 16 August that it was an 'awe-inspiring sight to see the boys charge and carry the Turks' trenches . . . There were many who never reached the trenches, blown to pieces with shells or riddled with machine-

[1] Vol. 2, p. 497.
[2] Mitchell Library, Sydney, T. J. McKinley, letter.

guns and rifles. I was in it and saw it all. Men were killed and wounded on every side of me. The 4th Battalion went in with 843 and came out with 283.'[3]

Lieut-Colonel C. R. Duke, then a private in the 4th Battalion, vividly remembers the checking of equipment and then the march into the forward trench from which two-man foxholes had been dug still further forward. 'The tension as we waited for the whistle was unbearable. We had some seventy or eighty yards to go and as the fire grew hotter we might have been doubling over crisp straw as this was the impression the noise of the firing made on me. We had to go straight to the third-line trench over the top of the others. I got to this trench absolutely exhausted and was regaining my breath when a big Turk came charging along being pursued by two Australians; as he passed me I shot him in the back. Immediately we met more Turks and I made an attempt to bayonet one but my bayonet stuck in his leather equipment and as he was about to shoot me, he himself was shot by a rifle fired over my shoulder. I fired at a dark head peering from around the traverse and two bombs came back in reply. I was paralysed with fear waiting for them to explode but none of us was seriously hurt. We got on to the firestep to face Turks apparently about to attack when enfilade fire hit us all, killing six and leaving two of us wounded.'

From the position in the Australian line known as the Pimple, the bewildering delay was clearly observed, as the troops stood on, or ran along, the earth-covered pine roof searching for a way in, while those who inadvertently moved in front of the loopholes were of course killed. The attacking troops fired into the loopholes and through such holes as they could make in the cover. In the maze of twisting communication trenches behind the main trench, parties of men were chased, bombed or bayonetted into corners or behind bends from which they waited to fire upon the first enemy troops who appeared.

The Australian official historian describes how the Australians quickly learned to carry their rifles vertically around the bends to avoid giving the split-second warning of a gleaming bayonet. There is ample evidence of the fearless catching and returning of enemy bombs in the closely confined fighting, and of men with a hand smashed still attempting to catch and throw the bombs back. Under these conditions there was no time for the normal practice of throwing greatcoats or slightly filled sandbags on to the smouldering bombs.

[3] The figures for the 4th Battalion given in the Australian official history shows 474 losses out of 742 attackers. 3rd Battalion losses were even heavier. (See vol. 2, p. 566.)

L. W. Graham remembers that many of the dead of both sides who choked the trenches were dragged into some of the Turkish communication trenches, which were then sealed off. Two men whom he saw had bayonetted each other simultaneously and remained impaled together. Keysor and another man in his battalion had particularly distinguished themselves in this bombing, which had to be done from the firestep, as the Turkish trench which they held was so deep. A piece of burning rope was used to light the home-made bombs, but in catching the Turkish bombs a number of men lost a hand.

Seven Australians earned the Victoria Cross for their bravery in this attack, which drew in all the immediate Turkish reserves, but the Australian losses had been extremely severe. In the feint attacks on the following day these losses were to be sadly increased. These attacks took place against German Officer's Trench, at the Nek, at Pope's and at Quinn's. They were launched without the benefit of success at Chunuk Bair and each involved harrowingly disadvantageous conditions. Against German Officer's Trench not only was the thin roof of the underground forward trench, from which the assault was to be launched, in danger from the three mine explosions timed to go off before the attack, but Turkish shelling gravely disrupted the movement of the troops as they assembled. It blocked trench sections and communication passages.

In the entire campaign it is difficult however to select an assault more cruelly futile than that at the Nek. Across a narrow open ledge the 8th and 10th Light Horse were to assault the more elevated Turkish line and its support trenches. The third and fourth of the four attacking lines were from the 10th Light Horse and they knew that they were to follow two lines which had been wiped out to a man. The intensive artillery preparation was stopped too soon, allowing the Turks to man their forward trench in time to direct a veritable hail of fire across the few yards separating them from the Australians. Of the first line, most were killed within the first five yards of the attempt to leave their own trench and few from the second line got much further. With the distressing wreckage of dead, dying and wounded encumbering their movement in the trench, the 10th Light Horse then took up positions on the firestep for their assault, reaching to grasp the pegs knocked into the earth to help them to get out of the deep Turkish-dug trench. The youngest man in the regiment, C. H. Williams, finding himself between the sergeant and the sergeant major, was told that there was no hope for them and that he must lie down immediately he got out of the trench. Once out, he was in fact pulled down and, with a small party which had taken similar action, he found cover in a slight dip. They stayed there until dark and then crawled back.

Enie Bain was on the left in the fourth line and his brother, a sergeant major, was more to the right, but: 'I saw and heard him moving along the line calling to the men to get ready and that they would be up on Baby 700 for breakfast. Well, the right of the line did go over the top and my brother was killed. We were not ordered out of the trenches as orders to cancel the fourth-line attack in view of the massacre reached us just in time. I was soon told that my brother had been brought in dying. I didn't get to him in time and all there was left for me to do was to bury him and write to his wife.' Two pairs of brothers were killed in the same attack. Perhaps thirty or forty yards had had to be covered, and chance, even against the solid curtain of fire, allowed a very small number of men to reach the enemy parapet. Those who got inside were killed, one heroically planting his signal flag to be clearly seen for a short while sticking up from the trench. A number of men crouched up against the parapet between the firing loops. They could see bayonets and brown arms above them but, until they were bombed, they continued lobbing bombs backwards into the trench.

With the fall of night a straggling number of wounded attempted to crawl sideways into cover or directly back to the Australian line past dead and dying. Failure at the Nek enabled the Turks, who had suffered virtually no casualties, to enfilade disastrously the Royal Welch Fusilier attack on the right towards the Chessboard and in addition to this the first-line Australian attack at Quinn's was as costly a failure as that suffered at the Nek. These attacks had been launched without the essential, planned pre-condition of successful progress in the leftward flanking attack. There seems to be no parallel on the Peninsula to this case of men going so knowingly to their deaths. To read in the Australian official history the detailed, moving account of officers and men given time to be aware of the immediacy of their death, and not merely of danger, is a disturbing and humbling experience. In the attack at the Nek, and in particular for those in the second, third and fourth lines, that comforting, if unrealistic, feeling that 'it can't happen to me' was totally removed from the men involved. The evidence of what was about to happen to them was before their own eyes. There was no wavering and every man steeled himself sufficiently for what was to be the supreme sacrifice. That the attack might serve as a microcosm of the appalling futility of warfare, and of trench warfare in particular, and of the intolerable burden borne by every man, does not rob the men of their surpassing nobility in death. A senior officer, writing a letter of sympathy to the parents of Lieutenant W. E. Addison,[4] killed in the attack on Hill 60, wondered 'whether a splendid death like his is not more a matter for congratulation than of condolence', and across the ocean of time which separates us from 1915, the meaning behind such an arresting sentiment can be appreciated by those familiar with events at the Nek in the early morning of the 7 August.

The complicated and interrelated movements in the flank attack and resultant four-day battle at Anzac are covered with meticulous accuracy in the Australian official history and no attempt will be made here to retell something already so brilliantly covered. It is nevertheless possible within a general framework to be aware of the differing nature of unit experience by looking at the evidence from individuals involved in separated sectors of the attack and at various periods before its final withdrawal in the face of the Turkish counter-attack.

The assault up the Aghyl, Chailak and Sazli Beit Deres, which was the key to the whole offensive, necessitated the clearing of the foot-hill approaches to the three gullies. The men were as fully briefed as available information allowed and there was a sense of purpose and qualified optimism in the air which rejuvenated men made old by dysentery and privation. For 6 August, A. L. Guppy entered in his diary: 'All officers and N.C.O.s were lined up today and General Monash told us something of what our next job is going to be. Our company officers then showed us on maps how we were to carry out our work and told us all the plans . . . and now at dusk we, with full water bottles and two days' rations, are awaiting orders to move. The boys are all in great spirits in the expectations of another move after the inactivity of the last weeks. It is strange the feelings that possess men on the eve of an action.'[5]

Lieutenant A. N. Oakey was to earn the M.C. for his work directing a party of New Zealand engineers using a ship's grapnel as silently as possible to pull clear the wire entanglements at the bottom of the Chailak Dere. They came under fire from an enfilading trench but nevertheless removed five out of the six bays of timber and wire. With the Otago Mounted Rifles leading the initial attack on the foot-hills below the Chailak Dere was Trooper M. A. Richards. 'We moved into the creek but the Turks must have had wind of our intended attack: just as we got into the creek they opened fire . . . we did not fire a shot as we went out without any cartridge in our rifles. We were told to take the place with the bayonet and by jove we did in great style . . . two Turks came around a bush and I got them both.' His diary account shows the urgency with which the New Zealanders moved through the difficult country, having only very short rest spells before resuming the climb. In spite of this the anticipated time for the completion of this preparatory attack was two and a half hours longer than had been estimated.

Casualties had been quite heavy and it was difficult to find and move them in the dark to the field dressing station which had been established, according to Sgt. Cardno, in a captured Turkish officers' dugout. Later, as the wounded came flooding back from the heavy fighting on the 8th and 9th, the clearing stations got so crammed it became impossible to move the men down to the beach to ease the overcrowding and get medical attention for them under less hard-pressed conditions. The inadequacy of the hospital ship arrangements was regretfully accepted by Edney Moore of the Australian Army Medical Corps: 'We filled up two which are in now immediately and so far no others have turned up. It is awful to see poor fellows who it is impossible to help here, whereas if they could be got on a hospital boat, there is no doubt many lives could be saved.'

An especially moving sound during the evening of the 6th had been that of the Maori soldiers singing, in their splendid tongue, 'Jesu Lover of my Soul', after a service in which their chaplain had spoken to them of the special way in which the good name of the Maori people lay in their keeping. Later on the fiery 'Komate' of those same throats was to resound from the hill that they had captured. 'The war cry mingled strangely with the cheers of the Aucklanders.'[6]

The column which was to make use of the successful capture of the foot-hills was also largely composed of New Zealand troops, together with men of the 26th Indian Mountain Battery. By the Sazli Beit Dere and the Chailak Dere the infantrymen were to assault Chunuk Bair itself. It was during the night attack that a most unusual scene took place in which Turkish troops on Table Top actually helped men of the 8th Company Otago Battalion, commanded by Second Lieutenant Gibson Bishop, up the last yards, hugging and even kissing some of them presumably because they were glad to surrender and escape the continued misery. From here the New Zealanders moved up Rhododendron Spur and on to the slopes of Chunuk Bair, which was also under attack by the 10th Gurkhas. In the darkness however the Canterbury Battalion, moving up the Sazli

---

[6] Alexander Turnbull Library, Wellington (Misc. M.S. 1196, H. E. Browne, undated letter).

Beit Dere, had become lost. Private Hunter's diary is charitable in view of the frustration all must have felt. 'Came around to the valley between No. 1 and No. 3 outpost, advanced up there for nearly a mile and then came back again. The Heads got a bit mixed.'

Hunter's diary records that the Battalion got up to the head of the valley 'just at day break' and their entry into a blind side-gully resulted in the troops on the higher slopes being unsupported for any further advance.

To prepare the way for the much longer and more difficult movement of the attack up the Aghyl Dere, British troops secured the first objective. The main assaulting force consisted of Australians, New Zealanders, the 21st Indian Mountain Battery, Gurkhas and Sikhs. The timetable for this attack seemed to ignore the fact that a good deal of the ground was un-reconnoitred scrub and was likely to be extremely difficult to negotiate in the dark. Furthermore the organization of a long composite column in the broken ground was sure to be exceptionally demanding if speed, silence and contiguity were to be essential elements. In the event a 'short' cut proved disastrously ill-advised and further delays, interminable halts, fire from scattered and unseen enemies, had so seriously exhausted the troops that two Australian battalions dug in, unable to go further. It should be noted that these troops were not fresh to the Peninsula and were in a weakened condition as a result of widespread dysentery.

The Gurkhas and Sikhs, who were totally unfamiliar with the ground, had, with varying degrees of delay and loss of direction, taken up position to the right of the Australians and far short of the objectives that the column had been set. Even at the planning stage the unrealistic attempt to win Hill 971 reduced the chance of gaining and holding Chunuk Bair, the loss of which was in fact to prove decisive as Turkish reinforcements were to arrive here just in time to stem a local victory which had striking possibilities.

Within three days of the attack, Lieutenant Savory, with the 14th Sikhs, had written of the 'very high country covered with dense scrub in places sometimes six feet high and, as you can imagine, perfect for defence but damned hard for the attackers . . . none of us is very hard after three months of enforced inactivity in the trenches, and consequently when attacking up a very steep slope we all get so done up that we have to stop for a bit to rest.'

The frustrations of the 2/10th Gurkhas were expressed by one lieutenant who had been attached to them because his regiment, the 27th Punjabis, contained so many Moslems that it had been thought advisable not to send it to Gallipoli. 'Saturday, 7 August: Went wrong last night and never arrived, so had to take the hill by day. Did a charge with some N. Zealanders but never arrived – so stayed out with thirty men and about thirty New Zealanders until dark and then made our way in. Got some water somehow or other. Dossed down for night in a gully. Collected some survivors from another company who came in after dark. Scott wounded and missing. Stevenson, Birkbeck, Campbell killed.' The scrub had been so thick that it is recorded in the *History of the 5th Royal Gurkha Rifles*[7] that one man, unable to fire his rifle through it, had set an example by using his kukri to cut loopholes in the dried, prickly vegetation. It was the vicious nature of the thorns and snares on this scrub that an Australian, E. C. Skinner, referred to in a letter describing the necessity to drop quickly to the ground regardless of the discomfort, when there was need for cover or opportunity for rest. In the attack Second Lieutenant Cosby with some 1/5th Gurkhas got to within 200 yards of the summit. Here they were pinned down for the rest of the day by withering fire but managed to disengage and retire under cover of darkness.

For Colonel Marks[8] in the 13th Battalion A.I.F. the night march had provided constant problems of co-ordination, but in all the difficulties 'the Padre would insist upon staying at the head of the column with us. The night was fearfully dark and as we turned into the Aghyl Dere shots broke out from ridges on right and left. A platoon was detailed to clear each side, the men went in with the bayonet and nothing was heard but a few shrieks and some prisoners were immediately brought in . . . Our native guide and interpreter were continually being apprehended by our covering party and stood in imminent peril of their lives.' This diary included for the same day, 7 August, an interesting reference not merely to the discovery of a number of wells with clear, cool water but a farmhouse with bees and blackberries. 'Men robbed the hives with the aid of their gas helmets.' Among the prisoners taken by the Wellington Mounted Rifles were 'two young fellows, their father and his father, the latter a grey-haired patriot whose hand the son took whenever we shifted them'.[9]

On the 7th the delayed and weakened New Zealand and Gurkha attack failed to take Chunuk Bair. The left-flank attack and the conditions it faced are described in the British official history. 'The 4th Australian

---

[7] p. 313.

[8] Diary, Mitchell Library, Sydney.

[9] Alexander Turnbull Library, Wellington (Misc. M.S. 1196, H. E. Browne undated letter).

Brigade had not moved since dawn, and the Indian Brigade, widely scattered, had lost all cohesion. The heat of the day had been tropical, water was very scarce; and the New Army battalions, utterly un-accustomed to hill climbing and suffering acutely from thirst, had been tired out to no purpose.'[10] When the attack was resumed on the 8th, despite strong opposition frustrating the weary Australians, the 1/6th Gurkhas, later reinforced by British troops, got to within reach of the crest of Hill Q and New Zealand troops gained the top of Chunuk Bair. Enfilade fire severely reduced the number of British troops able to join the New Zealanders on Chunuk Bair and the latter were experiencing difficulty in digging in because of the rockiness of the ground. When the Turkish withdrawal was stemmed and reinforcements arrived, those troops forward of the crest were almost all killed.[11]

There was a desperate urgency for adequate communications and for immediate reinforcement. Under heavy rifle fire the small figure of Corporal C. R. G. Bassett repeatedly laid out new telephone wire and repaired it as it was damaged by shell-fire. This soldier whose chest measurements had failed two medical scrutinies, and who had been so concerned on 25 April whether he would be equal to the test he was to face was to be rewarded with the Victoria Cross for his courage during the long hours on Chunuk Bair. The work of the Wellington Battalion in holding much of the crest until they were relieved in the evening had been heroic. Successive short bayonet rushes were launched at the Turks to keep them at bay and the New Zealanders even had to vacate their own shallow trench when it became filled with their own dead and dying. Reinforced by the Auckland Mounted Rifles, the Wellingtons disguised their lack of ammunition, bombs and adequate support by the sheer aggression of their defence.

On Chunuk Bair the lack of water was a desperate problem, as was the impossibility of attending to isolated wounded. These men, if unable to find or scrape any cover, were hit repeatedly by shell-fire, machine-gun or rifle fire and bomb explosions, so that few survived. The unwounded were in no continuous line but rather in isolated groups where a degree of cover had been found or laboriously dug. Short of food, water, ammunition and close companionship as well as being under constant

---

[10] Vol. 2, p. 208.

[11] According to the Australian official history, vol. 2, p. 674, a Turkish sergeant narrowly averted the killing of eleven wounded New Zealanders captured in their forward trench. There is also evidence of a German officer stopping a similar atrocity during these attacks on the Sari Bair ridge (see p. 662).

fire, the prolongation of intolerable strain on this height matches with a different intensity the ferocity of Lone Pine and the acceptance of death at the Nek.

There was however to be a final tragedy to destroy the possibility of profit from the endurance of these men and it was not to be solely associated with the Turkish reinforcements moving up Hill Q and Chunuk Bair, nor with the disastrous absence of aggressive leadership at Suvla. In the renewal of the attack on these heights on the 9th, the 1/6th Gurkhas and some supporting South Lancashires took Hill Q, or at least the saddle between it and Chunuk Bair. An officer in the South Lancashires, G. R. Mott, led his men into a charge with his hunting horn and it was not until a retirement on the same day that he discovered 'my watch pocket had been shot through and my watch cut off the leather chain, also a small bottle of citronelle sent to me for flies, scattered to pieces . . . my equipment on the right side cut away badly and my puttees ripped in two pieces'. In the very moment of tremendous possibility opened up by this Gurkha and South Lancashire success, howitzer shells began bursting among them. The Australian official history asserts that there is no doubt that the shelling here had come from within the Anzac position.[12] At about the same time New Zealand troops were shelled from the same source. It was believed at the time, and is indeed recorded in diaries and letters, that the Gurkhas and New Zealanders had been shelled by the Navy. R. R. James[13] supports this view.

Whatever the truth of the matter, the effect was disastrous. The demoralizing nature of this experience is clearly illustrated in the harrowing details of an undated letter written from hospital by a New Zealand survivor, H. E. Browne. He wrote of men flung into the air by the exploding shells, of silhouetted limbs outspread against the sky, and of a man unable to take the strain being told that he would be bayonetted if he did not shut up. 'Poor old Hughie Pringle was killed, his throat ripped by a piece [of shell] and presently there came groping past us Clutha McKenzie blinded. Young Mell Bull his jaw smashed and another unrecognizable. As they passed us their faces were covered in blood and seemed to hang in tatters . . . Physical fear is a strange thing. While all are more or less affected by it in a tight corner, most manage to contain it, but in some cases it causes them to lose all control over themselves.'[14]

For men who had seen the Turks running before their charge, as

[12] Vol. 2, p. 695.
[13] *Gallipoli*, pp. 286 ff.
[14] Alexander Turnbull Library, Wellington.

the Gurkhas, Warwicks, and South Lancashires had, and for the New Zealanders who had resisted every effort to throw them from their grimly held position, this shelling led to confusion, dismay and of course recrimination. The Turks, now in greater strength, counter-attacked on the morning of the 10th and both Chunuk Bair and the Pinnacle fell into their hands. The British units holding these positions were intermixed and their numerical strength was perhaps two thousand. The attack came when not all were in position and they were overwhelmed by wave upon wave of Turks advancing with the bayonet. This was a new phenomenon on the Peninsula and the terrain held by the British gave advantage to troops able to attack in sufficient numbers from several flanks at once in this manner. Those troops who remained against the onslaught were bayonetted. The Turks lost heavily too, especially when Captain Walling-ford's New Zealand machine-guns at the Apex were able to sweep the Turks with enfilade fire as they swarmed down the slope of Chunuk Bair towards the Farm. As far as British losses were concerned, of 890 men of the 10th Hants who went into action in this engagement, 508 were killed, wounded or missing. Perhaps the most pitiful fate was that of survivors of the 5th Wiltshires, who lay between the lines for a fortnight in the Sazli Beit Dere. Water was found from a spring but was apparently supplemented by some from sympathetic Turks who knew where they were but neither fired on them nor took them prisoner. In an attempt to escape, some were killed by the Australians who mistook them for the enemy, and others by the Turks, who had observed their dash. Two men managed to reach the New Zealanders and one, in his weakened condition, was carried out to help to locate and rescue the five remaining survivors.[15]

10 August did not see the end of the allied offensive. The Suvla attacks up to and including the major battle on the 21st to take Scimitar Hill and the W Hills have been mentioned and on the 21st an attempt was made to link Anzac to Suvla more securely by capturing Hill 60. This scarcely discernible rise was defended by a maze of trenches and had not been adequately photographed from the air. The composite force which attacked Hill 60 from Anzac, like the Yeomanry in their crossing of the Salt Lake on the same day and the 29th Division in their advance on the W Hills, was to suffer cruelly. Australian, New Zealand, Gurkha and British troops maintained their attack and renewed it on the 29th but the summit of the hill was not taken.

[15] *Official History of Australia in the War of 1914–18*, vol. 2, p. 714n., and W. G. Bavin, *Swindon's War Record*, John Drew, Swindon, 1922, p. 306.

Just before one of these attacks a New Zealander was approached by his closest friend, who, white and trembling, confided that he was afraid. The New Zealander, J. F. Rudd, did all he could to comfort his friend but the latter was sure he was soon to be killed. With final checking of ammunition and guns completed, 'I can still remember the feeling as we looked at our watches and saw the time creeping nearer to five o'clock. The whistle went and out hopped the first row of men and they fell like ninepins, then the second row went out and my friend Jack Bindon's premonition was fulfilled.' Fear of a different kind had been experienced a fortnight or so earlier by a sixteen-year-old New Zealander, N. R. Maxwell, who had falsely stated his age in order to get to Gallipoli. Given bullet-holed, blood-stained equipment on arrival he had fled to a side gully on 8 August and, once there, had manufactured some sapping work for himself to do. Found by an officer and ordered to get a rifle lying behind some corpses, the young soldier was still further unnerved by the voice of the nearest 'corpse' admonishing him, 'put that bloody rifle down, digger. We're not all dead here.'

Conditions on Hill 60 were grim. The bodies of Turks had to be used to make parapets at the rear of the captured trenches, which were of course facing the wrong way. Deepening the trench enabled the bodies to be covered but, as the heat aided decay, dark smudges appeared, discolouring the sandy clay. A blackened hand would show, or perhaps a foot, and fat maggots dropped from them on to the rations of the living. Further horror in the attack on Hill 60 lay in the scrub catching fire, burning wounded and setting off the grenades some of the dead and wounded had been carrying. In the close bombing work Second Lieutenant Throssell's cool gallantry described in the Australian official history,[16] in leading the defence of an exposed position, is yet another example of sustained, inspiring courage combined with the virtues of swift reactions and a practical response to each problem which faced the small party of six or more men. With this narrow but costly failure, the allied attacks on the Peninsula fronts end. As a Gloucestershire soldier was to write to the Rector of Dyrham, 'progress is very slow but it always is a very hard job to put a man out of his home'.[17]

On 2 September the Turkish Lieut-Colonel Fahrettin Altay wrote to his father: 'The hopes of the British have collapsed. Will they bring up

[16] Vol. 2, pp. 758 ff.
[17] Letter of George Moss, 21 September 1915, Blathwayte Papers, Gloucestershire County Record Office.

fresh troops, perhaps Italian, and land them on the old beaches – or elsewhere? We are used to it and let them come if they like. In one respect it helps our soldiers, who strip all the British dead of their boots, and now have fine British boots on their own feet . . . When the rains begin, unpleasant as they will be in our trenches and saps, they will be far worse for the British. For they will be stuck in the marshes and swamps on the low ground, and the rain and the floods pouring down the ravines that descend from our lines will swamp them.' The accuracy of this officer's assessment of British strategic hopes is matched by that of his prediction of the winter discomforts which would bring new miseries to the allied troops, now without prospect of doing more than holding on.

For most of the reinforcements packed in the troopships en route for the Peninsula, the voyage, though not without considerable discomfort in the foetid atmosphere of the lower decks and the apprehension of submarine attack, was the most thrilling experience of their lives. Volunteers to a man as far as the British were concerned, with a boyish infectious confidence, many were fascinated by the sights in Valetta harbour in Malta, the oriental smells at Alexandria, as much a part of the scene as the domes and minarets, the small boats laden with fruit and souvenirs for which haggling became a necessary talent.

Many letters deal with the fundamental problem of *mal de mer*, more frequently referred to as 'feeding the fishes'. An R.A.M.C. private, Stanley Parker-Bird, wrote with frank disdain for the sufferings of others: 'I am happy to be able to say that although nearly all the fellows have been very much indisposed, I have not been affected in the slightest ... I am enjoying the trip immensely and only wish it were to be for a few more weeks, for it is really grand to lie on the deck and do nothing. Now that the boys are getting well again we are arranging for concerts and deck sports so we shall spin the time out very well.' There were injections against cholera and typhoid to be endured, but once in Alexandria and Mustapha Camp, unless the men moved straight on to Mudros or the Peninsula, there was sea-bathing and trips into Alexandria, where a Y.M.C.A. provided tea, bread and butter and three fried eggs for two piastres (in those days fivepence).

There were however other sights and scenes in Alexandria which, attracting some men, profoundly shocked others. Of Cairo, Sergeant Morris wrote his immediate impression in a notebook to accompany his diary. 'While I was in Mena Camp I paid a visit one Sunday afternoon to the vilest place on earth, the Wazza bazaar. As I went through the narrow streets and dirty lanes, I was almost overcome with the vile scenes and nauseating smells. Leaning from the windows of their dens were women of every nationality – excepting English and American – who pestered the passer by with their solicitations: "British Tommee very good, very nice, my house very clean. Come on, come in." Besides the houses of the prostitutes there are also the "show houses". In here native women arrayed in the gaudy finery of the East sit in disgusting positions, or dance some vile form of native dance which is nothing more or less than a series of immoral antics. I was sickened and pained to think that human beings would descend so low as to yield their members, servants to iniquity in such a form.'

For those encamped at Mudros awaiting transportation to the Peninsula there were none of the temptations or repulsions of Egypt. J. C. Attwood, on landing from the troopship, spent two nights without groundsheet, blankets or tent, and for a good deal longer had no easy access to washing, shaving or drinking water. He remains convinced that it was this absence of organization which made so many men ready prey to the dysentery universal on the Peninsula itself.

Captain E. D. Wolton, of the 1/5 Battalion of the Suffolk Regiment, remembers the wonderful send-off the people of Watford gave the battalion. The townspeople even carried their kitbags to the station, and on their train journey to Liverpool they saw a large board outside a factory with the words 'All you who are going out to fight, we wish you God's speed'. Wolton's voyage was in the huge *Aquitania* which carried about 7,000 men. Thankfully, his deck (C) had access to the fresh air. As the lights of Merseyside faded and amid thoughts of what would happen to the three Wolton brothers on board and sadness at leaving relatives and friends, he felt above all satisfaction that at last 'we were to share the hardships and dangers that our own comrades had borne for so many months'. Nevertheless Wolton also recalls the chastening interchange with a troopship of Australians returning to Gallipoli. The new troops cheerfully yelled 'No!' to the Australian chant 'Are we downhearted?' and thus left themselves open to the rejoinder 'then you bloody soon will be'.

Not all the ships arrived safely. One of the saddest features of the Cape Helles monument is the rows of names of men drowned in the torpedoing of the *Royal Edward*,[1] which sank in the Eastern Mediterranean on 13 August with a loss of over 850 lives. A. T. Fraser,[2] in the Border Regiment, was in a deck chair on the afterdeck starboard side when suddenly dozens of men ran past him from port to starboard. The

---

[1] A more distant tragedy, but one related to Gallipoli, was that of the accident to the troop train at Gretna in which so many Royal Scots bound for the Peninsula were killed.

[2] Mr Fraser writes that only those detailed for duties inside the ship were allowed to remain below decks after breakfast and there were probably 200 on those duties, plus 200 crew.

explosion came before he had time to ask what was the matter. 'The ship had no escort and we had not been ordered to have our life-belts with us. The hundreds on deck ran below to get their life-belts and hundreds below would have met them on the way up. I shared a cabin accessible from the deck I was on and I raced there to get my life-belt and ran to my life-boat station which was on the starboard side. As the men arrived they fell in in two ranks. Already the ship was listing and this prevented our boats from being lowered, so we were ordered to jump for it. I saw no panic, but of course one can imagine what was happening on the inside stairs. I swam away from the ship and turned to see the funnels leaning towards me. When they reached the sea, all the soot was belched out, there was a loud whoosh and the ship sank. No explosion, no surge. So I was alone. The little waves were such that in the trough you saw nothing, on the crest you saw a few yards. The water was warm. I wondered if there were sharks.'

Fraser found some wood to rest on and he was joined by a seaman, an older man who had twice previously been torpedoed. This brought the young Scot confidence. An upturned *Royal Edward* life-boat was to provide seventeen of the survivors with a little more security though in what Fraser calls a half-hourly recurring turbulence the boat turned over, offering them conventional but completely water-logged accommodation every alternate half-hour but at least providing them with something to do. There was no singing and little conversation. The first ship that passed hailed the scattered men and promised to signal for help. It could not stop, as it had high explosives for Lemnos.[3] Some of the men became depressed and showed unwillingness to clamber back in the life-boat when it overturned, but on each occasion all were persuaded. Finally the hospital ship *Soudan* arrived to pick them up in her life-boats, and at two o'clock Fraser was safely aboard her after just under five hours in the sea. He remembers that 'a large number of men lost their false teeth as we were constantly sick in the sea – and these men were sent back to England. We, the younger ones, were clothed and kitted and on another ship three days later for Gallipoli.'

The inexperience of fifteen-year-old James Houston (2nd Lowland Field Ambulance) led him to strip himself of all his clothes once he reached an upturned collapsible boat. Naked and shivering, he waited for rescue as drowned men floated by, their legs out of the water, the body below supported by an incorrectly worn life-belt. John Crighton (87th

---

[3] A New Zealander, C. McBeath, on board the troopship *Alnwick Castle* recalls his ship passing the sinking *Royal Edward* without stopping.

Field Ambulance Reinforcements) put to good effect the advice he had been given by his father who had been torpedoed earlier in the war. He dived immediately into the sea, swam well away from the ship and then alternately swam and trod water till he was rescued.

On 2 September the transport *Southland*, carrying Australian troops for the Peninsula, was torpedoed within sight of Strati Island, forty miles south of Lemnos. Some men were killed in the torpedo explosion but nearly all the soldiers and crew were rescued by ships which came up in support, and a skeleton force of crew and volunteers from the soldiers kept the ship afloat and guided her safely into Mudros harbour.

For many men the journey was to be made in the reverse direction, to hospitals in Egypt, Malta, Gibraltar or Britain. Their stay on the Peninsula had been cut short by wounds or by dysentery, and their voyage was made in hospital ships. After the discomforts of the Peninsula these men were often overwhelmed by the sheer luxury of a bed and clean white sheets and by the attention of the British and Australian nurses, who in retrospect seem to have been uniformly beautiful in their angelic ministrations. S. B. French, who was at Suvla, recalled the two hospital ships anchored off shore. 'Both were of course painted brilliant white with a red cross marked on the side. One was the *Roselart Castle*. At night, on duty in the trenches, one gazed out to sea and there were the two great ships brilliantly lit from stem to stern. It always brought a lump to my throat. I eventually finished up on the *Roselart Castle* with a flesh wound plus enteric and dysentery. You can imagine my reaction once again to lie in a bunk with clean sheets after weeks of living like a savage. We naturally needed some cleaning up. Socks came off almost taking the skin with them and of course we were full of lice.'

The journey from shore to ship was often uncomfortable and even hazardous. James Barnet (2nd Lowland Field Ambulance) has recorded that 'stretcher cases had to be loaded on to the ship's boats with the thwarts boarded over. These were then towed out by a picket boat with two of us in charge. On arrival at the hospital ship a cage or box with openings for stretcher handles on two sides, and a rope from each corner would be lowered. We had the task of loading each stretcher, mindful all the time of our boat's bumping against the ship's side and the rise and fall of our respective levels.'

The demanding and indeed potentially dangerous work of nursing Gallipoli cases both in Egypt and on board hospital ships is clearly recorded in the diary of Sister Speedy from New Zealand. At the

Deaconess Hospital in Alexandria during August, 'there was no such thing as getting off duty. It was a case of go on from 7 a.m. till 11 p.m., 12 or 1 a.m. and perhaps 2 a.m.' In September the diary notes the death of Miss Smailes, Miss Chadwick and Sister Hawken from dysentery, Sister Griffiths in an ambulance crash at a level crossing, Miss Rockell after an operation, and then, on 1 November 1915, 'ten of the 36 sisters are missing' believed drowned in the torpedoing of the *Marquette* on its way to Salonika. There are however far more entries dealing with the bravery of her patients with severe wounds or weakening dysentery.

R. B. Gillett, wounded in the first week of the landing and transported on the hospital ship *Delta*, remembers that the engines were stopped at intervals and one offered up a prayer for the unknown casualty who had not survived his wounds and was being committed to the deep. Charles Mackintosh, badly frostbitten at Suvla, was filled with self-disgust at the black liquid coming out of his blistered feet when he crawled on hands and knees to the latrine from his shipboard bed.

Mrs G. A. Hale was a nurse on board the liner *Aquitania*, which was used at the end of the campaign as a hospital ship, and this vessel took on board many of the frostbite cases. 'Each man was allotted a cot before arrival on board so there was no overcrowding, but in the bay of Biscay there was a terrible storm in which the plate-glass windows on the upper deck were smashed and the seas poured in. On the lower decks where the patients' cots were stapled to the floor, the violence of the storm wrenched many of the staples out. One odd thing I recollect very clearly was that practically nobody was seasick. I am still stirred today by the poignant memory of the ship's little chapel, crowded with staff and a few ambulant patients, with the sound of their voices singing "Eternal Father strong to save" with all the fervour and gratitude they could muster.'

The contemporary account of C. R. S. Saunders shows how fortunate he was to experience life aboard a hospital ship. 'An order came around that a man was wanted to accompany Second Lieutenant Wedgwood Benn M.P., who was being invalided away with jaundice. I applied for the post and obtained it. That was about the luckiest thing I have done since the war started. We boarded the hospital ship *Valdivia*. What a treat it was to be amongst the light and warmth of this spotlessly clean ship. They gave me sleeping quarters with the hospital orderlies and I was given some food. I remember devouring piles of bread and butter, cheese, cakes and a lovely hot cup of cocoa. How I slept and how bad I felt the next day. I think I slept the next two days right off. Recovering,

I visited my officer, but he was so well attended to by the nurses that there was absolutely nothing for me to do.'

On 5 October a War Office circular memorandum was issued to Medical Officers and nurses on hospital ships and ambulance carriers. 'It has been brought to the notice of Sir Ian Hamilton that, here and there, on Hospital Ships and Ambulance Carriers, Medical Officers and Nurses have allowed themselves to become too seriously impressed by the stories of young officers and men who have come on board sick or wounded. It is natural under the circumstances that these tales should be over-coloured; it is natural also that contact with so much suffering should incline the listeners to sympathy; but it is certain also that, whether from the standpoint of the individual sick or of the military operations as a whole, such enervating influences should be resisted. All grades and degrees of the medical staff must make it a point of professional honour to maintain a hearty tone of optimism calculated to raise rather than lower the confidence and courage of the fighting men who have been temporarily committed to their charge.'[4]

On board the hospital ship *Delta* C. D. Selsby kept a diary which gives an account of his experience from his embarkation. '15 October. Had a good hot bath and then went to bed. The first time for about three months. Had a fair night's rest but aching all over.' Selsby enjoyed his Bovril, custard, sweets, bread, butter and marmalade and cocoa, the books and cigarettes provided and the Chaplain's administration of Holy Communion. He found the ward very hot and stifling but was too weak to stay on deck. His entry for 19 October reports '30 dead on board of dysentery'. The wound card attached to him read 'Persistent diarrhoea', which cannot convey to anyone who had not endured it the debilitation suffered by the 1915 victims of the 'Turkey Trot'. Selsby was to survive and to reach Queen Mary's Military Hospital at Whalley in Lancashire in time for the Christmas celebrations, which included a denominational service, a cinema exhibition, Clayton le Moors prize band, a 'Grand Concert', where appropriately a Mr Critchley sang 'The Crown' and 'There's only one England', but above all a Christmas dinner. The menu card shows each of the items ticked off by the young soldier: soup, roast beef and Yorkshire pudding, roast pork and savoury and apple sauce (unticked), boiled potatoes, vegetables, plum pudding, brandy sauce, mince pies and dessert, beside which Selsby pencilled in 'bananas, oranges and apples'.

A good deal less pleasant are the professional reactions to some of

[4]   Vice-Admiral Limpus papers, National Maritime Museum.

the makeshift hospital ship arrangements recorded in the diary of
Naval Surgeon Lorimer. '30 June 1915: When I got to the *Saturnia*
I found the whole ship packed with wounded, lying about anywhere, no
order, nor anybody in charge apparently. The wounds had not been looked
at for 48 hours at least, and in that climate were in an awful state, live
maggots in many . . . The other naval surgeons who had arrived were
all working independently as there was nobody to give instructions.
The M.O. of ship was at dinner when I wanted to report for duty and had
apparently chucked his hand in. It made one ashamed of the medical
organization of the Army.' The Dardanelles Commission Report noted
that the arrangements for dealing with the transport of the wounded
were until August in a very unsatisfactory state and that the 'terrible
story of the *Saturnia* [was] a most extraordinary indication of the
absence of organization'.[5]

Some left the Peninsula during the campaign for other reasons.
According to a document in the French Military Archives at Vincennes[6]
the French General Bailloud communicated to the War Minister on
9 July that reports from the Colonel commanding the depot at Mudros
stated that a certain number of officers recently arrived from France
had not the physical aptitude or morale for service in the Orient. One
had to be evacuated within a few days of his arrival. The Colonel considered that some of these men had come having been 'attracted by the
mirage of a trip to the Orient', and Bailloud asks that the next batch
should be more carefully examined. Hamilton was to have something
of the same problem with the leadership of IXth Corps at Suvla.

[5] Dardanelles Commission Report, Part 2, p. 95.
[6] C.E.O., Premier Bureau 20 N 15.

The Reverend H. C. Foster, the Reverend O. Creighton and Ernest Raymond[1] have all written of their experiences as padres on the Peninsula and of their attempt, under adverse conditions, to give decent Christian burial to the killed, among whom there were of course frequently men with whom they had breakfasted that day or had exchanged a regular cheerful word. Foster relates that the question of the burial of the Turks led to a conference of chaplains at which, after 'quite an animated debate, it was agreed that no Mohammedan should be buried without a short service in which the Lord's Prayer should form a part'.[2] In his published diary[3] Creighton gave an indication of how soon after the landings cemeteries were established and other places were designated as such. '11 May: When we got to the cemetery at six, it was to find he had been buried some hours before . . . so I just said a few prayers over the grave, and went with the two majors to see about a piece of ground being railed off as a Lancashire Fusilier burying place, where some day a memorial might be erected above the beach where they made their famous landing.' It is clear that some units had the opportunity and concern to arrange and record meticulously the burial of their men. Such a unit was the Royal Naval Division Engineers, whose members took photographs and drew plans of the wooden-cross-marked graves and have been able to compare the positions with those in the Official War Grave cemeteries which were developed from the makeshift ones of active service.

Of course for many men, perhaps particularly at Anzac and in the tangled scrub of Gully Ravine, or in the wider open Suvla plain, with its shallow gullies leading from the amphitheatre of the Kiretch Tepe, Tekke Tepe and Sari Bair ridge, there could be no known grave. Human remains are still being uncovered at Anzac, where the author in 1972 saw the newly discovered bones of six men, and found the skull of another at the mouth of Gully Ravine. Of those wounded and then burned to

---

[1] H. C. Foster, *At Antwerp and in the Dardanelles*; O. Creighton *With the 29th Division*; E. Raymond, *The Story of My Days*.

[2] p. 115.

[3] pp. 88 ff.

death in the August scrub fires in the Suvla attack and perhaps some
of those to be drowned or frozen to death in the storm and frost of late
November, no identifiable remains would be recovered, so that the post-
war headstone merely commemorates their death and not the immediate
presence of their remains. Lance-Corporal Tait, of the Northumberland
Fusiliers, was killed in August at Suvla, though his wife was informed in
September that he had been 'wounded' and in October that he was
'wounded and missing'. In March of the following year there came two
contradictory accounts of how he had been killed. In May 1916 she was
warned that in accepting an Army pension instead of an Army separation
allowance 'this must not be taken as any proof of the death of your
husband'. It is scarcely surprising that for long after the war Mrs Tait
could not accept that her husband had been killed.

A good deal has been written about the so called 'lost army of Gallipoli',
the Sandringham Company of the 5th Royal Norfolk Regiment which
disappeared without trace in an attack in August. The mystery may in
fact have been solved four years later when a War Graves unit found
a grave containing 180 men of whom 122 were Royal Norfolks, but sinister
rumours have been reported that the men had all been shot in the head
and that the watch of the commanding officer Captain Beck had turned
up in a Constantinople shop window and had been bought and returned
to the Beck family.[4] But the disappearance of so many men and the
reported manner in which they had been killed make this a special case,
and further research of a difficult nature would be needed to solve the
mystery beyond all reasonable doubt.[5]

An acceptance of death and of wounds was an acceptance of reality
and it is this accommodation to the existing situation which from the
diary records would seem a more accurate analysis of the soldier's attitude
to death than the common idea that he became 'hardened to it'. The
latter implies an insensitive coarsened brutality which goes well with
the theatrical bravado implied in the familiar stories of shaking hands
with the stiff hand protruding from a trench wall or parapet of which a
body formed a part. The diary of Eric Wettern unconsciously provides
perhaps a truer reflection of the soldier's attitude to death. '23 June:
Section III party caught by shrapnel on mule track returning from work
in the evening. Nunn and Mason killed outright. Ledbrook and Serg.
Goodwin wounded. Bad day for our section. Nunn and Mason buried

---

[4] *The Gallipolian*, No. 13 (1973) and No. 14 (1974).
[5] A report in the Australian *Sun-Herald*, 29 July 1973, describes a cloud seen above the
troops and considers the possibility that this was an unidentified flying object.

in new cemetery in evening. Everybody upset. 24 June: Sorting out Nunn's kit. Busy till late with various correspondence. Treacle for tea. 25 June: Mail in. Still no papers. Got rice from Frenchmen. Ledbrook died from wounds – funeral in evening in new cemetery next to Nunn and Mason. 12 July: Webster killed by shrapnel in comm. trench – just starting out to work. Bombardment continued all day . . . huge mail in evening. Got my parcels at last. One in bits. Supper party with Murphy, Dixon, Thomas and Harris – rice, pineapple and coffee. Webster's funeral after dark – next to Nunn and Mason. 18 July: Feeling rotten. Stayed in dugout and slept all day. Kept off grub. W.C. with seat to it near incinerator! Great luxury. Patronized it all day.'

There are many stories of men having a premonition of swiftly approaching death and of this premonition being fulfilled. It is idle to deny that men feared death, though still more they may have feared disfiguring wounds or a wound involving the loss of their manhood. Naturally in open conversation most men would affect a devil-may-care attitude, and the pessimist was always the butt of fun and sometimes a perverse source of encouragement. But occasionally in letters home, despite the sincere attempt to shield the reality of war from the anxious families, the consciousness of the proximity of death breaks through. B. H. A. Eames wrote the briefest of letters home after the attack of 21 August at Suvla. 'My dear Mother, a short note to tell you we have been into action. We took part in a very big battle last Saturday and Sunday and am sorry to say the regiment lost very heavily. I came through alright, but I can tell you it was very hell. Am very fit. I cannot say much due to the censor. Much love to all, Basil.'

The letters of Second Lieutenant Duckworth, who was killed on 7 August, are filled with a thinly disguised preoccupation with death. On 15 July he wrote, 'Mother says "quite a lot of officers lost". Figures may interest you. Twenty-eight officers left Cairo with the Company and four of these are left.' On 25 July: 'Was interested to read about Grandpa's will in the paper. It was the first I heard about it. I seem to get a watch after Dad's death – by which token I hope it is a long time before I get it – but I was thinking that if he sent me the watch now and he took it after my death it might be a fairer arrangement under the present crisis! However, we'll hope not.' On 29 July: 'Fifty-one weeks now since we mobilized and three months since we landed here, and we seem as far away from seeing home as ever. However, I hope the powers that be will be moved to pity for the remnants of this miserable Division and send a tug boat for them . . . Life is a daily misery and there is no news . . . Afraid this letter isn't very cheery but St Peter himself would be a crank under these conditions and I'm no Job.' 4 August: 'I should like to see Rochdale again. However we must hope for the best.'

Eric Duckworth's last letter was written to his mother on 5 August, two days before he was killed. 'Little enough did I think twelve months ago today that on the anniversary of mobilization I should be writing you from a hole in the Gallipoli Peninsula, not having seen you for ten and a half months, and to the tune of 75-mm. guns. However you never know your luck, and I may see you in time to celebrate my twentieth birthday at home, though as things look at present, there's not much chance of that.'

Routine and Discipline

It is undoubtedly true that soldiers on the Peninsula, borne down by dysentery, nervous and physical debility, long periods of enervating boredom and shorter periods of intense strain, were supported by more than individual qualities and the undoubted strength of fellowship moulded out of the demanding conditions. The common denominator which did so much to keep men going was Army routine. The significant insignificance of General Routine Orders[1] illustrates that while in some matters, for example dress, there had to be flexible adaptability, in others the structure of Army life demanded regulations. Proper attention to administrative procedure, to the listing of stores and equipment and to the relationship between ranks helped to defeat sloppiness and irresponsibility and did much to provide the individual and the unit with a solid basis for ordered, purposeful, morale-sustaining activity.

It is of course easy in the light of changed circumstances today to ridicule many of the orders solemnly issued in 1915 and perhaps some of them deserve such treatment. But one is then left with still less to answer the challenging question of how the men of the M.E.F. 'stuck it' and 'stuck it' so well.

'139 Q.M.G. 11.5.15. Postal. The Postmaster General has arranged for the free delivery in all parts of the British Empire of unpaid or insufficiently paid letters from the Mediterranean Expeditionary Force.'

'179 Q.M.G. 20.5.15. Curtain Flaps for Caps. The issue of a curtain flap for caps at the rate of one per man is approved. Units will submit indents accordingly.'

'315 Q.M.G. 28.6.15. Equipment. The waist belt belonging to the web or bandolier equipment is only to be used for the purpose for which it is issued. It is not to be worn as a belt for keeping up the trousers.'

'37 Q.M.G. 10.4.15. Disposal of kits of Officers and Other Ranks who are deceased, missing, prisoners of war, sick or wounded . . . A sword if sent with kit should be so secured that it cannot fall out in transit.'

'122 A.G. 7.5.15. Salutes. With reference to Standing Orders, Section 5(h), an impression seems to be prevalent among the troops that on active service the paying of compliments is suspended and considerable

[1] M.E.F. Official Papers (P.L.).

slackness has been observed in the matter of saluting. Officers commanding units will bring this matter to the notice of their men and it must be
clearly understood that except when actually employed in active operations, any relaxation in this respect will be met by suitable disciplinary
action.'

'The following daily rates of pay are authorized:

Officer Ranking as 2nd Lt.	7/6
Honorary Chaplain	Nil
Corporal	2/–
Man	1/–'

On 4 July, Eric Wettern wrote a letter which provides a light-hearted
but fair indication of life and routine on the Peninsula. 'Our company is
at last enjoying a much needed "rest" after about two months of firing
line work. It is about time too. The rest consists in working one day in
four, on communication work etc., so it's quite worth having. It doesn't
affect me however as I am still with Smith looking after the roll books
and the letters and doing all sorts of awful jobs . . . and I really was getting
fed up with wielding the shove and pickel all the time. Asiatic Annie is
trying to give us shocks again and has plonked about eight big 'uns round
about since I started this letter . . . on a Sunday evening too!

'The last few weeks we have spent in sapping, mainly in front of our
lines. It is a funny job and you don't want to put your head out and admire
the scenery. It is apt to be exciting especially at night and if there happen
to be any Turks messing around with bombs. It is also very monotonous–
barring the bomb part of it. A Turkish gentleman came over the top of
one of our saps one dark night. He gave our chaps a bit of a shock as they
didn't know whether the rest of the Turkish Army was coming too and
wondered whether they should stay and see. One or two just tickled him
with their bayonets a bit and then it turned out that he was tired of the
Army and had strolled over to us for a bit of a rest . . .

'The scrapping now is quite different from what it was at first and I
should imagine it is now very similar to Flanders. The trenches in some
places are only a few yards apart and our firing and reserve and communication trenches are an absolute maze. There must be miles and miles
of trench now – a large proportion of which we can proudly look upon as
our work. The difficulty we were soon up against was place names. We
went as long as we could with names like the Pink Farm . . . but they are
all ruins and have a knack of gradually disappearing as people pinch the

stones to improve their dugouts – and we as the odd job merchants have
started a special stencilling and name board department and it will soon
be possible to issue a directory. We have already got Oxford St and Clap-
ham Junction and Romanos and Piccadilly Circus. You can get a drink
at Romanos but they only keep one sort and you have to bring your own
bucket and a piece of rope. Some genius has by the way labelled our
camp Walmer Castle . . .

'I am not wanting anything in the clothes line at present but could do
with the following – small tube of ink tablets for fountain pen, carbolic
soap, a few letter cards, Gibbs shaving stick. As to luxuries anything in
the grub line is always welcome, cocoa and milk powder and tablets . . .
they don't make compressed whisky cubes do they? I have lately taken
to fancy cooking as a pastime. Our official diet is meat, bread or biscuit,
bacon, tea, jam, cheese, potatoes, with occasional rum, lime juice and
onions, and we get jolly sick of it (and from it) at times. So I have rigged
up a kitchen range of my own and go in for occasional variations such as
coffee, boiled rice, toast, Welsh rarebit, and that is about the extent of my
repertoire at present. Oh, I forgot bread and milk. The coffee and rice
we swop from the French for jam and the Nestles we can occasionally
buy when anyone happens to be going to the canteen which isn't very
often as it is a long way off and a fearful wait in the queue when you get
there . . . We get an occasional Taube dropping bombs, but he can't hit
a ten acre field, and anyway he never stops very long. I wish he would
stop a minute or two longer just once. I rather fancy though that we are
up to that game about fifty times to their once.'

On the Peninsula many of the crimes which would normally be expected
to lead to courts martial simply could not be committed. Absence without
leave and drunkenness might well be ranked as achievements under
Peninsula conditions, but of course various field punishments, including
the degrading No. 1 F.P., in which the prisoner was tied spreadeagled to
a gunwheel for a predetermined period and which was soon to be discon-
tinued, did have to be served. Among the General Routine Orders there
is a record of a commutation of death sentences for cowardice on five men
from the 1st Munster Fusiliers and one from the 4th Battalion the
Worcestershire Regiment. The Orders state that 'the General Commanding, seeing how gallantly the force was advancing against the enemy, felt
convinced that he might yet spare those who had been condemned without thereby endangering the lives of their comrades'.[2] In the period

---

[2] M.E.F. Official Papers (G.R.O. 131 A.G. 9, May 1915) (S.P.A.). The charge had
been 'behaving in such a manner as to show cowardice before the enemy'.

between Christmas 1915 and the Helles evacuation S. Blythman claims that his sergeant was shot at Y Gully by a firing squad after a court-martial sentence, but research into this and similar cases is made difficult by the restrictive conditions on the appropriate War Office records.

At Vincennes documentation is available concerning the French disciplinary record on the Peninsula. The details range from the severity of certain judgements to the bizarre instance of the report by Sous-Lieutenant Castel that a certain 'Maréchal des Logis was surprised by Trooper Parra at the moment when, in full light of day, he was embracing Trooper M—.[3] This took place in mid-August, but on 10 April, even before the French troops landed, one Jean Fischer was sentenced for desertion in the face of the enemy to twenty years' detention, military degradation and – in a somewhat mystifying rubbing of salt into his wounds – ten years without leave.[4] In the previous month an Algerian soldier was sentenced to three years' imprisonment for outrageous offences against a superior officer. Between 11 and 13 December 1915 a Senegalese soldier was charged and condemned to death for leaving his post in the face of the enemy by means of self-mutilation. General Brûlard considered but rejected commutation of the death sentence, and in the previous month there was no reprieve for Tirailleur Bedary Xarka Tamboura of the 57th Colonial Regiment. Lest an unfair impression should be given of a great degree of harshness in the French force, it may be added here that the Vincennes Archives also show General Bailloud writing to the Minister of War on 15 September: 'A Senegalese soldier named Bakary has been killed and his son (15) wounded . . . could you see he is, after recovery, put in a school for the children of soldiers.' Bailloud, it seems, may have been particularly attached to his Senegalese troops and he denied vigorously the implication of a War Office inquiry in August that it might be against the racial customs of these troops to take prisoners.[5]

It is a point worthy of note that there is an almost total absence of references to field punishments on the Peninsula in the recollections of several hundred British veterans and that there is a parallel absence in Peninsula diaries. For the Western Front this is not the case, despite the fact that special punishment camps like the Bull Ring at Étaples[6] could be kept away from the front-line troops. It may well be that the Peninsula

---

[3] French Military Archives, Vincennes (T.E.O. 20 N 17).
[4] ibid. (T.E.O. 20 N 14).
[5] ibid. (T.E.O. 20 N 14).
[6] Of course the Bull Ring was also a major training camp.

imposed its own discipline, but the whole question of Army discipline is one which needs careful consideration before valid observations can be made. Without any proper statistical comparison between the disciplinary record of a unit serving on the Peninsula and then serving on the Western Front it would not be possible to put forward firmly based conclusions. In any case there are so many variable factors that such an exercise would only have limited value. Having made due allowance for this, the personal evidence cited above suggests that the geography of the Peninsula and the stubbornness of the Turk produced a situation conducive to the maintenance of discipline while uncongenial to comfortable living.

Twenty-one French troops were taken prisoner at Kum Kale and one of them, a soldier in the 6th Regiment of Mixed Colonial Infantry, Marius Gondard, has given an account of his journey into captivity and his experiences as a Turkish prisoner of war. They were first taken to Chanak before crossing the Narrows and marching to the town of Gallipoli. From there they were taken by steamer to Constantinople and then to Afion Karahissar in Asia Minor (see Map 1, pp. 14–15), where they found already installed the surviving ten members of the crew of the French submarine *Saphir*. Later they were joined by thirteen soldiers taken at Helles and Anzac, and some French Marines. Later still the full complement of the French submarines *Mariotte* and *Turquoise* were to increase the Gallic predominance over the British at Afion Karahissar, until some of the English victims of the Kut surrender in Mesopotamia arrived in the summer of 1916. In 1915 the crews of the submarines *E 15* and *AE 2* were to add to the English and Australian contingents, but the camp was in fact principally occupied by Russians.

The food was mainly chick-peas and crushed wheat with very occasional and tiny pieces of mutton. It was scarcely sufficient, but the intervention of the American Ambassador obtained some money for each of the prisoners which enabled them to augment their meagre diet. When some of the prisoners were moved to a camp at Sivas, four Frenchmen escaped and got back to France via Russia, north to Archangel and thence to England and across the Channel.

In January 1916 the ranker prisoners suffered a cruelly cold railway journey to Belemidik camp, where they worked on the construction of the railway to Baghdad. Under the direction of Greek and Swiss engineers, tunnels were to be dug through the Taurus mountains. At this camp, accommodation and supervision conditions improved and enough money was earned to buy food in the camp shops. The prisoners even had facilities to cook for themselves. Nevertheless the climate was unhealthy, and typhus and dysentery claimed many victims, especially among the Russians, despite the work of an Armenian doctor, Boyadjian, whose medical training had been at Montpellier in France.

Sports were arranged at Easter 1918 and Gondard won the long jump.

The French came first, second and third in the obstacle race, won the three-legged race, and naturally won the frog-hopping race.[1] Australian victories in the egg-and-spoon race, the hundred yards and the veterans race emphasized the English failure to secure more than the tug of war, for which single event, alas, there was no prize. However, the English tended to win the football and rugby matches, so a particularly strong Australian always used to play for the French in order to even things up.

Among the papers kept by Gondard was a sheet of camp regulations which stated that anyone who tried to escape would be treated with the utmost severity and to stop an escape attempt a sentry would be obliged to use his weapon. It is pleasant to see from another document enumerating the provisions of an agreement between France and Turkey on the repatriation of prisoners that the French were prepared to exchange two Turks for every Frenchman.

One of the 4th Battalion the Worcester Regiment, captured in front of Krithia on 6 August, was a Private L. Moore, who had been badly wounded in the attack. He was taken by bullock cart to Constantinople, and by reason of the severity of his wounds from an exploding grenade this journey proved a nightmare. He and his fellow prisoners suffered the indignity of a humiliating parade through the streets. He needed prolonged hospital treatment in the city and watched from his window the endless traffic on the Golden Horn as he slowly recovered. He later worked on a section of the Constantinople–Baghdad railway as a German engineer's servant, and this brought privileges which considerably eased the conditions of his captivity.

Another Worcester Regiment prisoner, S. F. Lawrance, said that many died through the conditions of work in the tunnel, but as he was employed as a saddler he worked in the open air and furthermore, with others, had the opportunity to steal eggs and even chickens. According to Lawrance there was no systematic brutality and in fact a reasonable relationship existed between the prisoners and those German officers and guards who had fought in the war, but not with the elderly reservists. Lawrance received parcels of tins of meat and other food from the Lord Mayor's fund in Birmingham, the regimental fund and a Mrs Digby Bell. Most parcels were shared, though Lawrance, who admired the Australians in other ways, said that they were reluctant to share and one kept his bread with him wherever he went, even to the toilet in the corner of the room.

An Australian captured by what appeared to be a ruse at Anzac during the evening of the day of the landing has written a published

[1] *Course de grenouilles.*

account of his experience. R. F. Lushington, in *A Prisoner with the Turks, 1915–18*, describes how he was on the same steamer as the twenty-one Frenchmen captured at Kum Kale and he felt the shame of captivity. He suffered from the normal and accepted practice whereby Turkish officers beat their soldiers, who promptly behaved in the same fashion towards their prisoners. They were the first allied soldiers to reach the Turkish capital, though their entry was a triumph for the Turks rather than for the invaders. They were inspected by Liman von Sanders, who added to the seemingly consistent efforts to subvert the solidarity existing between the English and the French by expatiating on the sad manner in which the French had become the dupes of the English.

They left by rail for Afion Karahissar, the sailors from *AE 2* clothed in Turkish soldier's greatcoats, fezes and Turkish slippers. Lushington's account confirms the bad conditions described by Gondard. Stone-breaking was the main activity and the men grew weaker and weaker on the starvation diet until the American Ambassador's visit brought tinned foods, blankets and clothes.

Lushington's next camp was Changri, which they reached by marches, first to Angora and on again north-westwards. The marching was very taxing and on some days began at sunrise and lasted till eight or nine in the evening, the men 'lapping up water from the hoof prints of cattle which had been standing in wet ground'.

Conditions at Changri were grim, though Lushington does mention games of rugby. A prisoner would attempt to avoid manual labour by describing his trade or profession as 'goalkeeper', 'golf caddy' or 'diver'. A train journey and a march brought them to Belemidik for the railway construction work previously mentioned, which consisted of pushing trolley-loads of stones, carrying timber or hauling it up the steep hillside. Occasionally, through weakness or by design, they allowed the logs to career down the slope out of control, to be lost in the river below. Unlike Gondard, Lushington mentions only German overseers and engineers, and there is no reference to Greek or Swiss. The Germans celebrated with gusto the news they received of Jutland, and the allied soldiers, oppressed by bad news filtering through from several fronts, did their best to counter this with lusty singing of the National Anthem.

In August 1916 Lushington and two others escaped, climbed to the summit of the mountain range and made for Adana and the sea. Their freedom lasted thirteen days. They had almost reached the sea when they were captured, having travelled on foot nearly 150 miles. A filthy, crowded civilian prison with chained murderers and bastinadoed civilian prisoners was to be their reward. Dysentery secured Lushington a merciful transfer to hospital, where he met and was horrified by the condition of emaciated, exhausted British and Indian prisoners who had marched from surrendered Kut. They were tended by an American doctor and an Arab Christian doctor, and the work of these two men saved the lives of many, though the daily death toll was heavy.

A further spell of civilian imprisonment and then rail transfer to Afion Karahissar brought him to a camp undergoing the legendary regime of the commander, Maslum Bey. Prisoners were flogged, their illnesses neglected and their parcels ransacked. Lushington's ordeal had not ended, because he was to suffer harsh contracted labour to a German civilian, the unfulfilled possibility of an exchange of prisoners of war and grim conditions at camps at Ada Bazar and San Stephano. His book reminds one that to ignore the travail of captivity for the soldier taken on the Peninsula is to provide an incomplete picture of the Gallipoli experience.[2]

[2] A most unusual account of P.O.W. experience in Turkey has recently been published: Group Captain C. W. Hill's *The Spook and the Commandant*, William Kimber, 1975.

The seaplane support from the converted carrier *Ark Royal*, which had been active since the last days of February, was in April reinforced by No. 3 Squadron R.N.A.S. under the command of C. R. Samson, who had established an aerodrome on the island of Tenedos. In the early summer, Turkish positions and troop movements were regularly harassed by bombs and bundles of flêchettes, the small metal winged darts which surviving Turks still resent, though their aircraft, the German Tauben, were using the same rather ineffectual weapon on the allied positions. Ships and even submarines were bombed and torpedo attacks were successfully made with the Short floatplanes operating from the newly arrived carrier *Ben My Chree*. The *Mitchell Report*[1] fully details the successful work of attacking Turkish communications by air. 112-lb. bombs were used to attack the vital Maritza river railway bridge at Usün Koprü in November and in the same month Ferijik railway junction and Dedeagatch railway station were more successfully damaged, hindering Turkish communications through Bulgaria.

The Turkish sea supply bases and camps and the roads were also bombed, and a Turkish War Office report describes the panic among civilian workers caused by these raids. A Turkish captain told the Mitchell inquirers: 'On one occasion he saw a bomb burst among a party of twenty soldiers, resulting in fifteen killed and one wounded.' The destruction of a flour store in Gallipoli town is certainly likely to have affected bread rations to the Turkish troops defending the Peninsula. The French paid particular attention to store dumps near Kum Kale. A Turkish major admitted that allied aeroplane attacks had necessitated the moving by night of nearly all supplies and troops towards Anzac and Helles. Bomb and flêchette attacks dispersed convoys, wrecked carts, killed camels and caused long delays.

The French regularly bombed the important Soghanli Dere rest camp on the southern shore of the Peninsula, and the white Turkish tents had to be camouflaged, but the troops were finally forced to shelter from these attacks by living in dugouts or caves in the hills, so that it became a rest camp in name only.

[1] pp. 206 ff.

Of course the work of the aeroplanes was particularly linked to reconnaissance and spotting for the naval gunfire. That this was not always
developed to good effect is recollected by Rear-Admiral Delaye, who
flew as an observer in a French Maurice Farman from the French aerodrome at Tenedos. An entry in his log book shows that in sighting an
enemy submarine on 27 May he had almost certainly spotted the *U 21*,
which, having sunk the *Triumph* on the 25th, had that very morning
secured further prey in the form of the *Majestic* at Cape Helles. His report
however did not lead to the destruction of *U 21*, as she was not re-located
after Delaye's reconnaissance. He also recollects reporting that he saw
almost no opposition facing the British landing at Suvla of 7–9 August
while on patrol over the area during those three days.[2]

Delaye has described the perfect flying conditions over the Peninsula
till the late autumn. It was possible to fly at any time of the day and every
day. His reports had quite often to be made personally to General
Bailloud, the seventy-two-year-old commander of the French force on
the departure of d'Amade. The General's Chief of Staff, Colonel
Girodon, had on one particular occasion warned him not to speak too
loudly in case he disturbed the General, who was very tired. At the
precise moment of this warning both men were startled to hear Bailloud
calling out in full voice, 'Long live love and potatoes.'

Delaye was involved in co-operation with one of the newly arrived
British monitors, the high trajectory of whose shells was to prove better
at searching out Turkish ravine-sheltered gun positions than the flatter-
trajectory normal naval gun-fire, and the captain and the French aviators
worked closely together. Delaye remembers the English captain as
always being short of supplies, including even ink for his reports.
Delaye's commiseration that his paper work would thus be reduced
brought the sad rejoinder that he always had a plentiful supply of pencils.

Though he observed the fire of the English monitor, of the *Suffren*, the
Charlemagne, the *République* and of various other ships, Delaye's plane
was on only one occasion opposed by an enemy aircraft. The Frenchman
opened fire, but no real combat took place. In fact the German Tauben,[3]
so frequently mentioned in soldiers' diaries, were never able either by
number or by individual effectiveness seriously to inconvenience the
allied troops beyond their normal hardships. The German bombs were
only of 20-lb. weight, many were duds and none caused serious damage,

[2] The same evidence is recorded in R. Bell-Davies, *Sailor in the Air*.
[3] The *Mitchell Report*, p. 513, gives the types of aircraft as Gotha, Rumpler and later
Albatros, all tractor biplanes. Taube was a generic name for German monoplanes.

though eight men were wounded and five officers killed by them during the campaign.

The French squadron (98T) under the command of Captain Cesari had established itself on 1 May on the south coast of Tenedos, with the agreement of Commander Samson. The ground was flat and did not have to be specially prepared, but official documents show that at the end of August a certain Hafouz Ibrahim had still not received any 'compensation for the loss of grain in the fields used by the French'.[4]

A report[5] shows that by the 16 May two aeroplanes were assisting artillery observation, getting orders and necessary servicing from the makeshift landing ground above W beach at Cape Helles. Two more planes were photographing the Turkish trenches opposite the French as well as patrolling Erenkeui Bay, two were on general reconnaissance and one on bombing duties. By the end of September the French had eighteen planes (Maurice Farmans) flying from Tenedos and eight pilots for them. There was a large ground staff of eighty-four, but twenty-four were detached elsewhere.

Though flying conditions and visibility were so good, there were problems for the airmen in their work. Inland there were few easily distinguishable geographical or man-made features, and the maps were insufficiently detailed and accurate. The thick scrub afforded easy concealment and the terrain at Anzac was as confusing from the air as it was from the ground, as aerial photographs amply demonstrate. The improvised Turkish anti-aircraft fire became more effective and during the campaign successfully brought down five planes, while another was brought down by machine-gun fire. As the *Mitchell Report*[6] points out, there were further difficulties: 'observers were untrained, wireless telegraphy gear was not perfect, the aeroplanes were not fitted for carrying wireless transmission and the majority of fittings required had to be made locally.' The seaplanes of the *Ark Royal* did have wireless telegraphy and though sets were later installed in the land-based planes there were serious deficiencies in their quality.

A French army signaller, Émile Malcailloz, recollects an example of the sort of thing that could go wrong with these early experiments with morse-coded messages. Unable to distinguish the messages he was supposed to be receiving because an English ship was transmitting during a period allocated to the French, he used the emergency agreed signal for

[4] French Military Archives, Vincennes (C.E.O. 20 N 27 and 28).
[5] ibid.
[6] p. 503.

'shut up' to clear the air for his message. A day or so later indignant British naval inquiries tracked down the source of a terse signal to their flagship. The unfortunate Malcailloz was summoned for questioning, but the inquiry was fully satisfied with his explanation and good will was restored.

A site was selected for the Helles aerodrome as early as 30 April, but it was always under Turkish observation and planes did not as a rule remain overnight there but flew back to Tenedos, having been based in pairs at Helles for work during the day. From 29 June, Turkish fire prevented even this use of the Helles aerodrome and landings were made only in an emergency. (A dummy aeroplane here attracted 650 shells in October.) The latest of these landings was made by Second Lieutenant F. D. H. Bremner,[7] from the squadron based at Imbros. He had arrived at Imbros particularly well prepared, with letters of introduction to distinguished Greeks written by an acquaintance of his family, who was able in truth to point out that the young Bremner was a 'friend of the Prince of Wales'. Bremner also had, but did not use, a leather wallet in a waterproof case which contained doses of Savory and Moore's chlorodyne, morphine, quinine sulphate, calomel, cocoa extract and essence of ginger. The difficulty of January flying is indicated by an entry for 3 January in his log. 'We had one or two very bad bumps in places. Quite calm at 8,000. We had to give up owing to clouds getting too bad to see the target. Very badly blown about when near the ground so pancaked the last ten feet down. Got caught in a gust which gave me a bit of leeway so landed rather heavily on the back wheel.' On 6 January Bremner wrote, 'Towards the end Archie made some very good shooting. For the first time I did not mind a bit, even when the bursts were very close.'

While spotting for H.M.S. *Earl of Peterborough* on 8 January, though his engine was stuttering badly, he flew to investigate something noticed by the observer to the north of Krithia and, on returning, their plane was 'attacked by a Hun who came up unobserved behind and slightly above me. Did not know he was there till he started firing and even then did not realize at once what it was. As soon as I did realize I attempted to turn left to bring my Lewis to bear on him and just caught a glimpse of him over my left shoulder. He then disappeared behind me and again fired a few rounds, and apparently made a big right-handed sweep and made off in the direction of Chanak. He was too fast and nippy for me to bring my gun to bear on him, and the whole thing only lasted about thirty seconds!'

[7] Log, Imperial War Museum, and P.L.

Bremner described in this letter how he had attempted to follow, but finding his engine revs had dropped realized that he had been hit and, with no hope of reaching Imbros, made for Helles aerodrome. He can scarcely have been a welcome guest, because the last stages of the evacuation were under way. The plane was pushed into a dugout but would not go right in and of course the Turks were by now shelling it. With some mechanics and using a pick, shovel and sledgehammer they smashed the plane, as he was not, for obvious reasons, allowed to burn it. He left the Peninsula from a pier at W beach aboard a lighter at 0130 on the 9th to board the second last ship to leave the bay, the armed boarding steamer *Partridge*. In his letter home on 11 January Bremner understandably had to conclude, 'That is a full account of what happened up to five o'clock. After that I cannot say what happened, you will probably understand the reason why from the papers before you get this letter,' and the letter continues with an account of the first R.N.A.S. hockey match on Imbros during that afternoon.

The British aerodrome at Tenedos had been made by Greek labour, rental being paid for the ground and compensation for the vines which had to be dug up. The large Farman biplanes were landed in packing cases and, in an operation which seems almost biblical, the cases were hauled on rollers by the labourers and sailors up the slope from the shore and along the road to the new aerodrome. On Imbros there were two aerodromes. One, near the harbour, provided such a dangerous take-off because of its proximity to cliffs and consequent air currents that a move was made to Kephalo Point, which was constructed by Turkish prisoners. This second aerodrome was appropriately known as Kephalo Marsh because it was so near to the island's Salt Lake that in wet weather it could not be used. Though there were also aerodromes on Mitylene and on Rabbit Island, the Imbros aerodromes, eleven to sixteen miles distant from the three Peninsula fronts and in immediate proximity to M.E.F. G.H.Q. on the island itself, were obviously to have considerable advantages over the others.

Of the seven types of aeroplane used by the R.N.A.S. only the Maurice Farmans and the B.E.2s were able to do useful work continuously, though the wooden packing cases in which some of the aeroplanes had been brought did provide living accommodation for the men on Tenedos, the officers living in a small house and in tents. There is no doubt that the French squadron at Tenedos was far better equipped in every way, particularly with regard to spare parts, transport, workshop machinery, hangars and trained personnel. The arrival in July of six Nieuports, two more high-powered Maurice Farmans and four Henri Farmans considerably improved the British strength, but the Maurice Farman pusher-type biplane with 80 h.p., 100 h.p. or 110 h.p. Renault engine, provided the backbone of the land-based aeroplane work in the Dardanelles.[8]

The outstanding personality in the field of aviation was undoubtedly the short, stocky, bearded and somewhat irascible Commander Samson. Bremner remembers how the Commander's fury and voice were roused and his language debased by the sight of unauthorized personnel walking on the landing strip at Kephalo. Samson's standing orders are given in the official history[9] and they do reflect the image of a man of efficiency and aggression. That sound practical common sense was another factor is also apparent. Pilots were always to be armed with a revolver or pistol, observers were always to carry a rifle. Pilots and observers were to familiarize themselves with the photos of Turkish men of war described in the *World's Fighting Ships* – 'This book is in the office' 'Don't make wild statements . . . a small accurate report is worth pages of rhetoric giving no real information. If an enemy aeroplane is sighted attack it, reporting you are doing so if spotting. Don't try to do what is termed by some people "Stunt flying". This is not wanted for war and is not conduct required of an officer.'

In his contemporary private papers[10] Samson's confidence is always evident. On 19 April, having hit a howitzer with a bomb, his notes record: 'I was very pleased with myself, especially the first gun, as it was the result of a careful sighting shot.' 25 April was a 'wonderful sight and I will never forget it', but he was far from devoid of compassion as the 'corpses on the beaches and the blood in the water were sights that made you feel rather rotten sitting up there aloft with nothing to do except spotting the ship's fire'.

His notes for 25 April make compelling reading. 'The water was simply whipped into foam by the shells and bullets . . . the *Q.E.* was putting salvo after salvo into the town . . . you could, from the air, trace the tracks of the shells passing through the houses before they burst.' Samson's fame spread. An Australian with the 10th Battalion wrote to a friend as early as 19 May: 'We have the best English and French flyers here. One named Samson the Germans have offered £6,000 [for] dead or alive.'[11]

[8]   *Mitchell Report*, p. 519.
[9]   *The Official History of the War in the Air*, vol. 2, pp. 27–8.
[10] Imperial War Museum, Papers of Air Commodore Samson (D.2, Papers concerning the *Official History of the War in the Air*, Dardanelles, pp. 12, 14).
[11] South Australian State Archives, 10th Battalion A.I.F. unofficial letters (P.R.F. 272/9).

The death in a take-off crash of an officer named Collett clearly affected him deeply. 'He was burnt to death. His loss was a terrible loss to the squadron and I lost a great friend, he was absolutely irreplaceable. Chief Petty Officer Keogh, Jones and Robins displayed remarkable bravery in attempting to save him.' The tributes he paid to his men are paralleled by his admiration for those of his planes with Renault engines, 'which always [went] splendidly'.

By 11 November No. 3 Squadron, which had averaged seven pilots, had flown 143,000 miles and dropped 205 large and 543 small bombs on the Turks. For the next month or so they would be faced by terrible cold and many more flying clothes had to be worn. Samson wrote in his notes that he wished the so-called flying organizers in England could have a taste of this.

Samson made it a rule 'whenever possible that if anybody bombed my aerodrome, we always returned the visit immediately and gave them worse than they gave us'.[12] No. 3 Squadron was imbued with a spirit of determination reflected in their achievements and it is certainly tantalizing to consider what might have happened had Samson achieved complete success in bombing a Staff car which was, as appears from later evidence, carrying Kemal. Yet another hypothesis in the alluring game of considering how nearly the Peninsula was won!

Sadly one can pass to the evidence of the log of Admiral Portal for actuality rather than potentiality. As a sub-lieutenant on *Bacchante* Admiral Portal had already served at the Anzac and Suvla landings and became an R.N.A.S. observer in January 1916, flying from Imbros. His log for that month and for February makes an unintentionally ironic comment on the futility of the Gallipoli endeavour as his reconnaissance flights over Suvla, Anzac and Helles allow him to observe the Turks taking up the long-held allied positions. 'Tried to locate gun firing from Hunter Weston Hill. Ceased fire before we arrived.'

One pilot was deservedly singled out for the award of the Victoria Cross. On a raid to destroy the railway supply route from Bulgaria at Ferijik Junction one plane was damaged and had to land in Bulgarian territory. The pilot, Flight Sub-Lieutenant Smylie, set fire to his plane but, on seeing Lieutenant Davies preparing to land beside the burning plane, exploded the bomb still on his plane with pistol fire in order that it should not damage the plane preparing to land. Davies, though surprised by the explosion, landed nevertheless and as Bulgarian troops approached, Smylie was squeezed under the engine cowl to 'crouch on all fours be-

[12] C. R. Samson, *Fights and Flights*, p. 229.

tween the rudder bar and the engine bearers with his head bumping on the oil tank'.[13] Davies took off successfully and the two men arrived safely in Imbros. In his contemporary notes for 19 November Commander Samson wrote: 'one of the very finest feats of aeroplane warfare was carried out today by Davies . . . Davies already has the D.S.O. which he has earned twenty times over since. He should get the V.C. for this. We all think he deserves it.'[14]

Bell-Davies writes engagingly in his memoirs of his time in the Dardanelles,[15] when 'by a terrific fluke I landed a 100-lb. bomb right on the [German] hangar. The French squadron was just behind me and saw the bomb burst, so my reputation as a bomb-aimer soared with them.' He described the yellow fog through which on occasion landings had to be made at Cape Helles when the prevailing north-east winds blew the dust off the dried Peninsula. 'At the landing ground one had to turn without being blown over and taxi hastily downwind to the spot behind the mound before the Turkish shells arrived.' At the time of the Suvla landing he was told by the Flag Commander, Alexander Ramsey, that 'your rotten old aeroplanes will be no bloody good anyway,'[16] but his reconnaissance over Suvla, like Delaye's, showed the absence of strong opposition in the first days of the new landing. His memoirs include a description of creature comforts at Imbros – an aeroplane packing case divided into three rooms. 'The two end rooms we fitted with bunks and used as sleeping cabins; doors connected with the middle room which we used as a sitting room. Wash basins were made out of petrol cans fitted on hinged brackets which shot the dirty water outside. Windows were made from the glass of old photographic plates. We improved the oil-drum stove by building a proper fireplace in our sitting room with fire blocks and fire clay looted or rather salved from the old colliers which had been sunk to form a breakwater for the small-craft anchorage in Kephalo Bay. For fire bars we used tappet rods from wrecked gnome engines. In fact we were as well housed as possible to face a Gallipoli winter.'

The work of the men operating and observing from the kite balloons moored from the *Manica* and the *Hector*[17] must not be neglected. The

[13] R. Bell-Davies, *Sailor in the Air*, p. 135.

[14] Imperial War Museum, Papers of Air Commodore Samson (D.2, Papers concerning the *Official History of the War in the Air*, The Dardanelles Attack on Maritza Bridge, p. 15).

[15] p. 122.

[16] ibid., p. 127.

[17] *Hector* arrived at the Peninsula in July.

Manica had previously been involved in manure-carrying in the Manchester Ship Canal,[18] but quickly achieved distinction in spotting for the successful sinking by the *Queen Elizabeth* on 26 April of a Turkish transport seven miles from the British battleship. The only trained observer in the kite balloon section was Squadron Commander J. D. Mackworth, but, as kite balloons could stay up all day, the observer was in constant telephone communication and a target once sighted could be continually observed, the advantages for naval gunfire of this form of observation over aeroplanes was considerable. There were of course also disadvantages – the balloon could not be used on windy days, reached no great height and was vulnerable to air attack – and indeed submarine attack, because it could be operated only from a specially fitted and slow-moving ship. An official report pointed out a potentially disastrous problem for the *Manica*: 'A large shell bursting near the full gas tubes below decks showed that it was running an unnecessary risk of total destruction to the ship to keep them on board, and the gas-making and compressing plant was transferred to the tug *Rescue*.'

A submarine scout airship was also operated, first from Mudros and later from Imbros. It was at Imbros that the slow seaplane carrier *Ark Royal*, with its hangar for ten planes, had to be based from the time of the submarine scare rather than at its original base of operations, Tenedos. The diary of Flight Lieutenant G. R. Bromet chronicles both the tribulations and the less frequent but hard-earned achievements of the *Ark Royal*'s seaplanes and aeroplanes. On 17 February, the day the *Ark Royal* arrived at Tenedos, Bromet's seaplane was the only one of three to carry out a wireless trial patrol successfully. He reached 3,500 feet in twenty-six minutes and a maximum height of 4,500 feet. 'Before returning to base we dropped two bombs – one at Kum Kalessi which found its mark and one at Seddel Bahr which fell short. The enemy opened fire on us with field guns, rifles and machine-guns, but only managed to hit us seven times . . . The flight lasted for 1 hour 15 minutes.'

On 19 February he was spotting for H.M.S. *Cornwallis*, but the ship had ceased firing by the time he had reached the necessary ceiling. In a later patrol on the same day lack of fuel forced him down before he could spot for the *Inflexible*. When all the ships were ordered to fire at the same time, spotting was impossible. In recording his admiration for the 'plucky and wise' manner in which the Turkish gunners in the forts reserved their fire until the ships were within range, Bromet 'nevertheless considered that had our seaplanes been given the opportunity of control-

18 *The Official History of the War in the Air*, vol. 2, p. 33.

ling the gunfire of each individual ship it is quite certain that by 5 p.m. the Turks would have had no guns left'.

When the naval shelling was resumed on the 25th the sea was too rough for the seaplanes to take off, though Captain Kilner in Seaplane 136 did succeed in making a useful reconnaissance on the following day. Great care was needed in the handling of the seaplanes, as 'new machines and spares would take six weeks to arrive from England'. On 4 March an inlet valve rocker broke and pierced the propeller and the port float. Unable to climb higher than 2,000 feet and getting too close to Turkish troops at Yeni Shehr, Seaplane 172 came under small-arms fire and 'collected twenty-eight bullet holes, which served the silly old bitch right for refusing to climb to a safe height'.

The following day, 27 February, Bromet records that Seaplane 808 had spiralled and nose-dived into the sea. Astonishingly both the pilot, Flight Lieutenant Garnet, and the observer, Flight Commander Williamson, were rescued, Garnet holding the injured Williamson's head above water until the destroyer *Usk* arrived. In Seaplane 922, which took off immediately afterwards, Flight Lieutenant Douglas was shot in the calf and had to land, but a later flight, using searchlight communication from the *Ark Royal* and reply by wireless, successfully spotted for the *Queen Elizabeth*.

Bromet was very conscious of his dependence on the efforts of his mechanics: 'C.P.O. Finbow worked solidly on a difficult and annoying job for sixteen hours and I cannot praise him or Air Mechanic Somner too highly for their painstaking and successful work and for their cheery optimism throughout.'

The resentment felt by the seaplane pilots at the restrictions placed on their work and the consequent underestimation of their potential is revealed in numerous entries in Bromet's diary. 'The great interest taken by the Air Department in land machines is all very well but some of us would like to see a more intelligent interest taken in seaplanes.' In September, not long before he left the Dardanelles, he made the point more strongly: 'People laugh at seaplanes and ask what use are they. Why? Because they have only experienced and been able to compare the work done by *Ark Royal* (whose hard work had to be carried out with seven seaplanes of an inferior quality and with no spares) and Cmdr Samson's squadron (whose aerodrome we built and had ready when he arrived) of ten or more land machines supplemented by new ones when necessary. I allow that as things have worked out aeroplanes can do the Peninsular work better than we can, but one must not forget that the naval front extends from Enos right down to Smyrna and that had the campaign gone as it was expected to go aeroplanes would have been of little use owing to the necessarily rapid changes of aerodrome.'

As he was leaving the Peninsula in the first week of October, Bromet wrote that he had thoroughly enjoyed his eight months in the Aegean, but 'of course we only see the fun of war. The disgusting realities of the trenches do not touch us, although I have smelt them even in the air at 3 or 4,000 feet and seen the red fringe along the Helles shore.' It should perhaps be mentioned that Bromet had not always been so removed from close contact with danger. On 28 March the *Ark Royal* had been bombed by a German biplane, and Bromet confided to his diary that 'it is most disconcerting to have bombs dropped on one . . . I think one feels absolutely helpless when being attacked from above; I certainly did today after seeing the first bomb drop and when the second one exploded about twenty feet away from me I began to wonder where one might take shelter in the case of a future attack.' Fortunately for Bromet and the *Ark Royal* there was a general truth in a rhyme the seaplane pilot was to record during the campaign:

There's a game that some play for the whole of the day
Of dropping a bomb from the air,
And men grin with delight if they drop it aright,
A contingency only too rare.

For a final recollection of the *Ark Royal* we shall turn to Squadron Leader Teasdale, in 1915 a chief mechanic on board the carrier. He remembers that motor-boats had on occasion to traverse the chosen sea track to roughen it sufficiently for seaplane take-off. He also remembers seeing from the *Ark Royal*, at the time when the ship was based at Imbros, red-tabbed Staff officers commuting each morning and evening to and from the Peninsula armed for war with their briefcases.

A faster carrier, the *Ben My Chree*, arrived at the Dardanelles on 12 July after conversion from use as a Liverpool–Isle of Man passenger ferry. Unlike the *Ark Royal*, which had steam-driven hoists to winch the planes from their hangar in the hold, the *Ben My Chree* had an upper-deck hangar aft, with a good testing and repair workshop. On 12 August, Flight Commander C. H. K. Edmonds, in a Short seaplane from the carrier, scored a perfect torpedo hit on a large Turkish transport lying off Bulair, where the ship had already been damaged, probably by *E 14*. Though the ship was in water too shallow for sinking, Edmond's torpedo success, from only fifteen feet above sea level, was the first of its kind in the war. In his flight report Edmonds writes that, as he looked backwards, 'I observed the track of the torpedo, which struck the ship abreast the mainmast, the starboard side. The explosion sent a column of water and large fragments of the ship almost as high as the masthead . . . she appeared to have settled down a little by the stern when I ceased watching her.'[19] The official history[20] considers that the *Ben My Chree* was particularly valuable as a mobile self-contained air unit, but not the least of its achievements was one which could not have been anticipated, for the carrier rescued 694 troops and 121 crew from the torpedoed *Southland* thirty miles from Mudros on 2 September.

It is perhaps appropriate that a final incident concerning the war in the air should concern Commander Samson. His log for 6 August records that he was engaged in dropping propaganda pamphlets. Squadron Leader Teasdale has remarked that it was generally known in the *Ark Royal* and on the island of Imbros that Samson was so disgusted at having to fulfil this function that he dropped bombs on the soldiers picking up the leaflets. This curious recollection cannot be substantiated but, if it is true, the limited value of propaganda material in influencing morale must have been still more limited on that particular occasion.[21]

[19] *The Royal Naval Air Service 1914–18*, ed. S. W. Roskill, p. 222.
[20] *The Official History of the War in the Air*, vol. 2, p. 56.
[21] For the mismanagement of the seaplanes attached to the *Ark Royal*, see A. J. Marder, *From the Dardanelles to Oran*, pp. 7–11. Marder uses the unpublished memoirs of Group Captain H. A. Williamson, Second-in-Command and Senior Flying Officer in the *Ark Royal*. These papers are held in Churchill College, Cambridge.

20. Autumn Stagnation and the Onset of Winter

From September, at Anzac in particular, the character of the fighting and other activities changed. With an increasing readiness to live and let live above ground, the opposing forces dug deeply underground, defensively for dugouts and communication tunnels, offensively for mining activity.

Concerning Helles there is intriguing evidence in the diary and memory of Eric Wettern of an isolated tree with flags on it denoting an exceptionally quiet sector on the right, once held by the French and later by the R.N.D. At Anzac, where the trenches were in closer proximity, messages, cigarettes, jam, and the less popular bully beef were exchanged simply by lobbing them across the narrow no-man's land. To a very large extent the attitude towards the Turk had changed too. The letter dated 13 September of the wounded Colonel Brown in which he expressed admiration of the Turk who 'is a very fine soldier indeed and any one who thinks otherwise can be convinced by going out to Gallipoli for a week' is paralleled by many letters and diaries.

As the fighting slackened in intensity, health and living conditions naturally dominated all other impressions. On 20 September Padre McKenzie wrote that he was infuriated that parcels and clothing were lost to the 'thousands of thieves among the orderlies and soldiers who steal the parcels and help themselves'. Much more serious was the general condition of the troops, and in particular those at Anzac. A table of Gallipoli casualties and statistics in the official medical history shows that, while 47,803 British and Commonwealth troops were admitted into hospital with wounds, 128,708 were admitted as 'sick'.[1] Of the latter, nearly 50,000 were cases of dysentery, diarrhoea and enteric fever. Dysentery and related illnesses had become a very serious problem in July and conditions after the August battles were ideal for the spreading of the disease. At Helles, Anzac and Suvla men dragged themselves pathetically to the latrines and, with normal hygienic facilities inadequate, the problem increased daily. 'Passing slime and blood'[2] is a pathetic entry typical of diaries from all three fronts. J. G. Gasparich felt that 'my whole alimentary tract was on fire and was periodically being torn

[1] p. 203.
[2] A. S. Hutton, diary, 28 August 1915. South Australian State Library (D 4975).

from me. I was sent over to Imbros and housed in a great marquee with dozens of others in like state. We slept on the ground and were fed stew and tea which only made matters worse. We were forced by the sickness to visit the latrines every hour or so, each visit being made in agony. Some men were so weak that they crawled to the latrines and stayed there until they died. In the hospital ship to Alexandria the lavatory arrangements were totally inadequate and there were long queues of men in agony waiting at the crowded toilets. The Mohammedan-style squatting-toilets in a Cairo hospital adapted from an army barracks provided the final refinement to our torture.'

The New Zealander Captain T. R. Ritchie,[3] in his evidence to the Dardanelles Commission, affirmed that the saltiness and stringiness of the Fray Bentos corned beef, the insufficiency of condensed milk, the lack of arrowroot, the inadequate purification of the water and the absence of castor oil had all helped to further the disease, but, even more than the insanitary latrines, the fly menace was the greatest evil. 'We had the ordinary open latrines. The space in Monash Gully which was not under fire was very limited and it was very difficult getting sites for latrines. What I wanted to introduce was the pan system. We introduced it at Headquarters itself and it worked very well but we could not get the pans – in one case Capt. Home of the Wellington Bn fixed up latrines with a box cover over them so that no flies could get in.'

The experience of using the primitive latrines is recalled by F. C. Sillar, who contracted dysentery when in the front line at Helles early in November. 'I was compelled to go every ten minutes from my duty post to the latrine, which was formed in a short side trench leading back from the line. Here there were three buckets covered by wooden box lids with extremely sharp edges. Just behind this latrine we had a trench mortar firing about every two minutes. The Turkish equivalent kept firing to find and destroy our mortar. Shells were falling all around and some in the latrine space itself.' Sillar must have visited his scarcely peaceful haven many times during his four-day stint in the line. Incidentally the many photographs of troops bathing at W beach do not always show the large wooden structure built out from the cliffs into the sea. This structure was one answer to the problem of waste disposal, as it enabled the troops to perform their natural functions directly into the sea.

During the week ending 5 September, 7.5 per cent of the troops at Anzac were evacuated sick, while only 1.7 per cent of those at Suvla had fallen victim and 5.1 per cent of those at Helles. While these figures

[3] Alexander Turnbull Library, Wellington (Misc. M.S. 1428).

do provide an ironic comment on the much abused physique and general fitness of the New Army at Suvla,[4] it must be conceded that the geography of Anzac imposed special problems concerning the nature of the fighting there and the living conditions, both of which would directly influence the health of body and mind. Some of the Anzac troops were given a much needed rest at Lemnos, but those who remained, together with the replacements, were now heavily committed to digging deep dugouts against winter conditions and the anticipated increased supplies of enemy ammunition. The supplies came from the German-directed Turkish armament factories, as well as from the Central Powers through Bulgaria to Turkey once the full effect of Bulgaria's entry into the war on 6 September was felt.

In the absence of any heavy fighting, Anzac was a hive of activity in September and October. The work force building roads, piers and jetties on the beaches was augmented by Maltese and Egyptian labour and experiments were being carried out, unsuccessfully, with a small-gauge railway. In the front-line areas more sophisticated trench periscopes, telescopic-sighted rifles, silencers, catapults and individual stalking[5] in no-man's land were the rule. One refinement used on all three Gallipoli sectors was the steel plate firmly wedged into a section of a parapet. A spring-clipped shutter covered the observation and firing aperture for sniping at the opposition. An Australian War Memorial photograph of the surface of one such plate, pitted by bullet marks after a very short period of service, indicates both the need for such defence and the nerve needed to look and fire through the central spy hole.[6] A network of deep intercommunicating dugouts, as well as mine tunnels, was being moled underground. This mining was difficult and dangerous work. In the shortage of candles, slush lamps, consisting of a wick in oil or fat, gave out their dim light in the hot, shadowed, dusty galleries in which perspiring lamp-blacked faces paused anxiously in their own digging to listen for any sound of similar Turkish activity. When such sounds were identified, the danger signal was silence, denoting the enemy's readiness to fire his explosive charge. When one side broke into the other's tunnel, hastily erected sandbag barricades provided a cover to prepare charges to blow up the enemy tunnel while sentries fired into the blackness

---

[4] Of course some of the new British troops were at Anzac.

[5] *Official History of Australia in the War of 1914–18*, vol. 2, p. 812.

[6] Hypnosis was used successfully to cure the shell shock affecting a young Australian after narrow escapes while working from one of these bullet-proof shields. See W. Moore, *The Thin Yellow Line*, p. 97.

beyond the barrier. There was extensive mining activity at Helles too and both Joe Murray's *Gallipoli As I Saw It* and the Australian official history provide details of the danger of this work. The Australian A. L. Rutter retains today the speech impediment produced by the explosion in one mining tunnel in which he was working, and several documents testify to the heroism of those men who braved the poisonous fumes in the tunnels to rescue comrades who were overpowered by these gases.

Leading from a position known as the 'Western Birdcage' on the extreme left of the Helles front line was a tunnel which burrowed its way beneath no-man's land towards the Turkish front line. The 7th Manchesters had been busily engaged in clearing the spoil from the tunnel. The prone soldier dragged it towards him in a half-filled sandbag, eased it past his body and pushed it backwards towards the next man. It was hot, tiring work. Funnel-shaped air chimneys brought some light on to the work and by this illumination, aided by a candle, F. T. K. Woodworth used to read the *Strand Magazine* in periods of inactivity during a two-hour stint. When this particular tunnel was found and 'blown' by the Turks, twenty-eight men were killed.

The imagery of an ordinary soldier at one such scene is recalled by Ivor Birtwistle. As the bodies of sappers and those who had attempted a rescue were laid side by side just below where Birtwistle was sitting, the evening sun neared the sea beyond them, colouring the whole scene with gold, scarlet, pink and mauve. Across the purple sea lay the still darker island masses of Imbros and Samothrace. A man nudged him and said, looking towards the heart of the sunset, 'It looks as if those chaps had rushed into heaven in a hurry and had forgotten to shut the door.'

Except for a few tear-gas grenades at Anzac, gas was one refinement of war not used on the Peninsula, despite the wise precaution of issuing many troops with primitive gas helmets or hoods. Some units had to wear them for training periods and photographs of these exercises testify to the awareness of the danger of a surprise gas attack.

A temporary but unprofitable diversion was provided for troops of both sides by the target of migratory flights of geese, ducks and swallows, but on all three fronts the autumn was a period of relative quiescence, except underground. Raymond Weil, at Helles suffering from fever despite doses of quinine, confided in his diary for 29 September that it would suit him quite well if he was evacuated straight to France. Many of the French troops were in fact evacuated at the beginning of October and sent to assist the Serbians. In the same month the 10th Irish Division was sent from Suvla to Salonika. The French troops remaining at Helles included the Senegalese, the Colonials and the artillerymen.

At Helles on 1 October the R.N.D. Engineers Signal Company's trench magazine *Fag Ends* inquired, 'How long are we likely to occupy our new dugouts?' and 'Whether the Post Office will allow Xmas puddings to be sent to the Dardanelles at a reduced rate?' In the absence of intensive military activity such questions, jocular or more serious, became a preoccupation. Though the R.N.D. Engineers had constructional work to do, Eric Wettern's diary for September and October records days off, walks to the French lines, a concert in a dressing station, canteen committee meetings, a raffle, taking photos, and an occasional 'shrapnel for lunch'.

During the quieter periods it was natural that the soldier became particularly aware of the distance which separated him from family and friends at home. It was not merely by the receipt of letters that this distance could be diminished, it was in the writing of letters that the terraced house or the isolated farmstead could be brought closer. The letters of a Tasmanian artilleryman, Sergeant Alf Clennett, illustrate this point. Full of tenderly expressed understanding of the strain upon his mother, who had three boys serving on the Peninsula, Clennett unconsciously paints with imaginative insight the continuation of every-day life in an island still affectionately known today as 'Tassy' and mentioned in all the sergeant's letters. He expresses surprise and pleasure at the sale for a good price of 'Beauty', a horse 'getting well on towards her allotted span'. He feels regret that his ninety-year-old grandfather could not deliver his normal supply of fresh eggs to the grandsons on the Peninsula and also that his old grandfather's fence is not available for firewood. To his sister he writes to say how much he would like to be badgering them in the kitchen when they are making cakes and scones:

'Isn't it splendid the way the people shelled out on Australia Day? It is rather wonderful how they keep it up when times are so bad, but what a long way behind Launceston is. The Hobart people will crow about their victory this time, won't they? I notice South beat North at football too, another bang in the eye ... I am glad Guy had done pretty well with the apples and sheep and cattle. I suppose he will be spraying again before this reaches you and I wouldn't mind giving him a hand again if this scrap was over ... Thanks very much for sending us the violets, it is nice to see a flower again. I suppose the flowers are all out at home, how different to things here ... the photo of our [dogs] is very nice too. It is nice to see them all again. Monty evidently wanted to wag his tail at me . . . I suppose you had quite a lively time with the Archdeacon when he was down. I can just imagine I can hear his grand old laugh.'

For Sergeant Clennett, briefly visiting the rest camp at Mudros, the enjoyment of visiting some of the large naval vessels moored in the harbour would have been gladly exchanged for 'a trip round the old bay at home'. These letters, though laden to an unusual degree with wistful homesickness, are typical of many sent from the Peninsula at this period – seldom written in a manner to betray low morale but bearing a consistently recurring theme: 'How different things must look at home from this desolate place.' As early as 22 May, Merseysider Tom Sye was confiding in his diary: 'I have been indulging in a few daydreams . . . always my solace is in future anticipations – of days to come when, decently dressed, I shall again enjoy the luxuries of congenial companions and good food served up daintily. Again at times I derive joy from looking back. Little vignettes present themselves to my mind's eye – Betws-y-Coed, peaceful and beautiful; Douglas with its Port Jack and its wonderful summer days; Blackpool with its lights and thousand joys . . . little memories of nights of stars and gladness, of a room lit only by the flickering firelight and the shadows dancing over the walls where we two have sat and talked and dreamed the nights away.'

In the autumn and winter men newly arriving on the Peninsula, like J. M. L. Bogle, were struck by the lack of activity compared with the heroic deeds of which they had read: 'Our men seem to do so much less shooting than the Turks and . . . seem dog tired and worn out.' Within a day of his arrival at Helles, Bombardier Brown, who had served in France, was to write: 'Am posted to 66th Brigade H.Q. Staff and everything seems alright, in fact I could not have done better. Food simply grand, much better than we ever got in France and not half so much work to do.'

At Suvla, one of the day's sights was a horseman or a motor-bike rider running the gauntlet of the desultory shelling which threatened his route to Anzac and back with dispatches. With water supplies now properly provided and deeper entrenchments in use, life was less dangerous, but now boredom and a sense of purposelessness for the healthy were an erosion to morale, though not of course to such a dangerous degree as the effects of dysentery. J. C. Dart's diary entry for 3 September is a fair reflection of a general picture. 'Feeling fed up. Had a wash in a biscuit tin. Felt much refreshed. No mail, no tobacco. Sand blowing all over the place. Consequently we are all feeling down in the mouth.' When Newfoundland troops were landed as reinforcements at Suvla Bay their enthusiasm led them to scramble for the shrapnel balls or hot fragments of shell which had exploded over their heads. However, the problem of digging temporary dugouts in the fine, powdery sand near the beach soon took the edge off their keenness.

In fact the Peninsula held for its prisoners one last terrible trial, made no less severe by an awareness that it would have to be faced. So concerned were the War Office and the M.E.F. H.Q. about the problems of a harsh winter that an official meteorologist had been appointed. Neither he nor other experts accurately predicted the earliness of the winter storm, and its intensity found the troops completely unprepared. The prescient Lieutenant Carrington had written home on 15 August for warm woollen clothing, a balaclava cap and an oilskin sou'wester. On 7 September he noted that the weather was getting chilly and 'such things as bronchitis and tonsilitis are flying around'. He concluded with a statement the ironic significance of which he could not of course appreciate: 'Most people will go away during the winter for some reason or another so don't get alarmed.'

In early October storms damaged landing stages and small craft and at the end of the month the landing facilities at each sector suffered again. Some of the winter stores and protective clothing had not yet arrived and one consignment had been returned in error to Mudros. There were further gales in November and then, from the early evening of 26 November, the Suvla Sector War Diary of the 86th Brigade, 29th Division,[7] illustrates the terrible experience which was to befall those at Suvla and to some extent those at Anzac.

'1900. Very severe thunderstorm with very strong gale and torrents of rain.

'2000. All telephone communication was cut off and all dugouts flooded out.

'2100. Reported to Bde H.Q.s that all trenches were flooded, water had come in as though it had been a tidal wave, that many men must have been drowned, and few had been able to save their rifles and equipment. The men were standing up to their knees in water, behind the parados of the trenches.'

Next morning, under great difficulty, some rations were brought up for the men. They huddled together to try to get warm. 'A great deal of shrapnel was fired during the day, chiefly at parties of men who were

[7] P.R.O. W.O. 95 4310 XK 976.

given permission to leave the trenches, all in various states of exhaustion, to go to the ambulances. It was not expected that many of these men reached their destination and it is feared that a great number of men died from exposure.' Towards evening the weather got worse, developing into a snow blizzard with intense cold, and men were still struggling down to the ambulances in large numbers. The condition of the men still in the trenches grew worse as the blizzard continued throughout the night of the 27th–28th. The following day it remained intensely cold. On the 30th it is recorded that 'a number of trench boots were received. These are to prevent the men from getting frozen feet.'

The storm, blizzard and frost were to result in 280 deaths and 16,000 cases of frostbite and exposure. At Helles, even allowing for Eric Wettern's gift for understatement, the conditions were not too harsh. 'The Pig Sty [his dugout] let a few drops of water in but nothing much. Pretty cool alone in Pig Sty. Anxious moments but no serious trouble.' At Anzac the deep, well-constructed dugouts provided some protection and the lie of the land carried the water quickly down to the sea. Many Australians were seeing snow for the first time and were only prevented from admiring the white mantled beauty of the scene by the intense cold. Some, like N. Craven, made ice cream out of snow and condensed milk and there was even some snowballing. J. G. Gasparich shed his soaked greatcoat and remembers that it stood as a frozen, empty, stiff-standing sentinel for several days. Colonel Holmes remembers how the snow enabled better sighting of slight glimpses of Turks in their trenches or of their shadows, but for the Indian troops and for those moving on lower ground at Anzac the miseries of Suvla were shared.

Sapper Clifton of the 1st Field Company, New Zealand Engineers, tells in a letter[8] of having to go down from Rhododendron Ridge to collect fifteen mules and then lead them to Hill 60. It was pitch dark and bitterly cold, and the wind was blowing, so that the night was to become an experience that he would never forget. On the beach everything was in confusion and everywhere there was deep slush. The necessary ropes were almost frozen and gear had to be loaded and roped in the dark. Soon the party got split up. Carrying full packs, extra blankets and sheets, and rifles, they stumbled along in the dark. One man never arrived at his destination and frozen stragglers staggered in to fight for a place in the crowd of men around a small brazier.

'Turks walk about on top of trenches. Very few shots exchanged. Rain and snow at night. Men in awful state, some dying from exposure.' This

[8] Alexander Turnbull Library, Wellington.

diary entry by Nobby Clark outlines the conditions at Suvla on the 27th.

It is not accurate to say that there was no firing, as Turks and British stamped about outside their trenches trying to avoid the flood and generate some warmth, but certainly there was very little and in certain sectors none at all. 'The Turks apparently fared even worse than we did and were so cold that they got out of their trenches and walked about to keep warm, whereupon we shot as many as possible, poor devils,' records Second Lieutenant Savory. His 14th Sikhs had not been so badly affected by the state of affairs as had the Gurkhas, but the Indian troops were totally unaccustomed to such conditions. The history of the 10th Princess Mary's Own Gurkha Rifles[9] relates that the 2nd Battalion had 447 cases of frostbite. 'All these had to be evacuated, ten of the other ranks died and most of the others had to be invalided out of the service, many of them maimed for life.'

Down in the Suvla plain the flood had raced along the deres and into the trench system as a raging torrent carrying corpses of men and mules and every imaginable article of equipment. The famous Highland Barricade was swept away by the Azmak Dere, but by great good fortune a Scottish corporal of the Fife and Forfar Yeomanry, A. G. Brown, while surveying the flood, was sufficiently quick to grasp a floating box which proved to be from Fortnum and Mason. The contents included spirits, which helped his small party to keep alive. His blond-moustached sergeant had however been sniped through the head when he had got out of the trench and his face stared up at them from its tomb of frozen flood water for several days as they were forced to walk along the ice in the trench.

Charles Mackintosh was in the front-line trenches at Suvla just behind an advanced post known as Warwick Castle. His experience may be taken as illustrative of the suffering of many. He and his men were flooded out of their trenches when the torrent raced through, but they had managed to salvage some blankets and when the flood waters subsided below the firestep they clambered back in and endeavoured to keep warm. In the morning he saw a fellow officer in trenches full of water, shot as he clambered on top to consider where a drainage channel should be dug. Soon after this, cries for help came from the communication trench winding towards Warwick Castle. The trench was blocked with mud where it entered the main front-line trench so that the only way to help

---

[9] *Bugle and Kukri*, p. 108. An interesting comparison and contrast is contained in the *History of the 5th Royal Gurkha Rifles*, p. 268.

the unseen sufferer was over the top of the trench in full exposure to the Turks. 'I got out of the trench feeling as if the guns of the entire Turkish Army were turned on me and slithered over to where the head and shoulders of a man were showing over the mud in the communication trench.' Mackintosh, finding every effort to tug the man clear prove futile, had finally managed to get him out by dragging soaking sandbags to dump into piles in front and behind him, so that by standing on them directly above him he finally pulled him clear. Utterly exhausted and unable to face the dixie of rice which he was offered, as it clearly contained some of the remains of one of the men who had been killed in bringing it forward, Mackintosh now had to face the increasing cold which succeeded the storm.

He shared a dugout with a fellow officer who rocked and moaned throughout the night and in the morning the blizzard drowned almost every other sound, forcing snow down the throat of any mouth attempting to shout. One of his unfortunate companions appeared to be trying to sing, arousing Mackintosh's admiration. The singing seemed to change to snoring and then silence. When a corporal stretched across his officer to lift and force the body of the silent singer over the parapet, Mackintosh's protest was that of a man already losing full consciousness. He had taken off his boots so that he could wrap his puttees round his swollen feet and, finding that he could not walk, had crawled on his hands and knees towards a fire which was surrounded by Worcester Regiment officers. They gave him blackcurrant tea. He was carried down to the beach and after a further day there spent listening to the pained protests of a badly wounded man, every time a warship sent salvoes over their heads, he was stretchered off the Peninsula. As one of the serious frostbite cases, his Gallipoli service was now over. It was December and the final drama was approaching. Out of the suffering at Anzac and Suvla with all the attendant disorganization, it seems scarcely credible that within eighteen days every soldier would have been safely evacuated in an operation which compels admiration at every stage of planning and every level of execution.

Though the full Cabinet did not finally authorize the evacuation of
Anzac and Suvla until a meeting on 7 December, detailed planning had
begun on 22 November. On the Peninsula, rumours had for some time
bruited the likelihood of such a move. For many the November storm
seemed to make the evacuation more necessary and yet more difficult. At
Anzac in particular it was obvious to the ordinary soldiers that if the
Turks attacked while the withdrawal was taking place and succeeded in
commanding the heights above the beaches, serious losses would be
suffered. This must have been an important element in the meticulous adherence to the elaborate deception plans carried out during
December.

Some general impressions of the plan's execution do stand out from
the wealth of contemporary and recollected evidence. On the one hand
there was a general consciousness that the troops and their leaders had
shot their bolt, that their continued presence and suffering were to no
obvious purpose; on the other hand there was an unwillingness to accept
defeat. Dead comrades were being left behind with the 'affair' not
successfully accomplished. The soldier was not prepared to concede that
he had been defeated: outweighed by the combined forces of geography
and climate and well matched by the Turks, but not defeated, not
thrown off the Peninsula, would be an accurate summary of his attitude
judging from the evidence of letters, diaries and recollections. At the
same time he was conscious that to leave the field before the end of a
match constituted defeat and, while most would be content to leave the
varied privations of the Peninsula far behind them, the implication of
evacuation was a bitter pill. Naturally the increased activity, its unusual
nature combined with heightened tension and a sense of purpose, did
something to disguise the taste.

With the centre of the Turkish line at Anzac, that is the Nek, only 800
yards from North or Ocean Beach and within three hundred yards of
direct observation of the beach, the soldier least aware of anything other
than his immediate needs can scarcely have been ignorant of the difficulty
of getting off the Peninsula without a battle to hold the beach. Such a
battle would clearly be fought at an overwhelming disadvantage, and to

slip away silently from a position less than ten yards from Turks, whose conversation could be heard, seemed unrealistically optimistic.

The sick were evacuated first and then most of the field ambulance men; gunners went with their guns. This whittling down of the Anzac garrison, intended to appear as preparation for a reduced winter establishment, was done at night. The actual sequence of events at Anzac as they were noticed by the ranks could scarcely be better described than in the diary of New Zealander C. J. Walsh, though some of the detailed activities, like the making of dummy soldiers remembered by J. F. Rudd or the better-known water-operated rifles in the thinly held front line on the last night, find no mention.

'Thursday, 9 December 1915: Nothing of any interest going on. All companies on usual fatigues sapping, tunnelling etc. and making H.E. shelters. We used to call them funk holes but H.Q. objected and wanted them called H.E. shelters. Friday, 10 December 1915: All the morning the *Endymion*, *Doris* and *Bacchante* and a couple of monitors were pounding shell in as hard as they could go somewhere near Lone Pine. [This was because of the allied fear of what the Turkish batteries might do to the embarkation piers.] Saturday, 11 December 1915: Got first butter issue since leaving Egypt. Drew canteen stores. Very funny. Cigarette issue. Plenty of rumours floating round. Some of the artillery shipped away somewhere. Seems to be something doing. No more stores to be landed. A lot being sent away. All the sick sent away. Sunday, 12 December 1915: General rumours that we are going to evacuate all positions here. No outgoing mail allowed.

'Monday, 13 December 1915: Very heavy bombardment by both enemy and our side this morning. According to the latest "latrine" the allies are all going to quit and go home. 10th Light Horse, Otago Battalion and Field Ambulance all going away tonight. Auckland Battalion taken over 220 more yards of trench. Paul and I put in another phone this afternoon. It certainly looks as though we are going to evacuate. No more reinforcements or returned sick are to join up here. I'd like to know something. Lot of artillery, Gurkhas, Sikhs and Australians got away late. Tuesday, 14 December 1915: Heard that good things were to be had on the beach, got loaded up with jam and cheese and also a bag of cabbage and onions. Everything points to a complete evacuation. Railway being torn up. From our bivvy we can see about ten transports near Williams' Pier at 8.30 p.m. All lists for embarkation been made out. Wednesday, 15 December 1915: Got orders through that no bivvies are to be disturbed and all roofs are to be intact. On the beach the authorities are tipping out rum and whisky in Mule Gully and a terrible lot of rum etc. was tipped out and formed a pool. All hands were there with jam tins, dixies etc. lapping it up. Have just received final orders for H.Q. Signals. For last twenty-four hours seven men to remain to man phones and for last few hours I think it is going to be rather nervy. Password for tonight is Corkscrew. Thursday, 16 December 1915: Our H.Q. signals orders cancelled. Only two men are to stay and man the phones, Sgt Calame and myself. All barges busy getting troops off. The last ones to go are Walker's Ridge, Quinn's and Courtney's and all are to be heavily mined. Very busy at Williams' Pier. Password Strawberry. Friday, 17 December 1915: Just got orders through that all arrangements to be postponed twenty-four hours. Password Havelock. Very bright moonlight. Can see shipping as clear as day.

'Saturday, 18 December 1915: On 3 a.m. to 6 a.m. watch this morning. Went out about 5 a.m. to waken officers and saw a great glare in the direction of Anzac. Evidently the heads burning all stores etc. Seems fairly cheeky though.[1] Four aeroplanes up at once, evidently reconnoitring. At 9 p.m. most of the boys got away. Everything going satisfactorily – only occasional burst of fire disturbing the night. Turks been working hard all day improving fire trench. Password Malta. We are leaving everything as they stand. Our funk holes or at least H.E. shelters, once our pride and joy, are now half filled with all sorts of rubbish, empty bully tins, old socks, burnt paper, broken helios etc, Burnt all our intelligence department stuff such as old messages etc. Sunday, 19 December 1915: Last night all went well without a hitch. About twelve o'clock the nasty-tempered brutes of Turks started lobbing shells all over the place. Got orders to get into our funk holes. No damage done. Had a wash and clean up to celebrate what we fondly hope is our last day on Gallipoli. I'll feel quite at ease when I see the shores of Anzac fade away over the horizon. Things very quiet. Turks working hard on the defences. Am keeping the last two messages sent by Col. Plugge during Gallipoli campaign. 9 p.m. Report "All quiet". Password Cucumber. All the afternoon and tonight they are pouring it in somewhere evidently at Cape Helles. 10 p.m. Report "All quiet". 11 p.m. Report "Everything normal". Midnight report "Situation quite normal".

'Monday, 20 December 1915: Just had a tin of Maconochies, some cocoa and a nip of Northern Cream. I feel goodo now. Got word through to commence withdrawal. We cut off at 1.52. I waited for Paul and we got our gear and bashed things about a bit and started for Williams' Pier.

---

[1] This fire had been started accidentally and caused great anxiety because it was exactly the sort of obvious evacuation activity which it was hoped to avoid.

Got there and aboard the lighter at 2.30 a.m. Started to have a sleep and some Lieut-Col. stood on my face. Woke up and shook him up. Left pier and was put aboard Prince Abbas, left at 4.30 p.m. As we left, Suvla Bay was a mass of flames. Guns blown up on Walker's Ridge.'[2]

In the last week of November a brilliant though demanding exercise was the silent stunt. This nerve-racking experience is remembered by Colonel Holmes. In order to accustom the Turks to the quietness of an evacuation, all firing was to cease from the Anzac lines from 6 p.m. on 24 November to midnight on the 27th. The troops had to wait about in the trenches to deal with inquisitive Turks who crossed no-man's land. Such parties did come and even threw bombs into the Australian positions without reply, but in Holmes's sector one Turk had actually jumped down into the trench and had been bayonetted and his comrades bombed out. The only other feeling of nervousness Holmes experienced was in turning his back to the Turk and descending the winding paths to the beach for the evacuation. These paths had been marked with flour and direction changes shown by candles or shaded lanterns set into the sides of the trenches. Where the front lines were particularly close, the trench floors had been lain with torn blankets, boots had to be bound with sacking and metal accoutrements similarly silenced. Even the boards of the piers had been covered and hard ground paths broken up to make a less resounding surface.

The preparations were tried in rehearsal. Other means of deception such as carrying empty boxes back up to the heights, as if supplies were still being brought ashore, are remembered by men engaged in this work, such as C. J. Arnold. Mines were laid in carefully selected positions and rifles with an improvised self-acting mechanism were set up in nearly all sectors. A line was attached to the trigger of the rifle and then to an empty can suspended in a position which would cause it to apply pressure to the trigger when the can had been filled with water to a certain level. This was achieved by means of a second can, positioned above it and pierced with holes through which water dripped into the trigger-attached can. The key to all the preparations was to deceive the Turks with normality. On the very day of departure Colonel Marks noted accurately in his diary, 'Everything normal.'[3] The Turks were still out wiring, which was of course to the advantage of their enemy and the embarkation was 'very smooth and uneventful'. For some the tension showed in

[2] In fact this was a very big mine which is recalled today by veteran Turks as being an unsporting farewell gesture.

[3] Mitchell Library, Sydney.

9

privately confided nervousness. 'Should the Turks attack us tonight,' reflected M. E. Pearce, in his diary 'it will be almost certain death for all of us remaining on the Peninsula, however they will pay very dearly as we are ready for them.'[4] The path to the beach of a New Zealander, M. S. Galloway, led him beside some recently tended graves, near enough to read with a pang of anguish the name of a friend and fine Wellington rugby player whose splendid try in his last match in New Zealand provided an instant poignant recollection. J. G. Gasparich remembers the eerie echoing of his footsteps on an uncovered or unbroken path and then a sudden unnerving wail from the Turkish trenches, which their state of tension translated into a sign of an imminent attack.

In the event of a major engagement during the evacuation two fully equipped casualty clearing stations were to be left to cope with the seriously wounded who could not have been evacuated. Though the Australian official history[5] mentions that it was hoped that the Turks would allow both the wounded and the medical personnel to be collected on the day following, there is a letter from General Monash to his wife and daughter which implies that these men would be taken prisoner but that he had 'every confidence that in such an eventuality the Turks will play the game'.[6] Though no casualties or medical men had to be left, a gramophone and note were waiting for the Turks in one of the casualty clearing stations – the record ready for playing was of course 'Turkish Patrol'.

The last troops to leave were to see Suvla and Anzac lit up by the burning stores and mine explosions. It is perhaps not surprising that some of these troops were a little the worse for wear as a result of their unwillingness to waste all the rum which had been poured away.

The destruction of stores had not just been limited to rum, bully beef and ammunition. Those guns which had not been evacuated were so methodically destroyed that it was hoped they would not serve even as war trophies.[7] The need for secrecy meant that much could not be destroyed and had to be left to the Turks, but with a cricket match being played on the beach and normal troop and mule movements maintained till the last, deception had been brilliantly successful. The preparations

---

[4]   Mitchell Library, Sydney.
[5]   Vol. 2, p. 880.
[6]   La Trobe Library, Melbourne (MS 9456).
[7] Nevertheless in the Sunderland Polytechnic Archives there is an unpublished Turkish photograph of Turkish officers and men proudly assembled beside the barrel of one of the few big allied guns at Anzac.

had been meticulous and they had been responsibly executed to the last detail. Nevertheless the inestimable value of fine weather and a calm sea, which was to be even more critical to Britain twenty-five years later at Dunkirk, perhaps led the thoughtful soldier or sailor to reflections similar to Birdwood's diary entry for 20 December that he was 'grateful to Almighty God for the wonderful weather given us'.[8] On the last two nights twenty thousand troops had been evacuated with but two men wounded.

At Suvla there were huge dumps of stores to be destroyed because they could not be re-embarked in secret. Blankets and bayonets, boots and water bottles, socks and woollen gloves, tarpaulin sheets and even motor-bicycles were remorselessly thrown on the fire heaps, while near Kangaroo Pier, on another funeral pyre, were a full fortnight's rations for 40,000 men.[9] The preparations and procedure were the same as at Anzac, but there was considerable advantage at Suvla in the greater distance between the front lines and absence of major underground mining activity. Every gun, even those firing the normal amount of ammunition during the evening of the 19th, was evacuated and only on the Kiretch Tepe Ridge was there any delay in the orderly progress of men to the beaches. Despite this delay there was not a single casualty and every soldier was safely embarked.

With booby traps and contact mines laid both in front of them and behind them, Signaller F. Bradford had waited anxiously for the call 'G' which would order their withdrawal. He and his small party, waiting in the eerie darkness of the wide-open plain, actually began to fear that they had been forgotten when at last the call came through. 'I could never describe the feeling of relief when that signal came.' Andrew Brown, checking his sector, had casually kicked at what appeared to be a pile of rubbish in his way and had found it was their cook, scarcely conscious, hugging a rum jar. Private C. J. Bygrave had had to organize the pulling of a log of wood on two cartwheels to the front line to replace a gun being evacuated.

Lieut-Colonel Gething remembered that two nights before the evacuation all the kit which could be carried on the person in packs or haversack was sent to the beach. This included officers' valises, so they were left with just what they stood up in. 'I never saw my valise again. The men took a delight in slashing the sandbags as we destroyed all we could in our trenches. The only thing we left was the earthenware jug in which we

[8] Australian War Memorial, Canberra.
[9] *Official History: Gallipoli*, vol. 2, p. 453.

had kept our water cool during the hot days. We left it for the Turks, hoping it would serve them as well as it had served us. Sentimental soldiers that we were. I felt terribly lonely but there was too much for us to do to brood over this. We had to show ourselves all we could, draw water for the whole battalion, light and keep going all the cookhouse fires. After dark I had twenty-five men and we had to keep fire coming from as many firing bays as possible. I put a box of ammunition in the cook-house fire hoping it would last till after we had gone. On our way to the beach I remember above all the silence. Only heavy breathing and the occasional stumble of padded feet could be heard.'

The booby traps were not all of a metallic nature. Brigadier Rathbone confesses, with a degree of embarrassment, that his unit left a lethal mixture of rum and paraffin which may well have had a discomfortingly explosive effect of its own when the Turks drank to their victory. It may be wondered whether this potent mixture was not more likely than marmalade[10] to have caused the single Turkish fatality in the gorging of the edible stores left after the evacuations.

With the complete success of Anzac and Suvla, it must have seemed to those at Helles that they could scarcely expect to be so fortunate. Their diversionary bombardment and local attacks had helped to distract the Turks on 19 and 20 December, but the Turks, with increasing supplies of ammunition, were now able to concentrate their attention exclusively on Helles.

The Senegalese troops had all been withdrawn by 22 December and the final decision to withdraw the whole force came six days later, though plans were already being prepared for this expected eventuality. As at Suvla, Turkish observation of the entire area made concealment of the preparations as difficult as it was vital. Furthermore in terms of 'Gallipoli-distance' it was quite a time-consuming journey for the front-line troops, who had to wend their way through the maze of trenches to the evacuation beaches. If this front line were to be attacked during the evacuation of units in the rear or immediately after the vacation of the forward trenches, a successful rearguard action would be extremely difficult.

The French Colonial Brigade left the Peninsula on 2 January and 3 January, but the French batteries remained. The French stores, added to those of the British, presented an enormous problem, the only answer to which had to be destruction. Sadly this was the fate of many of the

N. 153. Revised Jan. 1914.

CERTIFICATE FOR WOUNDS AND HURTS.

These are to Certify the Right Honourable
the Lords Commissioners of the Admiralty that

(Name in full)   (Rank or Rating)   (Official or Regimental No.)

James Duncan Fitch   *A.B. R.N.V.R. 3184*

belonging to His Majesty's Ship *Drake Batt.*

being then actually upon His Majesty's Service in *action*

Here describe the particular duty.

in the Gallipoli Peninsular

Injured or Wounded?

was wounded on *8th May 1915.* by

Date

*an enemy rifle bullet which produced a compound
comminuted fracture of both bones of R. leg
resulting in slight permanent disability*

Here describe minutely the nature of the injury sustained and the manner in which it occurred — as required by Articles 1207, 1315 and 1354 of the King's Regulations.

"Sober" or not sober. *He was sober at the time.*

Personal Description Age about *24* years. Born at or near *London* Height *5 ft. 7 ins.*
Hair *Dark brown* Eyes *Dark Brown* Complexion *Fresh*

First certificate sealed in R.N. Hospital etc. being unable to obtain one from the proper source.

Particular marks or scars.

Date *6th September* 191 *5*

Signature of Commanding Officer of Ship
or of Coast Guard or Marine Division.

Rank

Signature of Person who
witnessed the accident.

Rank.

Signature of
Medical Officer.

Rank *Deputy Surgeon General*

N P 286/1913.
Adm. 166/1911.
D no. 89/11.
Sta 119/13.

NOTE:- The grant of a Hurt Certificate to a Petty Officer or Man is to be noted on his Service Certificate.

A lasting Gallipoli legacy: a bullet wound produces 'slight permanent disability' but the casualty was 'sober at the time'.

mules which had shared the suffering and labours of Peninsula service, to deserve a better end than the slaughter which now awaited them. The carrying-out of a smooth withdrawal was also hampered by very heavy Turkish shelling and an attack on the left of the line, but British naval gunfire did much to convince the Turks that there was no weakening in determination to hold on.

Evacuation rehearsals had taken place and tremendous efforts had gone into making the piers at W beach and the floating bridge at V beach sufficiently secure for the embarkation of nearly 17,000 men and 37 guns during the night of 8–9 January. Increasingly heavy seas, bringing damage to the piers and bridge and grounding a lighter, ensured that there were constant problems to be solved, such as the need for some troops awaiting evacuation at Gully Beach to march to W beach. As the last troops got away, a thunderous roar from the main ammunition dump signalled to the Turks that they were too late and that the well-nigh impossible had been achieved.

A private in the Royal Marines, W. C. Williamson, was in a privileged position during the last hours on the Peninsula, as he had to hand messages to the officer commanding the withdrawal, outlining details of unit progress at each stage. 'The officers sat in silence round a table with a candle in a bottle as their only light. The G.O.C. Embarkation read each message silently and passed it round. With the final message in, the Corps Chief of Staff, Brigadier-General Street, merely announced that we had better leave now, handed me two attaché cases and picked up my rifle which he himself carried. When we got to the rowing boat awaiting us, I could not help but be amused that a Staff officer, eyeing the considerable swell on the sea, began to give instructions to the naval Warrant Officer in charge of the boat, manned as it was by seamen of the Royal Navy.'

Midshipman Traill of the *Lord Nelson* had the task of searching for stragglers. Not relishing a cold dark swim ashore, he had astonishing luck when a ten-foot-long, flat-bottomed, carpeted Turkish pleasure punt bumped against his cutter and allowed an easy transfer for a dry examination of the coast. The punt, held on a line by the crew of the cutter, drifted against a breakwater in Morto Bay and Traill, revolver in hand, wandered along the beach calling 'Anybody about?' and hoping the reply would not be in Turkish. After some time the explosion of the ammunition dump at the very point of the Peninsula convinced him that his search for lost or harassed troops was no longer necessary. It was a sobering thought that he was probably alone in presenting the continued allied challenge to Constantinople. He quickly made his way back to the moored punt and so to the safety of the cutter.

On the Peninsula itself some soldiers had looted from the dumps shirts, vests and pants far in excess of their needs, remembered T. S. W. Jarvis. They were forced to jettison their surplus requirements on the long tiresome trail to the piers, as they were too much of an encumbrance. Philip Gething, fresh from the Suvla evacuation, experienced the very heavy Turkish bombardment of the 7th and, sheltering from the shrapnel balls, picked some of them up still hot from the shell burst. As much to raise his own morale as those of his men, he played marbles with them. He and his men were fortunate to be on the Gully Beach lighter which did get away on the night of the 8th, so that they did not have to endure the considerable physical and nervous strain of the march to W beach.

A. C. Pawson, evacuated on the 4th, wrote emphatically in his diary that he didn't care 'if I never see the Peninsula again – and I fancy all of us on board feel the same', but Eric Wettern's unit, the Royal Naval Division 2nd Field Company Engineers, was very much committed to a continued close acquaintance with terrain which had been its home since the last week in April. '5 January: Carrying stuff for barricades. Turks apparently spotted something and plonked a few big 'uns round about making a mess of trenches in two or three places. Had to get night working party from Howes to shift the muck. With Stout fixing up barricades got most of the work done. 6th: . . . Completing barricade arrangements. Fixed up everything to drop in instantly. Rehearsals with Rugg. 7th: . . . General rehearsal at 2. Attack by Turks on Fusilier Bluff preceded by bombardment of whole line. Shrapnel and Annie[11] in our sector. I went up to tie white tape on crinolines[12] and got a bit of it coming back. Rest of company left, leaving only ten of us. Part of firing line went off. 8th: . . . Hoods on our left moved out very quickly . . . straw down and muffled feet . . . 23.45: All moved out. We put down crinolines in front line . . . we put down umbrellas[13] and crinolines at Supports . . . Waited for Dumezil and bomb people at Ligne de Repli barricade. Further wait at Post 11 for Thompson. Then all down to Post 15. Eski. Longish wait for Blake. Barricaded road. Put gear on, proceeded down. Very quiet. Few French left round Camp des Oliviers. Via Cypresses to F.U.P. at

[11] 'Asiatic Annie', the Turkish gun firing across the Straits.
[12] A crinoline was a long pole with cross bars at each end, the whole construction wrapped round with barbed wire, and set ready to fall into and block saps and communication trenches.
[13] An umbrella was a smaller version of the same design.

Seddel Bahr – then in fours – slow progress over beached French warship on to destroyer *Grasshopper*. Like sardines, on board before 0300. Few dud shells from Annie. Out to sea. Bonfires started 0400 on all beaches and Turks started shelling like blazes and sending up red flares. Fine to watch it from a distance.'

This diarist, Eric Wettern, wrote to his brother on 15 January: 'I expect you are feeling fairly disgusted at home at our magnificent bunk from Gallipoli . . . As a matter of fact we aren't exactly sorry to leave dear old Gallipoli. I think we could have stuck it all right, though it was getting a bit warm, but I suppose they thought we should never do any good by staying there.'

At least one person however felt that the soldiers' efforts deserved appreciation. A West Australian schoolgirl sent a present of a notepad to 'a wounded Anzac soldier'. She thanked him for his 'kindness in going to the front. I am glad to hear that you soldiers have tried [your] very best to fight for the King and Country. I wish you will get better and go to fight again,' but she added with unaffected sincerity, 'I hope the war will end soon.'[14] As the Gallipoli soldier continued his war service for almost three more years on the Western Front, or in Mesopotamia, Salonika, Egypt or Palestine, he would echo and re-echo the schoolgirl's sentiment and in so doing he would unconsciously mock the high political hopes for the campaign in which he had first been associated.

---

[14] Letter by Lily Fagence, 20 April 1916, to R. A. Nicholas (P.L.). It is pleasant to know that in the 1970s through the aid of a Perth (W.A.) newspaper the Anzac veteran was able to meet the writer of the schoolgirl letter.

Appendix 1:   The Political Responsibility

There can be little doubt concerning the real author of the Gallipoli campaign. As First Lord of the Admiralty Winston Churchill had introduced the subject into War Council discussion on 25 November, and it was his forceful leadership in the War Council and in communication with the French Minister of Marine which saw it carried into effect. There is however equally no doubt that he had secured the support of his colleagues some of whom were later eager to disclaim a responsibility which nevertheless can be established.

Lord Kitchener gave his approval to a scheme which it was hoped would secure his country's interest in an area significant to the protection of India and Egypt. 'Left to himself [he] would have selected, as all his friends knew, some point in the Near East, and would have launched an attack with every man and gun and shell which could have been begged, borrowed or stolen from the Western Front.'[1] This judgement may have substance, but Kitchener ordered neither the General Staff, such as it was, nor the War Office to prepare a new detailed appraisal of a Gallipoli scheme. Furthermore he did not insist on a full examination of whether Britain could afford a major troop commitment additional to the enormous demands of the Western Front.

The Prime Minister himself must be criticized for presiding over discussions which were characterized by a lack of precision, though this seems a relatively small fault beside the irregularity and infrequency of formal War Council meetings in March, April and early May. The Foreign Secretary, Sir Edward Grey, accepted blame in his memoirs for not dealing forcefully with the diplomatic problems involved both in the preparatory planning and in the event of attendant success. Certainly little credit can be given to Grey for his prediction at the War Council of 8 January that the Turks would be paralysed with fear when they heard that the forts were being destroyed one by one.[2]

Lloyd George is recorded by Hankey as liking the plan when it was introduced on 8 January, but he was not to forget his resentment at the defeat of his Salonika–Serbian strategy as the Gallipoli campaign

[1] Reginald, Viscount Esher, *The Tragedy of Lord Kitchener*, p. 106.
[2] P.R.O. Cab. 22/1 3623.

stagnated. As early as 15 May Frances Stevenson, his secretary, recorded in her diary the contents of a note sent to her by Lloyd George, concerning Churchill and Gallipoli: 'It is the Nemesis of the man who has fought for the war for years. When the war came he saw in it the chance of success for himself and has accordingly entered on a risky campaign without caring a straw for the misery and hardship it would bring to thousands, in the hope that he would prove to be the outstanding man in this war.'[3] Hankey's notes, however, record no opposition by Lloyd George in the meetings at which the vital decisions were taken.

Fisher, the First Sea Lord, stifled his doubts, and boomed his approval for a grandiose design in the same area. Later he sat in official sulky silence while informally growling his disenchantment. He claimed that, from Jellicoe to the Admiralty charwomen, everyone knew of his opposition. This opposition grew into simmering fury as the scheme developed. As early as 19 January he wrote to Sir John Jellicoe, the Commander-in-Chief of the Grand Fleet: 'and now the Cabinet have decided on taking the Dardanelles solely with the Navy using fifteen battleships and thirty-other vessels and keeping out their three battle cruisers and a flotilla of destroyers – all urgently required at the decisive theatre at home! There is only one way out and that is to resign! But you say "No" which simply means I am a consenting party to that which I absolutely disapprove. I don't agree with one single step taken.'[4] This letter, one of several on the same theme, illustrates his equivocal position. The tragic influence of the split between Churchill and Fisher over Dardanelles policy remained a major factor in influencing the chances of success in the critical months until Fisher's resignation on 15 May.

Russian responsibility too should be noted: the decisive impulse towards Gallipoli had been a Russian request for help. There is in addition some irony in the thought that British success in the Dardanelles would have given Russia Constantinople, which British diplomatic, military and naval effort for a hundred years had striven to withhold.[5] George Cassar observes that not only did the British and French fail to agree on the political objectives to be secured but they never seriously considered whether Russia could help and if so by what means.[6] The assistance of the Russian cruiser *Askold* can scarcely be considered a major contribution to the allied naval and military commitment.

[3] A. J. P. Taylor, ed., *Lloyd George: A Diary of Frances Stevenson*, p. 50.
[4] A. J. Marder, *Fear God and Dreadnought*, vol. 3, p. 140.
[5] In March 1915 the British government conceded Russian rights to Constantinople.
[6] G. Cassar, *The French and the Dardanelles*, p. 2 of introduction.

The attractively loyal French support for what was essentially a British concept is remarkable. The French fell for Churchill's blandishments without consulting their Admiral in the Mediterranean, Boué de Lapeyrère, and without regard for their previously agreed primacy in this sea. A recent French source correctly outlines the Churchill logic. 'Churchill in his passion to succeed ignored advice which did not support his argument,'[7] but no contrary advice came from the French before the military landings in April.

Churchill knew that the pedigree of a British assault on the Straits was lengthy. Admiral Duckworth in 1807 had actually breached the Dardanelles but had been severely mauled on his return journey from an unyielding Constantinople. At the time of the Russo-Turkish war in the late 1870s there had been an examination of the problems associated with British involvement in the Dardanelles, and in 1907 a Joint Staff appreciation had seen too many obstacles in a combined operation to offer much chance of a worthwhile success. The Admiralty had however qualified the joint assessment by accepting that such an operation might be forced upon them and that, if this was the case, they were not as gloomy as the War Office appeared to be about the prospects.

The project was raised again in September 1914 as a result of the equivocal Turkish diplomatic stand and the escape of the *Goeben* and the *Breslau* through the Dardanelles to Constantinople. The British military attaché in Constantinople, Lieut-Col. Cunliffe Owen, prepared a paper on the subject and was quite clear that the 'more directions in which Great Britain's energies are scattered, so much the better for German policy'.[8] He drew attention to the need for British–Russian co-operation and suggested that the Persian Gulf might be a better place to strike than the Dardanelles.

As a result of this memorandum the question of the feasibility of an attack was studied by the Director of Military Operations at the War Office, General Callwell. His opinion was that 'considering the strength of the Turkish garrison and the large force already mobilized in European Turkey, he did not regard it as a feasible military operation and that he believed this to be the War Office view'.[9]

The background to Churchill's own ideas on the Dardanelles is interesting. He had sent a memorandum to the Cabinet in 1911 which stated that 'It is no longer possible to force the Dardanelles . . . nobody

---

[7]   Chack and Antier, *Histoire maritime*, vol. 2, p. 142.

[8]   P.R.O. WO/106/1462 2099.

[9]   P.R.O. WO/106/1463 2099.

would expose a modern fleet to such perils'.[10] He had conceded at the War Council on 25 November 1914 that an attack on the Gallipoli Peninsula would be 'a very difficult operation requiring a large force',[11] and he had written to Fisher on 10 December 1914 concerning the latter's projected Zeebrugge landing: 'I am shy of landings under fire . . . unless there is no other way.'[12] In view of such evidence, both Churchill's logic and his judgement seem exposed by his confident assertion at the War Council of 6 April that 'he anticipated no difficulty in effecting a landing'.[13]

Ashmead Bartlett seems to provide an acceptable analysis of the development of Churchill's thinking: 'It not infrequently happens that men of dominating imagination are apt to jump to the conclusion that successful accomplishment must follow as a natural corollary to a brilliant scheme which has suddenly germinated in their minds . . . Mr Churchill realized how far-reaching would be the result if Constantinople were captured, but there is little evidence that he ever carefully considered what forces were necessary to ensure victory or weighed the consequences of failure.'[14]

In considering whether the Gallipoli idea was a 'strategic conception surpassing others in promise',[15] it must surely be remembered that a proper consideration of the practical problems involved in the execution of a strategic conception is an essential part of such an evaluation. Granville Fortescue wrote that 'it is the lack of foresight shown by the mind that conceived the plan of smashing a channel through to the Black Sea which is appalling'.[16] Fuller separates and then links the factors involved with devastating logic. 'As a problem of pure strategy it was brilliant. But without a powerful Greek army to back it, it was amateurish because England was not capable of fighting on two fronts and the British army was neither equipped nor trained to fight in a theatre such as Gallipoli.'[17]

It may be claimed that the true Gallipoli conception involved naval action alone and that only over-cautious leadership and unfortunate weather conditions robbed Churchill's idea of the success it deserved.

[10] M. Gilbert, *Winston S. Churchill*, vol. 3, p. 220 note.
[11] P.R.O. Cab. 22/1 3623.
[12] A. J. Marder, *Fear God and Dreadnought*, vol. 3, p. 91.
[13] P.R.O. Cab. 22/1 3623.
[14] Ashmead Bartlett, *The Uncensored Dardanelles*, p. 14.
[15] H. W. Nevinson, *The Dardanelles Campaign*, p. vii.
[16] G. Fortescue, *What of the Dardanelles?*, p. 23.
[17] J. F. C. Fuller, *Decisive Battles of the Western World*, vol. 3, p. 235.

A. J. Marder has argued persuasively that the stakes were sufficiently high to justify a renewal of the naval attack in April once the new Beagle Class destroyers were available for fast sweeping.[18] But had the allied squadron got through, it would then, almost certainly in a damaged condition, have had to deal with the German–Turkish fleet in the Sea of Marmara. If successful there, it would still have had to rely on internal revolutionary activity. The likelihood of Constantinople being shelled into submission does not seem great and the fleet was not equipped for a military occupation.

There is no generally accepted agreement on the likelihood of internal revolution bringing an end to the Turkish administration, despite American Ambassador Morgenthau's clear support of this view in his memoirs.[19] We are left therefore with the uneasy historical consideration of the allied ships, short of coal, oil, ammunition, food and water, having to withdraw. The return journey to the Aegean, with the Narrows unguarded by an allied military force, could scarcely have been less hazardous than the assault.

There are further practical matters which would appear to weaken the case for success being within reach of an assault by the Navy alone. The ineffectiveness of naval gunfire against coastal forts is one major point which does not seem to have been objectively examined. It was maintained at the time that the new development in long-range naval gunnery rendered obsolete the long-accepted dictum that ships were matched unequally against forts. It was anticipated that aeroplanes and balloon observation would compensate for the lack of adequate observation of fire effectiveness in long-range bombardment. Improved fire control and range-finding would assist in ensuring accuracy in firing at a stationary target from a ship as a dipping, rolling gun-platform. In the event the need for demolition by a shore party soon proved how limited were the results which could be expected from naval gunfire. The low-trajectory high-explosive shells, unless scoring – against the odds – a direct hit on a gun emplacement, merely plunged into the low, broad banks of earth which protected the guns of the forts.

The validity of striking at Turkey through the Dardanelles is a much more finely balanced issue than its chief protagonists affirm. Planning and

[18] A. J. Marder, *From the Dardanelles to Oran*, p. 32. See also the S.P.A. correspondence of Captain L. A. K. Boswell: 'The naval attack was a sound operation of war which failed for one reason only – that nobody until 19 March had seen how to deal with the mines. The Army is entirely irrelevant and only an enormous red herring.'

[19] H. Morgenthau, *Secrets of the Bosphorus*, p. 128.

practical considerations had been underestimated. As far as the involve-ment of the Army is concerned, the Gallipoli commitment was undertaken in the War Council at the very time when the Western Front Neuve Chapelle offensive was being planned. The official historian of the Gallipoli campaign accepted that planning for offensives on two fronts was unrealistic. In his memoirs Sir William Robertson, not of course an unbiased source, bemoans the failure of politicians and soldiers to agree on the decisive front. The French, even in their support of Gallipoli, had no doubt about which was the decisive front as far as they were concerned. Their Gallipoli Commander-in-Chief, General d'Amade, was informed within five days of landing on the Peninsula that despite his desperate need for ammunition 'the needs of the armies of the N.E. [Western Front] – always considerable and urgent – must take priority'.[20]

Examining the vital question of troop commitment, Fuller cryptically comments that 'No sooner had the Government made up their mind not to use troops than they decided to use them, and after they had arrived at this decision they decided to carry out the naval attack without them.'[21] The significance of this vacillating folly is exposed by Paul Guinn. 'In retrospect it is easy to see that the contrasting views and consequent semi-deliberate misunderstandings on the function of troops at the Dardanelles were largely responsible for the manifest inadequacy of the Mediterranean Expeditionary Force for the task it had actually to perform . . . were indeed responsible for the ultimate failure of the entire campaign.'[22]

An objective assessment of the chances of success would suggest that the grand strategy gains through allied victory ought to have been outstanding to justify the effort required to secure success and avoid a seriously damaging failure. This leads naturally to a final major considera-tion: the optimistic assessment of the influence on the overall war effort of success at Gallipoli.

Russian collapse would certainly have been delayed in the event of a decisive allied victory over the Turks. Austrian collapse would probably have been accelerated, but scarcely by a united Balkan coalition com-prised of such disparate elements. British food supplies would have been made somewhat more secure, but the idea of British naval power being exercised to a major extent up the Danube is far-fetched. There were not even suitable vessels to implement this idea, unless it is considered

---

[20] French Military Archives, Vincennes (C.E.O. 1 Bureau 20 N 15).
[21] *Decisive Battles of the Western World*, vol. 3, p. 238.
[22] *British Strategy and Politics 1914–18*, p. 61.

that Fisher's prized North Sea landing craft could have been used. There would have been a major economy of men and munitions through the closing of the Turkish fronts, but it is unsound to conclude that the available reinforcements for the Western Front would have led to a breakthrough there. It is idle to pretend that the full Gallipoli landing force of 75,000 would have made any significant difference had these troops been used in the 1915 attacks at Neuve Chapelle, Aubers Ridge or Loos, and it is equally idle to believe that victory at Gallipoli would have won the war on the Western Front at an earlier date. The enormous troop reinforcements for the Somme offensive were to achieve no significant success there in 1916. Australian and New Zealand troops as well as the R.N.D. and the 29th Division took part in this offensive. If it is claimed that this huge battle did bring valuable gains to the allies, the arguments for this are at best on contentious grounds. Victory in the west would be won by the tanks, by an infusion from America of men, materiel and morale into one side of the war-exhausted contestants, and by the Royal Navy's strangulation of the German economy and industrial war effort.[23]

As it was planned and carried out, the attack on the Dardanelles with its subsequent land campaign had no outstanding prospect of success and was backed by unrealistic hopes. A heavy price was to be paid for the pursuit of an elusive prospect. This is not to deny that some value resulted from the ensuing failure. The Turkish army had been drained of its strength. Turkish successes in Mesopotamia and in Egypt and Palestine in 1916 could not be exploited. Exhaustion with consequent defeat was to attend their efforts to combat 1917 British reinforcements on those fronts.[24] Nevertheless no sophistry can disguise the allied naval and military defeat in the Dardanelles and on the Gallipoli Peninsula. The ships attacked and withdrew, the soldiers landed and were withdrawn.

[23] Obviously the allied avoidance of military defeat on the Western Front in March–April 1918 and their American-reinforced offensive of August would feature prominently in any deeper consideration of this point.

[24] There are some who see the dividend of the 1915 investment being collected not in the First World War but in the success of the superbly planned and unified combined operation of the Normandy 'D-Day' landings. According to Mrs G. Shields, Sir Ian Hamilton's private secretary in 1916–17, the General himself believed this. It must however be pointed out that Britain's 1940 Norway expedition provided an embarrassing parallel in failure with Gallipoli; this suggests that the lessons of the 1915 failure still needed re-learning twenty-five years later.

Appendix 2:   The Military Responsibility

An examination of the leadership of Vice-Admiral de Robeck and General Sir Ian Hamilton from March 1915, when they took up supreme command, till the collapse of the August offensive, must take into consideration factors outside their control. If it is shown that from the start the scales had been weighed against them both by events prior to their appointment and by pressures from independent sources beyond their influence, then the significance of misjudgements which can be attributed to them must surely be lessened. It may well be added that a more sceptical examination of the anticipated consequences of victory would lead to a less prejudiced assessment of a failure seen exclusively in terms of poor leadership. From this standpoint it might be asked how critical were the errors of direction taken in pursuit of the unreachable?

I believe that the Gallipoli conception, its likelihood of success and the attendant consequences of victory are too often viewed as through the telescope of an optimistic astronomer who reports on what he would like to see rather than what he does see. I further suggest that in the case of de Robeck, events prior to his appointment considerably lessened his chance of success on 18 March and that there are strong arguments in defence of his supposedly pusillanimous failure to attack the Narrows again on 19 March or in the days immediately following. In the case of Sir Ian I feel even more strongly that he was overwhelmed with factors not of his making which eroded his chances of success. Nevertheless, as this work is not least a tribute to those over whom the Vice-Admiral, the General and their Staffs exercised sway, the question of errors in command must be considered. Certainly as far as the M.E.F. is concerned there were decisions which are questionable as well as serious errors of omission.

With Vice-Admiral Carden's final breakdown in health on 16 March, de Robeck, as he had been concerned with all the planning for the attack, was given full responsibility for it, but only one day before it was to be launched. In the attack he lost three battleships, had three more quite seriously damaged and suffered grievous casualties, largely as a result of the sinking of the *Bouvet*. The hard evidence to him was of Turkish preparedness and of the ineffectiveness of the allied shelling and mine-sweeping. He was not even sure whether his losses had been from land-fired torpedoes or from drifting mines. He knew nothing, on the evening of the 18th, of the serious depletion of Turkish ammunition, nor of the supposed panic in Constantinople. Even as he assured the Admiralty of his intention to resume the attack, he doubted the wisdom of such a decision. He had the newly appointed Commander of the Mediterranean Expeditionary Force with him ready jointly to undertake a mission now so clearly fraught with difficulty. For all his Chief of Staff's persistence – and Roger Keyes provoked some of the alarm in senior naval circles that the First Lord of the Admiralty did in political ones – there were strong arguments for awaiting the arrival of the M.E.F. With the support of naval guns, soldiers could be landed in strength to destroy the guns of the forts defending the minefields and hold the forts and heights above them to allow the mines to be swept undisturbed. De Robeck had scanty evidence in support of any contention that a resumption of the offensive would not be equally costly and indeed lead to the arrival of a damaged fleet, weakened in numbers, into the Marmara to face the *Goeben*, the *Breslau* and the Turkish fleet. A fear for the security of his supply line also appears more than reasonable.

In his book on Gallipoli, Sir Roger Keyes wrote that his examination of the Narrows after the action left him with a 'most indelible impression that we are in the presence of a beaten foe'.[1] That this examination had taken place in darkness from the deck of a single destroyer seems to reduce its significance. Similarly when Keyes writes that 'it only remained to us to organize a proper sweeping force and devise some means of dealing with drifting mines to reap the fruits of our efforts',[2] the problem of matching this sort of appraisal with the harsher deductions of reality invites sympathy for de Robeck. A. J. Marder, though sympathetic towards the school of thought which regrets the failure to renew the naval attack, accepts that Keyes was never one to see beyond the immediate next step and his judgement was clouded by his eagerness to get at the enemy.'[3]

The indictment of de Robeck is that he refused to be convinced that the organization of the new Beagle Class destroyer sweeping force gave him an opportunity to clear a sufficiently wide sweep to allow his ships to approach the inner forts and reduce them completely to ruins at close range. It can be further maintained that this could have been done

[1] *The Fight for Gallipoli*, p. 69.
[2] ibid.
[3] *From the Dardanelles to Oran*, p. 23.

early in April and without any troop involvement. In de Robeck's agreement at the 22 March conference on the *Queen Elizabeth* with Sir Ian
Hamilton and General Birdwood that the Navy would await Army
readiness for a combined operation, his detractors see the decisive
subordination of the Navy's role. This persuasive argument gathers
strength as we see neither on 25 April, nor in early May, nor in August
any serious attempt to force the Narrows. The Navy's acceptance of the
role of transporting, supplying and covering with gunfire the operations
of the troops is seen by de Robeck's critics as the seal upon his failure
to secure success by the obvious and most economical means. Liddell
Hart considers this a 'moot point',[4] but in any case the War Council
on 27 March supported the decision taken at the conference on the
Queen Elizabeth. The caution shown by de Robeck may be compared on
a lesser scale to that consistently maintained by Jellicoe with the Grand
Fleet. The sheer weight of responsibility at this level of command and
the additional competing pressures upon him of the First Lord of the
Admiralty and the First Sea Lord must be kept in mind. If the failure
to renew the attack deprived the Navy of an opportunity for Nelsonian
victory, if the scurrying back to Mudros of the big ships after the *U 21*'s
exploits appears undignified, de Robeck's assessments were based on a
realistic appraisal. His doubts about the soundness of Keyes's alluring
picture were crystallized in discussion with Hamilton and Birdwood. In
this way he came to the decision that the M.E.F. must be the essential
striking force of a combined operation to secure the Narrows and open the
way to Constantinople for the Naval Squadron.

A brief word may be added on the manner in which the Navy fulfilled
the role chosen by de Robeck. As there was no overall command structure,
however much good will there was within the two separate elements of
the combined force, the lack of any experience in working together was
made more serious by there being no ultimate authority. De Robeck can
scarcely be held responsible for this, but the handling of such problems
as wounded and water supply would have been considerably improved
under such a structure. As early as 20 May in a letter (now in the National
Maritime Museum, Greenwich) to Vice-Admiral Limpus, Vice-Admiral
Wemyss stressed the difficulties and disagreements over inter-service co-
operation. He criticized very severely the inadequacy of the army medical
arrangements and the decision of the General Staff in refusing to be based
on the Peninsula, but he saw the root of the problem as the Admiralty.
'The light-hearted way in which they allowed this tremendous operation

---

[4] *A History of the World War*, p. 186.

to be undertaken with no means beyond those which could be provided by the ships of the Fleet and thereby curtailing their effective use, is nothing less than criminal.' Beside the weaknesses in the work of the Navy, however, must be set pioneering success in many aspects of inter-service co-operation, the supreme achievement of which lies in the administrative and executive handling of the evacuations.

For Sir Ian Hamilton, the millstones around his neck from the outset, and the subsequent externally imposed limitations on his freedom of action, proved cruel burdens. He and his Staff had an incredibly short time to prepare an operation unprecedented in nature and in size. His army was scattered, his knowledge and experience of the Turks and of their land was negligible. There was a constantly pressing need for speed on the one hand which was to wage damaging war with the need for thoroughness on the other. His force had insufficient troops and was short of engineers, artillery, ammunition and embarkation stores. He was jealously prevented from having the newly developed protected landing craft and the whole venture was never unanimously backed. With the War Council divided and Kitchener under anti-Gallipoli pressure, Hamilton's endowment had crippling clauses which were likely to inhibit its fruitful fulfilment. Above all was the time-lag after 18 March or indeed after February, when the Navy had demonstrated beyond doubt the allied commitment to the Dardanelles. The essential need for surprise in such an operation was thus put out of the question even had the secrecy of troop movements in the Eastern Mediterranean been possible.

It had been said that the allied plans underestimated the defensive fighting qualities of the Turks, and Hamilton's maintained optimism, in view of his failure to achieve victory quickly, has been seen by some as evidence of his being out of touch with reality. In fact Hamilton had no illusions about the difficulty of his assignment, and his Special Force Order to the troops before the April landings, for all its eloquence, is no lyrical appeal for glory without sacrifice. The reverse side of the good coin of Hamilton's optimism is revealed in his almost apologetic request for reinforcements. In the small numbers for which he asked may be seen one of the reasons for their arrival in relatively small numbers and too late for his enormous task. The influence of his loyalty to Kitchener, amounting to awe, was just one of the inherent difficulties consequent upon his appointment. Hamilton never allowed his immediate 'on the spot' knowledge and responsibility for the campaign to redress the imbalance of this relationship with Kitchener.

The Commander-in-Chief was in a position to influence the following elements within the campaign: adequate reconnaissance for a shrewd choice of the landing beaches, the degree of supervision he would exercise over his subordinate commanders, the adaptation of his broad strategy to meet any initial check and the placement of reinforcements accordingly, the decision where to launch a new offensive with major reinforcements and the personal influence he would win over the chain of command down to the humble private. For the choice of his Staff and the efficiency of their work he must also accept some responsibility. Though each of these areas will be considered, there was a dual factor which embraces all and which does much to explain Hamilton's failure to wrest achievement out of the morass of problems. By training and predilection Hamilton believed in conferring real responsibility on his Staff and his subordinate commanders and he exuded confidence in the likelihood of their success. He lacked both the capacity and the will to lead the expedition at every stage of its planning and execution. To give subordinates free rein if they are of outstanding ability in administration, tactical appreciation or in leading men, is essential under large-scale campaign conditions; but if these men prove defective, the Commander-in-Chief must swiftly interpose his authority. In the M.E.F. there proved to be too many commanders of this poor quality in times of critical significance and Hamilton's system of devolution was cruelly exposed.

The choice of landing areas was limited by the size of his force, the rocky coastline and the inbuilt task of aiding the Navy in capturing the Narrows. In fact Kitchener's instructions to him on 13 March 'strongly deprecated' the occupation of the Asiatic shore.[5] For such reasons, separately or together, the Asiatic shore of the Dardanelles or the mainland itself were out of the question. It must be remembered that the allied force of four British divisions and one French was 'actually inferior in strength to the enemy in a situation where the inherent preponderance of defensive over offensive power was multiplied by the natural difficulties of the terrain'.[6]

The landing had to be made on the Peninsula, but on the Aegean side for adequate protection from the Turkish forts of the Narrows. If the Gulf of Saros at Bulair looked geographically inviting, it was also the most obvious place for a landing to be expected. A landing here would be of little assistance to the Navy, as cutting the narrow neck of the Peninsula did not immediately threaten the forts of the Narrows, which

[5] I. B. M. Hamilton, *The Happy Warrior*, p. 282.
[6] B. Liddell Hart, *History of the Great War*, p. 186.

could still be supplied by sea. The same could be said for Birdwood's initial preference for Enos. There were further disadvantages, such as the difficulty of co-operation here with the Navy, the strength of the Turkish defensive preparations and the fact that, in the movement towards the forts of the Narrows, the rear of the landing force would be exposed to attack from reinforcements dispatched by sea or land from Constantinople.

Some of these disadvantages, notably the distance from the Narrows and the question of naval co-operation, removed Suvla Bay from consideration at this time. Hamilton, appreciating the danger of the dispersal of his forces, nevertheless decided that the key to the problem remained the Narrows. He chose therefore five beaches at Helles which would disperse and perhaps confuse the Turks. Quite reasonably he assessed that they would be heavily committed to defending the area north of Gaba Tepe. This area offered a relatively short crossing of the Peninsula nearer to the vital Narrows than Suvla offered and of course far nearer than Bulair. To confuse the Turks still further, a diversionary landing on the Asiatic shore was to be carried out and two further diversions, one at Bulair, threatened. There is imagination and logic in such an assessment, which was made from as thorough a reconnaissance as was possible. The smallness of the beaches was another argument for the dispersal of his forces and the only point which might be made is that the difficulties of co-ordinating several landings would be a major problem. To get a large force ashore as quickly as possible at Helles made the use of several beaches essential.

R. R. James makes the point that Hamilton's Staff did not know of Cunliffe Owen's detailed memorandum on the Dardanelles defences and that in mapping they were hopelessly unprepared. It may be wondered how Hamilton could insist on having intelligence information that he did not know existed: to have refused to act without adequate briefing material would have cost the expedition invaluable time even if it had not cost him his position. Hamilton's own reconnaissance and the information available to him resulted in plans acceptable to Birdwood, though the Australian official historian maintains that in retrospect the only chance of success which Hamilton had with such a force was to throw it suddenly from Gaba Tepe at the Narrows and trust to surprise to carry it through before the enemy could be reinforced.[7] The supporting effect of the naval gunfire which could be employed at Helles was overestimated, but of course only the April and May experience would prove this.

[7] Vol. 1, p. 604.

At the Helles landings there is little doubt that the overall command lacked awareness of the considerable opportunity afforded to exploit the Y-beach landing and to divert troops intended for V and W to Y beach. The failure to capitalize on the lack of initial opposition at Y and to insist on the vigorous pursuit of a link between S and X undoubtedly contributed to the heavy casualties at V and W and to the loss of any chance of an early capture of Krithia and Achi Baba. The 29th Divisional Commander, Hunter-Weston, could have made such decisions, but committed, as he chose to be, at the tip of the Peninsula he saw no such opportunity. Hamilton saw Y beach from the *Queen Elizabeth* and later in the morning sent a message to Hunter-Weston suggesting the sending of troops to reinforce those at Y. Hunter-Weston was not disposed to alter the original plans and Hamilton refrained from making such an order over the Divisional Commander's head. This was a decision well within his compass and an opportunity was lost. He must also accept some responsibility for the woefully inadequate preparations for the wounded in both April and August and the water problem intimately associated with the Suvla tragedy.

Hamilton chose to rely on his small G.H.Q. Staff and it was completely unable to deal with the volume and complexity of administrative problems. It was folly to leave his administrative Staff in Egypt, as remote in miles as they were in Hamilton's esteem, and the G.H.Q. Staff in the exercise of almost total sway over organizational matters made serious errors through sheer lack of experience. Some of the errors were to be exposed officially. The Dardanelles Commission was to inquire searchingly into the provisions for wounded and found the attempt of the G.H.Q. Staff to prepare plans for the evacuation of wounded without reference to the Director of Medical Services had been ill-advised.[8] With masterly understatement the Commission reported that 'the greater part of the sufferings of the wounded in the first days after the landing seem to us to have been inevitable, but there seems to have been some want of organization in the control of the boats and barges carrying wounded to the hospital ships and transports, which occasioned delay in their embarkation'.[9]

The use of the first reinforcements to strengthen the attack on Krithia rather than reinforce Anzac seems reasonable in view of Hamilton's decision that Helles must be the concentrated heart of his attack and that the small beach-head at Anzac was unsuitable at that stage to take large-

[8] See the Dardanelles Commission Report, Part II, General Conclusions, No. 25.
[9] General Conclusions, No. 26.

scale reinforcements and deploy them for attack. The casualties sustained in these frontal assaults were grimly depressing, yet the knowledge of similar costly failures on the Western Front demonstrates that criticism of Hamilton or Hunter-Weston must take into consideration the total failure to that date of finding an answer to trench warfare. For the August offensive however, Hamilton designed an imaginative conception, switching this concentration from Helles to Anzac in co-ordination with a new landing at Suvla and merely a diversionary offensive at Helles.

The surprise achieved at Suvla and the narrowness of the failure at Anzac are fair witness to the shrewdness of the concept. It must be admitted that this demanded a very high degree of co-ordinated efficiency and physical effort from tired Australasian and Indian troops and raw British troops, together with new Indian troops also unfamiliar with the terrain. This burden was made much heavier by the failure at Suvla to attack vigorously and profit from the initial surprise and weak Turkish defence. Both the Dardanelles Commission Report[10] and Major-General Fuller[11] consider the plan faulty because of the weakened physical condition of some of the men and the 'half-trained state' of the others, but other historians consider this challenging plan the campaign's single example of realistic daring offering hope of success. Nevertheless, whatever merits or demerits the plan contained, the defeat of the August offensive maintained the previous pattern of subordinate inefficiency, with Hamilton failing to intervene in time. Ironically the Dardanelles Commission Report considered that 'Sir Frederick Stopford's difficulties were increased by the intervention of Sir Ian Hamilton'.[12]

He had had little alternative to accepting Stopford[13] as Commander of the IXth Corps, though he had asked for Lieut-General Rawlinson or Major-General Byng. He had still less opportunity to object beforehand to the appointment of the sadly ineffective Hammersley[14] or Lindley[15] or Sitwell.[16] The system of appointment and seniority stands condemned by their promotion as it does in the case of other elderly generals with neither the physical endurance nor the recent service experience to command in the field in a modern war. It might be added here that Godley's command of the Anzac attack also left much to be desired.

[10] General Conclusions, No. 6.
[11] *Decisive Battles of the Western World*, vol. 3, p. 247.
[12] General Conclusions, No. 8.
[13] Lieut-General Hon. Sir F. Stopford.
[14] Major-General F. Hammersley, 11th Division.
[15] Major-General Hon. J. E. Lindley, 53rd Division.
[16] Brigadier-General W. H. Sitwell, 34th Brigade.

But Hamilton was Commander-in-Chief, with all the responsibility which that entails. His passion for secrecy, which led to the under-briefing of almost all concerned, his pliant acceptance of Stopford's objections to the immediate drive for Chocolate Hill and the W Hills and his delay before insisting on vigorous attack at Suvla seem incredible in that so much hung on taking advantage of the surprise gained. He was in a position to see his plans pursued with determination and he chose to dally fatally while they were being ruined irretrievably by feeble leadership. This was carrying devolution of authority to a final degree of absurdity. All defence of the Commander-in-Chief, like sandcastles before the tide, is washed away by the Suvla events. In his final instructions to Stopford, Hamilton had stressed that the main objective was to secure Suvla Bay and 'this insistence that the landing was the objective was the greatest error of all, and the root cause of the eventual disaster: for in itself it was a means and not an end'.[17] Undeniably he had waited long for his reinforcements and he had suffered from less than loyal political, War Office and finally unofficial press backing, but his fate was justifiably, even if sadly, sealed by Suvla.

Hamilton, for all his attractive personal and considerable professional qualities, had failed to inspire his generals with his own optimistic enthusiasm. It is given to few to have the essential magnetism to inspire in any personal way the individual members of large armies and Hamilton did not achieve this distinction. To the men of the M.E.F. he was a distant shadowy figure, not one indeed to attract the ridicule or the venom felt for some, but certainly not held in the warm affection or awe reserved for others. It has been established that he did visit the Peninsula on numerous occasions from his Imbros H.Q. and that he had toured areas of the trench systems, but he remained for most, as was perhaps to be expected, as remote as Imbros.

As the Gallipoli conception, planning and execution will continue to be examined while man retains an interest in his past, the mystery of Gallipoli should not fade. For a charismatic mystery Gallipoli remains at every level. From time to time authoritative accounts have been written clearly demonstrating one opposing case after another but will anyone conclusively explain and so dismiss the unanimity expressed by the survivors of W beach, of the Haricot or of Quinn's Post, of the Daisy Patch, of the Vineyard, of Lone Pine or of the crossing of the Suvla Plain that they were glad to have been there? Among those who

[17] J. F. C. Fuller, *Decisive Battles of the Western World*, vol. 3, p. 248.

had served on the Peninsula, a feeling had been born that they had participated in a great venture. In years of reflection the feeling has been forged into a conviction held with pride. A struggle fit to rank with any ancient epic had been fought on a singularly dramatic stage and perhaps in a strangely timeless way, despite the refinement of modern warfare. There is indeed neither insensitivity nor vainglory in the Gallipoli veteran's profound satisfaction that 'he was there'.

Bibliography

(Place of publication is London unless otherwise stated)

Official Histories

The Official History of the Great War: Military Operations, Gallipoli, vols. 1 and 2, Brig.-Gen. C. F. Aspinall-Oglander, Heinemann, 1929, 1932.
The Official History of the Great War: Naval Operations, vols. 1 and 2, Sir Julian S. Corbett, Longmans Green, 1921, 1923.
General History of Medical Services in the Great War, vol. 4, Sir W. Macpherson and T. Mitchell, H.M.S.O., 1924.
The Official History of the Great War: Casualties and Medical Statistics, Maj. T. J. Mitchell and Miss G. M. Smith, H.M.S.O., 1932.
The Official History of the War in the Air, vol. 2, H. A. Jones, Clarendon Press, Oxford, 1928.
Sir Ian Hamilton's Despatches from the Dardanelles, George Newnes, undated.
The Official History of Australia in the War of 1914–18, vols. 1 and 2, C. E. W. Bean, Angus and Robertson, Sydney, 1921, 1924.
The New Zealanders at Gallipoli, Maj. F. Waite, Whitcombe and Tombs, Auckland, 1919.

Early Histories and Appreciations

Adcock, A. St John, *Australasia Triumphant*, Simpkin, Marshall and Hamilton, Sydney, 1916.
Bartlett, E. Ashmead, *The Uncensored Dardanelles*, Hutchinson, 1928.
Callwell, Maj.-Gen. Sir C. E., *The Dardanelles*, Constable, 1924.
Cavill, H. W., *Imperishable Anzacs*, William Brooks, Sydney, 1916.
Dardanelles and Their Story, The, 'By the author of *The Real Kaiser*', A. Melrose Ltd, 1915.
Fortescue, Granville, *What of the Dardanelles?*, Hodder and Stoughton, 1915.
Head, Lieut-Col. C. O., *A Glance at Gallipoli*, Eyre and Spottiswoode, 1931.
Herbert, A. P., *The Secret Battle*, Methuen, 1919.
Masefield, John, *Gallipoli*, Heinemann, 1916.
Mitchell Report, The, Report on the Enemy Defence of the Dardanelles Straits, The Dardanelles Committee, 1921.
Morley, Sir James Headlam, *Studies in Diplomatic History*, Methuen, 1930.
Moseley, S. A., *The Truth about the Dardanelles*, Cassell, 1916.
Nevinson, H. W., *The Dardanelles Campaign*, Nisbet, 1918.
Story of the Anzacs, The, James Ingram and Son, Melbourne, 1917.
Wemyss, Admiral of the Fleet Lord Wester, *The Navy in the Dardanelles Campaign*, Hodder and Stoughton, 1924.
Wilkinson, N., *The Dardanelles: Colour Sketches from Gallipoli*, Longmans, 1916.

Recent Histories

Bush, Eric, *Gallipoli*, Allen and Unwin, 1975.
Cassar, G. H., *The French and the Dardanelles*, Allen and Unwin, 1971.
James, R. R., *Gallipoli*, Batsford, 1965.
Keyes, Admiral of the Fleet Sir Roger, *The Fight for Gallipoli*, Eyre and Spottiswoode, 1941.
McLaughlin, R., *The Escape of the Goeben*, Seeley Service, London, 1974.
Marder, A. J., *From the Dardanelles to Oran*, Oxford University Press, 1974.
Moorehead, Alan, *Gallipoli*, Hamish Hamilton, 1956.
North, J., *The Fading Vision*, Faber and Faber, 1936.
Pearl, Cyril, *Anzac Newsreel*, Ure Smith, Sydney, and A. H. and A. W. Reed, Wellington, 1963.

Memoirs and Published Diaries

Aston, Sir George, *The Secret Service*, Faber and Faber, 1930.
Beaverbrook, Lord, *Politicians and the War*, Butterworth, 1928, 1932.
Fisher, Admiral of the Fleet Lord, *Memories*, Hodder and Stoughton, 1919.
Grey of Fallodon, *Twenty-Five Years*, Hodder and Stoughton, 1925.
Hamilton, Sir Ian, *Gallipoli Diary*, Arnold, 1920.
Lloyd George, David, *War Diaries*, Nicholas and Watson, 1933.
Robertson, Sir William, *Soldiers and Statesmen*, Cassell, 1926.
Sazanov, Serge, *The Fateful Years 1909–1916*, Cape, 1928.
Scott, C. P., *The Political Diaries 1911–1928*, ed. T. Wilson, Collins, 1970.
Taylor, A. J. P., ed., *Lloyd George: A Diary of Frances Stevenson*, Hutchinson, 1971.

Biographies

Bean, C. E. W., *Two Men I Knew: William Bridges and Brudenell White, Founders of the A.I.F.*, Angus and Robertson, Sydney, 1957.
Esher, Reginald Viscount, *The Tragedy of Lord Kitchener*, Murray, 1921.
Germains, V. W., *The Tragedy of Winston Churchill*, Hurst and Blackett, 1931.
Gilbert, M., *Winston S. Churchill*, vol. 3, Heinemann, 1971.
Hamilton, I. B. M., *The Happy Warrior (Gen. Sir Ian Hamilton)*, Cassell, 1966.
Higgins, T., *Winston Churchill and the Dardanelles*, Heinemann, 1964.
Magnus, P., *Kitchener: Portrait of an Imperialist*, Murray, 1958.
Marder, A. J., ed., *Fear God and Dreadnought* (Correspondence of Admiral Fisher, vol. 3), Cape, 1959.
Oglander, C. A., *Roger Keyes*, Hogarth, 1951.
Robbins, K., *Sir Edward Grey*, Cassell, 1970.
Roskill, S., *Hankey: Man of Secrets*, vol. 1, Collins, 1970.
Taylor, A. J. P., and others, *Churchill: Four Faces and the Man*, Allen Lane, 1969.

General, Military and Naval History

Bean, C. E. W., *Anzac to Amiens*, Halstead Press, Sydney, 1946.
Bird, Sir W. D., *The Direction of War*, Cambridge University Press, 1925.

Chambers, F. P., *The War behind the War*, Faber and Faber, 1939.
Chatterton, E. Keble, *Seas of Adventure*, Hurst and Blackett, 1936.
Churchill, W. S., *The World Crisis*, Thornton and Butterworth, 1923.
Fuller, Maj.-Gen. J. F. C., *The Decisive Battles of the Western World*, vol. 3, Eyre and Spottiswoode, 1956.
Gammage, Bill, *The Broken Years: Australian Soldiers in the Great War*, Australian National University Press, Canberra, 1974.
Guinn, P., *British Strategy and Politics*, Clarendon Press, Oxford, 1965.
Hankey, Lord, *The Supreme Command*, vols. 1 and 2, Allen and Unwin, 1961.
Howard, M., *The Continental Commitment*, Penguin Books, 1974.
Liddell Hart, B., *A History of the World War*, Faber and Faber, 1930.
Marder, A. J., *From the Dreadnought to Scapa Flow*, vol. 2, O.U.P., 1965.
Moore, W., *The Thin Yellow Line*, Leo Cooper, 1974.
Robson, L. L., *The First A.I.F.*, Melbourne University Press, 1970.
Woodward, Sir L., *Great Britain and the War of 1914–18*, Butler and Tanner, Frome and London, 1967.

Turkish and German Accounts

Armstrong, H. C., *Grey Wolf*, Arthur Barker, 1932.
Benoist-Mechin, *Mustapha Kemal*, Albin-Michel, Paris, 1954.
Castle, W. T. F., *Grand Turk*, Hutchinson, 1943.
Hersing, Korvetten Kapitän Otto, *U 21 Rettet die Dardanellen*, Hase and Koehler, Leipzig, 1932.
History of Turkish Operations in the World War, Military Publication 1338, Istanbul, 1921 (French tr., Capt. M. Larcher, 1924).
Kannengiesser Pasha, *The Campaign in Gallipoli*, Hutchinson, 1927.
Morgenthau, Henry, *Secrets of the Bosphorus*, c. 1920.
Sanders, Liman von, *Five Years in Turkey*, U.S. Naval Institute, 1927.

See also under Articles, etc., below

French Accounts

Bayle, X. Torau, *La Campagne des Dardanelles*, Chiron, Paris, 1920.
Chack, P., and Antier, Jean-Jacques, *Histoire maritime de la Première Guerre Mondiale*, vol. 2, *Méditerranée*, France-Empire, Paris, 1970.
David, Robert, *Le Drame ignoré de l'armée d'orient*, Plon, Paris, 1927.
Delage, E., *The Tragedy of the Dardanelles*, Butler and Tanner, 1932.
Ducasse, A., *Balkans 1914–18*, Robert Laffont, Paris, 1964.
Faurie, Capitaine, *La Guerre Joyeuse*, privately published, n.d.
Gouin, G., *L'Armée d'orient des Dardanelles au Danube*, Rotogravure S.A., Geneva, 1931.
Peandeleu, Dr, *Aux Dardanelles à Lemnos*, Imprimerie du Patronage Saint Pierre, Nice, 1920.
Roux, Fr Charles, *L'Expédition des Dardanelles*, Armand Colin, Paris, 1920.
Stienon, Charles, *L'Expédition des Dardanelles*, Châpelot, Paris, 1916.
Testis, *L'Expédition des Dardanelles*, Payot, Paris, 1917.

Uncensored Letters from the Dardanelles, by a French Medical Officer, Heinemann, 1916.
L'illustration and *Le Miroir* for 1915.

See also under Articles, etc., below

Unit Histories etc.

Belford, W. C., *Legs Eleven* (History of the 11th Bn A.I.F.), Imperial Printing Company, Perth, 1940.

Boinowski, L., ed., *Tasmania's War Record 1914–18*, J. Walch, Hobart, 1925.

Burrows, J. W., *Essex Units in the War 1914–18*, vol. 1, *1st Bn The Essex Regiment*, J. H. Burrows, Southend, n.d., *c.* 1924.

Burton, 2nd Lieut O. E., *The Auckland Regiment N.Z.E.F. 1914–18*, Whitcombe and Tombs, Auckland, 1922.

Byrne, A. E., *Official History of the Otago Regiment in the Great War*, J. Wilkie, Dunedin, n.d.

Carew, T., *The Royal Norfolk Regiment*, Hamish Hamilton, 1967.

Collett, Col. H. B., *The 28th: A Record of War Service with the A.I.F.*, Perth, 1922.

Cooper, Maj. B., *The (Tenth) Irish Division in Gallipoli*, Herbert Jenkins, 1918.

Cowan, James, *The Maoris in the Great War*, Whitcombe and Tombs, Auckland, 1926.

Creighton, Rev. O., *With the 29th Division in Gallipoli*, Longmans, 1916.

Crutchley, C. E., ed., *Machine Gunner 1914–18*, Mercury Press, Northampton, 1973.

Davidson, G., *The Incomparable 29th and the River Clyde*, J. G. Bisset, Aberdeen, 1919.

Fergusson, Capt. D., *The History of the Canterbury Regiment N.Z.E.F.*, Whitcombe and Tombs, Auckland, 1921.

Geary, Lieut S., *The Collingwood Battalion, Royal Naval Division*, F. J. Parsons, Hastings, 1920.

Gibbon, F. P., *The 42nd East Lancashire Division 1914–18*, Country Life, 1920.

Gorman, Capt. E., *With the 22nd: A History of the 22nd Battalion, A.I.F.*, H. H. Champion, Melbourne, 1919.

Hammond, E. W., *History of the 11th Light Horse Regiment*, William Brooks, Brisbane, 1942.

History of the 5th Royal Gurkha Rifles, privately published, Gale and Polden, Aldershot, 1929.

History of the Old 2/4 Battalion, City of London Regiment, Royal Fusiliers, Westminster Press, 1919.

Hurst, C. B., *With the Manchesters in the East*, Manchester University Press, 1918.

Jerrold, D., *The Hawke Battalion*, Benn, 1925.

With the Royal Naval Division, Hutchinson, 1923.

Johnson, Lieut-Col. R. M., *The 29th Divisional Artillery War Record and Honours Book*, R.A. Institution, 1921.

Kahan, H. J., *The 28th Battalion A.I.F.*, privately published, Perth, 1969.

Kingsford, C. L., *The Story of the Royal Warwickshire Regiment*, George Newnes, 1921.

Lock, C. R. L., *The Fighting 10th*, Webb and Son, Adelaide, 1936.

Longmore, Capt. C., *The Old Sixteenth: Being a Record of the 16th Bn A.I.F. during the Great War 1914–18*, Perth, probably 1921.

MacKenzie, Lieut-Col. K. W., *The Story of the 17th Battalion A.I.F. in the Great War*, Chipping Newspapers, Sidney, 1946.

Midwinter, C., *Memoirs of the 32nd Field Ambulance, 10th Irish Division*, privately published, 1933.
Mullaly, Col. B. R., *Bugle and Kukri: The Story of the 10th Princess Mary's Own Gurkha Rifles*, Blackwood, Edinburgh, 1957.
Newton, L. W., *The Story of the 12th*, J. Walch, Hobart, 1925.
Olden, Lieut-Col. A. C. N., *Westralian Cavalry in the War (The Story of the 10th Light Horse)*, Alexander McCubbin, Melbourne, n.d.
Patterson, Lieut-Col. H., *With the Zionists in Gallipoli*, Hutchinson, 1916.
Roskill, S. W., ed., *The Naval Air Service 1914–18*, Navy Records Society, 1969.
Stout, T., *With the Royal Division Engineers*, privately published, 1930.
Third East Anglian Field Ambulance 1914–1919, Wyman, n.d.
Thompson, C. W., Maj.-Gen., *Records of the Dorset Yeomanry 1914–19*, F. Bennet, Sherborne, 1921.
With the Royal Naval Division: A Souvenir, W. H. Smith, 1915.
Wren, E., *Randwick to Hargicourt (History of the 3rd Battalion A.I.F.)*, R. G. McDonald, Sydney, 1935.
Wyrall, E., *The East Yorkshire Regiment in the Great War 1914–18*, Harrison, 1918.
Zion Mule Corps, The, Israeli War Veterans' Association pamphlet, 1965.

Personal Accounts: The Army

Allanson, Lieut-Col. C., *Diary*, privately published, n.d.
Andrews, M., *Canon's Folly*, Michael Joseph, 1974.
Behrend, A., *Make Me a Soldier*, Eyre and Spottiswoode, 1961.
Benson, Sir Irving, *The Man with the Donkey*, Hodder and Stoughton, 1965.
Blackledge, W. J., and Digger Craven, *Peninsula of Death*, Samson Low, n.d.
Condliffe, J. B., *Te Rangi Hiroa: The Life of Sir Peter Buck*, Whitcombe and Tombs, Christchurch, 1971.
Cutlack, F. M., ed., *The Monash Letters: The War Letters of General Monash*, Angus and Robertson, Sydney, 1934.
Darlington, Sir Henry, *Letters from Helles*, Longmans, 1936.
Douglas, A., *My Diary 1915: Walmer to the Dardanelles*, privately published, n.d.
Eades, F., ed., *The War Diary and Letters of Corporal Tom Eades 1915–17*, Cambridge Aids to Learning, 1973.
Edmonds, H. J., *Norman Dewhust M.C.*, H. J. Edmonds, Brussels, 1968.
Ewing, W., *From Gallipoli to Baghdad*, Hodder and Stoughton, 1918.
Foster, Rev. H. C., *At Antwerp and in the Dardanelles*, Mills and Boon, 1918.
Graham, Maj. J. G., *Gallipoli Diary*, Allen and Unwin, 1918.
Hand-Newton, C. T., *A Physician in Peace and War*, N. M. Peryer, Christchurch, 1967.
Hargrave, J., *The Suvla Bay Landing*, Macdonald, 1964.
Herbert, The Hon. Aubrey, *Mons, Anzac and Kut*, Hutchinson, *c.* 1930.
Lushington, R. F., *A Prisoner with the Turks, 1915–1918*, Simpkin, Marshall, Hamilton, and Kent, 1923.
McCustra, Trooper L., *Gallipoli Days and Nights*, Hodder and Stoughton, 1916.
Mackenzie, Compton, *Gallipoli Memories*, Cassell, 1929.
Malthus, Cecil, *Anzac: A Retrospect*, Whitcombe and Tombs, Christchurch, 1965.
Murray, J., *Gallipoli As I Saw It*, William Kimber, 1965.
Raymond, Ernest, *The Story of My Days*, Cassell, 1968.

Sparrow, G., and McBean Ross, J. N., *On Four Fronts with the Royal Naval Division*, Hodder and Stoughton, 1918.
Stevens, K. M., *Maungatapere: A History and Reminiscence*, The Advocate, Whangarei, New Zealand, n.d.
Teichman, Capt. O., *The Diary of a Yeomanry M.O.*, Fisher Unwin, 1921.
Watkins, C., *Lost Endeavour*, privately published, 1968.

Personal Accounts: The Navy and Royal Naval Air Service

Bell-Davies, Vice-Admiral Richard, *Sailor in the Air*, Peter Davies, 1967.
Brodie, C. G., *Forlorn Hope 1915*, Frederick Books, 1956.
Bush, Capt. E. W., *Bless Our Ship*, Allen and Unwin, 1958.
Carr, W. G., *By Guess and by God*, Hutchinson, 1930.
From Dartmouth to the Dardanelles: A Midshipman's Log, ed. by his mother, Heinemann, 1916.
Godfrey, Admiral, J. H., *The Naval Memoirs*, vol. 2, 1915–19, privately published, 1964.
Halpern, P. G., ed., *The Keyes Papers, vol. 1, 1914–18*, Navy Records Society, 1972.
Lockyer, Capt. H. C., *The Tragedy of the Battle of the Beaches*, privately published, revised edn 1936.
Price, W. H., *With the Fleet in the Dardanelles*, Andrew Melrose, 1915.
Samson, Air Commodore C. R., *Fights and Flights*, Benn, 1930.
Shankland, Peter, and Hunter, Anthony, *Dardanelles Patrol*, Collins, 1964.
Stewart, A. T., and Peshall, C. J. E., *The Immortal Gamble*, A. C. Black, 1917.

Articles, Commemorative Publications, Veterans' Bulletins

Allen, Capt. C. R. G., 'A Ghost from Gallipoli', *Journal of the Royal United Services Institute*, May 1963.
Anon., 'The Work of a Trawler in the Aegean Sea', *Naval Review*, vol. 6, 1918.
Augstein, R., 'Deutschlands Fahne auf dem Bosporus', *Der Spiegel*, 48, 24 November 1969.
Auphan, P., 'Un Cinquantenaire: L'Expédition des Dardanelles', *Écrits de Paris*, April 1965.
'Australians at Gallipoli, The', *Australian Journal of Science*, vol. 32, no. 9.
'Battle for the Dardanelles, 18 March 1915', *La Mer*, 1915.
Boswell, Capt. L. A. K., 'The Immortal Gamble', *Journal of the Royal United Services Institute*, January 1965.
Carcopino, G., 'Les Français à l'assaut des Dardanelles', *Historama*, 238, September 1971.
'Dardanelles, Les', *Provence Marseille Magazine*, 193, 13 April 1965.
Farmer, Lieut.-Col. H. M., 'The Gallipoli Campaign 1915 from the Point of View of a Regimental Officer', lecture reprinted in *Journal of the Royal United Services Institute*, November 1923.
'Forcement des Dardanelles, Le', *Revue Maritime*, 237.
MacMunn, Lieut.-Gen. Sir George, 'The Lines of Communication in the Dardanelles', *Army Quarterly*, April 1930.

Mohl, Korvetten Kapitän Hans von, 'Auf U-Boots – Vorposten in Kleinasien', *Der Deutsch-Afrikaner*, Pretoria, 1930.
Purnell's History of the First World War (1970-   ):
    Barker, A. J., 'The Dardanelles, Turkish Reaction', 1, 26, 1971.
    'Gallipoli: A Turkish View from Memoirs of Mustapha Kemal Pasha', 2, 12, 1971.
    Kemp, Lieut-Cdr P., 'Submarines in the Marmara', 3, 1, 1971.
    Liddell Hart, Capt. B., 'Gallipoli Judgement', 3, 9, 1971.
    Schurmann, D., 'Easterners v. Westerners', 1, 26, 1971.
    Schurmann, D., 'Suvla Bay', 3, 6, 1971.
    Selby, J., 'The Dardanelles, First Naval Assault', 1, 26, 1971.
    Sheppard, Lieut-Col., 'Gallipoli, The Generals', 3, 1, 1971.
    Vader, J., 'The Anzacs', 3, 6, 1971.
    Wright, R., 'Gallipoli, The Second Stage', 3, 1, 1971.
    Wykes, Alan, 'First Landing at Gallipoli', 1, 26, 1971.
    Wykes, Alan, 'Gallipoli, Evacuation and Withdrawal', 3, 9, 1971.
Smith, Capt. B. H., R.N., 'Dardanelles Details', *Naval Review*, vol. 24, 1936.
Striedinger, Col. O., 'Cape Helles – A Retrospect', *R.A.S.C. Quarterly*, vol. 12, 1924.
Trumpener, U., 'Liman von Sanders and the German Ottoman Alliance', *J.C.H.*, vol. 1, no. 4, 1966.
Williams, Dr Orlo, 'The Evacuation of the Dardanelles', *National Review*, 1920.

Anzac 50 Years Ago, Weekly News (New Zealand) commemorative issue, April 1965.
Auckland Heroes of the Dardanelles, N.Z. Advertising and Publishing Co., Auckland, 1915.
Australian and New Zealand Expeditionary Forces Assemblage at and Departure from Albany, Western Australia, The, Albany Advertiser, W. Australia, 1915.
Gallipoli Recalled: The Spirit of Anzac, Wellington Gallipoli Veterans' Association, 1955.
New Zealand at the Dardanelles, special war issue of the Weekly Press, Christchurch, September 1915.
New Zealand's Part in the War: An Appreciation, Auckland Weekly News, November 1918.
New Zealand's Roll of Honour, Auckland Weekly News, 1915.
Western Mail War Souvenir, Perth, W. Australia, 1915.

Artilleur, L', no. 72, 1963; no. 93, 1968.
Book of the Sixth Highland Light Infantry: Souvenir Booklet, 1918.
Bulletin des anciens des Dardanelles, Le, no. 8, 1968, and subsequent triennial issues.
Gallipolian, The, journal of the Gallipoli Association 1969–76, three issues annually.
Highland Light Infantry Chronicle, The, article on Gallipoli by Lieut-Col. G. Bishop.
Journal of the 6th Queen Elizabeth's Own Gurkha Rifles, Regimental Association, 1971–2.
Legs Eleven Minor, 11th and 2/11th Australian Imperial Force Battalion's Association newsletter.
Second Battalion A.I.F. Bulletins.
Stand To, journal of the Australian Capital Territory Branch of the Returned Services League.

Newspapers and Trench News Sheets, etc.

Various national and local daily newspapers, 1915–16.
1915 Navy news sheets: *The Aquatint, The Tenedos Times, The Tahitian Tatler, The Akabarbarian, The Clan (MacGillivray) News.*
1915 Army news sheets: *The Dardanelles Driveller, The Peninsular Press, The 7th Manchester Sentry.*
The Anzac Book, 1916.

Sunderland Polytechnic Unpublished Dissertations

Lightfoot, M., *The Lancashire Fusiliers at Gallipoli* (Teacher's Certificate), 1970.
Jones, G. R., *Naval Aspects of the Gallipoli Campaign* (Teacher's Certificate), 1970.
Lindley, M., *The Gallipoli Experience* (Teacher's Certificate), 1971.
Shafto, M., *The Gallipoli Conception and Execution* (B. of Ed.), 1972.

Poetry

Dennis, C. J., *The Moods of Ginger Mick*, Angus and Robertson, Sydney, 1916.
Herbert, A. P., *Half Hours at Helles*, Blackwell, Oxford, 1916.
Skeyhill, T., *Soldier Songs from Anzac*, G. Robertson, Melbourne, n.d.

Fiction

'Billjim', *The Coo-ee Contingent*, Cassell, n.d.
Brereton, Capt., *At Grips with the Turks*, Blackie, *c.* 1930.
Cooper, J. B., *Co-oo-ee*, Hodder and Stoughton, 1916.
Hope, Stanton, *Richer Dust: A Story of Gallipoli*, Jarrolds, *c.* 1930.
Raymond, E., *Tell England*, Cassell, 1922.
   The Quiet Shore, Cassell, 1958.

Pilgrimage Accounts

Allen, T., *The Tracks They Trod*, Herbert Joseph, 1932.
Hay, Ian, *The Ships of Remembrance: Gallipoli–Salonika*, Hodder and Stoughton, n.d.
Holmes, Jessie, *A Pilgrimage to Gallipoli*, Alexander Ousely, n.d.
Hope, Stanton, *Gallipoli Revisited*, privately published, 1931.
Pemberton, T. J., *Gallipoli Today*, Benn, 1926.
Return to Gallipoli, B.B.C. script, 1965.

Unpublished Sources:

I. AUTHOR'S ARCHIVES HELD AT SUNDERLAND POLYTECHNIC

(A complete list of the material relating to Gallipoli in the author's possession. 1915 rank and unit given when known)

Abbreviations

Diaries = D; Letters = L; Photographs = P; Various papers = VP; Books = B; Souvenir objects = O; Recollections in manuscript = RM; Recollections in typescript = RT; Tape-recorded recollections = RR.

British

Aitcheson, B. S., 2nd Lieut, Royal Munster Fusiliers: D, VP, O
Ashcroft, G., Pte, 87th Bde Fld Amb.: P, RR
Attwood, J. C. Sgt, 2nd Royal Fusiliers, 86th Bde, 29th Div.: R, RT
Auger, E., Sgt, R.A.M.C. Fld Amb., London Mounted Brigade: P, O, RM, and Spr Moore-Jones prints
Aumonier, W. W., Pte, R.A.M.C., 3 East Anglian Fld Amb. 161st Bde, 54th Div.: RT
Austin, J., Pte, 6th Green Howards, 11th Div.: RR
Baillie, J. S., Harland & Wolf 1914, building dummy battleships: RR
Banner, Maj. E. H. W., T.D., Chairman of the Gallipoli Association: contact with large number of British veterans
Barnes, H., Spr, R.E., 39th Bde, 13th Div.: RM, RT
Barnet, J., Pte, 2nd Lowland Fld Amb. R.A.M.C., 52nd Div.: VP, RM, and photos of Pte Handyside of same unit
Bartlett, Sqd Ldr, D.S.C.: Letters of his brother, Capt. R. N. O. Bartlett, 6th Bn East Lancs.
Batcheller, R. A., West Kent Yeomanry: B, RM, RR
Bates, R. B., Cpl, 1/3rd Welsh Field Ambulance (T), 159 Bde, 53rd Div.: O
Battersby, W.: RM, RT
Bennett, J. B., Pte, 1/3rd East Anglian Fld Amb. R.A.M.C., 54th Div.: RT
Bentham, Wing Cdr J., Sub-Lieut, R.N.V.R., R.N.D. *Hood*: D, VP, P, RR
Bialeck, S., 1/5th Royal Scots: RM
Bird, W. Parker, L/Cpl, R.A.M.C., 29th Div.: D, O, VP, L, P, RR
Blackmore, W. C., Pte, R.M.L.I. R.M. Bde, 29th Div.: RM
Blythman, S. W., Pte, Wiltshire Rgt: RM, RR
Bogle, Col. J. M. L., M.C., T.D., 1/2nd Fld Coy R.E., 42nd Div.: D
Boon, W. H., Stoker, Petty Officer, H.M.S. *Prince of Wales*: RM

Booth, L. G. C., Lieut, 3rd Coy of London Yeomanry: P, VP
Boswell, Capt. L. A. K., R.N., Midshipman, H.M.S. *Irresistible* and H.M.S. *Queen Elizabeth*: B, RT, RR, P, VP
Bradford, F., L/Cpl, 6th Yorks., 11th Div.: RM, RR, B
Brand, C. W., Tpr, London Yeomanry: L, RT
Brayley, Capt. C. E. W., M.B.E., Pte, R.A.M.C. 40th Fld Amb.: L
Bremner, Flt Cdr F. D. H., R.N.A.S. No. 2 Wing: P, RR, O, VP, L
Bromet, Air Vice Marshal Sir Geoffrey, K.B.E., C.B., D.S.O., Sub-Lieut, R.N.A.S., H.M.S. *Ark Royal*: D, P, VP, maps, RR
Brown, A., Gnr, R.F.A.: D
Brown, Lieut-Col. A. G., Cpl, 1st Fife and Forfar Yeomanry: RM, RR, P
Broughton, R., R.N.D. Signal Coy: RT
Buchanan, Cdr A. G., Midshipman, H.M.S. *Prince George*: P, D
Bullock, E. W., H.M.S. *Inflexible*: RT
Burgess, W., Pte, R.M.L.I.: RM
Burrows, Cdr E. Allison, R.D., R.N.R., Assist. Paymaster R.N.R., H.M.S. *Partridge*: P, L, RT
Bush, Capt. E., D.S.O**, D.S.C., Midshipman, H.M.S. *Bacchante*: B, RR
Bygrave, C. J., Cpl, R.F.A. 55th Bde, 10th Div.: RM
Calvert, J. J., Seaman, R.N.D. *Collingwood* Bn: O
Calvert, J. S., Sgt, R.E., IX Corps: O
Capper, Mrs R.: P
Carr, J., Pte, W. Yorks. Rgt: RR
Carter, B. W., Warrant Officer, 4th Norfolk Rgt, 54th Div.: RM
Cave, W. G., Chief Petty Officer, H.M.S. *Dublin*: RM, P, O
Chadwick, J., Cpl, R. Monmouth R.E., 29th Div.: RM
Chainey, H. G., Sgt, R.A.M.C. 3rd East Anglian Fld Amb., 54th Div.: L
Chapman, Mrs D.: diary of her father, W. Reay, in the R.N.D. (Medical Unit), and books
Chapman, H. S., Pte Bandsman, 7th Essex Rgt, 54th Div.: P, RT
Chapman, J., Sgt, R.F.A., 11th Div.: RR
Childerley, F., Pte, 54th Cyclist Coy: VP, RM
Churchill, Capt. C. F. H., Midshipman, H.M.S. *London*: RM
Clark, W., Pte, 3rd London Rgt Royal Fusiliers: RM, D, P, B
Clarke, H. F. M., Pte, 2/10th Bn The Middlesex Rgt: RT
Clarke, Capt. A. W., C.B.E., D.S.O., R.N., Midshipman, H.M.S. *Implacable* and S.S. *Arcadian*: D, P, RM, RT, RR
Coan, T. H., Pte, 1/3rd East Lancs. Fld Amb., 42nd Div.: VP, RM
Cobb, A. H. K., Paymaster Sub-Lieut, H.M.S. *Bacchante*: D, RR, VP
Cockell, R. A., Spr, R.N.D. Eng., 1st Fld Coy: D, VP, RR
Collingridge, Brig. H. V., 2nd Lieut, 1/6th Gurkha Rifles: L
Common, J., Pte, K.O.S.B.: VP
Constable, W. Briggs, 2nd Lieut, R.F.A.: RT
Cook, Col. R., Surrey Yeomanry: P, RT, RR
Cooper, T., Stoker, R.N.: RR
Coppard, E. G., Sig., R.E. Signals: RT
Cory, R., Leading Seaman, *Drake* Bn R.N.D.: RM, maps
Cosby, Brig. N. R. C., 2nd Lieut, 1/5th Royal Gurkha Rifles: B, RT

Gray, J., R.N.A.S.: RR
Grayken, E., H.M.S. *Irresistible* and Monitor *M30*: RM
Grimshaw, Lieut-Col. J. E., V.C., Pte, 1st Bn Lancs. Fusiliers, 29th Div.: RR
Haigh, Lieut-Col. J., 1st Royal Inniskilling Fusiliers, 29th Div.: O, D, RT, RR
Hale, Mrs G. A., nurse on hospital ship *Aquitania*: RM
Hall, S. A., Sgt, 1st Lancs. Fusiliers, 29th Div.: RM
Hamilton, Mrs M.: photos and books of her R.N. husband
Hammond, G. H., Sgt, attached Royal Warwicks Reg.: diary given by his widow
Harding, Field-Marshal Lord, G.C.B., C.B.E., D.S.O., M.C., 2nd Lieut, County of London
    Yeomanry: RR
Hargreaves, Cdr W. D. R., Midshipman, H.M.S. *Sapphire*: RM
Harris, E., H.M.S. *Lord Nelson*: RM
Harris, E. S., Pte, 2/1st Bn London Rgt Royal Fusiliers: RT, VP
Harris, H., R.A.M.C. 1st West Lancs, Fld Amb.: RT
Harrison, W., L/Cpl, 5th Manchester Rgt: VP, RR
Hart, N., Lieut, Gurkha Rifles: L
Hartshorne, Lieut-Col. N. H., M.C., S. Staffs. Rgt, 11th Div.: P, RT
Hazlewood, A, Pte, 87th Fld Amb., 29th Div.: D, RM
Heath, G. W., Sick Berth C.P.O., H.M.S. *Beryl* and G.H.Q.: VP, L, RT
Hedley, Maj.-Gen. R. C. O.: assistance in attempt to trace Gurkha survivors
Henson, W. T., Chief Petty Officer, H.M.S. *Agamemnon* and H.M.S. *Swiftsure*: RM, P
Hepworth, C. R., Gnr, R.F.A.: RM
Hibberd, A. S., M.B.E., 2nd Lieut, 5th Dorset Yeomanry: RM, RR
Hibbs, J., Pte, Royal Newfoundland Rgt: RT
Hicks, G., Sgt, Royal Newfoundland Rgt: RT
Holbrook, Cdr N. D., V.C., R.N., Lieut-Cdr, H.M. Submarine *B 11*: RR
Hole, Maj., 2nd Lieut, Royal 1st Devon Yeomanry: RR, VP, P, B, maps
Hole, C. A., Pte, 1/7th Essex Rgt, 54th Div.: L
Holvey, F. G., Seaman, H.M.S. *Cornwall*: P, RM
Hooper, Capt. J., R.N.R. Officer Arm. Mcht., Cruiser *Sarnia*: RR
Hope, Capt. G., Captain of H.M.S. *Queen Elizabeth*: VP
Horridge, Major G. B., T.D., 1/5th Lancs. Fusiliers, 125th Bde, 42nd Div.: maps, RM,
    RR
Houston, J. S., Pte, 2nd Lowland Fld Amb. R.A.M.C.: P, RM, VP
Hunnam, H. E., Dvr, 14th Siege Battery, R.G.A.: D, RR
Hutchings, Major E. L., L/Cpl, 2/10th Middlesex Rgt: RM, RR
Huttenbach, Col. N. H., 2nd Lieut, R.F.A. R.H.A.: RM, RR
Jameson, Maj.-Gen. T., C.B.E., D.S.O., officer in R.M. R.N.D.: P, RM
Jarvis, Major T. S. W., O.B.E., 2nd Lieut, 6th Manchesters: RM
Jebens, Major F. J., 2nd Royal Fusiliers, 29th Div.: RR
Johns, P.V.: RM
Johnson, J. M., Pte, R.M.L.I. (Plymouth Div.): RM, RR
Jones, C., Pte, 87th Fld Amb., 29th Div.: RM
Jordan, T. C., Cpl, 2nd S.W. Borderers, 29th Div.: RR
Kay, T., Spr, R. E.: RM
Keeler, G. E., Seaman, H.M.S. *Lord Nelson*: D
Keogh, W., Sherwood Foresters: RM, RR
Kerr, H. C., M.M., Petty Officer, R.N.D. *Hawke* Bn: RM

Kettles, A., Cpl, Scottish Horse Fld Amb.: P
King, F. H., Pte, R.A.M.C., 29th Div.: RM
King, W. F., Sgt, R.E. 29th Div.: P, RM
Laidlaw, Lieut-Col. R. F. E., Order of the Nile, Acting Capt., 1st Royal Munster
    Fusiliers, 29th Div.: P, RT
Lamb, D. J., Gnr, R.G.A., 4th Highland Mtd Bde, 29th Div.: B, RM, RR
Lane, W. O., Sgt, R.A.P.C., H.Q. 29th Div.: RM
Lawes, Lieut-Col. J. O.: assistance in attempt to trace Gurkha survivors
Lawrance, S. F., Pte, 4th Bn Worcester Rgt, 29th Div.: RR
Lawrence, Lieut-Col. L. B., Cpl and A.Q.M.S., 5th Royal Inniskilling Fusiliers, 10th
    Div.: RR
Ledger, G. C., Pte, R.A.M.C., 11th Div.: RR
Lee, Capt. A. B., 3rd Officer, H.M.T. *S29*: RR, O
Lightfoot, Brig., 2nd Lieut, Middlesex Rgt: RM, P
Lindberg, Lieut-Col. C. H., 2nd Lieut, 8th Northumberland Fusiliers, 11th Div.: L,
    RM, RR
Lines, W. P., R.Q.M.S., 6th Bn Royal Welch Fusiliers: RM
Lissenburg, Capt. D. N. Meneaud, Trmptr, Sig., R.F.A. 97th Bty, 147th Bde, 29th
    Div.: RT, RR, P
Livingstone, W., Colour Sgt, Fife and Forfar Yeomanry: RT
Lloyd, Mrs B.: husband's Gallipoli P.O.W. souvenir
Longley-Cook, Vice-Admiral E. W., C.B., C.B.E., D.S.O.: D, L, RM, VP, P, RR
Lorimer, Mrs I.: photo and diary of father-in-law, ship's surgeon Dr Lorimer
Lowe, E. A. H., 2nd Lieut, Dorset Yeomanry: P, RM
Luck, J. E., 3rd Writer R.N., H.M.S. *Lord Nelson* and H.M.S. *Triad*: D, P, VP, RM, RR
Lugg, W. W., M.M., Gnr, R.F.A., 58th Bde, 11th Div.: RM, RR
Lynden-Bell, Lieut-Col. L. A.: typescript memoirs of Major-Gen. Sir A. Lynden-Bell
Lyster, Capt. H. N., M.B.E., M.C., 3rd City of London Royal Fusiliers: RT, RR
McConnell, B. A., L/Cpl, 1st Royal Inniskilling Fusiliers, 29th Div.: O, RM, RR
McFetridge, Lieut-Col. C. H. T.,: assistance in attempt to trace Indian Brigade material
Mackintosh, C., O.B.E., 2nd Lieut, 9th Warwicks Rgt, 39th Bde, 13 Div.: RM, RR, B
MacMillan, Gen. Sir Gordon, K.C.B., K.C.V.O., C.B.E., D.S.O., MC** memoirs of Col. I.
    Campbell, Maj. 2nd Lovat Scouts
McPherson, A., Lancs. Fusiliers (A.S.C.): RM
Mankin, Capt. J., Tpr, 3rd County of London Yeomanry: B, P, RM, maps, O
Mann, W. S., R.N.D.: RM
Mansergh, Vice Admiral Sir Aubrey, K.B.E., C.B. D.S.C., Midshipman H.M.S. *Queen*:
    RM, RR
May, P. P., Leading Seaman H.M.S. *Triumph* and H.M.S. *Lydiard*: P, RT, RR
Mayne, C. F., Surgeon Lieut, R.N., R.N.D. 2nd Fld Amb.: RR
Mead, Maj. W. G., Cpl, R.E. Signals, 9th Army Corps H.Q.: RT, RR
Measures, E. C., Seaman, H.M.S. *Euryalus*: RR
Metcalf, Capt. J. Savile, Midshipman, H.M.S. *Triumph*: RT
Millar, W., Pte, 2/1st City of London Royal Fusiliers: D
Millard, R. F., Lieut, Border Rgt, 29th Div.: VP, B
Minter, C. J.: P
Monaghan, H., Fld Amb., 29th Div.: RM
Moore, L., Pte, 4th Worcester Rgt, 29th Div.: RM, RR

Moore, R. E., Tpr, Suffolk Yeomanry, 54th Div.: P, RR
Moore, Capt. R. W., Ship's Writer, H.M.S. *Euryalus*: RT
Moore, W. C., M.S.M., I.S.M., Bty Sgt Maj., R.F.A. 26th Fld Bty, 17th Bde: P, RT
Morgan, R. E., Sgt, 7th Royal Welch Fusiliers, 158th Bde, 53rd Div.: RM
Morris, Canon A., Sgt, Scottish Horse Yeomanry: D, VP
Moseley, G. F., Chief Petty Officer, Med., R.N., H.M.S. *Prince of Wales*: D, RR
Mott, Maj. G. R., 6/3rd South Lancs. Rgt, 13th Div.: D, RR
Moulds, H., Spr, R.E. Signals: D, RR
Moyle, S. J., L/S, R.N.D. *Drake*: RM
Murray, J., Pte, 4th K.O.S.B. Rgt: RM
Murray, J., L/S., R.N.D. *Hood* Bn: D, VP, RT, RR
Murray, J.N.C., Pte, Lovat Scouts M.G.C.: RM
Murrie, R. A., Pte, Royal Scots, 29th Div.: RR
Nathan, Lord: photographs of his father's Yeomanry service at Suvla
Nevinson, H. K. B., 2nd Lieut, Manchester Rgt: VP, L, P (sent by his sister, Miss B. Nevinson)
Newman, I. H., Spr, 496 Fld Coy (Kent) Royal Engineers: O
Newstead, J., Pte, 6th Yorks.: RR
Nightingall, C. W., Tpr, Surrey Q.M.R. Yeomanry, 29th Div.: L, RT
Noon, M. J., Eng. Sub-Lieut, H.M.F.M. *Princess Ina*: O, VP, RR
Ollive, L. H., Spr, R.E. Signals, 29th Div.: VP, RM, RR
O'Neill, W., R.N.R., H.M.S. *Bacchante*: D
Oren, B., L/Cpl, West Riding Fld Coy, R.E., 29th Div.: RR
Osborne, N.: RM
Palmer, R., Lieut, R.E.: VP, maps, P
Parker, H. G., C.B.E., M.M., Sgt, R.E. Signals, 54th Div.: RM, RT, RR
Parnham, W. J., R.M. Plymouth: D, RM (including letter of Gallipoli recollections from Lieut-Col. C. F. Jerram, C.M.G., D.S.O.)
Pawson, H. W. G., diaries of father, H. A. C. Pawson, 2nd Lieut, Sherwood Rangers
Penwarden, Flying Officer H. G., Cpl, 1st Royal Devon Yeomanry: RM, P, VP
Peterson, H., Pte, 87th Fld Amb., 29th Div.: RM
Pickthall, A. P., Pte, 87th Fld Amb., 29th Div.: RM, P, L, D, VP
Pilling, A., Pte, 6th Lancs. Fusiliers, 42nd Div.: RM
Pilling, H., Pte, 6th Lancs. Fusiliers, 42nd Div.: RM
Pippet, B. C., Ldg Seaman, R.N.D. *Hawke* Bn: RM
Pope, S. A., Kent Yeomanry: RM
Portal, Admiral Sir Reginald, K.C.B., C.B., D.S.C., Lieut, H.M.S. *Bacchante*: P, RR
Powell-Price, Lieut-Col. the Rev. E., M.C., T.D., Capt., 7th Royal Welch Fusiliers, 53rd Div.: RM, RR
Price, D.: photos of Australian soldier I. Davies
Prynne, Maj. H. Fellowes, Cpl, 2nd County of London Yeomanry: RT, P, RR
Pyne, Maj.: letters of his father, W. M. Pyne, Lieut-Col., R.E.
Rackham, Brig. B. B., C.B.E., M.C., D.L., R.N.D. *Hawke* Bn: VP, B, RR
Rathbone, Brig. R., O.B.E., Lieut, 6th Royal N. Lancs. Rgt, 38th Bde, 13th Div.: RT, RM
Raymond, Ernest, Capt., R.A.C. Ch.D. C.F., 126th Bde, 42nd Div.: RR
Rees, T., Pte, 2nd Bn South Wales Borderers: D, RM, RR
Richards, I., Dvr, R.E., 29th Div.: RR
Richardson, R., R.N.D.: RR

Tolley, J. W., Pte, 39th Fld Amb., R.A.M.C., 38th Bde, 13th Div.: RM
Tomkinson, C. R., Pte, 87th Fld Amb., 29th Div.: D
Traill, Air Vice Marshal T., C.B., O.B.E., D.F.C., Midshipman, H.M.S. *Lord Nelson*: map, RT, RR
Traynor, F. W., R.A.M.C., 11th C.C.S., 29th Div.: VP, RT, RM, RR
Trotman, C. L., Seaman, R.N.D. *Drake*: RM
Turnbull, W., Pte, 1/4th K.O.S.B.: RM, VP
Turner, H. H., Pte, A/QM, Portsmouth Bn R. Marines, R.N.D.: RT, RM
Tysall, Capt. E., Spr, R.E. Signals attached 1st Div. A.I.F.: RR
Vallat, Capt. K. W.: letters of his uncle, Lieut-Cdr H. K. L. Shaw, H.M.S. *Minerva*
Verschoyle, Maj. T., M.C., 5th Royal Inniskilling Fusiliers, 10th Div.: D, RM, RR, O, and translation of 1915 Turkish letters
Vetch, Cdr H. A., R.N.R., Midshipman, H.M.S. *Prince of Wales*: VP, P, RR
Walker, N., Pte, Manchester Rgt: B
Ward, A. L., Pte, 2/10th Middlesex Rgt, 53rd Div.: RM
Ward, F., Spr, R.E. Signals, 29th Div.: P
Ward, M., Tpr, Dorset Yeomanry: RT
Ward, R. Ogier: copy of letter to *The Times* 1936 re British influence in Turkey 1914
War Graves Commission, Commonwealth: assistance with field work on the Peninsula
Watkins, C., 6th Lancs. Fusiliers, 42nd Div.: RT, RR
Watson, Lieut-Col. D. B., M.C., 2nd Lieut, 2/10th Middlesex Rgt, 53rd Div.: D, P, VP, RR
Weakford, S. A., Spr, R.E. Signals, 29th Div.: RM
Weaver, E., H.M.S. *Amethyst*: RT
Wettern, Capt. E., Spr, No. 2 Fld Coy R.N.D. Engineers: VP, O, B,P, D, L, RT, RR,maps
Whittall, Maj. H. M., D.S.O., Lieut. R.M., R.N.D., attached 29th Div.: RM, RT, RR
Whyte, A. L. G., S/S, R.A.M.C., 1/3rd E. Anglian Fld Amb., 54th Div.: D, L, RT, B, RR
Wicks, Maj., Sgt, 2nd Royal Fusiliers, 29th Div.: RR
William-Powlett, Vice-Admiral Sir P., K.C., K.C.M.G., C.B.E., D.S.O., Midshipman, H.M.S. *Vengeance* and H.M.S. *Beagle*: D, P, RR
Williams, Cdr A. M., C.B.E., D.S.C., Midshipman, H.M.S. *Euryalus*: RT, RR, P
Williamson, Capt. W. Corbett, Pte, R.M., R.N.D. Corps H.Q.: VP, RT, RR
Willis, E. F., Pte, R.M.L.I. (Chatham): D, P, VP, RR
Wilsdon, Mrs S.: P
Wilson, A. E., Seaman, R.N.D. *Nelson*: VP, D, RR
Wilson, Cdr H., O.B.E., D.S.C., Midshipman, H.M.S. *Euryalus*: P, D, RR , L
Winkcup, S., Pte, A.S.C.: RR
Wolton, Capt. E. D., Lieut, 1/5th Suffolk Rgt T.F., 43rd Bde: L, RR, B, RT, RM
Wood, H. C., Quartermaster Sergeant, R.N.D. Engineers: D
Wood, J., Seaman R.N.D. *Anson* Bn: RR
Wood, W. G., Gnr, R.F.A.: RM
Woodworth, F. T. K., Lieut, 7th Manchester Rgt, 42nd Div.: O and papers of F. Bamber, 7th Manchester Rgt

Australian

Alexander, Maj. A., Lieut, 10th Bn: RR
Allchin, Lieut-Col. E. F., Sig. Sgt, 10th Bn: RR
Alston, The Rev. E. C., Pte, 12 Bn: VP, RM

Andrews, Canon M., Pte, 1st Fld Amb.: RR
Arnold, C. J., Pte, 4th Bn: RR
Bachtold, Brig. H., Capt, 1st Fld Coy Engineers, 1st Div.: RR, L, P
Bailey, H. R., Pte, 19th Bn: RR
Bain, E., Sgt, 10th Light Horse: RT, RR
Barton, W., Bugler, 2nd Bn: RM, RR
Bell, Mrs J. R.: letters, photos, equipment and various papers of her husband (Lieut, 12th Bn Reinforcements in 1915)
Bells, Mrs N. C.: diary of her uncle, G. P. Edwards, Tpr, 1st Light Horse
Berrisford, F., Pte, 8th Bn: RR
Bertwistle, W. H., Lieut, 27th Bn, Machine-Gun Section: D, RR
Bevan, T. G., Tpr, 3rd Light Horse: RM
Birtwistle, I. T., O.B.E., Lieut, 22nd Bn: D, RR
Bradford, J. C., Acting Sgt, 7th Light Horse: RR
Bradshaw, W. A., L/Cpl, 10th Bn: RR
Brearley, S., Sgt, 8th Bn, 1st Australian Div.: RM
Briggs, C. H., Gnr, 9th Btn, 1st Australian Div.: RR
Brown, A. E.: Tpr, 12th Light Horse: RR
Brown, J. A., Lieut, 10th Light Horse: RM
Brownell, Mrs P. J.: diary of her husband, Gnr Brownell, A.I.F.
Burgess, Pte, 17th Bn: RR, B
Burrows, G., Spr, 1st Fld Coy Engineers, 1st Div.: RR, P
Butcher, Maj. M. G., Tpr, 3rd Light Horse: RR, P, O
Champion, Dr B., Pte, 1st Bn: RR
Chequer, Mrs S. D.: letter extracts from her father, Pte H. A. Fildes, 12th Bn
Clark, W.: diary and typescript recollections of his father, Pte W. M. Clark, 10th Bn
Coley, L., Tpr, 12th Light Horse: RR, D
Costello, B. de, Gnr, 8th Bn, 1st Australian Div.: RT
Craven, N., Pte, 20th Bn: RR
Crook, Miss M., nursing Gallipoli wounded in Egypt: RM
Curlewis, G. C., M.B.E., J.P., 2nd Lieut, 16th Bn: RR
Cutler, Brig. R. V., M.B.E., M.C., Capt., 2nd Fld Coy Engineers, 1st Div.: RM
Deacon, Mrs F. M.: photos and various papers of her father, A. F. Waite, Spr, 3rd Fld Coy Engineers
Dorrington, Mrs P.: 1914-18 personal effects of her husband (Lieut, 1915)
Duke, Lieut-Col. C. R., Pte, 4th Bn: RT
Elliot, Mrs A. G., as Sister Gordon King, A.A.N.S.: RR, VP
Evans, C., L/Cpl, 12th Bn: RM
Evans, M. C., Tpr, 1st Light Horse Fld Amb.: D, VP, O, L, RT, RR
Fergusson, Brig. M. A., Bdr, 3rd Fld Battery A.F.A.: RR
Fitzmaurice, J., D.C.M., Capt., 10th Light Horse: VP, RR, and cuttings book of Gallipoli service of Throssell, V.C.
Frankcombe, L., Pte, 12th Bn: RM
Fry, A., Gnr, 8th Battery: RM, RT
Good, C. B., Pte, 12th Bn: RR
Gordon, Wing Commander J. R., Lieut, 10th Bn: RR
Graham, L. W., Pte, 1st Bn: RR
Greer, W. F., Gnr, 1st Battery, 1st Bde F.A.: RR, VP

Grove, Mrs M.: diaries of her husband, G. C. Grove, Lieut, 2nd Fld Coy Engineers, 1st Div.

Hamilton, W. L., 2nd Lieut, Australian A.S.C.: RM

Hansen, Mrs K.: diary of V. D. Hansen, 12th Bn

Hart, W., Cpl, 16th Bn: RR

Heathcote, Mrs P.: B

Hetherington, J. W., 3rd Bde Infantry: RM

Hitch, H. V., Pte, 11th Bn: RR

Hocking, F. R.: assistance in tracing Victorian veterans and Gallipoli photos

Holmes, Col. B, D.S.O., Capt., 17th Bn: RR, B, L, VP

Howe, W., Pte, 12th Bn: RR

Hudson, H. H., Pte, 7th Bn: O, RT

Jackson, N., Pte, 1st Bn: RR

Jackson, T., Pte, 28th Bn: O, RR

Jarvis, H.: Australian 1915 newpaper

Johnson, B. M., Pte, 4th Bn: RR

Johnston, R., Driver, 8th Battery, 1st Australian Div.: RM

Jones, A. E., Cpl, 7th Bn: P, RT, RR

Jones, R. L., Pte, 11th Bn: O, P, B, RR

Joyce, A. E., Pte, 9th Bn: D, RR

Kahan, H. K., Major, Sig., 28th Bn: RR, B, P

Keast, Mrs A.: diary, VP and RM of her husband, Pte J. R. T. Keast, 11th Bn

Kennedy, F.A., M.B.E., assistance in making contact with Australian veterans

Kent, Mrs M.: Gallipoli photographs of her uncle, Staff Sgt A. W. Ross, Australian Postal Corps

Kirk, A. K., Lieut, 6th Bn: P

Lanagan, J., Pte, 16th Bn: VP

Lapthorne, R., M.M., Pte, 12th Bn: RR, O, P

Lawless, F. A.: diary of his father, C. J. Lawless, 4th Fld Amb.

Logue, L. J., and Woolf, G.: typescript extracts from diary of G. A. Lamerton, 1st A.I.F.

Lovett, L., Bdr, 9th Battery A.F.A., 1st Div.: RR, P, VP and letters of Sgt A. J. Clennett, 9th Battery A.F.A.

Lowth, C., Gnr, 8th Battery A.F.A., 1st Div.: RR

MacGregor, J. H., Pte, 18th Bn: RR, VP

Mackenzie, H. K., Cpl, 3rd Bde Infantry: RT

Mackenzie, J. P., Sgt, 16th Bn: RR

McKinlay, Col. J. L., O.B.E., M.M., Spr, 1st Div. Sig. Coy: P, RT, RR

Mackintosh, S. J., Pte, 2nd Bn: RR

McLennan, W., Tpr, 2nd Light Horse: P, RR, RM

McNeill, Brig. J. G. D., Capt, 5th Light Horse: RR, P

Manuel, Mrs: letters of father, private in 11th Bn

Mayne, E. L., Gnr, 1st Brigade Ammunition Column, A.F.A.: RR

Minogue, F., 10th Light Horse and Imp. Camel Corps in Egypt and Palestine: B

Molloy, T. J., Pte, 1st Bn: RR

Moore, J.: papers, photographs, diary and paybook of his father, E. Moore, 1st A.A.M.C.

Morris, A. P., 1st Light Horse Fld Amb.: RM

Mortimer, Mrs M.: letters and communion chalice of her father, Chaplain W. Mackenzie, 4th Bn

Nicholas, R. A., M.B.E., Pte, Hospital Transport Corps, A.I.F.: L, RR, VP

Nixon, R.: assistance in tracing N.S.W. veterans

Oakes, D. S. M., Spr, 1st Fld Coy Engineers, 1st Div.: RR

Oliver, A. J., Tpr, 3rd Light Horse: P

Orr, H., Sgt, 16th Bn: RR

Parkes, Cobden, 2nd Lieut, 1st Bn: D, RM, RR

Paterson, W. W., 3rd Infantry Bde: letter made available by G. A. Radnell

Pickford, Mrs: letter to, and diary of, V. Frankcombe, 15th Bn

Pinkerton, R., Gnr, 3rd Battery A.F.A., 1st Div.: RR

Rabbidge, A., Tpr, 2nd Light Horse: P, RM

Radnell, G. A., Pte, 8th Bn: RM, RT, D, B, VP

Rutter, A. L., Sgt, 26th Bn: RR

Scudds, H., Pte, 10th Bn: RM

Sharman, C. A., Pte, 26th Bn, Machine-Gun Section: P, VP, RR

Sharp, F. H., L/Cpl, Sig., 12th Bn: B, RR, P, VP

Shaw, Lieut-Col. G. D., M.C., V.D., Lieut, 28th Bn: RT, RR, and assistance in meeting West Australian veterans

Sinclair, C. G., Pte, 24th Bn: RT, L

Skinner, E. C.: letters of his father, Pte E. C. Skinner, 16th Bn

Smith, T. S., Pte, 2nd Bn: RR, RT

Smythe, C. D.: letter of his uncle, Pte H. A. Smythe, 3rd Bn, and help in contacting N.S.W. veterans

Smythe, V., Lieut, 4th Bn: RM

Stagles, W., Pte, 11th Bn: VP, P, O, RT, RR

Sutton, S.: P

Sykes, P. W., Pte, 4th Australian Fld Amb.: RT, RR

Syme, J., Tpr, 10th Light Horse: RR

Thyer, Brig. W., 2nd Div. Sig. Coy: RT, L

Turner, F. G., Pte, 3rd Infantry Bde: RM

Walker, J. A., Cpl, 19th Bn: RR

Watson, Lieut-Col. S. H., Capt., 2nd Div. Sig. Coy: RR, RT, including diary extracts from Sgt Both

Westbrook, F. E., Gnr, 2nd Battery A.F.A.: RR and 1915 poetry

White, W. F., Tpr, 7th Light Horse: RR, P

Williams, C. H., Tpr, 10th Light Horse: RR

Williams, S. M., L/Cpl, 11th Bn: VP, O, RR

Wilson, W. J., Pte, 12th Bn: VP, RR

Wordsworth, Maj.-Gen. R. H., C.B., C.B.E., Lieut, 1st Light Horse: RR, P

Young, Mrs H.: letters of her father, G. C. Killner, 1st Light Horse Fld Amb.

Young, O. C., Bugler, 16th Bn: B, RR, P

New Zealand

Aiken, F. W., Sgt, Div. Sig. Coy, N.Z. Engineers: RT, RR

Algie, D. C.: diary and VP of C. S. Algie, Lieut, Auckland Bn

Anderson, J. A., Pte, Canterbury Bn: RR

Angus, W. M., Pte, 2nd Div. Train (later attached to R.N.A.S.): RR, P
Armstrong, N. J., Tpr, Auckland Mtd Rifles: RR, VP
Barclay, W. P., Pte, Div. H.Q.: RR
Bassett, C. R. G., V.C., Cpl, N.Z. Div. Sig. Coy: RR, RT
Batchelor, E. H. S., Lieut, Canterbury Bn: RR
Bell, W. A., Pte, 1st Wellington Bn: RR
Berry, H. N., Tpr, Auckland Mtd Rifles: D, O
Bishop, Lieut-Col. Gibson, M.C., 1st Lieut, Otago Bn: VP, RM, P, RR
Blanks, A. D., Tpr, Auckland Mtd Rifles: RR, P
Bloor, Mrs N.: photographs of Gnr T. H. Sutherland, N.Z.F.A.
Blue, J., Pte, Canterbury Bn, Machine-Gun Section: RR
Brown, B. B.: letter of father, Col. C.H.J. Brown, Canterbury Bn
Brown, A. S., Pte, 1st Otago Bn: RR
Canton, C. H., Pte, Wellington Bn: RR, map, B
Cates, Mrs M.: diary of her father-in-law, C. Cates, N.Z. Medical Corps
Chambers, M. S.: letter of his brother, Major S. Chambers, Wellington Mtd Rifles
Claridge, C. J., Pte, 3rd Auckland Bn: VP, D, RR, RM
Claridge, Mrs H. K.: diary of her father, Sgt G. Cardno, N.Z. Medical Corps
Clark, N., Driver, N.Z.A.S.C.: RT, RM
Clunies Ross, S., Gnr, 1st Battery N.Z.F.A.: RR
Colwell, Mrs B.: assistance in taping N.Z. veterans and in gathering original material
Comyns, Miss D.: letter and diary extracts of her brother, L/Cpl C. L. Comyns, 1st
   Wellington Bn
Cooper, E. A. J.: letters and diary of his father, Pte A. F. Cooper, Wellington Bn
Currey, A. A., Bdr, 1st Battery N.Z.F.A.: L, RM, RR, map
Davie, R., Pte, Wellington Bn: RT
Davies, Mrs: typescript memoirs of her husband, a N.Z. infantryman taken P.O.W. on
   the Peninsula
Edwards, G. L.: diaries of Bugler A. Bayne, Wellington Bn
Elsom, C., Spr, 1st Fld Coy, N.Z. Engineers: RR
Evans, Mrs C. A., Gallipoli veteran's widow: P
Fagan, J. A., Pte, Auckland Bn: RR, D, VP and diary extracts from Pte H. B. Raudrop,
   Auckland Bn, and letter of F. W. Watson, Auckland Bn
Fenwick, C. E.: diary of his father, Lieut-Col. P. C. Fenwick, N.Z. Medical Corps,
   Deputy Assistant Director Medical Services
Fielden, E. R.: diary of his father, Bomb. H. R. Fielden, 3rd Battery N.Z.F.A.
Flamank, Mrs P. A.: diary and personal effects of her father, M. A. Richards, Tpr,
   Otago Mtd Rifles
Fleming, N., Sgt, N.Z. Medical Corps, 1st Fld Amb.: RR
Foord, W. H., Cpl, 1st Fld Coy, N.Z. Engineers: RR
Foote, F. J., Tpr, Auckland Mtd Rifles: RT, RR, VP
Furby, Maj. W. E. S., Capt., 1st Wellington Bn: RR
Galloway, Capt. M. S., M.C., O.B.E., Sgt, 1st Wellington Bn: RR
Garrett, H. G., Pte, Auckland Mtd Rifles: RR
Gasparich, J. G., Sgt, Canterbury Bn: RM
Geary, Capt. S. J., Cpl, 1st Auckland Bn: RR
Gollop, Miss G.: copy of diary of her father, C. T. Gollop, N.Z.F.A.
Gressen, Sir Kenneth, K.B.E., P.C., Major, 1st Canterbury Bn: RR

Griffin, Miss L.: photograph of her brother on the Peninsula
Harrigan, C. T., Pte, 1st Otago Bn: RR, VP, B
Harris, Capt. R. H., Sgt, 1st Auckland Bn: RR, RM, RT, O
Hatrick, H. K., Cpl, Auckland Mtd Rifles: L, VP, map
Hawke, H.: diary of his father, E. Hawke, Cpl, 1st Canterbury Bn
Hayden, C. R., Infantryman: RM
Hilston, Mrs A.: VP
Honnor, D. W.: letters of his uncle, E. H. Honnor, Infantry Officer
Hood, J., Pte, N.Z. Medical Corps: RR
Horneman, J., Infantryman: RM
Howard, H.: P
Howe, O. W., Pte, Auckland Bn: RR
Hughes, F. W., L/Cpl, N.Z.F.A.: RR
Hunter, H. G., Pte, 1st Canterbury Bn: D, P, RR
Jenkin, H. C., Sgt, N.Z.F.A.: RR
Jenkins, M. E., Sgt, Canterbury Mtd Rifles: RR
Jennings, A. G., M.C., Sgt, 1st Wellington Bn: D, VP, P, RR
Jennings, Col. W. I. K., D.S.O., Capt., Otago Bn: RR
Keesing, H. W., Pte, N.Z. Medical Corps: D
Latimer, L. H., Pte, 1st Otago Bn: RR
Leaman, A. W. H., Tpr, Canterbury Mtd Rifles: RR, map, P
Leary, L., Pte, 1st Wellington Bn: RT
Little, Mrs E. E.: diary and photographs of her husband, D. A. Little, 1st Canterbury Bn
Lush, A., Spr, N.Z. Engineers: RT
Lyddiard, A. W., Pte, N.Z.F.A.: RR
McBeath, C., Sgt, Auckland Bn: RR, O
McCarthy, D. G., Pte, Otago Bn: RR
McCown, T. W.: diary of his brother-in-law in Wellington Bn (G. E. Littlejohn)
McKeith, E. G., Pte, 1st Canterbury Bn: RM
McMillan, J., Cpl, Canterbury Mtd Rifles: RT, P
McPherson, R., Gnr, N.Z.F.A.: RR
McRobie, J. D., Cpl, N.Z. Engineers: D, VP, RR
Mansfield, D. R., Sgt, 1st Fld Coy, N.Z. Engineers: RM, RR, D
Marris, Capt. A., Pte, Canterbury Bn, Machine-Gun Section: RR, P, B, VP, D, O
Maxwell, N. R., Pte, 1st Auckland Bn: RR, VP, L
May, Miss E. M. H., photos of her brother George May and friend Joe McBride in the Auckland Bn
Morgan, G. M., L/Cpl, Canterbury Mtd Rifles: RR
Morton, family of Capt. A. B., Staff Capt., N.Z. Staff Corps: diary and papers relating to his death on the Peninsula
Muir, Mrs A., widow of a Gallipoli veteran: B
Murphy, Col. W., C.B.E., M.C., J.P., Pte, 1st Otago Bn: RT and assistance in contacting N.Z. veterans
Murray, A., Infantryman: RT
Murton, W., Pte, 1st Fld Amb., N.Z. Medical Corps: RM
Oakey, Lieut-Col. A. N., M.C., Lieut, Field Troop N.Z. Engineers: RR
Palmer, H. V., Pte, Canterbury Bn: B, D, RT, RR

Palmer, J., Tpr, Auckland Mtd Rifles: RR, VP, B
Park, Air Marshal Sir Keith, G.C.B., K.B.E., M.C., D.F.C., 2nd Lieut, N.Z.F.A. and attached R.F.A.: RR
Parker, Lieut-Col. F. W., O.B.E., Capt., R.N.Z.A.S.C.: RM, RR, P
Parsons, M., Tpr, Canterbury Mtd Rifles: RR
Pennefather, Capt. S. S., D.C.M., Pte Wellington Bn: RR
Pether, Mrs K.: book and memoirs of her father, N. Clark Dunner, N.Z.F.A.
Price, T. H., Spr, 3rd Fld Coy, N.Z. Engineers: RM
Potts, H. W., Pte, 1st Otago Bn: RR
Priestley, H. G. M., Cpl, N.Z. Medical Corps Fld Amb.: D
Purdie, Mrs M. E.: contemporary account of Pte R. D. Baker, Canterbury Bn
Rasmussen, H. P., Tpr, Canterbury Mtd Rifles: RR
Rawlings, Capt. C. H., M.C., T.D.: D, O, RR
Reece, J. C., Pte, 3rd Auckland Bn: RM
Roberts, J. J., Pte, 1st Wellington Bn: RR, VP
Robinson, A. E., Pte, Auckland Bn: B, L, RR
Rogers, F., Sgt, 1st Otago Bn: RM, P
Rogers, P., 1st Otago Bn: RR, RM
Rudd, J. F., L/Cpl, Canterbury Mtd Rifles, Machine-Gun Section: RM, D, P, RR
Ryan, W. C., Sgt Clerk, N.Z. Pay Corps: P, B
Seddon, G. H., Pte, 1st Otago Bn: RR
Skinner, J. S., Sgt, Otago Bn: RR
Smith, A., Pte, Wellington Bn: memoirs drawn up with assistance of M. Moorhead, RT
Smith, A. E. W., Pte, Canterbury Bn: RR
Smith, F. G.: Sapper Moore-Jones prints
Spence, F. G., 2nd Lieut, 5th Battery N.Z.F.A.: RM
Stacey, D. E., Pte, 1st Auckland Bn: RR
Stevens, K. M., Tpr, Auckland Mtd Rifles: VP, D, RR and published memoirs
Taverndale, F. W., Sgt, Wellington Bn: RR
Taylor, L. G., Pte, Canterbury Bn: D, RR
Thomas, C. W., Tpr, Auckland Mtd Rifles: RT, RM
Thompson, A. C., Pte, Canterbury Bn: VP, P
Twisleton, Miss N. G., letters of her father, an officer in the Otago Mtd Rifles, and diary of N.Z. Nursing Sister Speedy
Walsh, C. J., Pte, 1st Auckland Bn: D, RR
Watson, O. L., Pte, Canterbury Bn: P, RR
Weir, R. J., Pte, Wellington Bn: RR
Westenra, J.: RR
Whitcombe, A.: RR
Whiting, E. H., Pte, Canterbury Bn: RR
Williams, Mrs: B
Wilson, A. M., Pte, 1st Wellington Bn: RR
Winter, J. H., Tpr, Wellington Mtd Rifles: RR
Wyatt, A., Pte, Auckland Bn: P, RM
Wyatt, W. C.: P
Young, Mrs A., widow of a Gallipoli veteran: 1915 gas mask

French

Albert, Augustin, Machine-Gun Coy, 312 Brigade: L, RT, RR
Bareille, J., Sgt, 4ième Rég. Mixte Colonial: VP, P, B
Baroli, Simple Soldat, 4ième Rég. de Zouaves: RR
Beurier, Dr F.: photographs of his father, a French army doctor, on the Peninsula, P, B
Blanc, Gen. (and Maj.-Gen. Belchem): assistance in contacting French veterans
Bollon, François, Simple Soldat, 6ième Rég. Colonial: VP, RM, RR
Bory, Jean Pierre, 105ième d'Artillerie Lourde: RM, RR
Deffez, Jean, Cannonier, battleship *Gaulois*: VP, D
Delaye, Contre Amiral, Enseigne de Vaisseau de Première Classe, French Air Squadron at Tenedos: RT, P, D, RR
Doin, Louis, Mountain Artillery: VP, RT, RR
Élie, Armand, Simple Soldat, 4ième Rég. Mixte Colonial: RM, RR
Evans, Maillard, battleship *Gaulois*: RM
Eymard, Jules, Radio Telegraphist at Kum Kale landing and on the Peninsula: P, RM, RR
Favot, L., Caporal, 175ième Rég. d'Infanterie: RR
Fournel, Adrien, Simple Soldat, 175ième Rég.: RR, VP, RM
Galline, F., Pharmacien at Seddel Bahr field hospital: RM, RR, L
Galoche, E. M., Caporal, 6ième d'Infanterie Colonial: RR
Garnier, Maître, 18ième Rég. d'Artillerie: RR
Giauffret, Simple Soldat, 4ième Rég. de Zouaves: RR
Gilormini, Jean, Sgt, 175ième Rég. de Marche: RR, B
Gondard, Maître, 6ième d'Infanterie Colonial: VP, RT, RR
Grammond, Mme Viricel de: diary of a member of the family who served on the Peninsula in the 2ième Zouaves
Gras, Henri, 3ième Bn, 1er Rég. de Marche d'Afrique: RT, RR
Guédet-Guépratte, Mme: complete private and official papers of Admiral Guépratte
Herkenne, Mme: documents and notes on service of her father in 3ième Zouaves
Hoaire, P. de la, Marine on *Argenfels*: RR
Jauras, Frederic, Matelot, battleship *Gaulois*: RM
Jomain, Simple Soldat, 6ième Rég. Colonial: RM, RR
Lucas, Contre Amiral, Enseigne de Vaisseau Première Classe, battleship *Gaulois*: P, RT, RR
Malcailloz, Émile, Caporal, 8ième Rég. du Génie (Télégraphistes): B, P, RT, RR
Massia, Simple Soldat, 4ième Rég. de Zouaves: RR
Medard, L., Simple Soldat, 30ième d'Artillerie Lourde: RR
Motreff, Ernest, minesweeper *Charrue*: P, B
Pastinelli, Matelot, battleship *St Louis*: RR
Payro, Sauveur, Matelot, battleship *Bouvet*: RR
Pegard, Marcel, Chef de Pièce, 45ième Batterie (75mm.), 17ième Rég.: D, P, L, VP, RM, RR
Pellet, Simple Soldat, 58ième Infanterie Mixte Colonial: RR
Petit, Marcel, battleship *Jaureguiberry*: VP, RT, RR
Pion, Fernand, minesweeper *Pioche*: L, RT
Roger, L., 176ième Rég. d'Infanterie: RM
Roux, Ernest, Caporal, 1er Rég. d'Artillerie, 33ième Batterie: RR, P

Roux, M. (de Chalons sur Saône): RR
Sagnier, René, Enseigne de Vaisseau de Première Classe, battleship *Suffren*: RT, RR
Seyeux, M., Midshipman, battleship *Gaulois*: D, RR
Sylvestre, A., Maréchal des Logis, 56ième Batterie d'Artillerie Lourde: VP, RT, RR, P, B
Thierry, Charles, Caporal, 176ième Rég. d'Infanterie: P, L, D. B. RR, O
Tournebise, Henri, Radio Télégraphiste: VP, P, RT, RR
Vallet, Pierre, Enseigne de Vaisseau Première Classe, battleship *Gaulois*: RT, RR
Vallières, S., Officier, 5ième Rég. Chasseurs d'Afrique: RR
Varcollier, H., Enseigne de Vaisseau in command of a supply vessel: RT, RR
Vincenti, M., Simple Soldat, Service de Santé: original water colours done while serving in French infantry on Peninsula
Weil, Commandant R., S. Lieut, 32ième Batterie, 8ième Rég. d'Artillerie: D, P, VP, RT, RR

Turkish

Abdurrahman, Mr: RR
Altay, General: original letters and taperecording
Arkayan, General Askir: RT, RR
Artun, Colonel S.: RR
Belen, General F.: RR
Ben, General O.: RR
Demirsu, Colonel: RR
Dilmen, Mr S.: RM, RR
Ozgen, Captain: RR
Savasman, Lieut-Col. A.: RR

Germany

Sources of Information

Bundesministerium der Verteidigung (Bonn)
Militärgeschichtliches Forschungsamt (Freiburg im Briesgau)
Bundesarchiv Militärarchiv (Bonn)
Deutsches Rotes Kreuz
Stadt Kiel: Der Magistrat Hauptamt
Verband Deutscher Soldaten (Bonn)
Marine Offizier Vereinigung (Bonn – Bad Godesberg)
Alte Adler Gemeinschaft (Bad Kissingen)
Alte Kameraden
Deutscher Soldatenbund Kyffhaüser e.v. (Wiesbaden)
Deutscher Marinebund e.v. (Wilhelmshaven)
Kameradschaftliche Vereinigung der Marineflieger
Western Front veterans and individuals, in particular Wolf Dieter Bach of Schwetzingen
Dr Ervin Liptai, Col. Cdr, War Museum and Institute, Budapest
Personal Contact
Hoffman, Jakob, S.M.S. *Goeben*: RT
Mertz, Heinz, S.M.S. *Goeben*: RT

Mohl, Hans von, S.M.S. *Breslau*, later on Admiral Souchon's staff: RT, RR
Pieper, Kontreadmiral Waldemar, Chief of Ordnance Inspection: typescript Ordnance
    Report provided by his daughter, Frau Irmgard Winckel
Thomsen-Oldenswort, Dr Waldemar, Hamidieh Battery and later A.D.C. to Admiral
    Pieper: RT

2. OTHER ARCHIVES

(Precise references are given in the footnotes for all documents quoted in the text)

British

Public Record Office, London

Notes on meetings of the War Council, the Dardanelles Committee and the War
    Committee, with Cabinet memoranda
War Office and Admiralty papers: appreciations, Kitchener–Hamilton correspondence,
    reports etc.
Mediterranean Expeditionary Force: orders, various papers and war diaries
Allied Squadron in Eastern Mediterranean: orders, various papers and ships' logs

Imperial War Museum, London

Mediterranean Expeditionary Force: orders and various papers
Allied Squadron in Eastern Mediterranean: orders and various papers
Dardanelles Commission Report, 1917

Acheson, Lieut, 2 letters (naval action in Dardanelles, 1915)
Berridge, Midshipman W. L., notes and letters
Birdwood, General, letters from Anzac to Col. Rintoul, rtd
Bremner, F. D. H., No. 3 Squadron, R.N.A.S., log book
Burge, Lieut-Col. N. O., R.M.L.I., letters
Clough, H., ship's surgeon, letters
Dawnay, Major G. P., M.E.F. H.Q. Staff officer, letters
Douglas-Jones, Capt. E. D., memoir of Suvla
Drewry, Midshipman, v.c., letters (V beach, Helles and Suvla landings)
Ford, J. E., R.M.L.I., diary
Jones, Rev. D., privately published diary (Suvla)
King-Wilson, Lieut, 'A Medical Officer's Memoirs'
Lisle, Gen. B. de, letter
Moreton, H. W., diary
Nightingale, Captain G. Warneford, 1st Royal Munster Fusiliers, letters
Samson, Air Commodore C. R., D.S.O., A.F.C., notes and various papers
Thompson, J., 42nd East Lancs. Div., memoirs

Centre for Military Archives, King's College, London

Letters and papers of Gen. Sir Ian Hamilton

National Maritime Museum, Greenwich

Vice-Admiral Sir Arthur Limpus, correspondence with de Robeck, Wemyss, Lord Methuen etc.
Captain Kelly of H.M.S. *Dublin*, proceedings and correspondence
Sir James Porter, Principal Hospital Transport Officer, various papers

Gloucestershire County Record Office

Letters of George Moss to the Rector of Dyrham (Blathwayte Papers)

Roxburgh Museum

Papers relating to the K.O.S.B. Regiment

J. M. Bruce, J. S. Leslie Aeroplane Photographic Collection (Scarborough)

French

French Military Archives, Château de Vincennes, Paris

Documentation on every aspect of the leadership and administration of the Corps Expéditionnaire d'Orient, its relation with the French Ministry of Defence and with the overall command of the M.E.F. H.Q., including plans of the Kum Kale landing of 25 April, reports on the Helles landing and fighting, reports on the French aerodrome at Tenedos, discipline, etc.

French Naval Archives, 3 Rue Octave Gérard, Paris

Official documentation on the allied naval attack of 18 March, especially the loss of the *Bouvet*. (The Musée de la Marine also has material on the *Bouvet*.)

Australian

The State Library, Adelaide, South Australia

Carew Reynell Papers: letters of 7 September 1915 from Birdwood to D. J. Byard on death of Reynell (PRG 29/22); letter written as a diary by Reynell, May 1915 (PRG 29/22)
A. S. Hutton diary for 1915 (D 4975)
Red Cross Repatriation Papers (227 SRG 76)
10th Battalion A.I.F. War Diary (PRG 272/8/1)
10th Battalion A.I.F. file of unofficial letters 1914–15 (PRG 272/9)
Various Gallipoli photos

La Trobe Library, Victoria State Library, Melbourne

Letter of Sgt R. M. Collins, 23rd Bn, to Minister of Defence, Senator Pearce, a friend of the Collins family, 8 November 1915 (Box 940/1 MS 8 133)
Special Instructions for action during suspension of arms, 24 May 1915 (Box 225/4 A). Presented by Sergeant A. Nicholas, 1st A.I.F.

John Monash, letters to wife and daughter, December 1915 (MS 9456)

Letters from Robert M. Calder describing May attack at Cape Helles and August offensive at Anzac (MS 9003)

National Archives, National Library, Canberra

Vasey Papers.

Fisher Papers, Dardanelles Commission Evidence (MS 2919 Series 7)

Murdoch Papers, correspondence with George Pearce, Minister of Defence, September 1915, and with Lloyd George, October 1915 (MS 2823)

Lord Novar Papers (Lord Novar, as Sir Ronald Ferguson, was the Australian Governor-General in 1914–15. He corresponded with both General Birdwood and General Bridges)

General Bridges' letter of 5 May 1915 to Lady Bridges

Royal Military College, Duntroon Canberra

Letters of Capt. Christopher Carrington, R.N.Z.F.A., 1914–15 (Carrington Papers, 7–11)

Australian War Memorial, Canberra

John Simpson Kirkpatrick, letters (AWM 749/80/7)

Diary of General Bridges (AWM 749/12/4)

Lieut-Col. Watson Papers (AWM 419/111/2)

Lord Birdwood Collection, diary for 1915, letters to Bridges, letter from Hamilton

Sgt R. H. Adams, M.M., 8th Bn, letters (AWM 181.11)

Lieut W. E. Addison, 18th Bn, letter written as a diary (AWM 181.11)

C.Q.M.S. A. L. Guppy, 14th Bn, typed extracts from diary (AWM 12.1.16)

Photographic archives

Mitchell Library, Sydney, N.S.W.

Cook, Thomas Murphy, Sgt, 1st Bn, diary

Evans, N. C., 1st Light Horse Fld Amb., letter

Gordon, A. D., 1st Fld Amb., diary account

Hall, Peter, 2nd Stationary Hospital, letter of 2 May 1915 describing voyage of *Seang Choon* to Alexandria

Hellman, A. L., 1st Div. Sig. Coy, diary

Keary, J., 18th Bn, diary

McKinlay, T. J., 8th Bn, letter describing August attack at Lone Pine

Marks, Col. D., 13th Bn, diary

Morris, Sgt. A. P. K., 1st Light Horse, stretcher-bearer, diary

Nixon, Robert Rex, 4th Bn, letters

Nixon, Rupert, 13th Bn, letters

O'Hare, A., 19th Bn, diary

Pearce, M. E., 1st Light Horse, diary

Ruskin, Alfred, of H.M.A.S. *Sydney*, log for 1914 re *Emden*

Wagstaff, Brig.-Gen. C. M., report of attack of 18/19 May to 6 a.m., 20 May

New Zealand

The Alexander Turnbull Library, Wellington

Browne, H. E., Wellington Mtd Rifles, diary (Misc. M.S. 1196)
Clifton, Spr E. C., 1st Fld Coy, N.Z.E.F., diary
Gascoigne, J. W., letters, diary, pay book (Misc. Papers 1007, File 5)
Jones, A. T., diary, January 1915
Melvill, William, papers (M.S. Papers 244, File 10) (N.Z. and Aust. Div. Evacuation Orders)
Paul, J., letter to E. C. Walmsley, 1 June 1915 (Misc. Man. ALS161)
Ritchie, T. R., diary and evidence to the Dardanelles Commission (Misc. M.S. 1428)
Tuck, G. A., diary for 1914–15 (M.S. 1914–18)
Wilson, Sir James A., papers, letters from Gen. Godley, in command N.Z. and Aust. Div., and letter from J. W. Marshall (M.S. Papers 137, folder 12 B)

New Zealand National Archives, Wellington

War Diary, General Staff, N.Z. and Aust. Div.: Nibrunesi Point Raid report, Birdwood/Godley correspondence, Godley/Sir James Allan (Min. of Defence) correspondence
R.N.D. G.S.O.2 War Diary (Lieut-Cdr B. Freyburg, o/c *Hood* Bn, report 26 April 1915)
N.Z. and Aust. Div., General Routine Orders, daily reports, General Staff messages
Private diary of General Braithwaite
The Auckland Bn War Diary

Christchurch Public Library, The New Zealand Room, South Island

The Canterbury Infantry Bn War Diary
J. L. Anderson, 1915 diary
Editions of *The Press*, Christchurch daily newspaper

Index

Verschoyle, Major T., 194, 195
Vinh Long, French transport, 137
Viricel, Claudius, 183

W-beach landing, 132–7
W Hills, 189, 209
Waite, Capt., Suvla raid report, 148
Waite, Major F., 66
Walker, Gen., 189
Walker's Ridge, 101, 151, 256, 257
Wallingford, Capt., 209
Walsh, Pte C. J., at landing, 111; at evacuation, 255–7
War Council, 33–5, 59, 265, 268, 270, 274, 275
War graves, 219–20
Warwick Castle post, 252–3
Wasser riot, 79, 82–3
Water, lack of, 195, 206–7, 209
Waterlow, Lieut, 104
Wear, H.M.S., 53
Weaver, E., 47
Wehrle, Col., 50
Weil, Commandant R., 65; in Egypt, 87, 91n; at second battle for Krithia, 143–5; at third battle for Krithia, 175–6; fever, 247
Weir, Lieut-Col. S. P., 150n
Welch, W. J., 107
Wellington Mounted Rifles, 206–7
Wemyss, Adml Lord Wester, 97, 274
Wettern, Spr Eric, enlistment, 64; training, 70–71, 89; at Anzac in April, 108; at third battle for Krithia, 176; on

Peninsula, 220–21, 224–5, 244, 248, 251; at evacuation, 262
Whittall family, 49
William-Powlett, Midshipman (later Vice-Adml Sir P.), February 1915, 37, 38, 41, 46; 18 March 1915, 53–4; S-beach landing, 125; 167n
Williams, Cdr A. M., 134
Williams, C. H., 201–2
Williams' Pier, 255–6
Williamson, Flt Cdr, 241
Williamson, Capt. W. Corbett, 181n, 261–2
Wilson, A. E., 64; at Saros diversion, 136
Wilson, Capt., 131
Wilson, Midshipman (later Cdr) H., at W-beach landing, 133–4
Wiltshires, 209
Winter, 250–53
Wolton, Capt. E. D., 195, 213
Wolverine, H.M.S., 42
Wood, Gnr W. G., 64
Woodward, Brig.-Gen., 98
Woodworth, Lieut F. T. K., 183, 247
Worcestershire Regiment, 133, 225, 229
Wyrall, E., 194n

X-beach landing, 123–4

Y-beach landing, 119–23
York and Lancaster Regiment, 194

Zeki, Major, 114
Zion Mule Corps, 156